Palgrave Studies in Crea

Series Editors
Vlad Petre Glăveanu
Department of Psychology
Webster University
Geneva, Switzerland

Brady Wagoner
Communication and Psychology
Aalborg University
Aalborg, Denmark

Both creativity and culture are areas that have experienced a rapid growth in interest in recent years. Moreover, there is a growing interest today in understanding creativity as a socio-cultural phenomenon and culture as a transformative, dynamic process. Creativity has traditionally been considered an exceptional quality that only a few people (truly) possess, a cognitive or personality trait 'residing' inside the mind of the creative individual. Conversely, culture has often been seen as 'outside' the person and described as a set of 'things' such as norms, beliefs, values, objects, and so on. The current literature shows a trend towards a different understanding, which recognises the psycho-socio-cultural nature of creative expression and the creative quality of appropriating and participating in culture. Our new, interdisciplinary series Palgrave Studies in Creativity and Culture intends to advance our knowledge of both creativity and cultural studies from the forefront of theory and research within the emerging cultural psychology of creativity, and the intersection between psychology, anthropology, sociology, education, business, and cultural studies. Palgrave Studies in Creativity and Culture is accepting proposals for monographs, Palgrave Pivots and edited collections that bring together creativity and culture. The series has a broader focus than simply the cultural approach to creativity, and is unified by a basic set of premises about creativity and cultural phenomena.

More information about this series at
http://www.palgrave.com/gp/series/14640

Ruth Richards

Everyday Creativity and the Healthy Mind

Dynamic New Paths for Self and Society

palgrave
macmillan

Ruth Richards
Psychology
Saybrook University
Oakland, CA, USA

Palgrave Studies in Creativity and Culture
ISBN 978-1-137-55765-0   (hardcover)   ISBN 978-1-137-55766-7   (eBook)
ISBN 978-1-349-71840-5   (softcover)
https://doi.org/10.1057/978-1-137-55766-7

Library of Congress Control Number: 2018946267

This Palgrave Macmillan imprint is published by the registered company Springer Nature Limited
The registered company address is: The Campus, 4 Crinan Street, London, N1 9XW, United Kingdom

Praise for *Everyday Creativity and the Healthy Mind.*

"The human community desperately needs new ways of thinking about the individual and the community, the common good, the creative good, our place in the world. Our health and wellbeing depend on the kind of innovative thinking found in abundance in this book. Dr. Ruth Richards poses powerful questions and provides concrete pointers as well as expansive and profound visions of what could be. I hope the reader will feel empowered and excited by the ideas and stories in this wonderful and brilliant book."
    —Judith V. Jordan, *Director, Jean Baker Miller Institute, Wellesley College and Assistant Professor, Harvard Medical School, USA*

"Dr. Ruth Richards's years of study of everyday creativity shine through in this new volume. She synthesizes a multitude of theories and resources, making everyday creativity truly accessible to everyone—bringing new hope to a world very much in need of healing."
    —Susan Borkin, *psychotherapist and author of* The Healing Power of Writing *and* When Your Heart Speaks, Take Good Notes

"A wonderful book. We are taken on a delightful exploration into the creativity that each of us, knowingly or unknowingly, harbors in our everyday lives. It is rife with examples of attitudes, actions, and situations that enrich each of our days with expressions of the joy of living."

—Allan Combs, *Doshi Professor of Consciousness Studies, California Institute of Integral Studies, USA. Authored books include* The Radiance of Being *(Best Book Award, Scientific and Medical Network of the UK)*

"This is not the usual creativity book. Rather than viewing creativity as something you do, this book makes it clear that a key part of creativity is about who you are. What a refreshing take on creativity and its linkages to well-being and a life well lived."

—Scott Barry Kaufman, *author and editor of books including* Wired to Create: Unraveling the Mysteries of the Creative Mind

"*Everyday Creativity and the Healthy Mind* is Ruth Richards's latest and hugely compelling exploration of the relationship between creativity and health. Seeking to bring a more 'qualitative' feel for the subject, this big book captures the attention from the get-go. At times confessional, intimate, joyous, funny, playful, challenging, direct, provocative, deep, and wide-ranging, it is always engaging, run-through with erudition, and just 'pops' with ideas on every page."

—Nick Wilson, *Reader in Creativity, Arts & Cultural Management, King's College London, UK. Co-Editor (with Lee Martin)*, Palgrave Handbook of Creativity at Work

"Enhancing human potential is a theme that has spawned numerous books and essays over the past several decades, but Ruth Richards has given it an original spin. In this provocative book, she digs deep and soars high to suggest ways that individuals can transform themselves and their social environment. *Everyday Creativity and the Healthy Mind* is bound to change the lives of many of its readers and, if its suggestions are followed, the direction of their world as well."

—Stanley Krippner, *Alan Watts Professor of Psychology, Saybrook University, USA. Recipient of the 2002 American Psychological Association Award for Distinguished Contributions to the International Advancement of Psychology*

"This book helps us see creativity as a way of life—that in fact we *are* the phenomenon of creativity itself. Taking a physiological, psychological, spiritual, and environmental approach, Dr. Richards eloquently describes the emergent processes revealed in all aspects of daily life, if only we become aware. Cooking a meal, working in a garden, telling a story to a child are as creatively important as painting a picture or writing a poem. Dr. Richards provides ideas for increasing our ability to be creative. She also explains how the emotional and physical benefits of living creatively leads to a healthier life—and ultimately can contribute to the evolutionary future of humanity."

—Marie diCowden, *Ph.D. Clinical Psychologist, Neuropsychologist, Saybrook University, USA. Founder of Biscayne Institute of Health and Living*

"Ruth Richards draws on her extensive experience as a clinician and a leading researcher on creativity. Her book is based on solid scientific information, yet is engaging to read and provides wise practical advice on how to lead a more creative and fulfilling life."

—Dennis Kinney, *Senior Research Psychologist, McLean Hospital, Belmont, USA*

"Of all academic treatises, the topic of creativity should ideally be treated in ways that are novel, creative, and linked to the process of living. In this remarkable book, Ruth Richards achieves these goals. She walks us through a surprisingly diverse wonderland in which creativity appears in the practices of ordinary living. In fact, life itself is an inherently creative process expressing itself in the nuances and rewards of relationships and in the recognition and appreciation of beauty. The range of topics goes from finding the meanings of one's identity to employing the process to transform destructive problems presented by the environment. This book is itself a creative adventure."

—Marc Pilisuk, *Professor Emeritus, The University of California, USA. Books include* The Hidden Structure of Violence, Peace Movements Worldwide *and* The Healing Web: Social Networks and Human Survival

"Dr. Richards has long used her psychological and medical training in the passionate pursuit of health—of helping people to live deeper and more satisfying lives as individuals and communities. This book helps readers move toward happier healthier living through learning to be more present in the moment, and creatively aware of possibilities. This often results in finding new openness, meaning, interconnection, and challenge. The book provides pathways to enhancing experience and appreciation of life, in surprising ways."

—Steven R. Pritzker, *Faculty, Saybrook University, USA. Former Prizewinning Hollywood Television Writer and co-editor of the* Encyclopedia of Creativity

"For years, I focused every last ounce of my creativity on writing poetry and chronicling remote corners of consciousness. Dr. Ruth Richards teaches all of us obsessed artists how possible—and necessary—it is for creativity to suffuse every moment of our lives, and at the same time she uncovers the often simple thought processes that underlie both everyday and artistic creativity."
—Michael Ruby, *Author of* American Songbook *(poems) and* Memories, Dreams and Inner Voices

"'All prayer begins in silence.'—Mother Teresa. It is with this silencing, not just radio, television, and cell phones, but the obsessive thoughts, the 'ya ya's' that keep us from the inner quiet, that our aliveness and creativity is born. Ruth Richards's book provides a path to silencing ourselves, and opening to the mysteries of consciousness, so our creativity can flourish."
—Roger Cunningham, *Faculty, Psychology, Bronx Community College, USA and Co-Founder, Encompass New Opera Theatre, New York, USA*

"Dr. Ruth Richards draws on longstanding scholarship to assert that creativity is available to us all. Her enthusiasm is infectious as she shows how to recognize and nurture our potential for everyday creativity—for our own good and the good of the world."
—Shan Guisinger, *Clinical psychologist, and Faculty Affiliate, University of Montana, USA. Theoretician in evolutionary psychology, and author of the Adapted-to-Flee-Famine Hypothesis in anorexia nervosa*

"Ruth Richards has been in the forefront of studying creativity and its relationships with both health and illness for years, leading the development of the Lifetime Creativity Scales and the construct of Everyday Creativity. This has allowed us to measure and understand the creativity of everyday activities of people at work and play, not just the great artist or scientific genius. In this book, Dr. Richards builds on her career as clinician and scientist, exploring in detail how creativity works, illuminating implications for human health and wellness, and explaining how each of us can tap into creative processes so as to enrich, deepen, and better our daily lives."
—David Schuldberg, *Professor of Psychology, University of Montana, USA. Visiting Professor di Chiara Fama, 2016, and the Erasmus+ Program, 2017 and 2018, Universita a degli Studi di Firenze, Italy, and President of the Society for Chaos Theory in Psychology and the Life Sciences*

"A new book on everyday creativity by Ruth Richards is a call for celebration. Here is a unique dynamic and process look that can change how we see our lives."

—James C. Kaufman, *Professor of Educational Psychology, Neag School of Education, University of Connecticut, USA. Lyricist/Librettist for the Off-Broadway musical* Discovering Magenta

"In her exciting and informative new book, Dr. Ruth Richards gives us an entirely new view of creativity in our lives, our relationships, and in our world. We realize that we, as human beings, are inherently creative. There is boundless originality in our everyday life, and this creativity has shaped human culture since the dawn of history. Richards also reveals how the creative aspects of our daily lives not only transform us but can profoundly alter the interrelated environment in which we live."

—Tobi Zausner, *Faculty, Saybrook University, USA. Author of* When Walls Become Doorways: Creativity and the Transforming Illness *and a visual artist with works in national and international collections*

"Dr. Richards, who has devoted her life to the study of creativity, has given us a book that combines scholarly examination of creativity research with encouragement to all of us who may at times unknowingly incorporate creativity into our everyday activities. She offers insight into the importance of creativity to health and wellness, and intersperses this writing with witty and personal anecdotes that inspire and sometimes amuse the reader, who cannot help but apply them in their 'everyday life.'"

—Antoinette Jakobi, *Associate Professor of Psychiatry, University of Rochester Medical School, USA*

"Creativity is increasingly recognized as a valuable commodity. These days it could even be the most important asset for both individuals and humanity. Yet too often the benefits of creativity are end results, outcomes, products of the creative process. Ruth Richards gives us a much broader, more accurate, and useful view of creativity. She explains how it is directly related to our health, our relationships, our happiness, and even our conception of life's meaning. She offers a convincing view that creativity is a part of each of our lives, every day, and that process is as valuable as product. Richards has provided us with a volume that is engaging, practical, and based on accepted ideas from the science of creativity."

—Mark Runco, *Founding Editor of the Creativity Research Journal, Distinguished Research Fellow, American Institute for Behavioral Research & Technology, USA and author of* Creativity: Theories and Themes: Research, Development, and Practice

"This book provides timely and fascinating insights into creativity, and Professor Richards forensically demonstrates that creative ability is something we all possess and can use *every day*. The book contains a wealth of theoretical and practical insights that both advance thought on creativity and show how vital an understanding of our creative capabilities can be for our well-being. Importantly, it explores the creative mind in ways that laboratory studies have struggled to capture, through drawing on individual experiences of creativity in a variety of settings. This book is an essential read for those studying creativity, as well as those interested in understanding the myriad of ways our creative potential can actualise."

—Lee Martin, *Associate Professor of Creativity, Centre for Cultural and Media Policy Studies, University of Warwick, UK*

"This is a beautiful book—a dynamic book about the processes of creativity and everyday life. It is hopeful about the human condition, with creativity at the heart of it. Richards, in a novel fashion, interweaves a broad spectrum of viewpoints, theories, philosophies, literature, research, and personal life experiences into a grand synthesis with implications about how to live and grow. Plus, the book is interesting and fun to read. A truly original contribution to the field."

—Sandra W. Russ, *Distinguished University Professor, Case Western Reserve University, USA. Author of amongst others* Pretend Play in Childhood: Foundation of Adult Creativity *and* Affect and Creativity: The Role of Affect and Play in the Creative Process

"Dr. Richards's book offers an urgent appeal to expand our views of what it means to express creativity in life. She reminds us that creativity is our birthright, and can also be important for our health and personal growth. She arouses the reader's curiosity to find 'oneself as a process-in-motion, an open system in an interconnected dynamic cosmos.' Read this book and find the chance to expand your creative palette, walk with your muse, discover your personal creative recipe, and express your creative power."

—Terri Goslin-Jones, *Chair Creativity Studies Specialization, College of Social Sciences, Saybrook University, USA. Board Member of the International Expressive Arts Therapy Association*

For Joey and Jake
Creative young adults with their lives ahead of them
and other family, friends, and companions on life's path
Plus all those who have come before
Toward a more joyous and healthy future

Foreword

In studying everyday creativity, Dr. Ruth Richards is the "go to" person and she has given us a precious gift in this book. She has been studying this topic for many years and is one of the world's experts on everyday creativity, providing a brilliant, positive and hopeful examination of what constitutes creativity. In this book Ruth serves as a guide (sometimes a very playful guide at that!), as a curious questioner, inviting us, in style and with asides, to join her in this project.

The book shines with a spirit of inquiry. It does more than simply impart knowledge. Dr. Richards illuminates the ways in which we all can participate in creative moments, perhaps even building creative lives. This book walks us through important theories about creativity and presents us with rich and intriguing data. According to Dr. Richards, the two criteria of everyday creativity are originality and meaningfulness. The potential benefits of everyday creativity for us include awareness, openness, health, caring and collaboration to name a few.

This book encourages us to look beyond existing categories in psychology, philosophy and spirituality. It unfailingly takes into account not just the person but the context. Dr. Richards asks not just how can we support our own personal creativity but how can we "design environments to bring out the best in us." This recognition of the part that context plays in creativity supports movement away from highly individualistic explanations of creativity. In this emphasis there is convergence with relational theories of human development and wellbeing.

The book digs deep, questioning: What is our human nature? Why must we continually frame our understanding in closed systems when life is filled with change and uncertainty? When we try to control the uncertainty, we resign ourselves to old templates, often old pessimism. We get stuck in repetition or stagnancy. Being open is like breathing in or breathing out. Open, fresh, now, life-giving. New each moment!

Close to my own heart is the importance of openness and responsiveness; these are at the core of empathy. Where and how is something new and meaningful brought into being? In relatedness, in responding to the newness born in connection (with people, with animals, with nature, with a higher power). When mutual change benefits both people in a relationship, we move beyond the dualities of self versus other, selfless versus selfish. This is creative movement. We are open to being changed (that can be alarming or comforting). "This too shall pass." Creativity is curtailed by status quo, static labels, linear mindsets. Being present, open, mindful and curious contribute to a kind of unfolding, aliveness—the blossoming of new possibilities, the development of deeper potential. Not only do we find resonance and growth in human relationships but in our interactions with the natural world, in the opening of our hearts to moments of beauty.

Everyday creativity is built around openness and increasing awareness of our interconnected being. Recently I had the privilege of being on a panel of five eminent scholars from the Harvard Medical School and His Holiness, the Dalai Lama. We were to explore the topic of psychotherapy and meditation. Although many important points were made, it was the quality of *being* that his Holiness brought that most moved me and stayed with me. Compassion, curiosity, a deep sense of connection and infinite kindness emanated from this smiling, laughing, loving wise man. I wish I could say the same about us scholars there, at best struggling to calm our prickly egos, at worst going all out to prove our intelligence and worthiness. His smiling, humble interactions with us provided an opening into hope. Perhaps we could come to an awareness of our common humanity, our interconnectedness. And with such insight, perhaps empathy and compassion could come center stage, creating healthy individuals and growth supporting environments.

In the last decade neuroscience has confirmed that connection with others is essential for human wellbeing. We are wired to connect. We need growth-fostering relationships the same way we need air and water. We experience the pain of exclusion in the same way that we experience physical pain or absence of oxygen. Functional MRIs attest to the neurobiology of relationship, to our essential, lifelong need of others. Too often this biological interdependence is dismissed as "soft," a sign of deficiency. Now we have bedrock data: we grow through and toward relationship throughout the lifespan. Exclusion and isolation hurt.

In connecting, we often face the unknown. We share the possibility of creating something new. But we all need to be supported when we move into new realms. We need to create a culture that embraces creativity and openness to difference and honors our longing to learn, to grow with others. We need to support the development of connectivity, a sense of being a part of something larger—whether it be community or the natural world. Overemphasis in our culture on separation and on becoming autonomous has led to widespread suffering, devastating levels of "loneliness" and depression. We need to develop a healthier culture. Revising our emphasis on individualistic models of development would contribute to an increasing sense of wellbeing.

This book is packed with ideas and wisdom. But more importantly it invites us to question and wonder and open to uncertainty. It is a book to read in its entirety but then to return to as an ongoing source of possibility and encouragement. My hope for the reader is that you will come away from this book with renewed inklings of your own everyday creative energy. I hope you will see movement into the open moments of life. And I hope questions will have arisen for you about your own creativity and how to pass the benefits of that on to others.

I believe creativity is nourished in relatedness, whether it be in internal conversations with old friends and mentors, real interactions with today's family and friends, or in the awe and wonder of a particularly spectacular sunset. Somehow we are changed in a good way, and that change can ripple out to touch others. We are relational beings. We are selves-in-world (or selves-in-relation). The human community desperately needs new ways of thinking about the individual and the community, the common good, the creative good, our place in the world. Our health and wellbeing depend on the kind of innovative thinking found in abundance in this book. Dr. Ruth Richards poses powerful questions and provides concrete pointers as well as expansive and profound visions of what could be. I hope the reader will feel empowered and excited by the ideas and stories in this wonderful and brilliant book.

Jean Baker Miller Institute   Judith V. Jordan
Wellesley College
Wellesley, MA, USA

Harvard Medical School
Boston, MA

Judith V. Jordan, Ph.D., Director, Jean Baker Miller Institute, Wellesley College, Asst. Professor, Harvard Medical School, and Co-Developer of Relational-Cultural Theory (RCT). She has lectured and conducted workshops nationally and internationally, and has appeared on the Oprah Winfrey Show. Her awards include Winner of the 2010 Distinguished Psychologist Award from the American Psychological Association (APA) for outstanding lifetime contributions to the field of psychotherapy. She was honored to be included among five eminent scholars in dialogue with His Holiness the Dalai Lama. Dr. Jordan is author, co-author and editor of books including (author) *Relational-Cultural Therapy*, 2nd Edition, APA Books, 2018. Series co-editor Jon Carlson lauded RCT as "one of the ten most important psychological theories today."

Acknowledgements

Never was a statement more true—about the essential parts of so many people without whom this work would have taken a different form or might not exist at all. In our complex, multilayered, dynamic and interdependent world, there are endless strands of influence we may never even know, or whose importance emerges only later: the great-grandparent barely remembered from infancy, the grandmother who gave a young girl book and crayons and encouragement, the father who showed how to develop pictures, and the mother who made fractal graphs of investments without even knowing that is what they were! The second grade teacher with name now forgotten—although I know that my daughter's second grade teacher, Doug, was a huge force for that fortunate class. This was from the opening daily song with his guitar accompaniment, to sharing his own second grade memories, to the early village with a barter system he had the kids construct (creating their own personalized figures and enacting a culture and economy in miniature), to how he had us, on parents' night, visualize ourselves back in second grade. His classroom came alive.

In that vein, here are some marvelous people, and powerful direct, and sometimes subtle, influences, persons still with us and others no longer present; they have each been central in their own ways to this work happening. They are presented alphabetically, with the understanding that there are numerous others as well, sometimes fully unsuspected. As we do our own work, we never know where our influence will take root.

With great thanks to you all including Fred Abraham, Maria Benet, Abbe Blum, Anna Joy Brown, Roland Brown, Brooklyn Waterfront Artists Coalition (www.BWAC.org), Jake Coffing, Allan Leslie Combs, Roger Cunningham, Marie DiCowden, Debbie Lee Dailey, Tom Eelkema, Fred Fulton, Helen Fulton, Terri Goslin-Jones, Tom Greening, Sylvia Gretchen, Shan Guisinger, Patti Hagan, Harold Hanham, Ruth Soule Arnon Hanham, Sandra Hoey, Toni Jakobi, Judith Jordan, James Zachary Holtz, Seymour Kety, Hyunmoon Kim, Dennis Kinney, Stanley Krippner, Virginia Latham, Edith Leslie, Lael Leslie, Christopher Lord, Steven Matthysse, Jonathan Matson, Nellie McCool, Ann Merzel, John David Miller, Alice Wilson Milne, Jonathan Milne, Thich Minh Duc, Ursula Monroe, Delmont Morrison, Shirley Morrison, Marta Davidovich Ockuly, Karen Packard, Judy Perani, Marc Pilisuk, Phyllis Pilisuk, Steven Pritzker, Susan Reed, Nancy Rhodes, Chet Richards, Dexter (Rick) Richards, Dexter Richards, Jr., Louise Taylor Richards, Dexter Richards, Donna Berlier Richards, Lauren Jo Richards-Ruby, William (Chip) Richards, Ruth Eleanor Fulton Richards, Linda Riebel, Andy Ross, Michael Handler Ruby, Mark Runco, Sandra Russ, Gregory Russell, Sandow Sacks Ruby, David Schuldberg, Jerome Singer, Kathleen Spivack, Deborah Strohbeen, John Strohbeen, Louise Lu Sundararajan, Khenchen Tsewang Gyatso Rinpoche, Suzanne Tuckey, Karma Lekshe Tsomo, Chia Tze, Laura Gellman Tze, Tobi Zausner, Eric Zeise, Fred Zeise, and Karl Zeise.

Finally, huge thanks to Palgrave Macmillan for their visionary publishing, including the fine editorial staff Nicola Jones and assistant Elizabeth Forrest for accepting the project, and Grace Jackson and assistant Joanna O'Neill for valuable help along the way. Thanks too to Laura de Grasse for the striking cover, and other talented Palgrave production staff, including Ganesh Ekambaram, Charanya Manoharan, and Tom Steendam for their quality work. This publishing program and its series, Palgrave Studies in Creativity and Culture, offer products which truly can help to change the world.

Contents

About the Author

Ruth Richards, educational psychologist and Board Certified psychiatrist, is professor at Saybrook University in Creativity Studies, and Consciousness, Spirituality, and Integrative Health. She has studied creativity in educational, clinical, social action, and spiritual contexts, as well as issues in aesthetics and awareness, consciousness studies, and chaos and complexity theories. Dr. Richards has authored numerous papers and chapters and a monograph, and has edited/co-edited two books: *Eminent Creativity, Everyday Creativity, and Health* (with Mark Runco) and *Everyday Creativity and New Views of Human Nature,* as well as writing *Everyday Creativity: Coping and Thriving in the 21st Century.* She is currently coediting, *Nonlinear Psychology: Keys to Chaos and Creativity in Mind and Life* (David Schuldberg, Editor in Chief, with Shan Guisiinger). She was also principal investigator and author (with Dennis Kinney and others) for *The Lifetime Creativity Scales.* Dr. Richards is on three editorial boards, for *Psychology, Creativity, and the Arts, The Creativity Research Journal,* and *The Journal of Humanistic Psychology.* She is Fellow of the American Psychological Association (APA) and, in 2009, Dr. Richards won the Rudolf Arnheim Award for Outstanding Lifetime Achievement in Psychology and the Arts from Division 10 of the APA. A concern of hers is whether everyday creative process can bring each of us, as a creative *person,* to greater health and purpose, offering new ways to be present with ourselves, each other, our larger world, and life's possibilities.

1

Introduction

Health for self, health for the world? This is our hope here. Along with imparting some healthful and joyous creativity, and seeing how this happens. Here too are ways to see oneself—fully and finally—as a highly creative person, a bit of a miracle, really, carrying a universal capacity, which is our very birthright.

Everyday Creativity and the Healthy Mind puts forth a more dynamic view of creativity, our "originality of everyday life," as both process and way of life, and part of our universal human heritage. Here is our "phenotypical plasticity" as per evolutionary biologist Theodosius Dobzhansky, the vast and innumerable ways we can manifest and live within our inherent boundaries.[1] We change in each moment, and so does our world, and what we can creatively offer. Each moment is new—and how much more delightful, healthy, and *important* it can be for us to live this way. Truly we can come alive.

© The Author(s) 2018
R. Richards, *Everyday Creativity and the Healthy Mind*,
Palgrave Studies in Creativity and Culture,
https://doi.org/10.1057/978-1-137-55766-7_1

We Turn the Camera Around

These chapters are framed by the "Four Ps of Creativity"[2]—Creative Product (the outcome) and then Process, Person, and finally Press of the Environment. After a look at creative product (object, idea, performance, etc) *we turn the camera around*. We look back at the creative person (that is, each one of us), and what we are doing, the creative process. We also look carefully at environments which on the one hand can help us blossom (think of a favorite and supportive teacher), on the other can kill our creativity (think of a negative judgmental boss). We also take a longer if speculative evolutionary view of how creativity came to be, in humans, in an emergent cosmos—and why this may be the most important time for it right now.

One may ask: What is this creative process, and what is it *doing for us?* What is it *evoking* from us? Can it change us? Expand our potential, unfold our inherent capacities? Can we discover parts of self we never suspected? Might our creating bring us new insights, beyond the creative product, both deeply into our selves and outwardly into our world? Can it change our relationships to others, our chances for intimacy, our wonder at life, awareness of beauty? Can it perhaps change us to be more caring, giving people; can it *change us for the better?* Since we humans can also change our environments to suit us, we consider too this incredible power, both for our own happier, healthier development and for living in a more caring and less crazy world.

Creating What?: Most Anything!

We humans are not primarily creatures of instinct who, for instance, build our homes in the same way. Throughout countless ages and around the world, we have made houses, dwellings, palaces, gathering places, shelters, meeting halls, cathedrals, temples of every size, shape and color, and from steamy deserts to icy tundra. We have created arts, music, rituals, language, traditions, cultures, belief systems, and much more. Our everyday creativity helps keep us alive—whether escaping a dangerous pursuer (and we have such examples later), and finding our way to safety when lost in the mountains. Our creativity helps us cope and survive—and also to find out what we are surviving *for*.

Everyday creativity is identified with two criteria only: *originality* and *meaningfulness*—it is new, and it is understandable. Beyond that, any activity can qualify. Whether we are landscaping the yard, fixing the car, instructing our child, advising a friend, or making a gourmet dinner out of some bare leftovers, we can be invoking our everyday creativity. Yet how many people know this? It need not be a "traditionally creative" activity to "count" though it may be one (e.g., painting, writing, scientific discovery).

In fact, seeing creativity throughout our lives involved opening our own eyes. With Dennis Kinney and others at Harvard Medical School and McLean Hospital we developed and validated our *Lifetime Creativity Scales* to assess this "originality" through intensive interviews; our group ended up with high reliability and construct validity for the ratings, yet still found great complexity at first in identifying the creativity in a vast range of daily activities.[3] For instance, aspects of homemaking or home repairs one might normally take for granted. Or starting a rotating story with children at bedtime.

We found we began looking at the world differently. The "originality of everyday life" began appearing in places we might have missed it before![4] If we, looking deliberately, did not even see it, it is not surprising that many people do not stop and acknowledge their own ways of being creative, and give themselves credit, when it has *not even been named* or acknowledged by others. Hence their creativity can *go under-recognized, under-developed, and under-rewarded.* Then what happens?

"I am not creative!" they say. "I cannot paint a picture!" How tragic this is. They are closing a door. Their creative potential will go unnoticed, when it could become recognized and more powerful than it ever was before.

Aside from the intrinsic joy that can come from our personal creativity (especially on the good days). I am also aware of these huge health benefits—and meanwhile how they are not very well known. Also unknown are various ways that more creative living can help us together, and help to improve our world. My intent here is to bring the background and benefits forward, plus a more "qualitative" feel for the subject, so more people can find and understand their own creativity and its power. That is the reason for this book.

Longstanding Study of Creativity—and Next Steps

I am an educational psychologist, Board Certified Psychiatrist, professor, researcher, writer, parent of a creative young adult daughter, and an occasional visual artist. I play three instruments badly (although that doesn't stop me), and sing reasonably well. My background also includes sciences and math, with a B.S. in physics (with distinction, receiving an NSF Fellowship in biophysics).

I became credentialed to teach physics, math, and art at the secondary level, before becoming interested in the psychology of creativity, and remarkably seeing that creativity, broadly defined, could apply to sciences, arts, and pretty much anything else. That was a huge insight (although others had had it, including philosopher John Dewey. Plus eminent researchers such as J.P. Guilford and Frank Barron). Yet I, along with many others, was still equating "art and creativity."

In education I started wondering why the priority was often to help a student get 100% on somebody's test, and not to make up questions of their own!

I have studied some aspect of creativity ever since, through studies for a Ph.D. and M.D., whether in education, medicine, clinical psychiatry, including issues of psychopathology, mind-body medicine, humanistic and positive psychology, Eastern philosophy, social action, consciousness studies and spirituality, aesthetics and awareness, or chaos and complexity theories. I am a practicing Buddhist, also from an Interfaith context and group,[5] and this in turn has brought further depth and understanding to how I and others can see creativity.

Over the years I have published numerous papers, chapters, and a monograph on creativity, and was principal author of *The Lifetime Creativity Scales*.[6] Do know I wrote an early "lost" book on everyday creativity, *Everyday Creativity: Coping and Thriving in the 21st Century*[7] (now found! available on Amazon) and have published two edited others, *Eminent Creativity, Everyday Creativity, and Health* (with Mark Runco), and another, *Everyday Creativity and New Views of Human Nature,* as below. I was privileged in 2009 to win the Rudolf Arnheim Award from Div. 10 of the American Psychological Association for Outstanding Lifetime Achievement in Psychology and the Arts.

Among issues that have concerned me over the years as clinician and academic, is the contrast between evident benefits of creativity, and certain misunderstandings and stereotypes which persist today. Let us stress the universality of creativity (vs. occasional special appearance, limiting it to a few) and the many rich connections (often misunderstood) with health. Especially now, when we as individuals, cultures, and a global culture can use new hope and new healing, it seems time to take another look.

Precursor Edited Book—and This Volume

This new book, *Everyday Creativity and the Healthy Mind,* picks up in part on 12 integrating themes from that last volume, *Everyday Creativity and New Views of Human Nature: Psychological, Social and Spiritual Perspectives.* Emerging from the chapters, in a formal qualitative analysis, were 12 integrating themes. Chapter contributors, well-known in the field, were chosen to address both individual creativity and social issues. The themes, listed under "Twelve Potential Benefits of Living More Creatively," are Conscious, Dynamic, Open, Healthy, Nondefensive, Integrating, Caring, Observing Actively, Collaborative, Androgynous, Developing, and Brave.[8]

A good time indeed to build on these findings and update knowledge about everyday creativity and its many benefits! Individually and socially—and, yes, spiritually as well[9] Plus to look more closely in areas not usually included in this type of book including empathy, relationships, beauty, and the sublime.

There is valuable literature here which crosses disciplines. Yet how, one might ask, could benefits of creativity coexist with seemingly paradoxical findings about creativity and creators—for instance where they are sometimes portrayed as "not normal"—nonconformists who are disar-rayed and marginalized, difficult, or frankly ill. How does this fit with creativity and healing? Or consider views of creators seeming too involved with self. Yet we are seeing ways creative styles can take one *beyond* self and even into universal themes and awareness. Looking more broadly our human greed, ignorance, or *lack* of reflection has exacerbated some serious global difficulties (e.g., Sixth Extinction,[10] or armed conflicts[11]); what if creativity can help? Can we encourage a path of self-develop-ment, and greater concern for others and the earth. Consider for instance humanistic psychologist Abraham Maslow in *Toward a Psychology of Being*, and his hierarchy of needs, with movement toward *self-actualiza-tion*; Maslow saw this self-actualizing person, moving toward higher human potential, and their *self-actualizing creativity* as very similar. Their virtues also include greater concern for all.

Paradoxes? Or is it just that life is more subtle and delicately balanced than some viewpoints or methods of analysis might suggest. Plus keep in mind that everyday creativity is *universal*. Let us hope it works in the service of health. Some serious misunderstandings or oversimplifica-tions need to be addressed. At the same time I have been co-editing a volume called *Nonlinear Psychology: Keys to Chaos and Creativity in Life and Mind* (Schuldberg, Richards, and Guisinger, eds.). The frame of chaos and complexity theory, has helped to unravel some of the contro-versy, while bringing the excitement of our topic of everyday creativity even more to life!

It is this author's pleasure to have *Everyday Creativity and the Healthy Mind* join the series "Palgrave Studies in Creativity and Culture," with series editors V.P. Glaveanu and B. Wagoner. The interest in creativity as a socio-cultural phenomenon, culture as a dynamic and complex process, and the multi-level and cross-disciplinary expanse of investigation is wel-come and far too rare. Too often creativity studies focus just on the indi-vidual. Meanwhile culture is thought to lie elsewhere. Yet one sees increasingly that it is all deeply interconnected, that we are dynamic open systems, and our highest creativity can draw expansively from all of life. Creativity is the inheritance of all of us—and also our business. It exists in a endless web with everything else.

The Chapters

Everyday Creativity and the Healthy Mind has seventeen chapters, including the Introduction, and is divided into six parts. Parts I through III, three chapters each, focus on aspects of the Four Ps of Creativity. These are New Openings (creative product), Aha! Moment (creative process) and Living Creatively (creative person and press). Parts IV through VI concern issues and topics less usual in the creativity literature, specifically Normal and Abnormal (including "compensatory advantage" in pathology), New Directions (relationships, beauty, the sublime, chaos theory and nuance), and Now What? (looking ahead, three possibilities for mind, plus an Afterword). Chapters include vignettes, relevant literature, and at times, illustrative examples that also allow the reader personally to try a creative activity. Although not a primary objective here, this allows for a "feel" for the topic, and for adding first-person qualitative and subjective inquiry to third person conveyed information. If ever there is a time to look within, and learn from our own experience, it would seem to be in the study of everyday creativity.

- **Part I, New Openings (Creative Product).** Here chapters include "Missing Worlds," on looking "without," and issues of altered consciousness, how perception itself is greatly limited, has many flavors, and how our experience can happen with mindful awareness, in the moment, and as a creative act. "Creative Palette," by contrast, is a look "within" at creative mind, imagery, conscious and unconscious, and integrated material then available for creativity (on the "palette"), in creative acts or in play. In "Change and Open Systems," one meets evolving complex interdependent systems (including you and me) in a world of change and surprise—an introduction to issues in chaos and complexity theory and especially "who we are" as open systems when functioning as creators.
- **Part II, Aha! Moment (Creative Process).** Chapters include "Moments of Insight," focused on the Butterfly Effect, with sensitivity to initial conditions, interdependence and feedback, with huge systems reconfigurations. Moving from a vignette showing global effects

of a single action in the world, discussion moves to the Aha! Effect in a creative mind. Next, in "Flavors of Mind" attention turns to neurological findings related to insight, along with state phenomena and the Default Mode of consciousness. Finally "Emergence of Life and Creativity" brings in evolution, speculating about emergence of life, then mind, and finally awareness and the meta-awareness to generate creative change, and finally weave it into a human future via *cultural* (vs. biological) evolution.

- **Part III Living Creatively (Creative Person and Press).** "Popcorn: A Model" highlights conditions for keeping creative insights and dynamic change going, as a personal style, first with a cognitive focus (within a welcoming affective set), including discussion of ongoing Divergent Thinking. "Creative Person" revisits this for personality traits, and other stylistic features including cognitive style. "Creative Space" shows environmental conditions that can not only spur creativity but open minds and change lives. Issues of delicate balances between multiple variables, within and between person and setting, nonlinearity and curvilinear relationships, and perhaps epigenetics, are important in this section.

- **Part IV Normal and Abnormal (Not What Some Think).** "Deep Sea Diving" concerns our personal unconscious mind and recruiting parts we can access while maintaining a delicate balance of openness and a loose adaptive control toward creative ends. Expressive writing and pretend play are examples, in this "balancing act." "New Normal" confronts negative stereotypes of creators in our culture but also class sizes, norms, and teacher issues that may misread or mislabel creative kids. A "new normal" defining self through process, awareness, dynamic change, risk, and growth has advantages for knowing self and truth telling in the world. Yet difference can be pathologized, creativity even confused with mild thought disorder. In "Creative (Compensatory) Advantage," one learns that a risk or diathesis for bipolar disorder or schizophrenia (plus spectrum disorders) in a family *can* have creative benefits. However creativity peaks most in the presence of relative health (state or trait). Further, romanticizing mental illness can be dangerous. Again here is a delicate nonlinear balance. Remember, "abnormal" needn't mean pathological; it can mean usefully exceptional.

- **Part V New Directions (Going Deeper).** "Empathy and Relational Creativity" concerns the often-forgotten presence of everyday creativity in the interpersonal domain, as we connect in direct, new, immediate, and authentic ways, develop understanding, empathize, change in response to each other. Empathy is central to us and to varied species; our mirror neurons help build it in. It is exemplified here beginning with a vignette about a hurricane. Charles Darwin, in an emphasis still unknown to some, wrote about empathy, cooperation, and love as central to our social species and survival. "Beauty, the Sublime, The Hidden" shows empathy can also exist with inanimate objects, even help create great art and science, as with Nobel Prize winner Barbara McClintock. Meanwhile mysteries of beauty draw us to awareness, also the sublime as per Kant—involving power, and the infinite, which brings awe, surpassing our senses and imagination. In "Fingerprints of Chaos, Nuance, and Creativity" we find, in visual forms of the breathtaking fractal forms of nature—such as the Mandelbrot Set— self-similar figures related to the microstructure of "chaotic attractors," foundations of our lives, found everywhere in clouds, trees, mountains, rivers, and our own bodies. They embody infinite series and thus recall the sublime, while meanwhile—in fractal views of memory— may help explain the mysterious draw of "nuance" in creativity. Virginia Woolf's creative process provides one example.
- **Part VI—Now What?** In "Higher Horizons: Three Views", aware that emergences can continue through time, we speculatively present three situations involving higher forms of consciousness. Two are based on case studies, the third on an organizational group example, with observations of process: (1) Abraham Maslow's "Transcenders" (beyond Self-Actualization); (2) Theory U from MIT, with group process including altered consciousness to help "bring in the future" in forward planning; (3) Bucke's Cosmic Consciousness, with Walt Whitman as exemplar. A further question is whether we can design environments to bring out the best in us. Finally in the "Afterword," presented here with a smile, the now global gifting of Smile Cards is presented—a creative initiative reflecting the Gift Economy. This shows another paradigm shift, so that we can finally ask: Just what is our human nature?

These issues and possibilities are very much based in a dynamic and interconnected nonlinear model of world and creator-in-world. I hope *Everyday Creativity and the Healthy Mind* will stimulate your thinking on these and other questions, while engaging and enhancing your own creativity.

Notes

1. Dobzhansky, *Mankind Evolving*, 320. We now include epigenetic effects among multiple complex interactions between genotypes, phenotype, culture, and the larger environment.
2. Richards, "Four Ps of Creativity," 733.
3. Richards, Kinney, Benet, and Merzel, "Assessing Everyday Creativity, 476.
4. Richards, "Everyday Creativity: Our Hidden Potential," 29.
5. www.AhimsaBerkeley.org.
6. Richards, Kinney, Benet, and Merzel, "Assessing Everyday Creativity," and Richards, Kinney, Lunde, Benet, and Merzel, "Creativity in Manic-Depressives..." for an important application. The scales themselves are found in Kinney, Richards, and Southam, "Everyday Creativity: Its Assessment and *The Lifetime Creativity Scales*," 285.
7. Richards, *Everyday Creativity: Coping and Thriving in the 21st Century.*
8. Richards, "Twelve Potential Benefits...," 290. The benefits are listed in the table and discussed in detail.
9. Kaufman, *Wired to Create*. Also see Milne, *GO! The Art of Change*, and Richards, ed., *Everyday Creativity.*
10. Kolbert, *The Sixth Extinction: An Unnatural History.* From 2014. Plus from almost two decades before, Leakey and Lewin, *The Sixth Extinction.*
11. Pilisuk and Rountree, *The Hidden Structure of Violence.* Important documentation and analysis in a world in conflict.

Part I

NEW OPENINGS
(Creative *Product*: 1st of Four P's)

2

Missing Worlds

Although we say that mountains belong to the country, actually, they belong to those who love them.
Eihei Dogen

Wearing our experiential human "blinders," we humans can miss worlds of experience "out there" including the brilliance of the present moment. This is due to varied states of consciousness, conceptual frames, attentional issues, preconceptions, memories, expectations, and more. This opens a discussion of everyday creative vision and living, and awareness of options, while revisiting our *process*, priorities, and—in a triumph for human conscious evolution—our chance to adapt and change.

The Missing World

Here is an event that stopped me cold.[1]

I'm rather good at maps. I'm also good at using a GPS device. But I forgot the maps and here we were, late afternoon, last day of vacation, my daughter

© The Author(s) 2018
R. Richards, *Everyday Creativity and the Healthy Mind*,
Palgrave Studies in Creativity and Culture,
https://doi.org/10.1057/978-1-137-55766-7_2

my cousin and I, driving along a two-lane highway in midstate Oregon. No other car in sight, and the sun had just gone down. Where was that charming little village?

It was supposed to be right along this river. We drove on, farther and farther into the unknown, river always at left as our guide. We kept passing farms and fields and scattered houses and now a few lights were coming out. In my head, I was doing a litany of self-criticism: Why didn't we start earlier, leave more time, have lunch sooner, save dessert for the little town, bring the map, and on and on and on, a list of all we did wrong—reliving it as if that could help us now. My cousin and I were both impatient and stressed. My daughter, at least, was happy in the back seat, text messaging a friend. I pull up on the shoulder of the road to think.

Just then—WOW! Amazing! A new scene had appeared. A new slide projected on a screen. Where did it come from?

Look! LOOK! I insisted. Even my daughter looked up. Right there, out of nowhere: a magical misty landscape. Fields moving off to infinity in muted purples and pastels, fuzzy in the haze, with clusters of tall lush trees, darkening and receding in the dusk. I turned the car engine off. All was silent in the hot summer air. Beside us a plum-colored river barely moved between a border of trees, its dark lazy water reflecting the last light of day.

How breathtaking! This landscape had cast a spell. We sat in the silence of an indrawn breath. Where had it been? If I had seen even a trace of this beauty while driving along, not a neuron had registered it, no mental bell had rung so that the conscious mind could stop and take a look. I had missed it all. We all had missed it.

We miss a lot. Almost everything, in fact, in our world. Our task-focused filters take care of that, selecting only what we need. We need to get to work. Have some lunch. Find that report. Water the garden. Go out on a date. We see what we need to see, often for purposes of survival—or survival of the species. Gregory Bateson, speaking of beauty, said aesthetic judgment is selection of a fact. We create the sight even as we become conscious of it. We do not simply see it. In our daily lives, who or what is doing the selecting? And why? Is this predetermined? Can we—in the here and now—make a change? Can we see further? Can we see better? Can we even better our world?

Opening our vision is a first step in Everyday Creativity.

Looking back now, this was a startling experience. How much more—every minute of every day—are we all missing? Just imagine, I thought, what more there might be Often, to be sure, this screening of experience is for good reason. Perhaps we want to focus on our driving. To stay on the road. Then again, what are we driving (or living) *for?*

This reflection, for me, opens readily into issues of *everyday creativity*, which I have studied and researched for years, in education, mental health, social action, consciousness and spirituality. The discussion below is followed by two examples of "blinders" which we may, instead of being aware and broadly appreciative, can mindlessly, apply to our lives. In the next section are addressed issues of conscious awareness, and mindfulness as a vital remedy in our deeper experiencing—plus as enhancers of creativity and so much more. This chapter ends with several posted comments on www.awakin.org/?tid=778, which I find very moving, from readers' own experiences and reactions to the Oregon Roads vignette above.

Everyday Creativity

Seeing as Creative: Or Not

Our *everyday creativity*,[2] our "originality of everyday life," when viewed an outcome, involves just two aspects being (a) <u>original</u>, new, or unusual, and having (b) <u>meaningfulness</u>, not in some profound sense, but simply that it not be fully accidental or random, and is able to communicate. If, at a picnic, if we accidentally drop a jar of jam on the pavement and it creates sparking purple grape-colored shapes and fragments, if the abstract pattern stops us, and we say, "oh my!" then ponder it perhaps including drops of jam that escaped further away, or whatever our conscious experience may be—this is no longer a random or accidental event, any more than a(nother) scene from nature. (We too are nature!). The moment is far from meaningless (it is a wonder).[3]

Our noticing, looking, observing, for one, can be creative—or not. A painter can choose and frame in their mind a brilliant scene to work with. Perhaps a sunset. Implied too in a choice are other qualities of the person or their process, some central indeed, absolutely necessary, including conscious awareness. (If we are on "automatic pilot" we won't be creating a lot!)

Another common and popular pair of criteria for creativity is originality with *usefulness*, but we do not go there for these purposes. We are not making judgments of value on a "product" (object, idea, performance, etc.) at one point in time; it is also laden with societal values plus time may well prove us wrong. Further, we are looking more, here anyway, for evidence of creativity-in-motion in the wake of a person. We seek the presence of freshness and originality within our lived experience—in this case, a scene experienced in the moment, new to us, new to the world—and not a special product designed to solve a particular problem.

Opening Up Options

Ok, then, we missed one view along the road. How serious is that, anyway?

Or are we missing something bigger, more general? Might we learn to open our experience a lot more, as our norm—for creativity, for a fuller life? That is the premise.

When people say, "Stop and smell the roses," is this perhaps some of the most powerful advice we can receive? Not just about the roses, per se, though let us indeed appreciate the world's beauty. Not just about laying off compulsive work (or something else we are thoughtlessly and maybe frantically doing, and for hours on end) to breathe and enjoy life and each other. Not even about an ongoing practice of being "alive in the present moment" (although we are very much for being present in our manifest reality, and aware of the greater realities in our world!).[4]

The issue here is not only about outcome, not only the creative (or uncreative) *product* or nature of our lived experience, but also of our *process*. How do we get here, stuck in this box, so remarkably constricted in our experience; how might we creatively open things up? How much can we transform things by being more conscious, aware, and self-aware, so as to open up alternatives, to have more choice in how we live! contemplating the figurative "blinders" we may be wearing, in this case, to encounter what we call "the world around us." Why this particular *content* in our experience, why this *process* that supplies it. Is there another world out there?

In what ways can we be more consciously aware of what we experience—and do not experience—rather than mindlessly and unconsciously accepting this as our "one reality." Surely we often do just that? Plus, all the easier to do, if assuming that it is other peoples' reality as well.

Creative Choices

A new awareness of process and choice can heighten our moment-to-moment creative experience, our capacity to feel alive, and be more spontaneous, interactive, flexible and richly aware of options in every moment. It turns out this can be more healthy than many other ways to live.[5] It can also, and already, include what we mean here by *everyday creativity*, or our "originality of everyday life." One need not make or produce something. One can bring more creative choice to one's lived experience.

If we were photographers, for instance, we might see vastly many more panoramas and scenes as we go down a street. We are not just looking for a turn signal, or a stop sign, but varied possibilities, for instance, scenes of beauty or social meaning; this issue is one of choice, plus we are aware there are multiple ways to frame the picture. Selections can be made for many reasons. Plus we need not stop with only one.

Originality and Meaningfulness

For *everyday creativity*, for outcomes (including the freshness of our observations, as well as our activities) to meet criteria of *originality* and *meaningfulness* need not be rare.[6] Our "originality of everyday life," can be present almost anywhere (although we may pass it by in places where it could have been valuable). You and I can be creatively present to life in writing a report, teaching a class, landscaping the yard, fixing the car, designing an experiment, counseling a friend, raising a child—as well as in more "traditionally creative" activities and areas of endeavor such as the arts or sciences. Everyday creativity is *less about what we do than how we do it.*

Our primary focus is not *eminent creativity* (where creative outcomes or the creator her/himself have received fame or social recognition,[7] albeit they are linked and everyday creativity is ongoing, most likely, in well-known creators as well as a precursor for further eminent creations). Still, eminence is not a guarantee of lasting quality or uniqueness or societal influence. Consider a painting (let us say) by a renowned and popular figure whose works fetches prices in the tens of thousands. It may have less originality and depth of meaning than a closeted and completely unknown painting done quietly at home. (I am actually thinking of someone here with canvases filed in a cabinet at-home, who is not—at least at present—seeking the spotlight.) Our creativity criteria are not about the spotlight![8]

Lifetime Creativity Scales

Question: Can one find everyday creativity throughout daily life and, if so, how will we know this? Some of us therefore sought a way, including this author (who had done a Ph.D. dissertation on creativity assessment) along with colleagues, including psychologist Dr. Dennis Kinney. We developed an in-depth, real-life and interview-based lifetime assessment at Harvard Medical School and McLean Hospital. We then extensively validated this "norm-referenced" approach (based on how unusual potential creations were—looking at both quality and quantity, and at work and leisure). We called the result The Lifetime Creativity Scales (LCS).[9] This development and validation process involved a large research and assessment group, hundreds of participants, multiple meetings, discussions, examples, determinations of inter-rater reliability, construct and predictive validity, and more; if you know assessments, this is a very big job. Beyond a report in *The Journal of Personality and Social Psychology*, he LCS itself was later published, and translated into languages including Portuguese (with back-translation as a check).[10] We were pleased that Daniel Goleman featured our LCS, and applications in mental health (to be discussed later) in the Tuesday *ScienceNews* section of the *New York Times*.[11]

This type of scale development is not easy by the way—to assess virtually any activity of everyday life, in a reliable and valid way.[12] If we want to "catch it all," this means almost *any* activity an individual might report The goal is to capture our "originality of everyday life," whatever it may be, and however it comes out, at work or at leisure, whether done quietly at home, or celebrated publicly on a big stage. We need to cast a large net here—to include within everyday creativity all that is possible. Activities are not always our first choice either, for example, very ingenious acts by delinquent youth, drug dealers, or financial con artists who rob us of long garnered savings. It is a further challenge to see what is original without being distracted by fame or notoriety. Everyday creativity raises some interesting issues.

Anywhere? As renowned creativity researcher Frank Barron once said, "Originality is almost habitual with highly creative people."[13] They are not just creative at the office and then flop in a chair at home (usually). They may still bring inspiration to making dinner, a favorite hobby, or home decorations. Or something more unlikely than these, for instance, doing a quick and clever repair on some broken eyeglasses.[14]

We have now morphed into talking about *creativity as "habitual," even as a way of life.* Whatever it is, they (or we), the creator, may tend to approach it differently. Sometimes the approach is highly unusual. For instance, our participants in validating the LCS included persons who brought mortally endangered refugees to safety in World War II, through creativity, risk, and courage; we even had a special historian-consultant for this aspect of our creativity ratings.[15] Consider also a parent who made clothes from scraps for her large family during tough times, and an auto-mechanic who *invented his own tools* to better do his work. What then about a parent who constructed a special chair for a disabled son, giving him greater options?

Creativity as Part of Who We Are

Interestingly, in these examples, we find, at minimum, creative *process* as well as *product*. (If it is fixing a car, our participant and someone else may both have fixed a car, and done so with excellence—but in very different ways.)

Also, this raises the issue of ongoing qualities for a creative *person*—is this so?—where it is said that "originality is almost habitual." Are there other such qualities, and what might they be? In fact, a very large literature exists on this very question. One example (see below and Chap. 9) is Openness to Experience. What other qualities might exist that transcend special talents, e.g., drawing talent, or musical expertise? Meanwhile it is important to acknowledge that special talents too have a place, in a specific area. Consider for example music. We will do better playing the piano (or composing) with a little experience[16] Yet let us suggest creative *potential* in the broader sense is the inheritance of all of us and part of being human[17]—and can be more important yet when it becomes a *way of life.*

A range of qualities appear to bridge fields, and are part of creative living. I was privileged to edit a book for the American Psychological Association called *Everyday Creativity and New Views of Human Nature: Psychological, Social, and Spiritual Perspectives*[18] with some remarkable contributors. For the concluding chapter, I did a qualitative content analysis of the integrating themes that emerged across contributions. The list of 12 included: conscious, open, non-defensive, dynamic, and integrating, among others—ant these are ones, I'd suggest, we might also want to find in a friend. As explored in this book, these can also benefit our own health and development.

Four Ps of Creativity: Perspectives on Product, Process, Person, Press

One can speak of The Four P's of Creativity—creative *product, process, person,* and also *press* (of the environment), four valuable perspectives or lenses we can use to explore creativity.[19] After all, we are interested in the big picture in this book. We turn the camera around from a creative outcome to look back—to look back at *us*—standing in the background, we who are doing the creating. The creating is not just changing the identified outcome (book, mural, office arrangement, teaching plan, whatever the goal) but *also the creator*, it also is changing *us*. For instance, if we are looking within our creative minds, if we are more open and non-defensive, may we become more comfortable with ourselves? We look at such questions throughout the book. We even posit—all else being equal—that living creatively *can* help us thrive, even become better more open and authentic people, more aware of life, and of others.[20]

"All else being equal" is very important here, since we do have many examples of thoughtless or self-involved creativity or frankly "malevolent creativity."[21] History provides numerous instances, as does a look around today. In what creative situations can one say a greater openness, non-defensiveness, and conscious awareness is apt to increase, and bring us more in touch with our better selves and the benefit of others? It seems expressive arts might be one area, among others that ask us to search within. Some types of teaching, or mentoring, could qualify. Yet many "core" creative qualities apply across fields, including science or math.[22]

The Fourth P is environmental *press*. The environment is greatly more important than some realize. Some might like to see themselves as singular, independent, and self-sufficient persons, but we are interconnected and subject to many influences. Just think of one's creativity with a stern and critical boss (or teacher or parent), compared to the experience risking a new and unique creative idea with an understanding supporter! The first reaction can even shut our creativity right down. Too often, over time, negative reactions convince some people that, creatively, they are "no good."

One can then verge into *epigenetics*, into ways our environment can call forth different potentials from us.[23] Environment is interacting here with our genotype, our DNA, differentially bringing out aspects of our potential. Aspects of how we manifest are drawn out in response to a larger context. This is not just about a teenager who is said to be conforming to a peer group—in an earlier era it might have involved smoking or overusing alcohol. More positively, one may think instead of a fresh employee, somehow drawn to a particular job opening who, encouraged to develop new skills, finds she is an absolute Internet whiz.

True enough, we, as creators and human beings, can *change* our environment, and not just respond to it. Yet it is meanwhile it is calling to, and very often changing, us.

In a more ongoing way, we have cultural evolution potentially on our side, so as to pass on and continue useful advances that we discover. Let us communicate that Internet hint! (Might it even "go viral"?) Is there a chance here—and most dedicated teachers would say a resounding YES!—to create educational conditions for different types of learning and change—including ones that can improve our lives, beliefs about self and others, and even the larger culture?

Please hold onto that one.

One can ask many new questions, once creativity can be assessed, our goal being again, not to miss that creative product, most anywhere it might emerge. Plus one can bring in the Four Ps, to look at the larger system and our role within it! We can research diverse questions: For instance what environments stimulate creativity for kids. (This refers to kids in general, not just young people who get designed "gifted"—and where sometimes this has less to do with creativity, than standardized test scores).[24] Or about ADHD and creativity—is there a relationship? Or ways of preventing bullying among youth, or providing equality of opportunity across groups. Deciding if one's personal relationship is a creative one. Plus, a great deal more.

For the LCS, Dr. Kinney and I, along with Maria Benet and Ann Merzel, looked at two aspects of everyday creativity: Peak Creativity and Extent (related to quality and quantity), assessing these separately at work and leisure, and overall. Setting can make a difference. How many people endure tedious work and come home and, quietly, do something marvelous. They may be chefs, artists, or artists in raising their children. We wanted to miss no one! We return later to many issues above, as found in everyday life, and in clinical situations.

Human Limitations or "Blinders" on Lived Experience

It is helpful to get a sense of our experiential restrictions. We cannot cover, here, all sensory and perceptual limitations or filters. Yet consider examples two types of "blinders" which—from a creativity perspective—can limit our experience. The first is visual, since this is the most dominant sense for most people. The points are also applicable to other senses such as hearing, smelling, tasting, or other muscular and physiological sensations, important for most of us.[25] Our perceptions can further open further a path to creative possibility—or can narrow our options. The examples here involve (a) alternations of consciousness, and looking within one state of consciousness, (b) attentional issues. You can even go online and try one puzzle yourself. Will you "see it"?

Alterations of Consciousness

Imagine. Worlds existing "out there" we don't even suspect. Yet meanwhile, do we think we see it all? I confess I do at times. Similarly many of us. Consider effects of alterations of consciousness. Change these and potentially change the movie!

As William James[26] (1901/1958), Father of American psychology, put it:

> … our normal waking consciousness, rational consciousness as we call it. is but one special type of consciousness, whilst all about it, parted from it by the filmiest of screens, there lie potential forms of consciousness entirely different. We may go through life without suspecting their existence; but apply the requisite stimulus, and at a touch they are there in all their completeness …. they forbid a premature closing of our accounts with reality.…

Baruss, citing pioneer Charles Tart's view, experientially defines an *altered state of consciousness* (ASC) as "a qualitative alteration in the overall pattern of mental functioning, such that the experiencer feels his (or her) consciousness is radically different from the way it functions ordinarily."[27] For Tart, this involved 14 varied dimensions including attention, perception, imagery, memory, emotions, arousal and more. Alternatively, Baruss offers three separate types of lenses, or ways of knowing, as "stable patterns of physiological, cognitive, and experiential events different from those of the ordinary waking state".[28]

Baruss stresses for ASCs, the *stability* and *distinctiveness* of such patterns. Altered states are more ongoing (if not as permanent as "traits" we link with people over time), and clearly distinguishable. Two common examples are deep sleep and dreaming. The looser construct of *alterations of consciousness*, does not require discrete and stable "states." These can even function as precursors to more stable states later on. For instance, we can stay open in a more ongoing way to experiences of beauty and wonder.

Note that characteristic and recurring states, as for instance in meditative experience[29] can even alter the physical brain. In meditation, EEG patterns include slow waves, not unlike patterns which can occur as well in insight-generation phases of creativity, discussed further later.[30] Hence we may well wonder if these can become more easy to access or more habitual.

Here, Baruss's term, *alterations of consciousness*, is used, being a little less strong than "altered states" (but often the same), to avoid certain controversies. Certain issues with ASCs, complex psychologically, remain debated, leading to issues and distinctions. For instance how does one classify hypnosis? Plus hypnosis may involve more than one process.

Still the concern here is not State A vs. B, but *to note these states exist at all in creative process*. They do exist, a rich multiplicity of experiential possibilities, some more transient, some more ongoing. How significant that altered consciousness is usually not mentioned in creativity literature.[31]

Do we already somehow know some of these alterations, know their "flavors"?[32] It seems possible. We boldly go further to ask whether creative aspirants can learn ways deliberately to "change channels" for creativity, in the moment, when the need arises. Some of us believe so—even if we could not necessarily state what happens in words. Willfully, and then how? With biofeedback? That might work. Here are possibilities worth researching. For the moment, though, let us note we may have rented more personal experiential channels from our cable supplier than we thought we had.

Selective Attention: When Parts of a Whole Go Invisible

Looking within one form of consciousness, we still miss a great deal. Here's a stunning example you can try yourself[33] The link is in the footnotes for Daniel Simons' and associates test of selective attention, a video on YouTube. If this is new to you, my guess is you will miss seeing the … had better not say. We do routinely put on blinders to some stimuli, very useful in our task-oriented life, where we need to focus on A not B. We are driving and do not want to miss the turnoff! But how amazing when we are fully blind to a dramatic event. Still we are almost always selecting in some way, often unconsciously. The demonstration above (which is also a well-researched effect—for instance 50% missed the event in one study, this may seem almost like a magic trick. These often operate on a related principle of distraction.

The above video shows a ball game with teams in black and white each trying to pass a ball to their teammates, while avoiding the other team. You have a task to do while watching. Suddenly, bounding into the middle, then boldly stopping mid-stage and beating his/her chest, is a (don't miss it!) figure which then exits in the opposite direction. Odds are excellent that you or the typical viewer never even see this figure. (Although you now have a major hint, you might still miss its appearance.) After this one is mastered, you are encouraged to play further YouTube videos from this group where a different "surprise" is used. Oops—they really did get me again!

Or on a more mundane note, picture yourself driving down a street, on a rainy day, and here are stores and signs, cars and traffic, lights and crosswalks, horns and whooshing cars in rain. Yet all you want is a cup of coffee. The rest fades into invisibility. How quickly—and almost as if floodlit—a sign for *Starbucks* (or another favorite venue) shines out. The need to have that coffee is dominant. Much more in the world goes invisible.

Opening Things Up with Awareness and Mindfulness

Mindfulness and Presence

Another way to encounter the world, whether on the Oregon country roads or an urban street where we are languishing for coffee, can be enlarged via Buddhist practice or wisdom of other Eastern traditions.[34] One can move from worries and experiences framed by memories of the past or future expectations, to an immersion, more broadly and without goal or judgment, in the present moment. One is *present*. One is more *mindful*.[35] If vastly more is still missed (and such remains our narrow slice of life), a great deal more can be noticed.

Many have heard of mindfulness meditation, which, for Vipassana practice (contemplative insight), most fully involves "non-discriminating, moment-to-moment bare awareness;"[36] A vital guideline asks us to "let go" of our engrained ways—here is the "essence of being, not doing— shedding the secondary enslavements of plans and contingencies, evaluations, and outcomes.[37]

Hence, so much for the coffee. Or the turn off the road. Focus was narrowed—we were searching for … something. Our conceptual mind assisted in focus, since we may have been looking for a specific sign, symbol, category (word *coffee*, picture of cup, logo of our favorite vendor, roadside stand, or passing diner). Interesting, when we give up a search, that mindful awareness might even feel good. Better than what we were feeling. Even if we still carry a few wisps of conceptual mind and its limiting experiences, this greater openness, and attendant *presence* can at times bring extraordinary joy. It is perhaps not surprising, as further discussed later, to find correlations with measures of creativity. Meta-analysis (a method combining many studies for stronger results) shows more association with some aspects of mindfulness than others.[38] Yet here, our purpose is to note the big picture. In general capacity for mindfulness can helps creativity. When seeking insight let us be broadly aware.

Meta-awareness, and Birth of Creativity

Here is a crucial feature, and triumph of evolution—nor is it just for creativity but in general—our *meta-awareness*: We are aware of what we are doing; this includes being aware of our own awareness! As with the Oregon Roads vignette, if we discover we have missed something, and if we care, we can moving forward, do something about it. With awareness we have a chance to open to experience, to expand our view, to look again, and to change. How amazing that we can do it.

With self-reflection then, we can consider, and we can re-consider. This also means we can see potential alternatives. We can imagine in our own minds—see next chapter for more on looking "within"—other ways that events could unfold. How revolutionary this is. One may understand how, in evolution, the extraordinary minds and brains of *Homo sapiens* really took off once we began developing such capabilities.[39]

With language or its alternatives (think arts, music, poetry, storytelling, pantomime—and let's add dreamwork[40]) we can also share discoveries with our fellows. We don't all need to discover each thing separately. They can enter the culture. They can be part of our "cultural evolution."[41] At times the price is survival itself.

Survival Itself

Picture two tribes in the frigid arctic winter. From a lightning strike, one group discovers fire, then how to preserve it, and even to rekindle it (not so easy). How quickly each hearth has a fire burning. The other tribe—well we can only hope.

Let us never take it for granted: that we humans can finally see ourselves, represent self and other, our acts, wishes, and possibilities, in our own minds. We are able to see, visualize, predict what we are doing (or what we can be drawn into doing, against our better judgment), and what might result. We can put it all out there symbolically, and potentially transform it. The colors are there on we here call our "creative palette" (this time a palette of life, and inner/outer experience and possibility).

This material is potentially available for new pictures. If we want, we can paint the picture differently another time. This is our next chapter.

Finding these capacities will require some practice, skill, time, and serious commitment, as with mindfulness training—or for that matter any capacity, including facility with visual arts, or everyday creative living. We all make our choices, and invest in what we value and need. Whatever that is, the main point is *having the choice. If we want, we can visualize alternatives and choose to live differently. Our personal creativity is born!*

Others Reflect on Their Experiences

I was moved by comments on www.awakin.org/?tid=778, including people sharing their own Aha! Moments, or renewed presence in a fuller experience of the world. Must we control or prejudge everything? Or can we meet life with wonder. Often, whether we are purposefully creating, or living life in predictable ways, the greatest wonders come unexpectedly. Interestingly the first respondent has ways of actively seeks these new experiences.[42] Seven excerpts follow, beginning with this one:

- … I developed a passion for taking off on a whim, just to see things I had never seen before …. these forays continued, not so much with the auto but with kayak or skis. (F.A.)

- … realize and see the true 'gifts' before us … where we are at … and living and being for the first time … no media reports, no distortions, no photo-shopping … (E.L.)

- … sometimes we must surrender to life …. we might be drawn off course …. but we need to have faith in knowing there is a purpose, a lesson …. in this case about developing awareness and appreciation for the blessings that surround us. (D.)

- I did a painting course last week. And ever since I have been looking at the world differently …. awed by all the lights blinking below me from the mountain road… (B.)

- Peace is all around us man, everchanging force of life to adapt to a world of misdeeds and misunderstood intentions... (J.)

- A longstanding joke with my kids is that I never get lost, when driving. If I lose sight of where I am .... they ask if we're on an adventure. (A.P.)

- I feel stuck ... am quite creative, innately, I think but .... can't get past the "have to" list ... am going to begin today .... small steps .... just observing my world, without judgment, simply... (A.)

Last Word and Next Steps

We have seen examples of limitations from our experiential "blinders," especially if we mindlessly accept them, and fail to move beyond, and expand our experience. Unfolding greater vision seems nicely bound up with everyday creativity, its openness, rich alternatives, ways of life that keep us mindful, seeking, and opening to the new. Examples here involved our "outer world," and the next chapter addresses our "inner world," our realms of mind and imagination. Yet we also see that inner and outer intertwine.

Notes

1. www.awakin.org/?tid=778. This vignette has 187,000 views, plus perceptive comments posted by readers.
2. Richards, "Everyday Creativity," 190.
3. Kinney, Richards, and Southam, "Everyday Creativity, Its Assessment, and The Lifetime Creativity Scales," 285.
4. Senge, Scharmer, Jaworski, and Flowers, *Presence.*
5. Richards, ed., *Everyday Creativity.*
6. Kinney, Richards, and Southam, "Everyday Creativity..." Also see Loori, *Zen of Creativity.*
7. Runco, Mark, and Ruth Richards, eds. *Eminent Creativity, Everyday Creativity, and Health.*
8. A friend does stunning spiritual paintings that are symbolic, archetypal, moving, and has shown widely in the past, but now is working more

privately. Is it any less impressive if it isn't publicly "out there" now (or had never been)?

9. Kinney, Richards, Southam, "Everyday Creeativity." Also figures such as John Dewey, and Abraham Maslow, prefigured in their writings what we are now calling everyday creativity.
10. Shansis, Fleck, Richards, Kinney, Izquierdo, Mattevi, Maldonado and Berlim, "das Escalas de Criatividade ao Longo da Vida."
11. Goleman, "New Index Illuminates the Creative Life," C1, C9.
12. E. Paul Torrance originated ratings of real-life creativity on a simpler scale and helped inspire us. Often assessments start with a refined group of creators. Starting with *everyone* reveals much that would have been missed.
13. Barron, *Creativity and Personal Freedom.*
14. As my creative daughter once did.
15. With all thanks to historian Dr. Ruth Soule Arnon Hanham.
16. Amabile, *Creativity in Context.*
17. Richards, ed. *Everyday Creativity*; Dobzhansky, *Mankind Evolving.*
18. Richards, ed. *Everyday Creativity.*
19. Richards, "Four Ps of Creativity," 733.
20. Richards, "A Creative Alchemy".
21. Cropley, Cropley, Kaufman, and Runco, *Dark Side of Creativity.*
22. Barron and Harrington, "Creativity, Intelligence, and Personality".
23. Moore, *The Developing Genome.*
24. Richards, "Who is Gifted and Talented?", 6.
25. Tart, *States of Consciousness.*
26. James, *Varieties of Religious Experience*, 298.
27. Baruss, *Alterations of Consciousness.*
28. Ibid., 8.
29. Goleman and Davidson, *Altered Traits*, 249.
30. Austin, *Zen and the Brain.*
31. Richards, "Everyday Creativity."
32. Richards and Goslin-Jones, "Everyday Creativity."
33. Simons and Chabris. "Selective Attention Test," www.theinvisiblegorilla.com.
34. Thich Nhat Hanh, *The Heart of the Buddha's Teaching.*
35. Shapiro and Carlson, *Art and Science of Mindfulness.*
36. Siegel, *The Mindful Brain*, 267.
37. Ibid., 243.

38. Richards and Goslin-Jones, "Everyday Creativity."
39. Developed further in Chap. 7.
40. Singer, *Imagery in Psychotherapy.*
41. Richards, "When Illness Yields Creativity," 517.
42. I know the first respondent who has done this for years, enjoying freshness of experience.

3

Creative Palette

[…] Long have you timidly waded, holding a plank by the shore,
Now I will you to be a bold swimmer,
To jump off in the midst of the sea, and rise again and nod to me
And shout, and laughingly dash with your hair.
Walt Whitman

Aware of our own *awareness*, let us stop, look, be present, and open our minds to self, life, and inner worlds—even if these seem, at times, to be foreign lands. Let us know creativity as a *process*, often with *unconscious* and developmentally primitive aspects. If we find exploring the hidden or the banished can be hard, discovery and integration can also be healing, even joyful. Plus, in connecting more deeply within and without, we can find our unique place in an evolving whole.

© The Author(s) 2018
R. Richards, *Everyday Creativity and the Healthy Mind,*
Palgrave Studies in Creativity and Culture,
https://doi.org/10.1057/978-1-137-55766-7_3

What Creative Palette?

Let us turn to issues in actively creating a *product* of our own, and the figurative "colors" we may use. One may contemplate our figurative *creative palette*, within the "creative deep"[1] of our unconscious mind, and the many colors—so to speak—of our creative possibilities going forward. Visual, auditory, and more. Here are sensory possibilities, as we uniquely appreciate them, and the structures we build around them with our minds, and these can be almost endless. Our *everyday creativity* can abound in all directions, drawing from the manifest world we have experienced and our worlds within, pulling from distant experience and even timeless archetypes up to our present experience, and future hopes and fantasies. This includes drawing from our libraries of memories, which are changing and reconfiguring in a dynamic mind. These are drawn from conscious and unconscious sources, including hopes (and fears), our affective lives, and imagined visions and possibilities (which, one recalls, we have built from our inner content and process, with limitations being only those of our own). Otherwise, we stand on the "borders of infinity," with possibilities abundant in our creative minds.

Imagery is key here, and a helpful characterization is provided by Lyn Freeman, from the 3rd edition of her *Mosby's Complementary and Alternative Medicine*.[2]

> **Imagery** is the thought process that invokes and uses the senses. These senses include vision, sound, smell, and taste, as well as the senses of movement, position, and touch. Virtually nothing exists in our experience that we do not image in some way, and these images can produce physiologic, biochemical, and immunologic changes in the body that affect health outcomes.

Since these images are more complex than a Polaroid photo or a recording of some theoretically objective stimulus—especially when originating in our inner imaginative quarters—let us add here, from the late mind-body medicine expert, Jeanne Achterberg[3]:

In the behavioral and social sciences, "image" is treated as an hypothetical construct, an intervening variable between the stiumulus/input and the response/output. As such the image finds itself in the quite respectable company of the other great issues studied: learning, motivation, memory, and perception …. the image is a putative event that is influenced by both the internal and external environment, or in a relationship between stimulus and response.

One finds a touchstone here within Buddhist philosophy. Perception involving one sense, let us say vision, brings together three aspects: sense organs, objects, and a sense-consciousness (eye, visual stimulus, process of seeing), whether in the moment or our later remembering or creating. The process is all of a piece; it all comes up together.

Why is this important? Let us not oversimplify our creative experience. We don't just see something "out there." Or "in here" either. The construction is complex and profound, drawing from an outer manifest reality and inner processes. "Inside" and "outside" are not so immutable or distinct.

Some of us, let us say, are gazing at a cheerful bubbling brook in the bright sunshine. Or that is how some of us, at least, see it. For each person, it is all an integrated whole, outer, inner, and process—although we may well imagine each person is looking at exactly the same scene. We each experience it in our own way—for instance, as with the last chapter, our own forms of selective attention. How amazed I was, for instance, when my daughter was young, had pencil and paper, and at a friend's house started drawing what I was sure would be the stunning view from the property. Not at all. She was fascinated with the curved and overlapping ceramic tiles on the roof of the house. She explained why these were so amazing.

For years, I showed a slide of this drawing in giving talks. We think we know what another is seeing. We may have a good idea—but at other times we may not have a clue!

There is more. Each perception, whatever it is, brings with it endless trails of associations and meanings, *for that individual,* histories, stories, feelings, concepts and primitive complexes of associations, drawing on our own inner worlds. Would it be a wonder some of us liked this cheerful and aesthetic experience of a bubbling brook while some other people didn't?

This is all part of our figurative *creative palette* of life—what we bring and what we create—our own expanse of remembered, imaginal and generative ingredients, toward our own creation, our palette of figurative colors. These go far beyond a visual artist's palette. Below we explore instances of this, but first….

Highlighting How Healthy This Can Be

A quick mention of creativity and health is worth adding, as we go deep, and perhaps find unexpected content. Freud, Jung, and others have extolled benefits of making the "unconscious conscious."[4] It also matters how this happens. Exploration needs to be done with sensitivity; who knows what surprises await. (We are speaking of healthy processes of self-discovery, here, whether on one's own or with others—not sudden or traumatic encounters that surprise and overwhelm, without needed support.)

Jung in fact recommended two steps for working with unconscious material, in his process of "active imagination." This process allows unconscious material to express itself, through emergence of forms including images. The first stage provides an opening through something like a meditative state, to suspend "rational critical faculties" and "give free rein to fantasy"; it can "bring things alive." In the second step, "consciousness takes the lead" in apprehending meaning.[5] Steps one and two can alternate rapidly or slowly (this resonates with other programs as well). Insights can move the individual toward personal integration and unity, through unconscious and even collective unconscious revelations. Do note that *unconscious* material here implies "certain events of which we have not consciously taken note … (which) have been absorbed subliminally."[6]

Mind-Body Boost

With successful processing, as we see further later, in Pennebaker's expressive writing research (this process too reveals unconscious material—in writing about very difficult past experience), there is a positive psychological boost. This is perhaps right away, but often later, from revelation and integrated understanding. Beyond that, measureable and remarkable changes have been found in mind-body indices. These include increased working memory (a reflection of more inner integration), and higher immune (T-cell) function than found in participants from a control group, and hence greater resistance to disease.[7] How amazing, our mind-body continuum.

Hence, we as creators may get a bonus. Not only is there realization of an original creative impulse, and a product we wanted to create, but another very notable product, namely: *beneficial changes in us*. There can be varied healthy mind-body effects on the creator—on you or on me.

Comparing Creative Palettes

Artist's Palette

This artist's palette is familiar perhaps. Imagine one in your "mind's eye": a curving board, perhaps oval, perhaps round, in blonde or dark wood, with a hole for one's thumb (held in the left hand, for a right handed artist) with colors arrayed around the outside. Red, blue, yellow, green, orange, purple, while and black, primaries and secondaries, light and dark, and more. Then we mix them and use them. The palette itself can become a work of art, with mixed, dabbed, swirled, used, and sometimes muddied, colors. Might this be true as well for our personal *creative palette* of mind and life? It can be another work of art—even including patterns of how we the Life Artist has been changed for the better.[8]

Creative Palette (of Life)

This next one can get wild. One sees, in theory, that here is everything we can draw upon—on our palette—everything now, in the past, in the imagined future, on nonexistent worlds and across fantasized galaxies, conscious and unconscious, memories, projections, imaginative constructions, virtual realities we can generate in numerous forms. Is he going to call me? Yep, that can be one too.

Images, fantasies, symbols, myths, archetypes—might this even get "transpersonal," drawing on deep cultural even human truths we all, as *H. sapiens,* harbor, found deep below consciousness, even a collective unconscious, reflecting our genetic and evolutionary history? Jungians among others work with this, bridging across time, world cultures, belief systems. In some form we know these. Great Mother archetype, Hero's Journey, and more.[9] Joseph Campbell's multiple books, including *The Hero with One-Thousand Faces.* Narratives of our personal lives are often organized by symbol and story.[10] Jung also believed archetypes in our dreams and some themes and myths can transcend time and civilizations, drawing on ancient and unconscious instincts from our evolutionary past.[11] Might we have encoded physically some wisdom across aeons of hominid evolution?

Notably, important discoveries have emerged from imagery in dreams and early hypnagogic states while falling asleep. Elias Howe, for example, invented the sewing machine after visualizing a spear in his dream, and one with a hole near the pointed top. The scientist, Kekule, in a hypnogogic moment, falling asleep before a fire, saw an ancient snake symbol; this led to the six-sided carbon ring that transformed organic chemistry.[12]

Re-creating and Healing Self

We live in a world of change and surprise. Our creative product is just one piece. Turning the camera around, our creative *product* will come to include us as well since we are all part of this picture and too are changing, each moment, in our larger setting, now we as the creative *person.* We do not, for instance, always know the stories of our lives—parts can be unconscious, hidden, subliminal. We are writing stories, and they may be powerful. Yet what stories do we meanwhile discover within.

Toward greater mental health, we may pursue these—reasons, among others, that we have art therapy, expressive writing, poetry therapy and more. The goal is more the artist than the art. And how it can help. These discoveries and experiences, our new insights and explorations, also become part of our creative palette. For depression, trauma, life threatening illness and much more, our creating can provide new perspectives, and a new sense of control and capacity to cope. We after all have drawn the picture (or told the tale), and we can change it.

We can all have hidden stories that don't reach consciousness, which may be unhelpful to us. For instance, beliefs about certain activities we once tried: I just can't do that! Forget this class! Alternative: I have always been resilient and can take on new challenges; I can handle this one too. Unconscious aspects may seem elusive, but often we can find them. Another option is Cognitive-Behavioral Therapy (or practice, and this can be done on one's own) which can help us directly uncover and alter key underlying beliefs and behaviors.[13] With new discoveries, entire new areas of the creative palette (of life), once dim or hidden, can suddenly open up, and become brilliant with figurative colors and possibilities.

Ongoing Development—Living by Symbols, by Story

How rich are the layered powers of mind! A symbol (more than a sign) can go very deep. Our "experiential mind," says Jerome Singer, "often encodes and stores our life events in symbolic or imagery forms, using the religious and cultural legends with which we've grown up..." There is also "special potential ... in the formation of life narratives."[14] With symbols, Singer gives one modern example that draws from earlier times, putting a "tiger in your tank"! What ancient associations.! Another, more recently, and so tragically, is new meaning for the symbol of a "mushroom" (a mushroom cloud). I have also seen people bring in grim war imagery in difficult personal stories. "I couldn't believe it. They really dropped a bomb on me."

I have been privileged to teach the wonderful course *Personal Mythology and Dreamwork,* which includes revisioning of one's past and further growth, while bringing to light some unconscious stories that have unknowingly shaped our lives. Here is a colorful path of discovery, as outlined by Feinstein and Krippner, in their book, *The Mythic Path.*[15] A five stage process includes practices, rituals, fairy tales, and other exercises, plus deep contacts with one's own wisdom figure (or higher power), which could be an ancestor or "inner shaman." This program (or related others[16]) can definitely bridge some unconscious barriers, if we are brave and motivated and truly want to understand our life stories, motives and choices. Creative *product* in this case, is very much also a renewed *creative person.*

Example: We may have been making sacrifices to become an astrophysicist or molecular biologist (nothing wrong with those choices, let us add!), but are we struggling simply because someone else wanted it? A rather unfortunate story, isn't it? Often stemming from some well-meaning parents, but parents with their own ideas. Even for their older offspring. We do tend to organize our lives by story, and may have unknowingly imbibed a narrative about our future lives, including careers, without really knowing it.

Now what do we actually want? Does it sound as if our personal mythology is a carefully guarded secret. In fact it is. We don't quite knows the secret—to the extent we have kept it from ourselves. A veiled and subliminal story also translates to dark spot on our *creative palette*—It is not usable material for future creativity if we do not know it is there, what it means, nor how we might change its message. As Feinstein and Krippner say[17]:

> Your personal mythology operates "behind the scenes" in your psyche. It shapes your every thought, perception, and action, bringing them to conform to an underlying story line. Most people cannot quite articulate this unfolding internal mythology, but it nonetheless directs the course of their lives.

Really? Does this sound like big trouble? What then is our own story? Perhaps it seems time to unearth it, to shine up one's creative palette of rich and *usable* life content. We can also revisit our option, in every moment, consciously to recreate our story and our own life.

Group Creating and Children's Play

One may turn to an under-recognized yet vital and pervasive area of healthy creative growth, and one often depending on story. Here is a form of creativity which can glow brightly on a creative palette for one's future life, even at times as a rehearsal: the effects of children's pretend play. How sad that I was literally told, years ago, that a certain school would have less time for this pretend play, once kids get "serious" in upper elementary school. This is when older kids start learning their "Three R's." (It is also, incidentally, a time kids' creativity scores may drop.)[18]

Sandra Russ whose major accomplishments include expanding the psychology of play, and developing *The Affect in Play Scale*, has found many significant relationships between pretend play and child and adult creativity—and involving both intellectual and emotional aspects.[19] One further question might be: Why aren't we adults playing more?

As for the kids: No!, we will not cut back on recess. At play, kids are learning to create in groups as well as individually, and as part of it, enhancing their social and emotional development, their emotional regulation, and ability to cope resiliently with diverse challenges. I am a space ranger, and here is my team. I am an invisible girl. We are a super-cool hard-driving hit-writing rock 'n roll band. Well whyever not "be" this?

There is little limit to what one can make up, in pretend play, except in one's imagination. So much one can be learning. (Even career planning.) Plus, overall, how to survive childhood and thrive in adulthood—and throughout one's life.

Please, let us put away those cellphones at recess!

Again, here are new and brilliant colors, figuratively speaking, thoughts, feelings, enthusiasms, play experiences to call upon for one's new imaginative possibilities—truly colors to last a lifetime—as placed on one's creative palette.

In the Forest: Rich Associations, Complex Webworks of Thought

Let us move to associative mind (think of how your mind can jump link by link, maybe taking a winding path, for instance in daydreaming); it can leave in its wake a rich webwork of associations branching in all directions, content for later creative discovery. Creative mind also can use and integrate many levels or developmental forms of processing, including some that were early or, as some say, primitive (see also Chap. 12). Some might think earlier modes are no longer needed, once we have mastered the likes of mature conceptual thinking, and hypothetico-deductive styles. Yet more primitive conceptual modes (see Chap. 9) and loose associative richness can weave mighty webs. "Intuition," whereby we arrive at a solution in a flash, without reasoning, is there as well, at all ages, and can call on multiple processes, including unconscious, procedural, holistic, nonverbal, and bodily knowing.[20]

For high creativity we can "have it all," merging capacities of mind of multiple forms and from different developmental origins.[21] As one example, consider the following, written originally for *New Directions in Child Development.* The aware creator can follows a dynamic flow into a fertile place in one's creative palette, where many other miracles are fluid and coalescing, and the new can be born.[22]

I. An Example

This is a particular place … tall sequoias to the heavens, dense ground beneath, cool, wet, s tray beams of sunlight flickering through tall boughs, hanging moss, the ground matted with needles, cones, brush, ground ferment, trails of soft slimy creatures. You stop, you listen to the silence. Not even the distant traffic is heard, so unusual that its absence is thundering. The song of a bird, the drop of high moisture, then it's still. One is enclosed, enwombed, in a forest that exceeds one's own scale even to imagine, one's mightiest parent, so comforting and natural that, indeed, on might always have been there.

II. Associating Through a Forest: The Content

How does one see this forest? It's not a sensory snapshot, taken verbatim, to be filed away. It is processed by its own creative process, in conjunction with everything related and remembered in one's past….

There are the stories about the forest you once heard, the summer trip with your family, the drives with your grandfather, the walks with your mother, the picture books, the postcards from a friend, … (a) segment of Star Wars, a two-week summer camp…. You may not consciously summon up all this history. You may not even summon up its feelings. You might not even be able to remember it consciously if you want to. But, somehow it is all there…

III. Associating Through a Forest: The Process

Now look at how these associations have formed, even below our awareness in the depths of the mind. We've gone beyond concepts and logic. We are swimming from oceans to grandmas to camping trips and walking slowly down a sunlit lane. These memories are borne on the tides of our feelings, and on the links of the most primitive of types of complexes and syncretic ties. Yet somehow these all connect, and so intimately and well.

One can indeed regress to an earlier level of development, and indeed to an altered of consciousness, and mentally swim most freely amongst the myriad content that is there. In this way, one can forge new connections that might never have arisen if one had stayed on the road and taken the well- traveled highways of concepts and structures and topic outlines.

Down here, in the primordial soup, one sees the snake bite its tail, and there is Kekule's concept of the carbon ring—six carbon atoms in a ring-like structure—shining through one's dream and heralding the basis for all organic chemistry.

Who Is Running This Show?

The creative magic depends on some mental oversight of the process. The creator (also) as director. Wallas outlined five heuristic stages of creative process, *preparation—incubation—intimation—illumination—verification.*[23] These involve getting ready—letting it gel—getting subtle hints an insight is coming—The Big Aha!—and pulling it together. We deal, later, with the last three, and especially *intimation* (which is sometimes left out of the "Three I's" in the middle). Right now, though, we look at the first step, *preparation,* as one readying one's creative palette, with a bit more on the step of *incubation.*

Preparing-I

We know our purpose—at least as it initially exists (it may change). This is after all our own creation and our own creative palette. We can get our materials ready, psychologically this time, our topic on the table; we ready our resources and even prepare for *incubation* to learn more. Tricky at times, as we, the creator, balance a loose executive control with what is a sort of creative deep sea diving into our subliminal or unconscious mind. Remember, that mind too is part of our creative palette! Perhaps there are kinks we need to work out, or a personal exploration not quite finished. At times, this is all a part of *preparation.*

   Sometimes warm ups can be useful—one can give them a try—as in, for a writer, journaling, blogging, talking with a friend, or writing morning pages, as per Julia Cameron's *Writer's Way*[24] Or, depending on the creator, one may make lists of steps (for organizing an event), sketches (for landscaping), scientific ideas (for teaching a class). This is bringing useful material front-and-center and closer to consciousness. We are putting out thoughts and feelings, interests and enthusiasms, even "seeds' of something more (which we may not yet fully understand but can unfold—see Chap. 16), on the creative palette; these possibilities are now more consciously available to us, and they sparkle in the sun. For some people (or people at certain times), this can be part of their *preparation.*

Preparing-II: Keeping the Psychic Doors Open

For us at other times—or also at the same time, simultaneous with the above—we may stay open to stumbling on creative "finds" as we go along, for instance, as part of our *incubation.* We may start hearing from our subliminal depths. What a thrill it can be when this happens. Odds are higher if we manifest qualities such as an "openness to experience" (OE) or lower "latent inhibition" (LI) that screens out seemingly irrelevant information.[25] Yet maybe it isn't all irrelevant. We might prefer those abundant choices! Low LI—thus letting much material through—has been found 7 times as often in research on high creators vs. others.[26] The good news here is that OE is not a fixed quality, one we have or not. Figuratively, it is like a trap door or secret passage to a deeper part of our extensive creative palette. We can cultivate more of this access.

Keeping One's Balance Throughout

One opens to inspiration while holding loose control. This links to the *balance* Neo-Freudians refer to as "regression in the service of the ego" (e.g., in balancing the brain's executive functions, with openness to subliminal content). Resonance is seen with aspects of Jung's "active imagination." The goal here is not to get overwhelmed on the one hand, or rigidly restricted on the other. One exercises a loose creative control, accessing material for adaptive use that is not quite conscious.[27] It means playing with this balance; being in executive control, while open to possibility.

How Integrated? Do We Use This Material? Or Does It Use Us?

A further caution. When are we psychologically free to engage with and work with this material in our creative minds? This very much depends on how attached are we are (how drawn in to the memories, past, history, ongoing issues, or future concerns, without truly being free, or able to let it go). Whatever colorful or moving content we have for our creating, however close it may be to conscious awareness and thus available for our usage, the material is only on our creative palette (among our usable colors of fantasy or life experience) *if we are also able to "use it."*

Not the case if it uses us.

Zen Master Thich Nhat Hanh[28] spoke about grasping or attachment, the result of pleasant feelings that become craving. With grasping or attachment, "we are caught in the thralls of the object."

Then we are not fully free to create. This is a central point.

Let's say we are contemplating a painful relationship from our past, perhaps for use in creative writing, or in counseling with another person. Yet we still feel strongly, are trapped in some way in our past, and the personal memories draw us away. They distract us, even absorb us. As in an inescapable reverie, we get caught, we get carried away. Or perhaps the past stimulates anxiety. As in the vignette about harried driving on the Oregon roads—everything is missed but the worry.

If, as creator, we are task-oriented and mindfully aware of our strong reactions, there is hope. If we are carried away, and our creative work distorted, then this material is not yet truly available for creativity, as part of our creative palette. There is inner work yet to do.

Jung's Three Issues

Jung mentioned three kinds of problems in "coming to terms with the unconscious" in working with patients, and their reactions, including: (a) "passing over into the so-called "free association" of Freud, whereupon the patient gets caught..." or, alternatively, where (b) "the patient evinces an exclusively aesthetic interest in them ... and remains stuck in ... phantasmagoria...," or, posing more of a danger, where (c) "the subliminal contents already possess such a high energy charge that, when afforded an outlet by active imagination, they may overpower the conscious mind...".[29]

If we are directing this show, we need to be able to manage the elements we bring into it.

Playing with Dynamic Mind

More Creative Latitude than We Knew?

There are also exceptions. In arts, for instance, if we can manage a loose creative control, and have had some practice, there may be times to go with our feelings, to let go temporarily, follow some fantasies, for instance, and see what will happen! The process says a lot about our underlying dynamic of mind. The concern is not about getting "carried away," if done on purpose and ultimately manageable. It is (as director) how to exercise deliberate and "loose control" to let things "run" for a time, and on purpose—but ultimately for the purpose of the creative effort.

Our minds are evolving, always in motion. Our creative palette is always in flux. This is one way we can use it—can adventurously go with the flow. Consider these examples.

Quick Examples

Our directorial role may be to let certain dramas run on their own—and remarkably even some scientific experiments! Nicola Tesla, the inventor, was superb at this. Tesla was said to conduct certain experiments in his mind. He actually and very exactingly set up certain conditions for machinery in his imagination! He then "came back" later to observe, to a level of great precision, if the machinery he was testing needed further adjustment.[30] The is truly remarkable example, and ability of one exceptional human being. Yet it shows what a mind may, below consciousness and direct observation, actually do.

In a related context, a writer of historical fiction I have interviewed will sometimes choose to get absorbed for a bit in a tale, dragged away into an imagined situation which has been assembled and set into motion.[31] This is done consciously yet in a sort of reverie. She particularly likes to create two historical characters in conflict and "let them go." What will they do? She ultimately has the ability—and loose executive control—to say "stop." Or to tweak conditions along the way, and let things continue. This is a more delicately balanced and ongoing variant on "regression in the service of the ego" amidst changing conditions. She may have a big smile on her face as she works. She can also be surprised at events.

For both scientist and writer, we see increasingly that the creative palette, the usable material for our creating, is not at all a fixed thing—but includes an evolving dynamic *process.*

Third example: emergent future for a book series? Our minds are always humming away. Yet this one really stopped me. Quite amazing—this large and hidden evolution within mind, which changed the work plans of author Ursula LeGuin. LeGuin is a favorite author of mine; she is called by some a science fiction and fantasy writer, which is certainly central; I see her also in part as a cultural anthropologist. LeGuin often sets up conditions to see how a setting, or characters within it, will fare. She literally creates cultures and worlds in her mind—witness *The Left Hand of Darkness* which has won multiple coveted awards[32] But I write here instead about her *Earthsea Trilogy* (and about Geb, the young wizard finding his way in his world).

LeGuin was asked repeatedly by fans to write a fourth *Earthsea* book, amidst this extended area of numerous islands, and colorful fantasy figures, to continue the trilogy. No, she had said. But one day, according to LeGuin she "went back to take a look." She checked—checked within her own mind—to see what was happening, how the lands of Earthsea were faring. What she saw stopped her, "Earthsea had *changed!*" LeGuin continued the *Earthsea* series.

In this way, our creative palette—the content and processes available for creativity—are more like www.YouTube.com than a still photograph. Things do change! And not always by our conscious design.

Life in Motion, Mind in Motion

As creators we learn to come alive in new ways. We can even find new inner (and outer) worlds within our creative palette. The palette is shimmering with energy, with motion, and can bring each of our senses alive—and even bring our conscious mind a surprise or two. We feel, we care, want, intuit, imagine—and, as noted, it is not always the conscious "us" who is doing it. Amazing? Furthermore, the creator too is in motion and is being changed by the process.

Our dynamic of self and "inner" world may make even more sense when we see ourselves in touch with, and even intimately entwined with, our so-called "outer" world, our dynamic surrounds, and can visualize ourselves, as in the next chapter, as open systems.

Summary and Next Steps

Hence "outside" and "inside" are not so separate after all! Our minds create, can even heal, using content and processes from our creative palette, generating near infinite worlds of imagination and possibility. Best though if we mindfully keep a loose overriding control. Use of imagery (conscious and unconscious) can draw on dynamic memory, mind-body senses, language, emotion, narrative, dream states, timeless symbols, archetypes and more, with its own dynamic flux. In the next chapter we ask what it can mean to find oneself as a process-in-motion, an open system in an interconnected dynamic cosmos.

Notes

1. Richards, "A Creative Alchemy," 125.
2. Freeman, *Mosby's Complementary and Alternative Medicine*, 252.

3. Achterberg, *Imagery in Healing*, 144.
4. Richards, "Relationships Between Creativity and Psychopathology."
5. Jung, Encountering Jung on Active Imagination, 10.
6. Mlodinow, *Subliminal*, 5, 15.
7. Pennebaker, Kiecolt-Glaser, and Glaser, "Confronting Traumatic Experience and Immunocompetence," in Runco and Richards eds., 295.
8. Richards, "A Creative Alchemy."
9. Jung, *The Essential Jung*, 108, 208.
10. Campbell, *The Hero with One-thousand Faces*. See also Feinstein and Krippner, *Personal Mythology and Dreamwork*.
11. Jung, *Active Imagination*, 5.
12. Jung, *Man and His Symbols*, 26; see also Krippner, on dreams and creativity, *Encyclopedia of Creativity*.
13. Beck, *Cognitive Behavioral Therapy, 2nd ed.*
14. Singer, *Imagery in Psychotherapy*, 163, 9.
15. David Feinstein and Stanley Krippner, *Mythic Path*.
16. McAdams, *Stories We Live By*.
17. Feinstein and Krippner, *Mythic Path*, vii.
18. Runco and Pritzker, *Encyclopedia of Creativity*.
19. Sandra Russ, *Pretend Play in Childhood*; Also Russ, "Pretend Play and Creativity," 396.
20. Richards, "Everyday Creativity—Process and Way of Life," 200; also see Marks-Tarlow, *Psyche's Veil*.
21. Richards, "Relationships Between Creativity and Psychopathology."
22. Richards, *Everyday Creativity: Coping and Thriving in the 21st Century.*
23. Wallas, *Art of Thought*, esp. 108.
24. Cameron, *Artists Way.*
25. Kaufman and Gregoire, *Wired to Create*, 81.
26. Ibid., 87.
27. Richards, "Relationships Between Creativity and Psychopathology."
28. Thich Nhat Hanh, *The Heart of the Buddha's Teaching*, 212.
29. Jung, *Encountering Jung on Active Imagination*, 42–43.
30. Tart, *States of Consciousness*, 143.
31. Richards, "Subtleties of Creative Longing."
32. LeGuin, *Left Hand of Darkness*. Sadly, Ursula LeGuin passed from this life on January 22, 2018. She was 88 years old.

4

Change and Open Systems

The air finds its way in everywhere,
Water passes through everything.
Lieh-Tzu (*The Yellow Emperor*)

… Where order in variety we see,
And where, though all things differ, all agree.
Alexander Pope

Our dynamic of self and world makes even more sense when we see our-selves in touch with, and even intimately connected and intertwined with, our larger surrounds. "Outside" and "inside" are not so separate. We our-selves are processes-in-motion. For many it is a new view of self-in-world, one linked to a larger worldview based in dynamic change and surprise. Our influences are many, and more evident, when we visualize ourselves as open systems.

© The Author(s) 2018
R. Richards, *Everyday Creativity and the Healthy Mind,*
Palgrave Studies in Creativity and Culture,
https://doi.org/10.1057/978-1-137-55766-7_4

Open Systems, Interconnection, and Us

In this chapter we expand the scope of awareness further to see (a) change and (b) interconnection; these offer us pathways more fully to access aworld in flux, and our deeper creativity.

Science of Change and Surprise

This is a new area for some people, yet one appearing ever more central to how creativity works, and to life in general—for us individually and together. It is more dynamic and interconnected, a more holistic and *emergent* way (with the term, *emergent*, having the popular meaning, "the whole is greater than the sum of its parts") to see life and world, and expand our appreciation of larger forces and systems.[1]

This is about: *chaos and complexity theories*—not so scary at all, not requiring any math for a conceptual understanding (see references both for simpler and more formal approaches, including Guastello and associates' publications for psychology and life sciences[2]). Meanwhile the principles are conceptual, metaphorical, and for you as an observer of life, probably quite intuitive to you. This is, after all, the way the world often works. Whether getting a job, making a good investment, or falling in love. Here, as one option, the future may involve a … *boom*! Sudden change. If I had not had emergency medical care after being struck by a car over 25 years ago (dreadful experience), you would not be reading this now.

Mathematician and chaos and complexity theorist Melanie Mitchell described the *chaos* part of complex dynamical systems in her prizewinning book, *Complexity: A Guided Tour*. "The *idea* of chaos is that there are some systems—*chaotic* systems—in which even miniscule uncertainties in measurements … can result in huge errors in long run prediction." This is called *sensitive dependence on initial conditions*. Weather, terrible storms and hurricanes, stock market drops (or booms), many are the examples. A wonderful post goes viral (or, alas, it is Fake News). Even aspects of family dynamics have been cited, or falling in love!

[3]Yet such chaos is not about randomness or anarchy. There is a deep and beautiful underlying order. Further, this occurs in a profoundly connected world with multiple interdependent systems, rich with feedback, interdependent and deterministic in its intricate interconnected effect. In fact, Dr. Mitchell says, where there are "large networks of components with no central control ... simple rules of operation give rise to complex collective behavior, sophisticated information processing, and adaptation via learning or evolution."[4] Indeed a way our own learning can happen![5]

These phenomena are often *not* linear. Not at all. However, some in social sciences have been stuck teaching a linear model.[6] Twice the force leads to twice the response? It is not always so. Examples abound. Hurricanes, and earthquakes, as mentioned, downpours, fires and mudslides.[7] But also some major, long-awaited social movements. Hashtag #MeToo surely empowered many, almost overnight, who have been silenced. Other beneficial instances, we might hope, include the emergent and self-organizing Internet (who foresaw this a mere 25 years ago—I for one didn't yet have an email) or the massed defenses of a working immune system (Prigogine got a Nobel Prize for relevant work). As British mathematician Ian Stewart put it[8]:

> Today's science shows that nature is relentlessly *non*linear.... If you draw a curve at random, you won't get a straight line .... (or) as the 18th century believed in a clockwork world, so did the mid-20th century in a linear one.

Or, from social scientists and chaos theorists Guastello and Liebovitch[9]:

> Psychology is not the first science to break out of the linear rut .... physical science made the transition more than a half-century ago.

At last, psychology and social sciences are beginning to make the shift.[10]

Constructs include "open systems" (note that those include *us*), further offering a chance to "go with the flow." Like an Aikido Master, we creators can learn better to see dynamic influences, at times following the currents, going with the flow, yet tweaking things slightly when most crucial. Seeing such patterns may also help us reframe, and quite usefully today, on a shrinking multicultural globe, our *worldview* and view of *self-in-world*. And hence our larger identities and belongingness and perhaps roles.

One practical systems example from Jeremy Rifkin is alarming and is finally beginning to be believed, how our global human carbon footprint has bounded higher and higher, and is still climbing (400 ppm in 2009, far above ranges for the past 650,000 years, with multiple ecosystems seriously affected).[11] Is this a "sudden" shift? Relatively speaking. Our geologically recent human effect on the countless aeons that proceded is very much that, not to mention a prediction that even the limiting goal of 450 ppm by 2050 won't happen with current practice. Temperature and tidal rises and multiple further eco-disasters are possible. Numerous lifeforms have perished and will perish in what has been called the Sixth Extinction.[12]

"Climate change deniers"? They do not know the research.

The good news—and there is some with these same complex dynamical systems models—is that we can still affect even such massive systems. Remember the situation is *not linear*. If we act, we humans might still manage major halts to these trends if not reverses, even relatively sudden shifts. With our information culture (and a positive attitude) just imagine if world awareness, belief, and change across populations could explode geometrically? We surely need to work together to stem things— and in a time of conflict and difference, to ease circumstances for people and groups at risk to help bring people to this table. Yet could it now occur; could effects take off exponentially? It is possible. Plus remember the situation is nonlinear and complex. By its very nature, we don't know the next step precisely; with *emergence* one never knows.

Creative Insight

We now return to one big hope, human creativity, in this context. Here are models and metaphors to help us better understand not just our world, but age old mysteries of mind and life, including the *Aha! Moment* (or sudden creative insight), including *chaotic bifurcations*, or changes, and emergence of new and creative solutions. Meanwhile advances also offer new learning opportunities for boosting our own creative potential—and at another level, or area, perhaps, the potency of what we offer.

Who Are We?

Chaos and complexity theories have opened new doors for viewing our creative self. Note how the complexity definition has changed: "once an ordinary noun describing objects with many interconnected parts..." it has now become a multi-branched field of science. Whatever the example—be markets, economies, organisms, Internet, "each of these complex systems exhibits a distinctive property called *emergence*, roughly described by the common phrase, '... the action of the whole is more than the sum of the actions of the parts.'"[13]

Within larger complex systems, forms of sudden bifurcation, or change, some of which led to the term, The Butterfly Effect (relative to those quick chaotic changes or bifurcations—initially for Lorenz's findings on our temperamental weather[14]), have also been called tipping points. The book Jurassic Park, and movie based on this, are further examples, even a film specifically called *The Butterfly Effect*. These phenomena have entered popular culture—and perhaps more on the scary end than on the hopeful one, such as proposed here. It is something to contemplate.

See the gorgeous fractal forms of "The Mandelbrot Set," from Benoit Mandelbrot, the Father of Fractal Geometry, generated by a very simple-looking formula, yet one that is applied recursively.[15] Variants of the Mandelbrot Set are now found everywhere including screensavers, calendars, and T-shirts. The figures can be breathtaking. Although formula-based, many also approximate forms found in nature.[16] In many ways this new science (along with its more dynamic, holistic, and interconnected worldview) is permeating our lives—including our aesthetic lives. It again may offer new horizons.

Let us focus now on us.

Changes 'R Us

The subtitle here is employed with homage to Toys 'R Us—known well I suspect to some parents reading this, and once an excellent resource—despite the recent demise of those colorful stores, with the advent of more online purchasing. Change is indeed the rule. In fact, we speak of accelerating change.

You have perhaps heard the indigenous saying "You can't step in the same river twice"? The water has moved on. We too have done this; we are not the same person twice. We may not look that different in the mirror. But we have changed from the start of this page. Plus tomorrow we may have our big creative insight! Then many things may never be the same. With nonlinear and emergent possibilities, as stated, one never knows. If things sound scary there is also—again around the corner—the eternal promise of hope. We are not, in theory, working on our own here, either. Donating $10 to a good cause may, at last, with efforts of others, be the Tipping Point.[17]

Meanwhile we humans are in many ways more aptly described as *processes* than *things*, truly as processes-in-motion, and as such, our existence is more allied to verbs than nouns. We are not static and seemingly unchanging objects—the way billiard balls might appear to some, bouncing imperviously off each other. (They change too!) Yet we humans are more visibly and quickly changing, living breathing eating, traveling, communicating, again, processes in motion. We hope we are meanwhile learning creatures, as well. And creative ones, too, being open to generating, and experiencing, the new.

How does it feel to be us? We too are evolving systems, emergent processes. With a composite and holistic identity. One might not imagine those dynamic undercurrents of our lives in a still photo, one showing us smiling, let us say, back as a child, as if life was always that way. Yet that child, at least, knews that s/he was growing! Who else says "I am 8-*and one half* years old now," or boasts, "Look how high I can reach." Adults more rarely ponder that they are aging and changing (and often shrinking). Nor does our dynamic process fit with some of the usual static language structure. Still we say: "I am tall." OK.

Self as Connected Process-in-Motion (or Self-in-World)

Key misunderstandings can arise in spiritual teachings about "non-self." It's not that "we" aren't "here," in our consensual reality, as some might put it. But what is "we" and what is "here." One misunderstanding involves the Buddhist "non-self"—which is not typically about nihilism, regarding self nor world.[18] We exist as much as that tree or flower does. But each is to us an identified structure we have conceptualized, yet also is intertwined profoundly within a greater whole—a view increasingly resonant with modern neuroscience and quantum mechanics, in concert with Eastern philosophies.[19] We can't literally talk about an *independent* self (not even for that billiard ball).

Thich Nhat Hanh has termed this phenomenon *interbeing*.[20]

We would not be who we are if born in a different family. Agree? Think about it.

How much are we influenced by each other? In ways small and large. In fact if it weren't for the chance advice of a friend, Tim wouldn't even have his career, never mind his rewarding job. If it weren't for a chance meeting (as told in a later chapter), a terrible war might have gone on for years. These examples fit with "The Butterfly Effect" in chaos theory. Or a type of *bifurcation* or sudden change. Example: The flapping of wings in Paris leads to a storm system over the greater Boston area ... remember all that snow?.[21]

Yet sudden change doesn't happen every day or for every butterfly.

We Belong to a Larger Emerging Picture

This is one small part of a larger interdependent picture. Here is the combined effect of months of snowfall, and the avalanche, started by the last snowflake. An "avalanche of mind" is a useful metaphor for when insight strikes, where that last piece of information closes a link, reconfigures a system, and it self-organizes in a different way. The earth is round and not flat. How that one changes everything else from science to history to theology.

Recall the earlier example of scientist Kekule's dream, dropping off in his chair by the fire, and suddenly seeing, very vividly and visually, the circle created by the snake, the Ouroborus biting its tail, and Kekule's waking to the chemical Aha! The six-sided carbon ring. What an incredible building block for organic life. An "avalanche of mind," a transformation of possibility. An option not really considered. It changed whole realms of a scientific field. Here, with the ring, is the symbol as well as an opening trumpet call for organic chemistry.

Nonlinear for sure!

Many other examples abound, smaller and less dramatic, throughout everyday life, as we reorganize the study, solve the broken pipe, craft a special dinner, make up a bedtime story with our child. Each has its varied Aha! moments, perhaps more than one. Metaphorically or literally, in each case, here is a creative insight, emerging suddenly from an evolving brain configuration; as with the last snowflake before the avalanche, everything can reconfigure with a crucial piece of information.

Yes—how nice when it works. There are other effects too. We have surely also had those days when, whatever we do, nothing seems to change! Alas. Shakespeare had something to say about this, too, and without benefit of a formal chaos and complexity theory, in *Julius Caesar*.

> There is a tide in the affairs of men;
> Which, taken at the flood, leads on to fortune;
> Omitted, all the voyage of their life;
> Is bound in shallows and in misery.

Who then is this so-called creative person? Who in fact are we? An embedded center of consciousness? A point of light in a changing cosmos?

We, you and I and the next person, are indeed identifiable entities in this manifest world, centers of consciousness each with a unique vantage point. If you don't believe it, check your Social Security Number or your last tax return. Someone thinks so. Yet we are moving targets. We may not be changing all that quickly or visibly. It's more obvious from ourselves at age 2 to now. Yet at this adult point, our friends will probably recognize us tomorrow (even though our clothes have changed, our smile is wider, and we're wearing a strange hat). We are *autopoieitic* or self-creating (and maintaining) wholes (as are cells, ecologies, and more).[22] Mitchell calls this a "self-maintaining process by which a system … functions as a whole to continually produce the components…" In fact, I will recognize you tomorrow. With aging, our hair may fall out but the original recipe (as I like to think about it) is pretty much the same.

Emergent is an important term for us and, to be sure for creativity, especially for those seemingly coming "out of nowhere" creative insights.

There are more gradual or ongoing phenomena as well. The birds flocking in an emergent group, and continuing on across the horizon. An organization which designates work groups for special projects, lets people self-select, where for a period they wander to different options, discuss, try this and that, and finally settle down. Interesting emergent phenomena are found here.[23]

Remember in *emergence*, "the whole is greater than the sum of its parts." Often we wouldn't even have guessed! That's what *emergence* is about. Each of us, ourselves, too, is a wonder that cannot be predicted from the individual atoms or molecules that we harbor (vs. the certainty of some with a reductionist view—as if we were a Lego toy[24]). When the new picture, model, discovery, insight, or other pattern emerges, how amazing it can do so right away! Wherever did it come from, and why didn't "we" know? It was somehow somewhere in our mind after all, was it not?, but not directly on the surface (in fact some deep mind-body mysteries may reside here). A couple of questions for later: Are there yet little clues we might find? Could we have known sooner?

We humans are continually changing in body and in mind as well— with each breath, and new piece of information—and the whole system can unfold, reform, transform, reconfigure. It can change, all together, and all at once. Plus effects can be physical as well as psychological. You speak and my mind, my brain, literally, alters! Neurons conduct electricity down the axons, dendrites branch richly between neurons to encode information. I want to remember this, and to that end, new dendrites grow to engrave the path.[25] Just because we don't always see it doesn't mean it isn't happening!

Regarding brain structure, there is good evidence that enriched early environments lead to much richer brain organization and webworks of connectivity within the central nervous system,[26] including more numerous and complex dendritic branches There is also support that such richness of connectivity may differ somewhat for arts and sciences among people of eminent renown for creativity.[27] Plus that's only the beginning when we bring in who we are, creatively—so as to keep on creating—our epigenetic influences (how environment calls on our genetic potential, or not), how our creative process can itself change us (and even help *heal us*), and more.

From Photo to YouTube to 3D Spectacular Systems

How often are we seeing, or trying to see, or imagine, or predict, in terms of *process*, of change, and seeking some of the deep interconnections one part may have with the next. We are not fully designed for this. We like to use names, to identify things, and our language helps support this.[28]

Is it a bit like going from that still photo where we are standing with a neighbor, to www.YouTube.com? In our video we are now running and jumping, albeit in two-dimensions. Add in the latest in virtual reality effects which can be quite amazing. We are living a new world, and in 3D or 4D if one adds in the dimension of time. Perhaps you believe virtual reality will never equal the "real thing" (though remember the film, *The Matrix*). Yet whatever the case, the immediate point is how differently we are processing, moving from the still photo to then landing in the midst— yes the midst—of a dynamic, new, and personally engaging scenario.

Context Can Be Everything

Nonverbally, holistically, were we using complex systems in imagining these phenomena? How often do we contemplate or visualize the layers of systems in which we personally are embedded (just a few being family, neighborhood, subculture, country, world). These help determine who are are, never mind what we will be doing tomorrow! If we still have our job, anyway.

Some people freeze at technical stereotypes about systems science, or at a need to hire expensive consultants who can make it clear. But we already know a lot about this—again, we live here too. We can think and imagine in a way that is interconnected and by nature dynamic. It is a set of capacities which might be emphasized more, let us suggest, along with predicting and creative thinking capacities, from grade school on![29]

Seana Moran is developing college programs of *proflexion* for visualizing alternative futures—and with the help of some of her students, produced a book of illustrations.[30] In an experimental middle school, my daughter visualized and visually mapped living systems from farm to city, to show how pollution is increased by Western practices such as factory faming. We can expand our systems awareness, including ability to see, hear, experience, in new and creative ways.

Interconnections: Pervasive and Subtle

Two Examples

Consider two further examples of a deep interconnection, the first in the realm of the material, the second involving thought and emotion. Would the first work in a elementary school? Colorful and illustrated teaching materials show cycles and circulating forms of water across the biosphere.[31]

1. Physical system we know well; raise your glass! Water makes a good and concrete example. It is everywhere, hopefully, and let us lift our glass! Remember, we are well over half water and would die of thirst in three days (and without air in 3 minutes!). Hopefully we are in healthy harmony with our world, including our ongoing metabolism with water in our life setting. Are we? Not in the recent droughts. Can we visualize a global water circulation?

Just one of many ways in which we are "open systems" in a give and take with our surrounds. With water, as per Thich Nhat Hanh[32] we are continuous with that water in a glass before us, never mind the clouds, the ocean, and the rain. We humans, plants, animals, living beings, are part of the greater metabolism of the phases and circulation of water as an environmental system ringing our entire earth.

In many other ways too, we are open systems, yet this next one seems especially poignant, as well as easier to visualize.

2. Power of mental/emotional connections. Add in the richness of human connection. (Now how is *that* transmitted?) Are you aware of the fate of many Romanian orphans, from troubled times in the 1980s, those babies in crowded orphanages? Due to massive overcrowding and inadequate help some babies lacked for being held, nurtured, attended to, and cared for.[33] For lack of caregivers, babies were too often left alone in their orphanage cribs. Some of these neglected babies, although fed and warm, physically withered and actually died. Or showed ongoing "failure to thrive." Failure, indeed, and even to the death. Nurturance, caring, love, is as important as water to each of us, or even more.

Conscious Decision to Expand Awareness—One Can Try It

Our focus has been on observations in the external and internal world, with an explicit mention of vision, although all senses are (and all experience and inner experience is) relevant. Like this author, some readers may be shocked to discover how much we have been missing, even vitally important in our worlds and lives. To learn that we are prepackaging and processing a limited and sometimes falsely framed set of perceptions. Charles Tart suggests one useful practice—whenever going through a certain doorway, to ask oneself, am I aware?[34] Maybe we'll need to put up a note though. Just in case our asking gets too habitual and fades away. Or in case we have a different mode of connection as in Example Two.

For creativity, we will want more awareness than sometimes is the case going through out routine-built, and hassle full, and mindless days. Perhaps we feel we are free and open to possibility, but did you know, by one study, the average person is looking at their cell phone—remarkable!—every 6-1/2 minutes?[35] Fun, maybe. But talk about being on a leash. Plus there is an addictive aspect—where for an enthusiast a cold turkey CellPhone holiday can evoke MRI results similar to craving in a sober drug addict.

Perhaps we feel we've gong no further than a space marked "Start" on a game playing board.

But NO! We have already made a giant step—and one that was giant long ago for hominids in evolution. First, awareness. Truly a triumph to be consciously aware of our tendencies, rules, and predilections to one condition or another, including our conscious awareness itself. It is the genius of human beings to develop such conscious awareness of what we do.[36] Plus then, to have a*wareness of our awareness*. This is our *meta-awareness*.[37] With this, we can now reflect on our own good and bad choices, strengths and limitations. Plus what we are seeing and what we may be missing.

We can know there is more. Much more.

We humans are in a world not just of biology and DNA or even epigenetics (where environment interacts with, and pulls different expressions from our DNA), but of learning and language and culture and cultural evolution. We humans have biological and cultural evolution and all mixtures in between.

With a new level of meta-awareness we can decide how to proceed to alter and open up our experience. And we can pass it on. We can expand the world we know and along with it, our creativity—indeed into infinite worlds of mind and imagination.

Once we know it can be done—and by us, by everyone, truly as our human birthright, we have reached a new freedom, a new realm of possibility. Here for us all to celebrate is is the birth of creativity.

Wait 'Til Tomorrow?

Wonderful, yes? Still, today it is too late and we head home for a relaxing evening. The day is over, we are done at work. We are back behind the wheel, pulling out of the parking lot, and getting hungry, more than ready to eat dinner. Now we are off the freeway, and out on a narrow road, with center line, turn off signs, all this grabs our attention. We have labeled these features (a long time ago), prioritize them (now), and obey them (automatically and without reservation).

Of course, all this is fine, and no one wants to run off the road. Yet the question remains as always, who/*what is choosing, and what are we missing?*

It is almost 6 p.m., and now consumed by the imagined taste of our meal, and our plan to flop in a chair, we mindlessly drive right past our creativity, while missing endless beauty, endless variety, unlimited opportunities, and life itself.

In Summary

we are interconnected, interdependent. Even the hermit. At times we are sensitive to small changes, be it new job, new love, or creative Aha! This affects both *worldview* and view of *self-in-world*. We exist, but not separate from our creative continuity with life. As emergent open systems, and deeply embedded, we are subject to the dramatic change and surprise of forces visible and invisible. This world is neither linear nor reductionistic (nor are we!) and wider vision offers hope. Looking broadly without and within, we find new clues to the mysteries of creativity and ourselves.

Notes

1. Morowitz, *Emergence of Everything*, 13, more formally defined as involving, "...novelties that follow from the system rules but cannot be predicted from properties of the components that make up the system."
2. Briggs and Peat, *Turbulent Mirror*; or Mitchell, *Complexity: A Guided Tour*, provide readable and colorful introductions. More formal treatments include Guastello, Pincus, and Koopmans's edited, *Chaos and Complexity in Psychology*, or (short but full) Smith, *Chaos* or Holland, *Complexity*, each from the Oxford *Very Short Introduction* series.
3. Mitchell, *Complexity*, 20.
4. Mitchell, 20, 13.
5. Singer, "Mental Processes and Brain Architecture." see Guastello one of first, in 1995, *Chaos, Catastrophe, and Human Affairs*.
6. Richards and Goslin-Jones, "Everyday Creativity."
7. Dreadful natural disasters, see Kluger and Haley, in *Time*, "A Perfect Storm." times, recently. One journalist called this a "bifurcation."
8. Stewart, *Does God Play Dice?* 74.
9. Guastello and Liebovitch, "Introduction to Nonlinear Dynamics," 1.
10. Reuter, "Ten Domains That Have Explained Creativity"; notably, both everyday creativity and chaos theory were mentioned in two of the ten domains. A forthcoming book, Schuldberg, Richards, Guisinger, eds. *Nonlinear Psychology*, presents nonlinear principles of chaos and complexity theory in relatively user-friendly ways for the social scientist; a related 2018 APA symposium brought this focus to a wide range of psychologists.
11. Rifkin, *Zero Marginal Cost Society*, 286.
12. Kolbert, *Sixth Extinction*.
13. Holland, *Complexity*, 1–2.
14. Gleick, *Chaos*, 16.
15. Briggs and Peat, *Turbulent Mirror*, 97.
16. Mandelbrot, *The Fractal Geometry of Nature*.
17. Richards, "Creative Alchemy," 130.
18. Thich Nhat Hanh, *Heart of the Buddha's Teachings*.
19. Ricard and Thuan, *Quantum and The Lotus*.
20. Thich Nhat Hanh, *What the Buddha Taught*, 154.
21. Guastello, Koopmans, and Pincus, *Chaos and Complexity in Psychology*.
22. Mitchell, *Complexity*, 298.

23. Owen, Dietz, and Gohring, "Strategies for Creating the Learning Organization."

24. Richards, "Relational Creativity."

25. Kolb, in Zimbardo, Johnson, and McCann, *Psychology Core Concepts*, 271.

26. Ibid.

27. Simonton, *Scientific Genius*.

28. Combs, "Consciousness: Chaotic and Strangely Attractive," 401.

29. Mitchell, *Complexity*, on new educational options including "K Forever".

30. Moran, *Ethical Ripples of Creativity and Innovation*.

31. Allaby, *The Environment* (nicely illustrated book for young people).

32. Thich Nhat Hanh, *Sun My Heart*.

33. Eisler, "Our Great Creative Challenge: Rethinking Human Nature— and Recreating Society," 267, 270–271.

34. Tart, *States of Consciousness*.

35. Kaufman and Gregoire, *Wired to Create*, 109. The average smartphone user checks the device every 6-1/2 minutes. Meanwhile, compare Schwantes, on "Steve Jobs's Advice," which was to do quite the opposite!

36. Morowitz, *Emergence of Everything. Homo sapiens* cannot necessarily take full credit. For instance, conscious awareness seems to have been present in great apes.

37. Siegel, *Mindful Brain*, 108.

Part II

AHA! MOMENT (Creative *Process*)

5

Moments of Insight

For the want of a nail the shoe was lost,
For the want of a shoe the horse was lost,
For the want of a horse the rider was lost,
For the want of a rider the battle was lost,
For the want of a battle the kingdom was lost,
All for the want of a horseshoe-nail.
Benjamin Franklin

We somehow learn—perhaps unawares—to be sensitive to a world of creative tipping points. Many are the background flickers of our days, ones we do not even notice. Yet others are larger, with a rare one even momentous, shifting lives, changing worlds. Like a martial artist, we can work with these intuitively, sensing the energies and balance, at times to tweak, advance, or divert events. These are our creative *Aha's*, our mental bifurcations, and a precious human piece of the "Butterfly Effect." What roles shall we give them in our own lives?

© The Author(s) 2018
R. Richards, *Everyday Creativity and the Healthy Mind,*
Palgrave Studies in Creativity and Culture,
https://doi.org/10.1057/978-1-137-55766-7_5

Here is our Butterfly Effect, as we live it—our experience of "sensitivity to initial conditions." The butterfly flaps its wings in Paris, as the saying goes, and a storm breaks over the Eastern USA (from recent weather, heaven forbid). It is not any butterfly, and not any day. This is the last puff of air, the last snowflake before the avalanche, the tipping point, the critical difference—the tweak in a huge interdependent global weather system, where each change resounds throughout the whole (extensive recursive feedback effect).[1] Benjamin Franklin's famous quote, above, is about another Butterfly, this one about an omitted act at a key point, for an army—and one which too changed everything. The kingdom was lost.

Our own creative piece—our insight, our Aha! Moment, coming at just the right time and place, and critically poised—may have its own effect, and hopefully one which, for many of us, will be *positive*. Agree with the decisions or not, a key story follows, and a true story, as exemplar, one I didn't hear until much later (and frankly, like the protagonist, after my own views had changed). It shows our Butterfly quite well—one we may even meet ourselves someday. Our sudden opportunity. What will we do? This one is drawn from several written sources[2] and a video which was 2010 Oscar Nominee for Best Documentary, *The Most Dangerous Man in America*.[3]

* * *

Many youth in the '50s were enthralled with the "Beat Generation" and authors like Jack Kerouac, whose well known writings included *On the Road* and *The Dharma Bums*. Being old enough myself, and a Californian, I even remember the black turtle neck sweaters, Left Bank Parisian berets, pointy beards, poetry in smoky cafes in San Francisco, Eastern religions and new social visions. The "Beat" writings were read by many—even including people in sharp suits and military uniforms. Daniel Ellsberg, former Marine officer, was one of these, now a defense analyst for the RAND Corporation.

Ellsberg had read *The Dharma Bums*, and then in 1961 found himself in Japan doing work for RAND. *Dharma Bums* gives a youthful Western take on Eastern philosophy, bring Buddhist wisdom and compassion to a generational shift in Western lifestyle and values. The book is based loosely on real people including Kerouac himself.

The key figure for this tale is poet Gary Snyder (as fictional Japhy Ryder) who, as Kerouac wrote, was a "kid from Eastern Oregon brought up in a log cabin…" who later "learned Chinese and Japanese and became an Oriental scholar and discovered the greatest Dharma Bums of them all…" the Eastern Zen masters of China and Japan. At book's end, Japhy (just like Snyder himself) takes off to Japan to become a Buddhist monk.

Perhaps we can now picture Ellsberg, a young man, in Tokyo on work, yet remembering Kerouac's description of the famous rock garden in a Kyoto Zen monastery. He travels to Kyoto. The year is 1961. Ellsberg's job involves analyzing the Pentagon's defense plans and nuclear strategies. Yet he takes a day off to see the Kyoto site, then going for a beer at a local bar.

Improbable? Who does he meet there, at this venue, but no other than "Japhy Ryder," that is, the same Buddhist monk and poet Gary Snyder, whom Ellsberg had read about. Snyder helps Ellsberg with a Japanese menu. Amazed, Ellsberg tells him, "You are the reason I am in Kyoto!"

They end up going to Snyder's place and talking for hours

Now please remember this example isn't primarily about military policy, nor acts of conscience. It is an example of "sensitive dependence on initial conditions." Yet it is also one of tremendous change and not just in individuals but of societies. It can happen. It still does. These are the tipping points of life.

Fast forward further into the '60s where, as you may recall, Ellsberg as analyst has run into shocking defense policy information on "Indochina." Turns out this has been withheld from the public across four presidential administrations. Ellsberg, who has been soldier and commanding officer in Vietnam as well as an analyst, has become increasingly uncomfortable with conduct of the war (including rising deployments and death toll, by war's end of 58,000 Americans and 2,000,000 Vietnamese).[4] America is being torn apart by dissent from college campuses to the streets.

Ellsberg has crucial information that the public lacks.

First, Ellsberg decides to share it with the Senate Foreign Relations Committee. Wanting greater response he then moves to make it public. Imagine copying 7000 pages of top-secret documents. These become the Pentagon Papers, and parts are first released publicly by *The New York Times*.[5]

It is here that Henry Kissinger tells Richard Nixon that Ellsberg is "the most dangerous man in America." He must be "stopped at all costs." One writer in the documentary film stresses that, "Ellsberg was "one person standing up to the greatest power on earth."

Ellsberg is *not stopped*—and he does not stop, putting conscience above career, He is even fearing for his life, or about getting life imprisonment, where he might never see his kids and family again, except from "behind a glass."

Before releasing the Pentagon Papers, Ellsberg makes his goodbyes. This includes making a trip to see the man, the former Buddhist monk, Gary Snyder, whom Ellsberg has so far met only once, that single time a whole decade before, in Kyoto. Gary Snyder, poet and philosopher, is now living, not in Japan, but on a farm in Nevada City, California, in the Sierra foothills.[6]

Ellsberg, with the unreleased Pentagon Papers still in his trunk, drives from the California coast to Snyder's farm for the second meeting he has ever had with this former monk.

History is changed.

Now, looking back—and looking at Ken Burns's multi-part new 2017 documentary on the Vietnam War[7]—one recalls The Pentagon Papers and their aftermath shook the world. Nixon's acts against Ellsberg ultimately led to Watergate, impeachment proceedings against the President and Nixon's resignation, and hastened an end to the war in Vietnam. Although Ellsberg initially received a sentence of 115 years in prison, it was dismissed in 1973 because of elected officials' "misconduct."

We cannot say for sure which snowflake started the avalanche that led to Ellsberg's act of conscience, or to the global response. But here were forces and counter-forces poised critically for change, awaiting a move that destabilized the whole. A ripple effect was felt around the globe.

This is a remarkable example of single input and massive response. "Sensitivity to initial conditions." It further illuminates of our complex interconnection and mutual influence as human beings, perhaps even issuing from one chance meeting. What does one do, when knowing secrets that could save millions of lives?[8]

*   *   *

For me, I write even now with a lump in my throat. Considering the death, the tragedy, the innocents murdered, the forces devastated, the napalm, destruction of a country, and secret military movements not even known to American citizens while their own sons may have died—plus the devastation of war in general, when we humans have capacity to find more creative solutions—for me, it is an example that rends the heart.

The igniting spark in this case was The Butterfly.

Aha! An Avalanche of Mind

Rolling Waves of Ahas!

Our creative Butterfly isn't on vacation this week; The Butterfly Effect is active all the time. As natural as the ocean, the weather, the turning of the earth. Little insights too, even tiny ones, exist and much more plentifully, not just the big ones. Perhaps we are apt to notice the big ones, and think that is all there is. But no. And we may develop sensitivity to the small, helping us too with managing the larger ones.[9] We view both here.

Big Ahas!

Let us hope we actually can embrace the big ones when the stakes can be so high.[10]

Long ago, Shakespeare wrote about such a larger dynamic. It is never just about ourselves alone. It is about us and the larger superstructure in which we are deeply interconnected. At certain key points an event, or our (in)action can change everything, as in Franklin's, "for lack of a nail…" the opening quotation. Meanwhile at other times, and despite all our efforts … nothing may happen. It seems fruitless, static, hopeless. I expect we've each, women and men who have lived in the world at all, sometime been there. Here is Shakespeare, from Julius Caesar[11]:

There is a tide in the affairs of men;
Which taken at the flood, leads on to fortune.
Omitted, all the voyage of their life;
Is bound in shallows and in misery.

Meanwhile the Little Ahas! Abound

In everyday daily life, our chances for insight are unending. We can switch the honey for the sugar in that recipe! Use the pliers to open the can. Make a costume from that curtain.

This "originality of everyday life" reflects our human nature, and our universal creative potential.[12] It reflects what Dobzhansky[13] called our *phenotypic plasticity*, our flexible manifestations within our genetic limits. Part of the genius of being human. We are not all creatures of instinct who do things the same way; we are not all building the same types of nests, using twigs and grass. We live all around the world in a sparkling diversity of dwellings, climates, colors, cultures, and lifestyles. How is this?

Everyday Creativity

We humans can flexibly shift, adapt, improvise, catch a brainstorm, ride an impulse, follow a feeling, try this and try that. We all of us come with this capacity, our *everyday creativity*. At times, it may even keep us alive—for instance, in fleeing a malicious figure who is pursuing us. We creativity researchers at McLean Hospital and Harvard Medical School, validating our Lifetime Creativity Scales, assessed similar situations once for WWII resistance fighters, helping refugees flee for their lives.[14]

Alas, though, that many of us have not even named our everyday creativity. If it remains unrecognized (or under-recognized), it can also easily stay underdeveloped. Plus, for sure, it can be under-rewarded. (These are the Three U's—under-recognized, under-developed, under-rewarded; important to remember for parents, school systems, and opinionated bosses).

Once we are aware, a different story can emerge. Let us also recall the benefits for health—and how evolution, indeed seems to favors the innovator.[15] As noted, we humans can be meta-aware. Aware of aware-ness. We can see how we know, why we act, and can choose anew, what to do, and in what way we want to live.

Top of the Mental Mountain

In any case, we humans are negentropic systems, in finding creativity! Energized, ready for the new. New order (at times in a flash) comes while exchanging energy and entropy with the outside world. We are highly charged with energy, able to move in an instant to a new solution, or new awareness. The human brain is not designed to be stuck and immobile at the bottom-of-some-barrel kind of energy sink, where we can't move or act. It is not a drop-down equilibrium of lassitude in a deep mental valley. In fact we get pleasure from challenge and accomplishment[16] often much more than timeless leisure. It we believe we can't think differently (or "think different" as Steve Jobs put it) it is not true. We are well equipped to do so—as part of our human, universal creative heritage—when we "free it."

If a particular reader is thinking Writer's Block, it is a good example. In fact, a "block" is precisely the issue. There is a barrier to our natural and open receptive brain state (See Chap. 6). We are generally still ready to go if we can unblock ourselves—are dynamically poised at an energy "high"[17] to jump in an instant to embrace the new—new ideas, thoughts, feelings, contents. It is our avalanche of mind.[18]

From this point (and the point and "we" are always changing), new places in mind and brain flash into existence. We encode new experience; at best, we continually live afresh.

"Try It Now": Asking Some Questions

To experience Aha! Moments more than before, now, one approach is to *ask yourself a new question, regularly, and do it even every hour* (also see Chap. 6). These can be about anything. Make it a habit! This can be about "problem finding" as per Mark Runco and colleagues. Something more can happen. One is putting the Aha! mechanism on general alert. It is opening to the new, welcoming new experience—and one's doing so can predict for creativity.[19]

Meeting New Paradigms

Aromas and Attractors

In powerful research, Skarda and Freeman[20] modeled brain data on olfactory cortex, showing how odors are recognized and recorded. We have "attractors" for example, citrus (big category) and then smaller appendages, or "wings," for lemons and oranges. Types of citrus. These are not little spots or spaces on a static physical brain map, but "attractors" in so-called phase space,[21] in mathematical representation, The attractors dynamically active and organizing our thoughts. They meanwhile change, they evolve, and often new ones are born.

Here is one. We are smelling lime. It's terrific. But what is it? It doesn't quite fit the citrus categories, above. Flash! We "keep" it as is! Now we have a new wing, or category, for "lime."

Caveat: Other Ways of Knowing

Note this is just one example, with a focus on categories, and the human conceptual mind. A triumph, and another part of our human genius. But not the whole picture.

Do not forget our intuition, whereby we "arrive at the solution of a problem *without* reasoning toward it."[22] Here is a sudden creative insight, seemingly out of nowhere. A direct experience "in the moment" can precede finding these constructed categories. One famous Zen story tells of enlightenment at the sound of a bird.[23] It's when we start analyzing it and boxing it in that its deeper truth can fade.

Our Ahas! can travel so much faster, sometimes joyfully. The glorious sunset in oranges and reds with stripes of purple and yellow and now we are gasping and pointing it out to each other, while standing on an ocean beach.[24] We don't compartmentalize it; we gasp in awe! Perhaps we even have a Maslovian "peak experience." "Divinity" say the Hindu Upanishads. An experience, at times, in some meditative and spiritual disciplines.[25] Our intuitive, immediate, nonverbal, unconscious, even collective unconscious experience—all is part of our larger picture and extended world of Ahas! Our creativity can be just as complex as we are, and possibly even as complex it gets.[26]

Nonlinear World

With new aromas and Aha! moments, we have departed the linear road, where twice the push leads to twice the response. There can be a huge change (*catastrophic* is the name for one type of sudden transformation, though the implication is about process, is not necessarily that the outcome is bad).[27] Or one finds sensitive, curvilinear, and more balanced ongoing change, amongst vast embedded systems. The dynamic of sudden change, though, is one we well know intuitively: falling in love, investing in the stock market, or watching a story go viral (hope it's not Fake News).

Some psychologists and systems scientists believe psychology is finally catching up with physics and other fields, as per Guastello and Liebovitch[28]:

> Psychology is not the first science to break out of the linear rut .... physical science made the transition more than a half-century ago.

Two nonlinear types of phenomena, to be reengaged in this book, in various ways, help us understand many surprising changes we encounter (a) the Aha!, we've been discussing and (b) the phenomenon of *emergence*, where—surprise!—"the whole is greater than the sum of its parts." That means we have met something we never could have predicted from the information given. It happens a lot. We live in a world of change and surprise. Our states of consciousness too, are self-organizing, and emergent. We are awake, now asleep, now in hynogogic reverie.[29]

Meanwhile others take a "reductionist" view, asserting we can know it all, and can predict it all too, if we can just know enough initial information. It linear; it is predictable, it is ours, as humans, to manage. Really?

We can build the entire world from the atoms on up, complete the whole structure, if we just know all the rules and starting conditions.[30] Or so they think.

So much that refutes it.[31] On the whole we humans—through ignorance, greed, or self-interest—haven't fully foreseen results of climate change (at least until sunken cities, floods, and hurricanes and other huge environmental shifts including loss of numerous species were inescapable).[32] This era of homo sapiens' freewheeling or heedless dominance may end up being named after us, but not as a compliment: the *Anthropocene.*

Paradigm Shift

Is it too late for a next step? Can *we* still shift? Be more mindful, reverse some of the damage? Can we work in concert with our living biosphere? The nonlinear complex adaptive systems models here suggest, for many of us, a paradigm shift in the making. With two colleagues, I have edited the book *Nonlinear Psychology: Keys to Chaos and Creativity in Mind and Nature*, with engaging experts as contributors, to do our part in bringing a interconnected, dynamic, holistic view more centrally to social sciences.[33] We also developed a related symposium for the 2018 Annual Meeting of the American Psychological Association.

The time is now. As Chaos Theorist and psychologist Sally Goerner put it[34]

> ... we stand at a turning point in human civilization, the magnitude of which we are only barely aware.... The bigger picture, of which chaos (Chaos Theory) is a part, is a physical understanding of how order evolves naturally, why change is inevitable, and what factors underlie transformation.

This shift is potentially a huge one in multiple areas, borne on our deeper and recurrent (feedback intensive) interconnection to each other and the world: a new view of who we are and what we are doing here. Everything counts. And everything changes. We can work with it but not know it all; we are not omniscient. Still with our self-reflection, creativity, and cultural (not just biological) evolution, we humans can be an influential and shining piece of a larger picture.

A closer look cannot come too soon, considering, for instance, renewed fears of nuclear war, where perhaps even a small hiccup (or Butterfly) could tip a balance toward global catastrophe.

Then, too, there is a bright side. (See Chap. 17) For us, if not for various Eastern and indigenous cultures, and world wisdom traditions, this is a different *worldview*.[35] As such (while not diminishing our own creativity) it calls for a new humility, along with, happily, the joys wonder, appreciation, and awe of this startling and surprising cosmos. We also come into a new view of *self-in-world*. One that also opens us more to appreciation of the wonders of life and—of greatest importance—to our own higher human potential.[36] Do we begin to understand what we can do? Remember … *with emergence, one never knows.*

Meanwhile, looking more deeply and fully, and with presence in the moment, we can find extraordinary beauty—perhaps unrecognized—everywhere around us. Beauty, hope, and with it, new vision and insight. As Dostoevsky put it,[37]

… beauty will save the world

It is worth our exploring this.

* * *

Summary

Aha! Moment. An avalanche!, collapse, reconfiguration, a complex systems shift triggered by that last snowflake. Similarly, that last datum. A big Aha! can sometimes yield devastating and spreading circles of effect. Far from rare, these keep happening. Yet, like avalanches, or earthquakes, the big ones occur less often. Still, how they change everything. There are very positive outcomes as well, and can we help further those? Learn more and join in the process? To live creatively and more consciously in this flow—seeing ourselves as processes—rather than resisting change? A big difference for "who are are," how it feels, and our view of *self-in-world*.

Notes

1. Gleick, *Chaos*, 22.
2. Sources include Peat, *Blackbird Night*, Kerouac, *Dharma Bums*, Ellsberg, *Secrets*, *The Most Dangerous Man in America—Daniel Ellsberg and the Pentagon Papers* (2009 Academy Award Nominee for Best Documentary, Directed by Judith Ehrlich and Rick Goldsmith). Admittedly, there are people, including some I know, who judge these events rather differently. The reader is asked, whatever your preferences or predilections, first to view this as a profound example of bifurcation, or The Butterfly Effect, a ripple effect that changed the world.
3. *Most Dangerous Man in America* (Video). If you believe there is no one absolute right or wrong, consider if there can be room for fruitful discussion of actions and alternatives in such a harmful and deceptive situation, recalling forces were alerted about "the most dangerous man in America." The film shows conditions that led to a brave step at great personal cost: major newspapers also took risks. I believe we can all benefit from dialogue in a larger context about criteria for ethical behavior. Do note Saybrook University awarded Daniel Ellsberg the Rollo May Prize for his courageous work.
4. Policy decisions can emerge, sometimes deceptively, from a powerful few. See Pilisuk, *Hidden Structure of Violence*.
5. *The New York Times* first published sections, later *The Washington Post*.
6. Nevada City is in California.
7. Burns and Novick, *The Vietnam War* (10-part documentary that premiered in September 2017 on PBS).
8. We can do is what we believe is right. At times it may not do much at all. At others—and especially in conjunction with like-minded others—there can be a tipping point. It might change everything.
9. Richards, *Everyday Creativity: Coping and Thriving in the 21st Century*, 190–192.
10. For many of us, the example above is tribute to courage, the human spirit, defense of human rights, democracy, and the willingness to take enormous risks to follow one's ethical imperatives for a greater good. Others, for their own reasons, would not have proceeded this way, and have commented to me on this material. Yet wherever one's view, here is a critical moment the Aikido Master would have seen as an opportunity. Example of an Aha! Moment.

11. Shakespeare, *Julius Caesar*.
12. Richards, *Everyday Creativity and New Views of Human Nature*.
13. Dobzhansky, *Mankind Evolving*.
14. Kinney, Richards, Southam, "Assessing Everyday Creativity…"
15. Richards, "Twelve Potential Benefits…", 290. Healthy benefits are best seen in Table 13, then each discussed.
16. Csikszentimihaly, *Creativity*, 110.
17. Guastello, Koopmans, Pincus, *Chaos and Complexity in Psychology*.
18. Abraham, "The Dynamics of Creativity and the Courage to Be"; Richards, "Everyday Creativity."
19. Kozbelt, Beghetto, and Runco, "Theories of Creativity," 34.
20. Skarda and Freeman, "How Brains Make Chaos in Order to Make Sense of the World."
21. Guastello, Koopmans, Pincus, *Chaos and Complexity in Psychology*.
22. Damasio in Richards, "Everyday Creativity," 200; also see Chap. 9.
23. *Surangama Sutra, Lankavatara Sutra*—moment when sensory experience leads to spiritual enlightenment.
24. Richards, "New Aesthetic for Environmental Awareness."
25. Maslow, *Farther Reaches of Human Nature*; Loori, *Zen of Creativity*.
26. Silvia, "Creativity is Undefinable, Controllable, and Everywhere." Includes importance of everyday sampling.
27. Abraham, "The Dynamics of Creativity and the Courage to Be."
28. Guastello and Liebovitch, "Introduction to Nonlinear Dynamics and Complexity," 1.
29. Combs, "Consciousness: Chaotic and Strangely Attractive," 404.
30. Richards, "Relational Creativity and Healing Potential," 301.
31. Roszak, Gomes, and Kanner, eds. *Ecopsychology: Restoring the Earth, Healing the Mind*.
32. Kolbert, *Sixth Extinction*.
33. Kuhn, *Structure of Scientific Revolutions*.
34. Goerner, "Chaos and Deep Ecology," 3.
35. Rao, *Consciousness Studies: Cross-Cultural Perspectives*.
36. With self-organization and emergence, we can have negative results—but since the outcome is unknown, there is a chance as well for hope and progress and understanding.
37. Dostoevsky in Dobzhansky, *Mankind Evolving*, 339. See later, for discussion of beauty.

6

Flavors of (Creative) Mind

I close my eyes in order to see
Paul Gauguin, Artist

*Toto, I've a feeling we're not in
Kansas anymore.*
Dorothy In *The Wizard of Oz*

Not always found in psychology books, our altered consciousness seems afoot here. Meditation, dreams, hypnagogic imagery, and more. We spend time with our muse, perhaps in a reverie by the fire, or on a walk. Wallas's stages of creative process are helpful, e.g., re incubation. Neuroscience brings another viewpoint. Word puzzles invoking insight have evoked distinct neuropsychological states, brain profiles, and subjective experiences. Is such experience familiar to you? Can people come to *feel* such states, even voluntarily "turn it on"? Might biofeedback or other technologies help? Add evidence for neural shifts, brain idling, a creative flash. Or views of unconscious and subtle mental states in *balance* with executive functioning. Careful. Do not pathologize these.

© The Author(s) 2018
R. Richards, *Everyday Creativity and the Healthy Mind*,
Palgrave Studies in Creativity and Culture,
https://doi.org/10.1057/978-1-137-55766-7_6

Flavors of Mind

Mind State and Creativity

How to evoke a mind state to tempt that Big Aha! We do know a bit about this and its challenges—even perhaps some things we ourselves may try. Happily some more of the forward looking psychology textbooks are beginning to cover consciousness studies including alterations of consciousness. One also finds some beginning forays into creativity, including dreams.[1] Our conscious states of mind can matter when creating (or trying to do so). Listen to no less than Rainer Maria Rilke, on a bad day, if we thought it always came easily[2]

> How far from me is the work, how far the angels!.... Please do not expect me to speak to you of my inner labor ... of all the reversals I will have to undergo in my struggle for concentration.

A Walk with the Muse

You have perhaps been advised about—after starting a project—taking a break, perhaps a walk with one's muse. In other words, about taking time off from one's hard conscious work, and why not invite the muse, that mystical source of inspiration, along? Whatever this may involve—and for some it might be playing music, or meditating, walking or dozing—this advice recalls Graham Wallas's[3] heuristic of five stages of creative process: preparation—incubation—intimation (stage often omitted)—illumination—verification. First we get ready, then (here it is!) take a deliberate break of some kind (that walk with the muse, a shower, a drive, making dinner, or something else unrelated). Next comes this stage often omitted in lists given as only four stages, where one may heed early subtle signs that something is coming (we return in force to this one later). Then yes it comes at last! The Big Aha! Finally, we pull it all together.

The reader who meditates may particularly appreciate proposed connections between meditation and creativity, as in the arts, and exemplified nicely in *The Zen of Creativity* by John Daido Loori, or Franck's "active meditation" in *Zen Seeing, Zen Drawing: Meditation in Action*.[4] Thich Nhat Hanh is said to meditate before his (wonderful) writings.[5] Some suggest a clear, calm, and one-pointed attention (shamatha) and/or more mindful and open awareness (vipassyana) may be linked in different ways to aspects of creativity![6] Whatever the form of meditation it is surely helpful for being present in the moment, very consciously aware, open and non-judgmental.

Process-oriented personal and social growth programs such as Natalie Rogers' Person Centered Expressive Arts[7] deliberately include meditation as one part of a multimodal expressive sequence, including movement, drawing, writing, improvisation, and more, to open to oneself and to the new.

Does it help? Surely it would if one is truly engaged—but not necessarily if busy judging their meditation!

Self-Organizing and Creative States

As noted there are many states, many alterations of consciousness,[8] be these sleeping, dreaming, ordinary waking, meditation or more. A new state can self-organize in a flash—and emerge—like the Aha! Moment—where the mind suddenly reconfigures, rather like tuning in to a new broadcasting channel.[9] There it is! After all, we may have sought sleep for hours and tossed and turned in bed. Yet suddenly it happens, and how do we know? Because we just woke up, hours later.

Do you, the reader, have any sense of a state, maybe a *flavor* of mind, you turn on, when you are seeking new ideas? If your first thought is no, please stay open to the question. Perhaps you know more than you realize, yet it is hard to put into words.

Dream Related States

Considerable creativity—including scientific—has come from images and insights in a dream or early sleep state.[10] (This is a reason to keep a journal directly by the bedside and write down your dreams). Productive times include REM sleep or hynagogic pre-sleep imagery. Hypnopompic states (upon waking) are occasionally mentioned. Fariba Bograzan[11] even uses lucid dreaming a cultivation of conscious awareness during the dream state, to paint incredible images of what is witnessed; we too can learn LD, for purposes including the spiritual, which Buddhist B. Alan Wallace, Bograzan and others, have done.[12]

Hypnagogic State

Back to that particularly special twilight state just before sleep—a *hypnogogic* state. See if you are (or can become) aware of it, yourself. When almost asleep, I for one can tell that sleep is about to happen. Strange images, maybe a sound. Next thing, I wake up.

Here again is scientist Kekule relaxing, before the fireplace, in his easy chair. He drops into a mental space, not quite asleep definitely not awake. Lazy, comfortable, warm and relaxed, and a flickering fire. Suddenly the image comes, the snake biting its tail and the transformative insight dawns, that benzene ring, those six carbon atoms, those alternating double bonds—not from calculations or hard study of one's textbooks, but—shimmering through an alteration of consciousness—as a direct creative insight.[13]

One hypnogogic trick was big help to Thomas Edison[14] who would take naps in chair, holding ball bearings loosely in his hand. They would drop at the first onset of sleep! Stop! Wake up. The time is here. Catch the creative insight, quickly!

Could we also train ourselves to enter creative insight states voluntarily through technologies such as biofeedback? Of great interest is research using both lived experience and neuroscience results, especially including EEG and fMRI results during a creative insight state. We can explore for signs of an alteration of consciousness. Or another special signature. Yet in this case, let us start by doing.

Try This

In studying creativity, personal experience is hugely valuable, providing another lens, and can be linked with diverse and external sources of data. There can be challenges in correlating these data sources. However, this approach, which some call "neurophenomenology," pioneered by Francisco Varela, offers new inroads into understanding mind and experience.[15]

In this case[16] a participant (you yourself are welcome to try) attempts a couple of word puzzles. There is no right way to do them either. Although there are some standard answers. If these puzzles aren't your favorite, no matter. Your lived experience is the point here—the observed *process* more than *product*. Two word games follow, and if new to you, please just play with each for a few moments. Get a feel for them.

(a) **Anagrams**. Make a word. Rearrange the letters. Example: GRANMAA. Ok, the two "AA's" were a clue and the GRANMA part a distractor! This one can make ANAGRAM. Now try DAPDEL. Take a moment. Did a solution pop out or did you reason to it? Or some of each, which often happens. If you had a *Poof!* or *Aha!* anywhere in there, *remember that feeling*. The point again isn't the answer, but to *notice the process(es)*. Try LOSOCH. (Hint: Put the two "O"s together. Did this hint spur an insight or a more analytic process? If there was an Aha!—what did that feel like? And—how strange it is, that sudden flash—where did that come from?)

(b) **Remote Associates**. A different task, after Sarnoff Mednick,[17] also with sudden "Aha!" potential. This time we start with three words that can relate in any way to a fourth. Example: HEART SUGAR SOUR (Answer #1: Sweet ... *sweet* heart, sugar is *sweet*, *sweet* and sour). Did an answer pop out and/or did you use analytic reasoning? That is, did you use *insight* and/or *analytic* strategies?[18] Try this one: FLAP TIRE BEANSTALK. Or another: SNOW WASH BLACK. (See chapter notes for further information.) If any one of these jumps out at you—*please remember that feeling.*

What Is the Brain Doing?

Meanwhile, picture that you are being monitored by an EEG or fMRI apparatus, while doing one of these tasks. After participants are done, the researchers separate people into one group who happened to use *insight* at some measured point (Aha! experience—by self-report), or *analytic* (again as experienced) or mixed modes during each key trial; the data is analyzed. You used mainly insight. Differences? *Definitely.*[19]

Martindale's[20] EEG work foreshadowed some of this years before, while correlating subjective and objective. He found with EEG, less frontal activity (key site for executive functioning—our balancing act), and lower cortical activation overall (less activity). There was relatively more right-sided (holistic, nonverbal, visual), and slower wave activity, including slow theta waves. Those nice slow theta waves found in other human activities, including meditation[21]; I even have a CD of "theta music"—said to induce such an "altered state, and I have used it in my teaching."[22]

Does this feel like your own creative experience? Might it make sense that if a writer, suddenly anxious and self-critical, loses the creative thread, that the theta waves have been blocked, and a rapid anxious beta-rhythm taken over?

Subjective Side of It

Martindale also asked about the participants' subjective experience, as well, their actual lived experience—while doing his own problem solving tasks.

What was the inner experience around the time of sudden insight?: A combination of defocused attention, associative thought, and multiple simultaneous representations. Here they were, more open, receptive, searching, loosely associating, letting possibilities tumble around, not necessarily in visual form. Yet there is dominance of holistic and nonverbal associative functions of the right side of the brain, the right-hemisphere. Here is Kekule's snake biting its tail—which by report was visual—perhaps rotating slowly, and magically, or flashing suddenly (Martindale reported multiple simultaneous images) high on an inner video screen! Meanwhile, let us take this so very seriously, opening the door to all organic chemistry.

"Take Home Message"

Other research[23] shows departures from one exact pattern and also more diverse patterns in brain waves and areas depending on exact task and assessment approach (plus remember there can be more than one state as well as solution mode). Still slow waves are overall a good thing.

Recently, Kounios and Beeman[24] (2015) summarized brain conditions for intuition and insight including "… remote associations, broad flexible attention, abstract thought, positive mood, a sense of psychological distance, and a promotion orientation."

To simplify, one might recall at least four qualities—two objective, two subjective:

(a) slower brain waves and
(b) more right-sided activity, linked to a
(c) diffuse associative state, and—how interesting—
(d) that we can really like doing this!

Alpha Flash! How Cool!

Here is more: A neurophenomenological Aha! This brings together creative experience and brain activity. And what activity!

Here is what Kounios and Beeman[25] call the Alpha Flash. Does this sound good? A key step before insight.

Backing up, we humans have five discernible brain states within ranges of frequencies of brain electrical activity[26] and it is usual to have a mixture at once. Yet a dominant frequency is the rule. Notable here is the alpha range, around 8–12 oscillations per second, as assessed by EEG or electroencephalogram. Alpha is seen, for instance, during waking and before the slower waves of sleep—theta waves of about 4–8 cycles per second linked to experiences including daydreaming, deep emotions, intuition, and moving into sleep. Delta is the slowest from about ½ to 4 cycles per second, linked to deep sleep.

Alpha, that 8–12 range, is related to relaxation, reverie, mindfulness, and types of meditation. Anna Wise, based on many EEG studies, has suggested it bridging from slower states of inner life to the faster brain states linked to response and thought in conventional reality, and is key in proposed mixture favoring creativity.[27] Alpha, as dominant, can be called a "default" state, or an "idling," a resting of mind, where attention is not strongly directed to outer intellectual demands nor logical conscious and critical thought, yet the person is awake, not asleep. Faster waves include beta, about 12 to 40 cycles per second, key for conscious, logical, intellectual activity. Gamma is faster along this scale, 40 to 100 cycles or so, for further information processing, learning, memory (and perhaps provide a background oscillating substrate binding our senses and processes together, at around 40 cycles per second). Now, back to the Alpha Flash.

The location in the brain is also important. In a previous step, according to Kounios and Beeman's work[28] one can measure precursors to this "Alpha Flash"! There is a visual rear-brain occipital moment, or EEG downshift, in the visual area, linked to those soon emergent promising creative alpha waves. It would appear the visual area is, in part, taken offline, toward something new.

In this "flash" of a brain instant, we then seeing the focal burst of alpha waves. (Notably, alphas flash out suddenly, but this is about emergence; they are not the fastest waves, slower than usual waking EEG patterns.) Hence potential initiation of the "brain idling" state. What happens next, then, a walk with the muse? Perhaps! Fascinating that a mental circuit interrupt appears to stop down one's visual input, and modulate the volume on the outside world—and quickly too. Now we are not looking out—but attending within.

Worth wondering about more of the finer detail. Why this change all of the sudden, a prelude to a creative solution. What further action below the surface—and broadly averaged surface EEG patterns, may have preceded this? Events are coming to a climax, subliminally, even if our conscious mind has not quite tracked it. The researchers colorfully call the next step a *brain blink*.[29]

Here it is! Within a second of the Alpha Flash. This time it is the right temporal lobe (focus shifts to a more holistic, visual, associative area). Now gamma waves are seen and Aha! An answer! Kounios[30] hypothesized:

> Alpha burst … brain idling … regulation of visual inputs … Insights (then) occur when subconsciously activated ideas pop into awareness …. aha!

Could certainly be. And with further and fascinating detail yet to be discovered.

Our Own Experience

Can we do this? "On demand" as the TV people say? Can we cultivate a brain state, learn when it helps and its particular *flavor?* One piece of Kounios et al.'s[31] report was beyond intriguing, that, prior to word tasks toward creative insight: *Some people seemed to turn this mental state on in advance.*

There are types of treatments designed to change brain activation while teaching the "feel" of a different state. Neurofeedback (or neurotherapy) for ADHD has received increasing attention.[32] It is adjunct to medication for one, and a treatment which the client can learn and can keep doing.[33] Actually, my daughter and I both tried this when a doctoral student of mine was working with kids with attention deficit problems to help them "play a video game with their minds." Could they cultivate mental control that could last beyond these sessions? We did it too: we kept a ball on a video screen bouncing *above* a line.

How did it happen? Good question. Yet we did it. With our minds. The kids evidently can love it. For creativity, can we also learn the feel of a slower right-sided associative brain aligned with looser executive functions—but not too much one way or the other—a delicate nonlinear, and magical, holistic balance, that can erupt in a *brain blink?*

Such findings raise questions, including: (a) whether there are recognizable *flavors,* so to speak, in our consciousness; whether (b) we can recognize and modulate these on our own for creative receptivity, if we train this capacity consciously; or (c) we can go further using neurofeedback or another method.

Question of Balance—Systems 1 and 2, Including the Default Network

Below, are two human modes of thought we all have. There may be individual differences in how we balance and use them.

"Brain Blink" is what Kounios and Beeman had called that EEG precursor to creative insight, or "brain idling," being offline for "outside" events. We may wonder what is happening "inside." The terms are colorful, and suggestive. Let us note the so-called Default Network, recognized and studied by Randy Buckner, Jessica Andrews-Hanna, and Daniel Schachter.[34] This is akin to the "idling" brain function in Kounios and Beeman, above. It is also the "thinking fast" part of Nobelist Daniel Kahneman's book *Thinking Fast and Thinking Slow.*[35] Kahneman elaborates on these so called System 1 and 2 options for brain function— where System 2 returns us to logical slower conceptual processing well-connected to our consensual reality. He suggests not getting too carried away by that fast System 1; it isn't always accurate. That's one side of it.

While Kahneman cautions us not to downplay our slower intellectual powers of reasoning, others such as Singer and Kaufman[36] remind us of the value of the faster system, the default mode, the idling function for creative thinking. Various other advantages are present too. The issue as always is finding the right balance. How do we orchestrate our alterations of consciousness? As per Kounios and Beeman, when is "idling" is more than idling, and a creative turning within, as in Wallas's incubation; how does it serves creative purpose?

Buckner and associates provide more detail on this internally focused mental activity, whether memory retrieval, envisioning the future or something else. They find multiple interacting subsystems, where two are first (from the medial temporal lobe) a subsystem providing memories and associations as building blocks, and another subsystem for flexible use of this information (medial prefrontal subsystem). Exciting work is coming from this.

Research by Epstein and Norris[37] has shown the experiential factor more related than the rational factor to not only performance measures of creativity, but also aesthetic judgment, humor, intuition—and with self-report measures of social popularity and—very interesting indeed for later (see Chap. 14)—with *empathy*.

Epstein and Norris noted importance, nonetheless, in their work, between a *balance* between Systems 1 and 2. Singer and Kaufman[38] summarized these and related findings, and also the relation of certain creativity measures that were used to Openness to Experience. They underscored importance of balance between Systems 1 and 2, and for general intelligence as well as creativity.

An important question for us, as creators, and for our subjective experience, is how we apply such findings in opening to our own creative inspiration.

Balancing Act of Mind

Let us again suggest the importance of *balance*—while also recalling the *nonlinearity* and sensitive weighing of subtle processes together in creativity! In the Systems 1 and 2 model, the Default Mode, System 1, has its rapid ease. It may feel right but is not always correct (yet evolution has often needed a quick call). Yet it opens new doors, brings forth new possibilities. It is a more automatic, fast system, experiential, biological, and can lead to some fast decisions. Sounds creative? It ought to. Yet our powerful slower system may bring good ideas to fruition. Although the Default Mode, System 1, connects with creativity, humor, aesthetic judgment and Intuition, among others, it cannot do everything by itself.

Hence, for the creator, it is about finding the right balancing act to merge the best of both.

Worth recalling again the neo-Freudian creativity term, "regression in the service of the ego." It seems resonant indeed, on the path to creative insight, and more colorfully, while on the same lines, with what we have called the balancing of creative deep sea diving into our unconscious mind balanced with loosely held executive functions.[39] The goal is creative possibilities used in adaptation to our manifest consensual reality.

Later, one can raise issues about normality—which Buckner and associates do as well—and questions of health vs. pathology, for instance where low *latent inhibition* (or less gating of new possibilities) is found both in severe illness and exceptional creativity. This does not make them the same! That added executive function, one will see, can make a huge difference.

That particularly shining predictor for creativity, namely Openness to Experience, is mentioned below. In research by Scott Barry Kaufman and colleagues[40] OE was the strongest predictor of an assessment of overall creative achievement compared to other factors such as IQ, divergent production (see Chap. 8) and various other personality features. But is it, with OE, "the more the better"? Careful!

Let us not overdose on something because it looks good, or pathologize something just because it seems different. Balance, the creative recipe, remains key. Groundbreaking creativity researcher, the late Frank Barron, put it well,[41]

> The creative person is both more primitive and more cultivated, more destructive and more constructive, occasionally crazier and yet adamantly saner, than the average person.

Openness to Experience (OE)

Here is a definition of Openness to Experience (OE) which helps explain its strong predictive power for creativity, also among the five major traits found in the Five Factor Model of Personality. From Costa and Widiger[42]:

> … active seeking and appreciation of experiences for their own sake. Open individuals are curious, imaginative, and willing to entertain novel ideas and unconventional values; they experience the whole gamut of emotions more vividly than do closed individuals.

I was pleased, awhile back, when I learned that OE had become part of a widely used Five Factor Theory of Personality. Whether or not one accepts the premise that only five factors can distinguish most of human variability between you and me and someone else, a creativity-related measure had finally made the cut! For years—and in my own doctoral dissertation as well—there were many more factors assessed in typical personality batteries. For instance, I used the 16 PF, the Cattell's 16 Personality

Factor assessment. Creativity prediction ended up as a complicated weighting of a number of these factors taken together.

The resonance, not surprisingly, between OE and the Default Network, or System 1, bodes well for the future. I find it significant to see "creativity" as a focus of psychological study coming to the fore, now, in recent years. Do keep OE and related capacities in mind as, next, we go back even before *H. sapiens,* and thinking to speculate about evolution, in the next chapter. At what point, and for what being(s) might Openness to Experience become possible?

Summary and Next Steps

This chapter looked at mental states, including dream states, and at System 1 and System 2 thinking in areas related to creativity. It also examined creatively receptive states from both experiential and neuroscience perspectives, and posed issues of balance between different aspects of mind in accessing and managing creative possibilities. One may speculate about when and why in hominid evolution such creative capacities emerged at all. Does our everyday creativity in fact, not only aid in survival, which seems evident, but also serve our larger and ongoing human genius and purpose? That is where we go next.

Notes

1. Zimbardo, Johnson, and McCann, *Psychology, Core Concepts.*
2. Rilke in Barron, Montuori, and Barron, *Creators on creating*, p. 53.
3. Wallas, *Art of Thought.*
4. Loori, *Zen of Creativity*; Franck, *Zen Seeing, Zen Drawing.*
5. Thich Minh Duc, personal communication, c. 2005.
6. Richards, "Everyday Creativity," 204 (shamatha, vipassyana).
7. Rogers, *Creative Connection*; Goslin-Jones and Herron, "Person-Centered Expressive Arts Therapy."
8. Baruss, *Alterations of Consciousness.*
9. Combs, "Consciousness...", 402.

10. Krippner, "Altered and Transitional States." Also see Gackenbach's classic book on lucid dreaming.
11. Bograzan, "Experiencing the Divine in the Lucid Dream State."
12. Wallace, *Dreaming Yourself Awake.*
13. Jung, *Man and His Symbols*, 26.
14. Walnut, "Power Napping for Creative Gems." Here is Edison's practice for creativity in hypnagogia.
15. Lutz and Thompson, "Neurophenomenology Integrating Subjective Experience and Brain Dynamics in the Neuroscience of Consciousness."
16. Kounios et al., "The origins of insight in resting brain activity." See Dacey and Lennon, *Understanding Creativity*, 154–156, for general task format.
17. Mednick, "Associative Basis of the Creative Process."
18. Subramamian et al., "Brain Mechanism for Facilitation of Insight by Positive Affect."
19. Fink and Benedek, "The Creative Brain," 212. Additional support.
20. Martindale, "Biological Bases of Creativity."
21. Austin, *Zen and the Brain.*
22. Two very relaxing CDs, Halpern, *Deep Alpha* (and) *Deep Theta 2.0.*
23. Vartanian, "Fostering Creativity: Insights from Neuroscience." Also includes working memory enhancement.
24. Kounios and Beeman, *Eureka Factor*, 204.
25. Ibid., 84.
26. Freeman, *Mosby's Complementary and Alternative Medicine*, 199, Table 7-2.
27. Wise, *High-Performance Mind.* Frequency patterns, individual and mixed, toward creativity and other outcomes.
28. Kounios and Beeman, *Eureka Factor*, 84.
29. Ibid., 87.
30. Kounios, Ibid., 86.
31. Kounios et al., "Origins of Insight…" Where some people seemed to turn the state on *in advance.*
32. Arns, Heinrich, and Strehl, "Evaluation of Neurofeedback in ADHD: The Long and Winding Road."
33. Ibid. Effects on inattention and impulsivity, medium effects on hyperactivity.
34. Buckner, Andrews-Hanna, and Schachter, "The Brain's Default Network."

35. Kahneman, *Thinking Fast and Thinking Slow.*
36. Singer and Kaufman, "The Creativity of Dual Process "System 1" Thinking."
37. Epstein and Norris, "Experiential Thinking Style: Its Facets and Relations With Objective and Subjective Criterion Measures." Importance includes the experiential factor breaking down into parts (intuition, emotionality, imagination) while a rational factor was relatively more intact.
38. Singer and Kaufman, "Creativity of Dual Processing..."
39. Richards, "Creative Alchemy," 125.
40. Kaufman and Gregoire, *Wired to Create*, p. 84.
41. Barron, *Creativity and Psychological Health*, 234.
42. Costa and Widiger, in Richards, "Twelve Potential Benefits...", 297.

7

Emergence of Life and Creativity

Here and elsewhere we shall not obtain the best insight into things
Until we actually see them growing from the beginning.
Aristotle

How can we begin to know the putative Big Bang or later steps? Yet scientific evidence paints a portrait of potential *emergences*, of matter, life, mind, and perhaps even a future stage, about which one may speculate. One can move from atoms, galaxies, worlds, life, organisms, mind, onward to a triumphant achievement for creativity—of awareness, and beyond that, of meta-awareness. Awareness of our awareness. This step is not about individuals in isolation. Cultural evolution enters, joins, interacts with biological evolution. We enter new worlds of possibility, futures we may choose. A Birth of Creativity. Aided by dreams, images, metaphors, symbols, archetypes, narrative, languages and memory, evolution of memes/information, and more. Nor are humans the only beings with such capacities. Might we hominids yet be poised for an eventual evolutionary leap—to higher mind, even a greater good? (If so, let us hurry.)

© The Author(s) 2018
R. Richards, *Everyday Creativity and the Healthy Mind*,
Palgrave Studies in Creativity and Culture,
https://doi.org/10.1057/978-1-137-55766-7_7

Could evolution—or what we think we humans know of it—help us see ourselves, our creativity, where this emerged, and now where it might take us? Albeit hugely speculative, one can learn from this exercise.

We explore in the footsteps of evolutionary scientists and theorists including renowned evolutionary biologist Theodosius Dobzhansky, biophysicist, chaos and complexity theorist, and natural philosopher, Harold Morowitz, and others, and drawing from perceptive review chapters.[1] In a few pages we cover almost 14 *billion* years of evolution from the putative Big Bang forward—although the reader is definitely encouraged to explore further. You and I surely weren't there as witnesses (albeit some of our atoms showed up rather quickly).

A major issue relevant to us humans (and perhaps other living beings) is presence of conditions and early evidence for a putative Birth of Creativity.

Are we now living out a story born in the mists of the past, with a purpose of which we are not fully aware? Let us ask this question. How might greater conscious awareness help us now?

Morowitz Explored 28 Examples and 14 Billion Years!

As Harold Morowitz framed it, "Evolution is the overall process while emergence characterizes the punctuations."[2] He chose 28 huge punctuations!

An impressive exercise of choice in itself—spanning many phases of physical evolution, emergence of life and mind. We give a much more limited taste here. Recall, in general, that for "emergent" events, whether the Internet, the infamous weather, or our health, there tends to be self-organization with a result where "the whole is greater than the sum of its parts." One cannot predict exactly what will happen. (For instance, we may hope there is not an emergent crisis in our own health next week—or for that matter in our healthcare system.) A more formal characterization of emergent properties from Morowitz[3]:

... emergent properties of the system .... (are) novelties that follow from the system rules but cannot be predicted from properties of the components...

If our brains were even larger and more complex than they are now (will it occur?—an ongoing theme and triumph of hominid evolution), might we be able to handle more data and sort events out to make accurate predictions? Likely not, even so, if we accept chaos and complexity theory and factors including vast numbers of interacting factors, sensitivity to initial conditions, quantum mechanical events, chance effects, and the nature of free will.[4] Nonetheless, a larger brain could be a real assistance. Computers, for instance, have helped in predicting the weather.

Emergences

From our human point of view, events have happened faster and faster over these huge time spans. Hence more emergences have occurred in "recent" times. Sally Goerner shows the energetics corresponding to the exponential increases in complexity, from the Milky Way onward. Appearance of the human brain far more than doubles what has gone before![5]

To repeat, we live in a world of change and surprise. We cannot necessarily predict and certainly cannot control a great many things (not even our jobs or schedules). If only such an awareness might help us become more humble, more in awe, more aware of the wonders of life, and better able to interact with our complex and not always predictable (and endangered) world. Yet this viewpoint is still not the norm. "We've got this one" we say. Oh really?

What May Have Happened

Putatively, over almost 14 billions years, in the Big Bang view, there was, first, a "primordial origin" (of unstated and one might well believe of unstatable nature). Then the so-called "Big Bang" with extraordinary manifestation postulated in the first three minutes (had there only been a science fiction clock and intervals to record it). Then progression through particles galaxies, stars, elements, planets, organisms, neurons, mammals, hominids, tools, language, agriculture, philosophy … and ….

These are parts of our Western scientific narrative, and with some good support. Yet other groups, cultures, and religions have their own cosmologies[6] which we might do well to acknowledge and explore, and dialogue with Eastern masters and sages—for instance going beyond the scientific evidence of our sense organs or conventional mind. Physicist David Bohm, for one, did this with J. Krishnamurti.[7] Nor would we presume such a series of emergences has come to an end. For those who don't believe they already "know it all" (a subset of people we have met, and whom we may have resembled at times!) there is a world of mystery out there. Hemingway expressed it well[8]:

"I know," said Nick.
"You don't know," said his father.

For instance, many scientists today agree that only about 4% of our universe consists of the matter that makes up you and me, the stars and planets![9] Ooops! Still a few missing pieces such as dark energy and dark matter. What has happened to the other 96%?

Evolution of Universe, Life, Mind

A universe somehow emerges, progresses through further complexity, physical matter comes forth and organizes, and finally, on our own planet, life appears (defined as forms that can grow, adapt, respond, and reproduce themselves).[10] What diverse and fantastic forms come to exist, all part of one mosaic of embedded dynamic layers—universe, galaxy, solar system, ecosystem, and our own back yard.

We jump beyond cells, and then multicellular life, ocean to land, and life forms including mammals (meanwhile recalling it is absolutely *not* "all about us"). Change occurs in diverse and more complex ways. "Our" progression is interestingly aligned with an upright bipedal stance (standing on our own two feet), along with growing brain size, or cranial capacity.[11]

"Recently": 1.8 Million Years Ago?

(This is definitely recent, on a 14 billion year timeline). Based on artifactual evidence, it took 5 million years for the arboreal, or tree dwelling, apes to become upright on the land and evolve into *Homo sapiens*.[12] At one time there may have been 12 related species that radiated out geographically including our particular form of *hominid*—*Homo sapiens*. Yet only one remained at the end. What happened?

Some reports follow just that one evolutionary line that eventuates in "us." Witness 1.8 million years ago, the ancestor called *Homo erectus*. The most notable change invovles brain size. With this ancestor, brain is said to have become a full 25% larger (and 75% of current size). Not yet, though, it is speculated, will one find "metacognition" (awareness of our thought—remember awareness of awareness, which can open new universes of imagination and possibility). We are watching for that one.

Other Capacities

Yet consider imitation, which has begun. This is no trifle at all; repetition requires a way to represent something and then to replicate it—similar to the recreation of *genes* in biology, yet this time these are new *memes*[13] or units of information. Plus this suggests a Theory of Mind—where you know your thoughts are different than mine, along with processes including reasoning, understanding, and honoring views of others. Also important are SRRLs (self-triggered recall and rehearsal loops). What a triumph. It become possible to call up and work with something without cues actually being present. Big advance. These living beings can think of something without it being in front of them. Plus taking memory further, it seems possible to include associative functions, and content addressable memory (we have passed some of this on in turn to our smarter computers, and artificial intelligence world).

Certainly, other species can have some of this. Although the evolutionary timeline isn't known, take for instance the "creative," long, complex, and developing songs found in humpback whales, individually and as group phenomena, with nonreversing changes seen from month to month. Even included are rhymelike structures and thematic material which have been proposed to act as a mnemonic device in an oral culture![14] Do we sometimes underestimate our fellow beings?

First Leap

Yet *Homo sapiens* is remarkable. The first huge leap in capacity was said to occur perhaps 600,000 to 150,000 years ago (a trifle again compared to that 14 billion year expanse), while enough of a qualitative leap from our sensory world to more abstract thought to change function greatly. "Gradualist" models say this *anatomical* modernity (the new big brain) was matched by *behavioral* modernity, moving along a path. New thinking, new actions.

"Second Big Bang"

A more sudden model, colorfully named the "Second Big Bang" by Mithen,[15] presents *behavioral* modernity as lagging the big brain a bit—until, suddenly!—a surge in capability occurred in the Upper Paleolithic, just 60,000 to 30,000 *years ago.* This matched further growth of the prefrontal cortex. (Recall its role in self-regulating in general, never mind the balancing, broadening, and organizing force in creativity.)

Onward with Creativity?

Without that time machine it is not certain we will ever know exact progress of each group. Some believe Neanderthals about 250,000 years ago seem already to have had a "germ" of representational thought[16]—a prerequisite for our colorful and creative imaginations. Interesting too are views of Neanderthal expertise with musical expression[17] for deeper and emotional communication.

Interesting by the way that many of us have about 3% Neanderthal heritage, reflecting some absorption by more dominant species. Hopefully we retained some of this musical aptitude.

Supporting another *gradualist* view, in the African Middle Stone Age, tens of thousands of years before this putative "Second Big Bang," appars evidence for specialized hunting tools, long distance trading, and various decorations and arts.[18] Here too then is higher mental capacity. Beyond the European tradition we do find other trajectories, and gradualist and sudden views will remain debated.[19] For the present purpose exact dates are less important than the emergence of capabilities in prehistory that may have jump-started our creativity, expanding human potential and vision today.

Drawing again from the 2nd Big Bang view: Cumulative and "rachet" development occurred, one advance building on another. There was "ability to reflect on representations and—note well this reported leap— to think about thinking."[20] At whatever turn, precisely, this is it! The doors are come open for awareness and change.

Here potentially too are tools, images, and symbolism in waking life, and think too about dream images, also in some parts of the world, substance induced, or other spiritually framed visions.[21] At what point would one anticipate the archetypal and transcultural images proposed by Jung?[22] Imagery was present at least 20,000 years before evidence of literacy.[23] With a strong oral, artistic, or written tradition comes the potential passing over time and space of discoveries and aesthetic expressions. If some inscribed things physically, others could communicate through oral stories, songs, legends, performances that also share with contemporary others and across time.

Biological and Cultural Evolution

Evolution is no longer just about DNA. It is about experiential knowledge, ways of living and exploring, and making meaning, for groups and individuals, passed on to new generations, for further development. Ways of life which can interact with our biological heritage. Hominids become self-reflective, and aware, not stuck with one way of living. One can change—hopefully for the better.[24]

Beyond initial discovery and use of fire (as per the example in Chap. 2) is now to remember how to keep making it, to kindle the fire early before the weather gets too cold, to tell one's neighbors (and kids and grandkids) how to do it for themselves.

Chance for heightened knowledge exchange would be expected with the origins of agriculture, a "knowledge-driven activity,"[25] with settling down of nomadic tribes, and enlarged group sizes, and division of labor. Bands of 30 to 40 hunters turned instead into settled groups of perhaps 300 individuals.[26] Emergence of agriculture across regions from Asia to Africa to the Americas, all ranging from 10,000 to 4000 years ago, suggests agriculture is "an emergent activity of societies of humans ... an activity of great consequences."[27]

Now "we" (that is, our earlier hominid ancestors) have capacities needed to manifest creatively promising openness to experience and to seek the new. Capacities appear to encompass the curiosity, appreciation, ability to image and imagine, and work with possibility. Recall again the definition.[28]

> ... active seeking and appreciation of experiences for their own sake. Open individuals are curious, imaginative, and willing to entertain novel ideas and unconventional values; they experience the whole gamut of emotions more vividly than do closed individuals.

As with Csikzentmihalyi's flow[29] (or, what is called, for an athlete, being "in the zone") which shows highly focused and engaged activity, at times beyond awareness of time, space, and self-concern, one sees that mastering a suitable creative challenge has very powerful intrinsic rewards for the creators. Creators enjoy and often prefer it. Surely such capacities enhance survival. Furthermore, not just to survive but also to thrive. Creative thinking and behavior appears to have been increasingly crucial in our human evolution, no less so today. For *Homo sapiens*, increasingly, creating is a very important evolutionary job.

Birth of Creativity

This comes not directly from our DNA, but from our minds. From possibilities symbolized, worked with, transformed into new possibilities. If creative styles typified certain individual *H. sapiens* more than others, this also resonates with individual differences today, and a diverse population with difference behavioral "niches" and interactions, roles and systems, toward a working creative society.[30]

Some individuals might become what we call "eminent creators" whose creative work has broad impact and changes a field or our culture, This is one role. Meanwhile their own "everyday creativity" would also continue. A higher creative level in the population would meanwhile likely raise odds of grassroots acceptance of new possibilities and cultural change.[31] Who are the "new adopters"? Will a community accept the changes? Prehistorically, was there some primitive equivalent of a Tony winning performance, best-selling book, or top award in science.[32] In any case, a systems issue. Worth recalling again systems literature and including Florida's[33] picture for *Rise of the Creative Culture*.

Values, Feelings, Collaborations, Caring: "The Lost Darwin"

Beyond cognitive or intellectual considerations, what about the rest? Charles Darwin did actually address this. This part of his work has won less recognition than other aspects.[34] In fact, Darwin can here be widely misunderstood, and his viewpoints misapplied.

Some cite Darwin as noting "nature is red in tooth and claw," as if there is no choice.

Even to support waging a war. Yet "survival of the fittest" was Herbert Spencer's term, and not Darwin's.[35] Moore and Desmond, in their introduction to *Descent of Man*, note that "... an extraneous 'Social Darwinsim' was born within sociology. This was Darwinian cut-throat competition applied directly to society, rather than nature." Yet this was not from Charles Darwin at all.

In fact, Darwin (who actually once studied for the ministry) in his later works, especially *The Descent of Man*—spoke to collaboration, sympathy (his word for empathy) and love. He mentioned *love* over 90 times in *Descent*. The family was cited as a central reason for this. We are many things, but also a species of collaborators, with family (or extended group) preserved in particular by strong bonds and caring. Darwin mentioned "survival of the fittest" only twice in *Descent*, once to apologize for the term.[36]

Is this, then, just about one's immediate family, or does it generalize to broader issues of culture and society. Key question. Darwin saw human nature as more broadly inclined, even mentioning Jesus's dictum, "Do unto others…" As with many world wisdom traditions, with greater compassion, and larger thinking beyond one's self-interest or own boundaries, it could be a different type of life and world.

Make Love Not War?

Well, not exactly. Or not yet.

Back to the species level: Where did all those species go? Of that group of 12 *Homo sapiens* (that is us) was the survivor, the winner, be it through winnowing from war, emigration, absorption, or multiple other causes. Gause's Principle states that no two species can co-inhabit the same niche. So called Competitive Exclusion leads to migration and other response often warfare, and extinction of one group (and also with absorption).[37]

Is this immutable law, from Gause, part of the dominant epigenetic patterns of the time (versus an inevitable sole law, finessing any other possibility). Here is calling forth of genetic potential by certain environmental conditions.[38] For 200,000 years, we have all been *Homo sapiens*, and with a common ancestor some call Lucy.[39] Yet do we "do unto others"? *Homo sapien* groups still battle and with a ferocity in-group which few other life forms show. Yet we are citizens of the world. Jeremy Rifkin in *The Empathic Civilization*, believes on this embattled shrinking globe we had better find a new and broader empathy fast.

Pseudospecies

We humans have same-species groups that pinpoint differences so severely that "the other" cannot inhabit the same space.[40] They could in theory interbreed but this is prohibited by *barriers that are nonbiological*, including scarce resources, religion, ideology, other factors. Very much the case in settling the North American continent. Terrible. One still sees it in the world today.

Not just a few groups either. On every continent. Throughout time. With occasional exceptions emerging from beings (e.g., two bird populations) finding different roles for coexistence in one limited space.[41] We could learn from those birds.

From Morowitz, "The principle of Competitive Exclusion, deep within the structure of modern ecological theory, is still applicable for *Homo sapiens*." Responses include forced emigration or banishment or separation (non-peaceful, non-collaborative), slavery, war, or outright genocide, rigid caste systems tied to occupations or roles.[42]

In part because of lessons learned in the painful history of South Africa, the United Nations and other bodies have *now rejected making a caste system an official government policy*.[43]

It follows for many persons that humane treatment of *all* beings is a natural extension—if we are deeply to care and empathize toward better treatment for all—and in 2014 a French amendment to the Civil Code recognized animals as sentient beings.[44] (Some painful conditions and practices were previously permitted in France, and still are, around the world.)

Diversity, Freedom, Creativity

All this is easy to say, perhaps. Taking cultural separation, what is wrong with cultural or ideological diversity, many say, with various initiative (after all, our so-called "melting pot" American society was founded on principles including freedom of speech and religion).[45] Yet this presumes compassion and fundamental respect for each other, at all times, our universal humanity (*Homo sapiens*) and others' ways of life. Not to kill banish or otherwise remove each other if we are in conflict.

How far have we evolved toward doing better? As Morowitz says[46]—how important this is!—if strong competition at one time would have led to the extinction of a group...

Now humans, having reflective thought and the power of choice are not bound to living (this) out…

Environment and Creativity

Can we—can humans as cultures—part of our cultural evolution, and with deeper knowledge of epigenetics, now create other conditions to draw differently from our genetic potential. Pfaff, for one, suggests we pursue this regarding altruism. We have a talent (albeit sometimes hidden) for it.[47]

Knowing of the species devastation that left *H. Sapiens* the sole "winner," how sad I was to read a highly empathetic quote from Mithen, in *The Singing Neanderthal*, suggesting we the readers move to the music of Brubeck and picture Homo ergaster "stomping, clapping, jumping, and twirling." We could, also…[48]

> … listen to a mother singing to her baby and imagine *Homo ergaster* doing the same…. When you next hear a choir … close your eyes … let an image … come … perhaps … the Neanderthals of Combe Grenal watching the river ice melt as a new spring arrives.

We being are so much more alike than we are different.

Can we then sing to each other? This is not for a moment to minimize the complexities. Yet, in case you haven't seen it, it is worth mentioning how shared music (and its cultural base) actually led to new mutual understanding in a fictional film,[49] showing deep and emotional new understanding, in one persistent and painful and ongoing conflict between groups. Meanwhile talented people I know[50] have in actuality used group process and arts to assist with coping and conflict resolution. We humans have a creative choice. Can we do a lot better than we did in prehistoric times?

Need Not Hurt—and Holds Huge Benefit

Worth highlighting a belief some continue holding, that our generous giving has to "hurt." The word "selfless" may sometimes connote that view—yet it certainly need not.[51] Kant for one contributed this belief, and even as some take it, that if it feels good it may not fully count.[52] Let us distinguish a self-interested giving "look at me giving!" from a true joy in helping another, as per the Four Immeasureables of Buddhism (loving-kindness, compassion, sympathetic joy, and equanimity). Here one delights in giving, for its own sake, for the helping, and also sees the benefit of helping all, not just a personal reference group. This orientation is presumably what helps us thrive, in a culture of caring, giving, and greater meaning. It is valued by varied spiritual groups. It is likely a key part of why, with such values, we might even live longer.[53]

Again a Balance—Not About Pain

Do we, as some do, watch out for self, while defending against others? Is the *sole* ideal a larger group, with "all for one and one for all." As Kennedy said, "Do not ask what your country can you can do, but what you can do for your country." Still we can take a day off and go to a movie.

There is also an excellent book by MacFarquahar, *Strangers Drowning*, about taking giving too far, to the detriment of the giver and close associates.[54]

Overall, balance might suggest we combine our personal sphere and benefit with a larger picture. Emmanuel Kant, suggested giving should involve some sacrifice, pain, self-denial, and *not* enjoyment.[55] We suggest a misunderstanding if the message is that giving will necessarily hurt. Overall, healthy balance suggests that it varies, yet a times may include a bit of both.

As Jeremy Rifkin suggests in *The Empathic Civilization*, our *empathy* is vital although it will take more than that to improve our overall situation; still, how auspicious the potential benefits for self and society in so doing. Rifkin adds to the scenario possible changes based on new informational and energy resources, even a new *industrial revolution*. Enter here as well higher *collaboration* along with our too common competition, and *balance* in ethics of caring and compassion, with justice and human rights. Let us have balancing of our immediate lives with larger systems and benefits of community, balancing present with our future.[56] Aside from intrinsic rewards for us, we can also seek community to help us continue—with its own huge rewards for health, happiness, and wellbeing, so as not to be immobilized from feeling helpless and unable to change anything on our own. It will take not only our unique creativity but a combined and co-creative effort.[57]

Looking Ahead: Wonder, Awe—and Butterfly Power?

Do we have a posited "conscious grasping for the future."[58] We pursue this further later in the book after a more practical look at creative process and person. Yet once again, whatever the forward prospects, creativity appears, for all of us, to be part of *our job*.

Remember, we can help shift our *cultural evolution. We can do so consciously.* (Our managing our genetic one, which some have suggested, is a bit more of a controversy.)

Later this book explores even more deeply whether (a) creativity is more naturally aligned with a life of meaning and caring (not to doubt the "other side" of destructive creativity here). Plus the important possibility some call an *evolution of consciousness.*[59] In going from matter to life to mind, will yet another (b) stage be forthcoming; is there really "something more."

Certainly much of the Western population,[60] attends, at least in behavior, to something higher. Some may call it, "the spiritual."[61] Recognizing the sparkling diversity of world cultures and paths, we recognize many ways to interpret this. Yet it can be argued—all else being equal—that the openness and truth-telling aspects of creativity, amongst much more, can help improve us and overall turn our actions toward a Greater Good.[62]

Humility, Wonder, Creative Power

Western scientist, and MacArthur Award winner, physician, and evolutionary biologist Stuart Kauffman, without calling on a particular religion or belief system, finds greater meaning in our newer understandings of science. His dynamic evolving complex systems view, in books such as, *Reinventing the Sacred*, and *Humanity in a Creative Universe.*[63] Resonant some might say with various Eastern views,[64] while bringing in new sciences. Yet a salient point is the mystery, our relative smallness in face of a vast and unpredictable, emergent whole. May this help us expand to a new worldview. Plus, perhaps, as well, some new epigenetic conditions for our human development. May we find new hope here.

Butterflies at Home and in the World

With our creativity, and the Butterfly Effects of our lives—sometimes we can do a world of good. It may give us a better day, or help our health, it may happen with our partner, kids, or in our backyard; it may change or community or travel across the country. Our opening example was risked and executed to change the world.

Yet change comes from all of us, and all the time. What is our piece? It may matter less what it is exactly than to keep trying. Creativity *is change*. It challenges some status quo. We don't always even know the effect either. We can only act.

One never knows; a tipping point may be near—again it may be our everyday creativity, in our own backyard. At the same time, it may reach further, or we may join a larger effort. The Women's March (globally) in 2016,[65] after the American presidential elections showed in a new way, the emergent power of groups. On the other hand, across continents, it took only four people originally to organize it. Four Butterflies. By choosing the right time and place and purpose, response was overwhelming.

Then we all did it.

Margaret Mead spoke in effect to these "tipping points" as well as to our individual empowerment. She said[66]

> Never doubt that a small group of thoughtful, committed citizens can change the world. Indeed, it is the only thing that ever has.

Dobzhansky ended his classic book on human evolution on a note of hope, looking at our higher human capacities.[67] We are still developing these and more! Can we see ourselves as…

> … not the centre of the universe …. (but an) ascending arrow of the great biological synthesis …. last-born, the keenest, the most complex, the most

subtle of the successive layers of life. This is nothing less than a fundamental vision. And I shall leave it at that.

Summary and Next Steps

Lost in the mists of time, we speculate on large outlines of evolving matter, life, mind. Scientific evidence supports potential *emergences*. With cultural evolution, joined with biological evolution, with self-awareness and meta-awareness (with seeing and developing potential of mind) H. sapiens enter new worlds of creating, near infinities of mind, design of futures, and birth of a full-blown creativity. This can both increasingly help humans survive and explore what they/we are surviving for. Modes of imagination and discovery include dreams, images, symbols, metaphors, archetypes, languages, increased social as well as individual memory and transmission, the power of memes/information. Other beings too have some of these. Nonetheless, might humans be poised for a new evolutionary leap? The next section moves to specifics of creative process and person, but the discussion returns later to these larger questions.

Notes

1. Major sources include Arons, "Standing Up For Humanity," Dobzhansky, *Mankind Evolving*, Gabora & Kaufman, "Evolutionary Approches to Creativity," Guastello, "Evolution of Human Systems," Kauffman, *At Home in the Universe*, Loye, "… Darwin, Evolution, and Creativity," Mithen, *The Singing Neanderthals*, Morowitz, *Emergence of Everything*.
2. Morowitz, *Emergence of Everything*, 37.
3. Ibid., 13.
4. Kauffman, *At Home in the Universe*, factors in evolution: self-organization, selection, chance, and design. Yet not deterministic. A colorful science fiction series by Isaac Asimov (*Foundation Series*) includes discovery of *achaotic equations* that could "predict the future," but in reality, we are still awaiting them.
5. Goerner, "Chaos and Deep Ecology," Richards, "Creativity, Chaos, Complexity, and Healthy Change." (Each contains Chaisson's speculative table of accelerating energy flow).

6. For example, Rao, *Consciousness Studies: Cross Cultural Perspectives*; Magee, ed., *Western Mysticism and Esotericism*, deChardin, *Phenomenon of Man*, Jamgon Kongtrul Lodro Taye, *Myriad Worlds ... Abhidharma, Kalachakra, an Dzog-chen.* Enomiya-Lassalle, *Living in the New Consciousness.*

7. Bohm and Krishnamurti, *Limits of Thought.*

8. Hemingway, quoted in Panek, *4% Universe*, iv.

9. Panek, *The 4% Universe: Dark Matter, Kark Energy, and the Race to Discover the Rest of Reality.*

10. www.biology-online.org/dictionary/life: Grow, metabolize, respond to stimuli, adapt, and reproduce.

11. Gabora and Kaufman, "Evolutionary Approaches..."

12. Arons, "Standing Up for Humanity," 181. Also sees upright posture having advantages of "far from equilibrium."

13. Richards, 1997, When Illness Yields Creativity, 489.

14. Payne, "Progressively Changing Songs of Humpback Whales;" also see Mithen, *Singing Neanderthals.*

15. Mithen, *Singing Neanderthals*, 253.

16. Gabora and Kaufman, "Evolutionary Approaches..."

17. Mithen, *Singing Neanderthals*, 205, 221. Emotional expression.

18. Gabora and Kaufman, "Evolutionary Approaches," Mithren, *Singing Neanderthals.*

19. Gabora and Kaufman, "Evolutionary Approaches."

20. Mithen, p. 283.

21. Harner, *Cave and Cosmos*, 37.

22. Jung, *Archetypes and the Collective Unconscious.*

23. Singer, *Imagery in Psychotherapy*, 19, imagery was present at least 20,000 years before evidence of literacy.

24. See Guastello, *Chaos, Catastrophe, and Human Affairs*; also a longstanding cooperative-competition balance.

25. Morowitz, *Emergence of Everything*, 165.

26. Ibid., 163.

27. Ibid., 164.

28. Richards, "Everyday Creativity," 297.

29. Csikszentimihalyi, *Creativity.*

30. Richards, "When Illness Yields Creativity," 513. Finding one's *niche.*

31. Ibid., 492.

32. Ibid.

33. Florida, *Rise of the Creative Class*; Sawyer, *Social Emergence*.
34. Keltner, *Born to be Good*, 16, 199; Gruber, *Darwin on Man*; Loye, "Telling the New Story."
35. De Waal, *Age of Empathy*, 30, Moore and Desmond, Introduction to *Descent of Man*, liv.
36. Loye, "Telling the New Story."
37. Morowitz, *Emergence of Everything*, 131.
38. Ibid., 148.
39. Mithen, *Singing Neanderthals*, 123.
40. Morowitz, Emergence of Everything, 148.
41. deWaal, *Age of Empathy*, Morowitz, *Emergence of Everything*, although there are exceptions, in some species, with divided roles within a single space.
42. Morowitc, Ibid., 150.
43. Ibid., 152.
44. Ricard, *A Plea for the Animals*, 272. Resonant issue when differentiating between groups of beings, with rights for some and lesser privileges, even painful treatment or death for others.
45. Pelosi, *Know Your Power*.
46. Morowitz, *Emergence of Everything*, 149.
47. Pfaff, *Altruistic Brain*.
48. Mithen, *Singing Neanderthals*, 276.
49. *The Other Son*, moving film, Israeli and Palestinian infants accidentally switched at birth, opened 2012 (France).
50. Dr. Ilene Serlin crosses cultures as part of the Trauma and the Arts group of the International Humanistic Psychology Association, including working with Syrian refugees in Jordan and Germany.
51. Thich Nhat Hanh, *Heart of the Buddha's Teaching*; HH Dalai Lama, *Beyond Religion*.
52. Kant in Richards, "New Aesthetic…" Also see Jordan, *Women's Growth in Connection*.
53. Could start with food, water, shelter, space, health services, human rights, peace, education, and more.
54. Larissa MacFarquhar. *Strangers Drowning*.
55. In Jordan, et al., *Women's Growth in Connection*.
56. Rifkin, *Empathic Civilization*.
57. Pilisuk, *Healing Web*. Rifkin, *Empathic Civilization*.
58. Morowitz, *Emergence of Everything*, 25.

59. For example, Richards, ed., *Everyday Creativity*, deChardin, *Phenomenon of Man*, Ornstein, *Evolution of Consciousness*.
60. Many have a spiritual interest/orientation although those with formal religious affiliation is shrinking. Health and wellbeing have less to do with formal attendance than connection, affiliation, and finding greater meaning. See Friedman and Martin, *The Longevity Project*.
61. Morowitz, 37.
62. Richards, "Creative Alchemy;" Keltner, *Born to Be Good*.
63. Kauffman, *Reinventing the Sacred; Humanity in a Creative Universe*.
64. Rao, *Consciousness Studies: Cross-Cultural Views*.
65. More than one million people rallied at women's marches around the world (January 2017). http://abcnews.go.com/Politics/womens-march-heads-washington-day-trumps-inauguration/story?id=44936042.
66. Margaret Mead understood working with those tipping points and bifurcations.
67. Dobzhansky, 348.

Part III

LIVING CREATIVELY
(Creative *Person* and *Press*)

8

"Popcorn": A Model (Ongoing Creative Insights)

... as a writer you're always surprised when you think of the right note or the right word. You think, 'Oh I didn't know I could—oh, that's good!' You know, writing's full of surprises for oneself.
Stephen Sondheim

In this chapter, "popcorn" is used as a model for a dynamic process of creation. In ongoing creativity, we generate and work with a series of sudden insights. Overall, things may go well (or not), yet each instant in itself is unpredictable. As with popcorn, we can raise the odds of an event, on the average at least—here, a sudden Aha!—by turning the heat up. We figuratively warm up the system with various maneuvers, including the group process of brainstorming, and individually-practiced divergent thinking tasks, while also looking at facilitating (or deadening) conditions. We seek at best a metaphoric (or actual) *edge-of-chaos*, a place in phase space where creativity may particularly flow. In effect we are "in the zone." We seek a delicate balance of qualities and conditions to help us optimize our creativity.

© The Author(s) 2018
R. Richards, *Everyday Creativity and the Healthy Mind*,
Palgrave Studies in Creativity and Culture,
https://doi.org/10.1057/978-1-137-55766-7_8

Popcorn: Keeping It Popping

This Chapter Starts with Us

It starts with the notion, "we are process"—a view of our *dynamic* identity. Among much else, we are processes in motion, we manifest change, we are part of life, which indeed is all about change. We may not think of ourselves this way, as we have said, perhaps more like a still shot (don't we look lovely?—as we picture ourselves in this static way) than a feature on YouTube.

Yet as computer scientist Marvin Minsky said[1]

The principal activities of brains are making changes in themselves.

We are designed for change. We also like it—at least at a reasonable level. Humans are happier when faced with a (doable) challenge than with something easy[2]; turn it around, and we are more creative when happy.[3] We can even have a "mixed affective state" from working with the dreadfully sad. We can deeply imbibe that sadness but at the same time even revel in our chance to know it, capture it, and (hooray) symbolically transform it. One basis of creative therapies.[4] Maybe a drawing, a story, a note to our friend; the situation moves and grows. It can change—and we can do it.

Keep It Going

Creativity *can keep going*, if we free ourselves from the constraints that can get in the way. If we are present, open, receptive—and beyond the self concerns that can be distracting, or paralyzing. If we are having fun. If we are engaged. Why not? It's OK to be wrong, and even required at times. Creating is part of our human job, and part of our play and work. Examples are below, and consider if this isn't a bit like popcorn. Yet how ow open are we to sudden and unannounced change?

Creative Process: Keep It Popping

A Useful Metaphor. The Pop! Is Our Creative Aha!

Master theatrical lyricist, Stephen Sondheim, was asking, before in the opening quote, in an interview with Lin-Manuel Miranda,[5] if he'd ever surprised himself in the writing process. What, Sondheim responded: All the time!

Oh come on, as a writer you're always surprised…

Pop!, Boom. Flash. We don't know when our Aha! will come, or where, or which kernel. Then, suddenly, it arrives. The Moment. The surprise. We can't predict it. Are we ok with this? It is surely creative. As one recalls a creative product meets criteria of being *original* and *meaningful*. This for sure is something we haven't seen before. Must have come from *somewhere*….

Playing the Odds

Yet for the moment, we will just play the odds. Like popcorn in the popper, if we take the right steps, action will happen, and somewhere, sometime soon. We put the kernels of corn inside—that is, we "*prepare*"—along perhaps with adding a little oil or salt. Then we put on the lid (to keep what happens roughly under control). We turn up the heat. It is an "*incubation*" period perhaps. Something is happening below the conscious mind, and to all those kernels too! Suddenly one of them goes *pop*! Who suspected? It is a creative "*illumination*," our popcorn insight.

Maybe over time we even get a random popcorn staccato of different ideas.

Open Systems, Examples and Practices: Creative Process

There is, as noted in Chap. 4, an *open systems* aspect to our identity in creating, in this world of change and surprise. We are continually changing. We take another breath. In some ways, now, we are a new person. The examples below are far from exhaustive but intended to give a feel for this.

As stated, we are in constant metabolism with our environment—whether eating, breathing or listening to each other. Day to day our "recipe" is still the same—I will recognize you on the street tomorrow—even with your new haircut. We are self-sustaining, *autopoeitic*, continuing while alive our central configuration, but we are already different, you, me, all of us, in some ways from the start of this paragraph.

How do we keep creating? Brain process is on our side! Creativity *will keep going*, if we can free ourselves from the constraints that can get in the way. Fears, anxieties, fixed ideas and more. It surely helps to live with openness to experience, in the present. Similarly to encounter or create some of the conditions below, in one's inner world and outer environment. At best, creating can help unfold a deeper part of our human potential. The approaches below are well-known and time-tested.[6]

1—"Brainstorming"

You've heard of this one, and perhaps even done it. Just keep throwing out those ideas. Below is a brainstorming example about a product name. What to call it? Alex Osborn's brainstorming adds group process, as well. From a nonlinear dynamical standpoint, as Keith Sawyer indicates, it even encourages new emergences at a group level.[7] Here is a new chemistry of creativity. We couldn't have predicted these emergent outcomes, by the very definition of "emergence." Furthermore, in this case, where they emerge from a group, we could not necessarily have come up with this alone.

Thus, one heats things up, while getting beyond inhibitions! Group energy and motivation can also raise attention and energy level. Beyond emergent magic, "hitchhiking" on others' thoughts can keep ideas flowing. Osborn, in 1953, first published his book, *Applied Imagination*, which has been repeatedly updated. Brainstorming has long been used in business contexts.[8] From Chap. 6, one might wonder if an EEG would show an "alteration of consciousness." One might even question neurological indicators of group synchronization,[9] Right now, imagine yourself in such a group.

Marketing Example

"What shall we call the new cereal." People pass pieces around and crunch on these:

"Donut crunch." OK, any others? (moderator writes it up on a flip chart). Ok, sugar rings. Right, happy bites. Or … ok yes! Cheery O's. Wait, someone says, what about this spelling! *Cheerios*! (Yep, it is a made up example).

What can we learn? For one, to just keep throwing those ideas out. Do not censor, do not judge. Have fun. Anything goes. Build on your neighbor's ideas, say whatever comes to mind. "Use your ANDs and not your BUTs." Follow the original "Brainstorming Rules."

No Judgment! (Not Yet)

It is worth repeating the admonition: No judgment. Think how crushing if you said, "Cheery O's" and someone said, "What? How can an 'O' be 'cheery;' that is a really dumb idea." (It happens) Down the drain the idea goes (and perhaps also a once eager person, who is now hiding out).

At best, then, keeping a safe uncritical space, which also means starting with a friendly and supportive work group! Not for to-the-death competitors. If there is no choice in who is present, it means making group process guidelines totally clear. (These persons too may learn something!)

Critic Goes Out for Coffee

In the marketing example, deciding on one single solution is a later and separate segment. Having generated many possibilities, here is where critical thinking can enter. One knows what *can* happen earlier in the process with our critic, that critical part of ourselves (and who can be readily a cause of Writer's Block, anxiety, despair, or that eight-year old incomplete novel going back in the drawer). "This stuff is just no good" the critic keeps saying. Another crumpled piece of paper is aimed at the wastebasket. Time to send that critic out for more coffee. The skills will be useful, but not yet.

Now some people (or perhaps we, eventually) can learn mind discipline to mix these modes, to orchestrate and alternate mental states more consciously, to generate ideas and choose along the way, without necessarily sending the critic out of the room—which is to say, out of our mind. This time the critic takes a back seat, mentally, until summoned. We, as creator, know what skills to bring in at each point. This is, however, a more advanced case—and even then, the plan does not always work.

Separating Off the Idea Generating

Hence it is easier to manage the first stage without interruption, to be "freewheeling," where "anything goes." To get all the candidate ideas are out there. Later one can put on a different hat (and likely a different state of consciousness, see Chap. 1), and decide which possibilities might be best "for a purpose." Not as good or bad ideas, in general, but how well they meet certain criteria. Maybe: *Cheerios*.

As in marketing. As in memorable. As in delicious. As in cheerfulness. As in attracting attention and selling a product.

2—Example: Divergent Thinking

This second example can be tried out individually, without a group. It draws on popular assessments of "creative thinking abilities" and in particular the Torrance Tests of Creative Thinking (TTCT) by E. Paul Torrance. Divergent thinking is relevant to creative *process*; this area has probably been researched more than any topic in the study of creativity.[10] There are certainly other approaches to explore as well.[11] Yet this one has an intuitive feel and also lends itself to programs of creativity enhancement.[12]

The original form of these assessments came in a more complex form from J.P. Guilford, and his three-dimensional Structure-of-Intellect Model.[13] Guilford's work and his Presidential address in 1950 to the American Psychological Association[14] began a major creativity assessment boom, with exponential increase in research and published papers using these methods. Others developed related measures, including Wallach and Kogan, whose approach I used along with selected Guilford tests for my own doctoral dissertation, one finding of which I will report below. For more information in general, do see a fine assessment resource by Kaufman, Plucker, and Baer, *Essentials of Creativity Assessment*,[15] as well as specific information on these and other measures, including background on testing principles and usage.

The Torrance Tests of Creative Thinking (TTCT) provide the most widely used creativity battery, for both verbal and figural assessment. It has now been used for decades, and works on a similar, personal brainstorming type, principle, in generating ideas. To get a feel for this, take 5 minutes (let us say—this is not quite a TTCT example, for copyright reasons[16]) and list all the ways you could use a tin can. Anything goes—right?

Why "Divergent"?

Because one is finding *many and many different* uses or possibilities for one stimulus. Or as Mark Runco put it, more generally, "Divergent thinking is cognition that leads in various directions."[17]

"Convergent" thinking, by contrast, seeks the one right answer, let's say 2+2 = ? (If you said 4, good for you! If you used divergent thinking you might also say 11—that is with base 3, yes?, sorry 'bout that! With divergent thinking, there is no "one right answer.")

Examples of uses for a tin can—use to: drink a glass of water, serve soup, cook vegetables, for a waterproof hat, a drum to beat, a pattern for drawing a circle on paper. Also: Cut it up to make jewelry. Connect two of them with twine for a walky talky. Use four for wheels on a toy car. (Yes you can use two or more, but the directions didn't say so. Is that fair?). Float the can as a boat. You get the idea.

Fluency, Flexibility, Originality, Elaboration

The list of ideas is the basis for multiple scores. Three of the four "scores," which are particularly popular, are **Fluency, Flexibility, and Originality**. Fluency (how many ideas), comes from counting them—"anything goes." Flexibility (how many different categories were used), comes from clustering; for instance the first three are all about food, where more categories shows more distinct ways of imagining the can—e.g., as wheels, or as a waterproof hat—a higher score reflects that variety. Originality (how relatively rare each idea is), uses a table of response commonality. How often do people tend to think of a particular use? A drum to beat? Not very common. The fourth score, Elaboration, adds detail to particular responses.

Originality Tends to Come Later

All else being equal, the more common responses come earlier in our lists. The tin can is used for drinking water—yes, rather a common response. Especially on a camping trip. If you want even more of the unusual answers, just keep on going. The more popular ones get used up. You may need to stop, and look in a new direction, but hang in there: How about: Use a big can with holes in the bottom to take a shower when in the woods.

For my own doctoral dissertation, awhile back, among other findings I discovered "fluency was necessary but not sufficient for originality."[18] It was not simply correlated with originality. I did scatterplots of relations between variables, and even scaled the creativity scores beforehand into a standard form (so that a skewed distribution could not create a false finding). Overall, *the more fluency, the more originality*. Not guaranteed, but it raises the odds (necessary but not sufficient). This finding suggests it may really pay to do those Julia Cameron "morning pages" before creative writing, or whatever other activity may comprise one's "warm up." The practice can bring on further originality. I won't say "use it or lose it," because that is not true. But if you do "use it," the results may get better and better!

I published a paper highlighting findings including this in *The Journal of Creative Behavior*.[19] J.P. Guilford himself earlier had related scatterplot findings and he commented in JCB on my article. Do note, by the way, that this journal and others, including *Psychology, Creativity, and the Arts* (PACA), and *the Creativity Research Journal* (CRJ) are good ones to consider in seeking the latest creativity research, including this sort of "psychometric" study. There are many modern studies on divergent thinking and not just with words but with images, and under varying assessment conditions. Performance can actually predict for measures of creativity years later, for young people, even into adulthood, and a remarkable *fifty years* in one TTCT follow-up study.[20] Although some people continue to debate how real-to-life these tasks are, important findings have resulted).[21] Kaufman and colleagues said of these assessments:

> ... there is a legitimate case to be made that divergent thinking is a key component of creativity and, more specifically, creative problem solving. Divergent thinking can be conceptualized as involving cognitive processes that help on produce multiple responses to open-ended questions or problems. DT is often contrasted with convergent thinking, in which cognitive processes are used to produce one or very few possible solutions....[22]

Well put, and all the more compelling are new results linking divergent thinking abilities to—remarkably—SNPS (pronounced "snips," single nucleotide polymorphisms), hence tied to distinct areas of DNA, in this case, related to the D2 dopamine receptor gene.[23] Hence one finds localization on the genome related to creative ideation. Remarkable. Although there are complexities in interpretation at level of finer structure, all of *fluency*, *flexibility*, and *originality* were involved! This is all the more significant because of evidence linking the neurotransmitter, dopamine, which Kaufman and Gregoire called the "neuromodulator of exploration,"[24] to Openness to Experience. Nice results. Yet do keep in mind there is no one quality, neurotransmitter, SNP, or skill for creativity. Different modes of functioning have their place in an overall balance. James Kaufman and colleagues, JP Guilford and others, acknowledge it is still a matter of *balance*. In brainstorming, one produces many ideas and then one chooses. There is a place for that openness and then for narrowing down. For a special issue of the *Creativity Research Journal* for the 50th anniversary of JP Guilford's famous Presidential address to the American Psychological Association, I wrote an article reinterpreting Guilford's model in a dynamic frame, showing many points of relevance to chaos and complexity theory.[25] More specifically, chaos theorist Fred Abraham has even proposed how a divergent and convergent balance might work, in chaos and complexity terms.[26]

Working Atmosphere Affects Creativity

Here is some critical of research,[27] which spawned many further studies. Directions can make a huge difference.[28] This is also very much about the environment that helps (or discourages) creativity. In this instance I also knew one investigator, Robert Dentler. Students—where college psychology students are often the participants in these research studies—were put randomly into two groups. A divergent thinking task was assigned to each; the goal as we've seen, to give many answers. Essentially in Group #1, they were told "anything goes, have fun" and etc. In Group #2 they were told in effect "only put down the *really good* ideas; be very careful in choosing them—just use the very best ones" and etc. Judgment was front and center—to evaluate every possible answer. To some, it sounded a bit scary; their inner critic had *not* gone out for coffee. (It can be hard to have a boss like that.)

Did the groups differ? Definitely. It was a telling result that the relative *originality* of the two groups was most notable. In what direction, would you guess? Might the second one, the "*really good ideas only*" group, do better at showing originality as instructed? (or in fact "relative unusualness" since unusual answers too got higher scores?) Nope—very much the contrary. In this study, the "have fun" group beat out the "be careful" group dramatically. By contrast, originality for Group #2 was rather poor. Thus in creating, we can relax and have a good time. Trying too hard can be fatal.

It was telling, as Marta Ockuly and I found in an Internet survey, that just one's own working *definition* of creativity, whether about *product* (had better be original!—hence judgment remains active) or *process*, tended to predict for attitudes about creativity and self.[29]

The Task Is Not Just Intellectual

These exercises, again, were examples, albeit using popular, and validated approaches. If you attempted these with some self-reflection you may have noticed qualities outside the cognitive or intellectual sphere that affected performance. These help create conditions for being creative, for us individually or in groups. Conditions include:

(a) in groups—supportive open collaborative environment
(b) an open explorative state of mind and, quite likely, a related "alteration of consciousness."
(c) willingness to take risks, and just let things come to mind—quite likely drawing from below the conscious mind
(d) a playfulness, spontaneity, having fun, while continuing to generate responses. The later responses are apt to be more colorful and original.
(e) A real willingness to be "wrong," where this is truly not even an issue to ponder, but part of accepted practice.
(f) a boycott, or at least partial boycott, on judgments, since bringing these in prematurely can shut down the flow of ideas.
(g) Flowing in general with the process of discovery, rather than a fixation on one response or another.

Hence this is far from a purely intellectual exercise. It draws on the whole person and is delicately poised within an encouraging, or discouraging, environment. We look at creative *person* and environmental *press* more shortly.

Chaos and Complexity

Considering Chaos and Complexity Theory and creativity, it is tempting to link parts of this process to idea generation at a putative "Edge of Chaos." Here is a rich cauldron of shifting possibilities, changing yet not randomly or chaotically, reflecting an underlying (and some would say) *beautiful* order. The flux allows for many solutions.

As noted earlier, David Schuldberg, Stan Guisinger, and I have coedited a book directed to the social scientist, called *Nonlinear Psychology: Keys to Chaos and Creativity in Mind and Nature.* My contributed chapter, "Chaos, Creativity, Complexity, and Healthy Change,"[30] includes the Edge of Chaos construct, and quotes two key innovators and their modeling work: Chris Langdon, from his groundbreaking 1990 paper, and then Stuart Kauffman, from his 1995, *At Home in the Universe.*

Does this "place" called *edge of chaos*, proposed in what is called phase space, mathematically, have a plausible "feel" for you? Do you believe you have ever hung out mentally in such a "place," intellectually speaking? If this were about sports, we might be talking about being "in the zone." Finding this sweet spot may be key!

Here is a metaphorical *edge of chaos.* Noted first by Langdon,[31] and elaborated for organic life by Kauffman[32] he described it as a "working hypothesis ... life evolves toward a regime that is poised between order and chaos." He continued, "Borrowing a metaphor, life may exist near a kind of phase transition .... too frozen (is) ... to rigid..." Yet if "too far into the gaseous ... not orderly enough..."

The highly creative thinker ends up, figuratively, right where some ice is forming but not yet rigid (a creative idea is coming to the fore), while nearby water close to freezing is still moving and promising yet other forms. Yet does one live in this place of ferment, or go only on weekdays? Do we have control? It gets interesting.

How to create conditions for such mental states and richness of possibility? Sir Ken Robinson,[33] a strong force in creativity education, believes—just as serious missteps with the world's ecology, have "squandered and damaged" our resources that there is a similar "calamity" with human resources in an ecology of creativity. Using "narrow forms of education" we have marginalized "... important talents and qualities."

Our educational systems can *transform* what students at all levels can accomplish. How can we help this to happen?

The next chapter goes further with qualities of the creative person, toward enhancing creative ferment, vision, and possibility; these are qualities we surely do *not* want to discourage.

Summary and Next Steps

We may picture ourselves as dynamic processes in motion—our bodies and very much our creative minds. We, and our world, can produce emergent marvels, unexpected creative products, as part of who we are. Or we can do so at least when we free our creative process. Can we get out of our own way? This chapter uses "popcorn" as a model to frame ongoing creative process, especially focused on early stages of: preparation, incubation, and then—Aha!—our insight or illumination. It also gives a feel for tasks that assess creative thinking (and reveal where we keep the popcorn popping). The next chapter explores qualities we may manifest, as creators, and settings that help engage this process and keep it going.

Notes

1. Minsky in Varela, Thompson, and Rosch, *The Embodied Mind*, 138.
2. Csikszentmihalyi, *Creativity.*
3. Kaufman and Gregoire, *Wired to Create.*
4. Richards, "Everyday Creativity"; Goslin-Jones and Richards, "Mysteries of Creative Process."
5. Sondheim quote: from interview with Lin Manuel Miranda, *Style Magazine, New York Times*, 10-22-2017.
6. Osborn, *Applied Imagination*; Kaufman et al. (Plucker, Baer).
7. Osborn, *Applied Imagination.*
8. An effective way to produce ideas through spontaneous group offerings; though at times group members can dominate process, there are many advantages to the group.
9. Strogatz, *Sync.*
10. Mark Runco. "Divergent Thinking, Creativity, and Ideation"; Guilford, *Nature of Human Intelligence.*
11. Kaufman, Plucker, Baer, *Creativity Assessment.*
12. Parnes, *Creative Behavior Guidebook.* One example of uses of the problem solving approach.
13. Torrance, *Torrance Tests of Creative Thinking.*

14. Guilford, "Creativity." See also Richards, "Millennium as Opportunity."
15. Kaufman, James, Jonathan Plucker, and John Baer. *Essentials of Creativity Assessment.*
16. TTCT needs to be purchased. Guilford's divergent production and other tests are found in *Nature of Human Intelligence.*
17. Runco cited in Kaufman, Plucker, and Baer, *Essentials of Creativity Assessment*, 17.
18. Ibid., 16.
19. Richards, "Comparison of Selected Guilford and Wallach-Kogan Tests of Creative Thinking in Conjunction With Measures of Intelligence."
20. TTCT prediction for personal creativity spanned *fifty years*. Runco et al., "...Fifty Year Follow-Up."
21. Multiple other assessment approaches are listed in Kaufman et al. and in Runco, *Creativity.*
22. Kaufman, Plucker, and Baer, *Creativity Assessment*, 16.
23. Yu, Qi, Shun Zhang, and Jinghuan Zhang. "Association of Dopamine D2 Receptor Gene with Creative Ideation."
24. Kaufman and Gregoire, *Wired to Create*, 85.
25. Richards, "Millennium as Opportunity."
26. Abraham, "Dynamics of Creativity..."
27. Dentler and Mackler, "Originality: Some Social and Personal Determinants." See Wallach and Kogan, "*Modes of Thinking in Young Children*," which initiated divergent thinking tests in very relaxed conditions.
28. Vernon, "Effects of Administration and Scoring..."; Gunvor Rand and Per Rand, "Effects of Working Atmosphere on Creativity." With some exceptions, as in the latter, where a subgroup did better under pressure, the relaxed conditions are overall conducive. Also see Beghetto and Kaufman, *Nurturing Creativity in the Classroom (1st and 2nd Eds.)*, Runco, *Creativity and Themes*, and Runco, "Divergent Thinking, Creativity, and Ideation."
29. Ockuly and Richards, "Loving or Fearing Creativity," showed power of imagined context on confidence about one's creativity, based on participants' views of how creativity is defined.
30. Richards, "Chaos, Creativity, and Healthy Change."
31. Langdon, "Computation at the Edge of Chaos."
32. Kauffman, *At Home in the Universe*, 26.
33. Robinson, *Out of Our Minds*, 285.

9

Creative Person

Instructions for living a life.
Pay attention.
Be astonished.
Tell about it.
Mary Oliver

What are we like?—What do we manifest as human beings and as creators? Here is a view that can keep us in that creative flow, keep the creativity going, the *popcorn popping*. Even when it is hard. This is based in our traits, predilections, intentions, discipline, passions. It is about our style, our habitual way of approaching life, our work, our play, our handling of challenges. This concerns our "personality," our cognitive, social, emotional, intentional, qualities and more, Nor need we think it is "too late" if we want more of a certain quality. The watchwords for us humans remain change and "plasticity." Creativity is our birthright, in part a survival capacity; its further ongoing and dynamic development will necessarily be part of that birthright.

© The Author(s) 2018
R. Richards, *Everyday Creativity and the Healthy Mind*,
Palgrave Studies in Creativity and Culture,
https://doi.org/10.1057/978-1-137-55766-7_9

Creative Person: Creative Style

The focus is on personal features and, taken together, on ongoing style—or, in view of varied schemata and ways we can adapt, to our style in a setting. Our thoughts, wishes, tendencies and actions in the world, what we seek and avoid, what we yearn to know, what we actively wish to pursue, how we like to relax, what we care about. A range of intellectual, social, emotional, and intentional qualities. This chapter even dares to give a couple of "lists" of researched traits linked with creativity, although some people may incorrectly think there is some checklist, or fixed profile—that there is one certain way to be.

This is not the purpose here. We look at a mosaic of qualities, portions of which are found statistically among highly creative people. Creative efforts differ, yet one finds some "core" regularities across domains, and beyond special capabilities.[1] As we explore our own patterns and the changing flux of our lives, we can learn from these.

The main point here is to suggest—to suggest strongly and in general, while offering a number of traits as examples—that it can be our personal qualities, including cognitive stylistic patterns,[2] beyond strictly intellectual abilities, that help us fire up our creative urges and keep our creativity going.[3] *One may call it the heat that keeps the popcorn popping.*

This is not, however, about some magic effect nor a simple direct relationship, where we add "A" and then "A causes C" (C = creativity.) Not such a simple linear model! ("A" can however "raise the odds" for "C.") Certainly many qualities cannot hurt our creativity (e.g., being present, curious, engaging the "openness to experience," raised earlier). Yet the recipe for any of us can be more complex. Our creative concerns emerge dynamically from a complex and multivariate picture of all that we are, and in a context.[4] We don't just simply "manifest more of 'A' and then are automatically more creative." (Although, on the other hand, practicing being creative may bring us more of "A"[5] Furthermore, once in awhile, that one trait is decisive; for example, with creative "risk-taking," if we are immobilized in our efforts, stalled, and a bit fearsome, some creative courage may make all the difference.)

Behavioral "Niches"

In any culture, furthermore, there are unique behavioral "niches" or roles for our creativity, within which people differ, and across diverse areas of endeavor[6]—e.g., in one's worklife, artist, scientist, teacher, entrepreneur. We are surely not all the same! As with brainstorming (here one might call it *cultural brainstorming*,[7] different people assume distinct roles, as in the two stages of brainstorming, but here dividing it between certain groups, where some people practice more divergent thinking, others more convergent thinking). Hence some people may be more "on the edge" in generating wild ideas (futurist, fiction writer, certain business consultants). Others may help mold the generated new into a practical, useable whole, closer to the second stage of brainstorming (e.g., gatekeepers, critics).[8] Creative risk-taking, for one, can take varied forms depending on role (e.g., being a community activist or a gardener; creative fantasy writer or literary critic).[9]

Between us, we humans manifest many flavors of creativity. Over the years, we explore and discover our own roles and predilections, hopefully finding our "fit" in a larger culture. In choosing we also further discover self: Do we lean toward the *future* (or the past), crave novelty and change vs. a more comfortable stability. What then is our chosen work, our parenting style, our goals for our leisure activity. There is room for numerous options. Or at least, this is so if we are challenging ourselves, and alive in the moment—if we are living a fulfilling life. (If we are unhappy, bored, mindlessly going through carbon copy days, or living a life of constant anxiety, a change seems in order.)

Meanwhile, who knows what we will be doing ten years from now? If "the constant is 'change,'" it is apt to be exponentially more so.[10] If the Internet was virtually unknown 25 years ago, can we even imagine what the next 20–25 years will bring?

Creative Person: And "Personality"

We explore qualities of the creative person, including *personality traits*, and also *cognitive style*, stylist modes of information processing or thinking related to ongoing personality trends.[11] One is observing a person, let us say, and sees them having a liking of and pull toward divergent thinking; for them, one answer is never good enough. What else can we offer, they might say? This tendency could be the combined result of qualities such as openness to experience, overinclusion, and others discussed below. Having such a mix (or another) might a bit *like turning the heat up under the popcorn.* That is, one is turning on creative brain functions (including perhaps alterations of consciousness).

Let us hear from Greg Feist, expert on creative personality, and his model of six latent variables for personality. First, Feist defines personality as a[12]

> Unique and relatively enduring set of behaviors, feelings, thought, and motives that characterize an individual.

We cannot of course cover everything in this huge field, but can hit some high points and give leads for the interested reader.

Feist's model (as a flow chart) begins with (a) a combination of epigenetic and genetic influences, then impacting (b) brain characteristics. This feeds into (c) four areas of function or types of traits, which further interact with each other, namely: Cognitive, social, Motivational-Affective, Clinical traits, finally (d) resulting in creative thought or behavior. Here we take examples of all but the clinical—which will occupy major parts of this *Everyday Creativity* book later on.

It will be helpful to start with *epigenetics.*

Epigenetics (interacting with genetics) as noted before by Moore,[13] *"refers to how genetic material is activated or deactivated—that is, expressed, in different contexts or situations."* Consider ancient Polynesians navigating vast oceans between tiny islands, and discovering new homes, voyagers who became brilliant at astronomy, reading clouds and weather and currents, and much more.

Some people believe we are somehow programmed by our DNA and that "the world out there" is a separate matter. We go forth to meet it. Others lean toward a more separate yet interacting relationship with our environment, while we the humans stay who we are. Now we do this, and change our environment like that. Yet we are still the same (strong and independent) Bob, Mary, Chris.

By contrast, in some ways we are servants of our environment, coming forth from our larger capacities or potential to meet it, as needs require, and are changed in turn. We live on a farm and rise early to start the day. We are urban sophisticated city dwellers. We live in a land beset by violence and danger and suicide bombers. We are each a product of, and an intrinsic part of, a larger evolving picture in which we are embedded. (Yet—remember—having self-awareness, we are not lost in this process, either, but can explore it and can still change the script, even dramatically.)

Interestingly, *epigenetics* was a word yielding only 46 references between 1964–2000 yet discussion is now everywhere.[14] Our environment not only "counts" but can one versus another can evoke very different possibilities from our storehouse of genetic potential. In what areas? Just name it: learning and memory, cancer, obesity, addiction, psychosis, aging and more. Further, these previously hidden mechanisms are even becoming important enough that the *"belief that experiences matter is likely to affect how we live our lives and how we treat those around us."*[15]

This is very important; we shall return to it in later chapters.

Meanwhile, and without or say-so or even knowledge, the environment helps draws option A or B out of us. Actually think of one's own life relationships, areas where one has lived, schools one has attended. So much has helped make us who we are. Powerful indeed when applied to the potential of humans for social change, for compassion, for altruism[16] or making vast leaps of whatever sort, via creativity.[17] Are we and our crazy world more malleable than we thought? That is the question.

On the downside (negative examples being yet further proof of these evolving interacting factors) one sees various disadvantaged groups, told they aren't any good at doing X. How deeply this can bias findings and switch off potential. Meanwhile members of this group quite readily could do X and exceptional feats far beyond.[18] Tragic is to put it mildly. (A *self-fulfilling prophecy*.)

While helping create better environments, to evoke something better, let us also turn off these more destructive conditions.

From Brain Characteristics to Traits that Influence Creativity

Within this context, then, genetic differences, as activated in a particular context, influence brain structures, consequences including varied temperamental differences. Feist divides these into the four areas above. Most importantly, given our Popcorn Model, he notes[19]:

> "… a particular constellation of personality traits function(s) to lower the thresholds of creative behavior, making it more rather that less likely." (He also notes how) "most models of personality now include some form of neuroscientific or biological component, and combined nature and nurture model are more the norm than exception." (and finally that comparable to) "interplay of nature and nurture at a genetic level, brain plasticity has done … at a neuroscientific level."

Hence, here is our Popcorn Model, and qualities of person that can lower the threshold, in this case for creativity. May the insights come, may the popcorn pop!

Further we again note use of *plasticity*—a term we met before. Today we exist in a wider world for "personality" research and factors influencing how we manifest, develop, and change. Evolutionary biologist Theodosius Dobzhansky saw our "phenotypic plasticity" as central to our human creativity and survival, as we also can today. Yet today we talk as well about biological plasticity, where the brain itself can change.

Certainly major changes can develop in childhood. Yet not only in childhood. Hopefully you have had the chance to see an older person who after a stroke who could not, perhaps, speak at all, or stand and walk (have seen both). Yet within six months, this person may have recovered much of this function.

We are dynamic miracles in motion.

Plus these mind-body qualities and dynamic interactions provide a critical mix that, in the Popcorn Model—per Chap. 8—can help *turn the creative heat up.*

Examples: Creators in Motion

A few researched personality traits or personal characteristics, linked to creativity, are given below, by way of example. Also added are a couple of lists. Attention is given to *Androgyny, Openness to Experience*, and *Tolerance of Ambiguity, Preference for Intuition*, and *Overinclusiveness*. These can help open creative mental doors, and three of these are not quite as common in the literature. OE however, as noted, has been more highly correlated with creative achievement than a range of other predictors including divergent thinking and other personality traits, and is front and center.[20]

Yet again, our main point here, is not about specifics as much as to suggest certain ongoing traits or personal tendencies may affect our creative popper, to "turn the creative heat up."

Examples

Examples draw on moments and quotes illustrating qualities of a creative person in motion, and bringing them a bit more to life.

First the late and amazing comedian Robin Williams, who could really get on a roll. A mind in motion. Our question is: How does this happen? What keeps it going? Not just one good idea either, but an ongoing cascade, while filled with fun and delight.

> And sometimes there are times when you're just on it—when you say the muse is with you and it's just flowing and that's when you know that the well is open again and you just put in the pipe and you stand back and say 'yes.'[21]

Or geneticist Barbara McClintock, who when the creative (and microscopic) doors were open and she could go right in to visualize and explore chromosomes firsthand; she would stay for awhile. (Later we return to Dr. McClintock and states of consciousness.) She said[22]:

I wasn't outside, I was down there. I was part of the system—I was even able to see the internal parts of the chromosome....

Look too at lyricist Stephen Sondheim quoted earlier.[23] Here is risk-taking, as an ongoing checkpoint. Not really about fear (wouldn't work). But relishing challenge. This *exploratory* quality, in fact, is central for high creators. Must we really keep doing the same old thing?

You shouldn't feel safe. You should feel, 'I don't know if I can write this.' That's what I mean by dangerous, and I think that's a good thing to do. Sacrifice something safe.

What to make of this? Powerful forces are at work here. This is from looking at *person*, only, without knowing a specific evoking context. Yet the conditions for scientific or artistic exploration tend to be fairly open an encouraging.

Personal Qualities: Examples of Lists

What are we manifesting, becoming?

Sandra Russ—one of the key creativity researchers who helped bring *affect* into a cognitive equation—in her book, *Pretend Play in Childhood*,[24] listed some evidence based and time tested personality traits, which would help maintain this momentum, including *tolerance of ambiguity, openness to experience, unconventional values, independence of judgment, curiosity, preference for complexity, risk-taking, self-confidence and intrinsic motivation.*

I had the privilege to edit *Everyday Creativity and New Views of Human Nature*, with remarkable contributors, for the American Psychological Association; our own group of 12 integrating themes/varied personal qualities, developed through qualitative analysis, were also very *healthy*, and oriented as well toward healthy cultures (*health* being one of themes) also including *dynamic, conscious, open, non-defensive, integrating, observing actively, caring, collaborative, developing, brave, and androgynous.* "Androgynous" is given as an example directly below.

Examples: Personal Qualities to Encourage Creativity

Freedom from Sex-Role Stereotyping or *Androgyny*

Androgyny[25] has emerged repeatedly over the years, and is not about being stereotypically male or female. Or stereotypically anything. Rather, it is about *not* being boxed in by stereotypes of any kind (can also apply to other classifications such as ethnicity, or socioeconomic status). Our androgynous creator can laugh and cry, be emotional and rational, intuitive and logical, subjective and objective—can be free (or become freer) to be more fully human.[26]

We need not be restrained by gender stereotypes—which Sandra Bem saw as a form of functional fixety[27] She noted how, in the past, discourse on masculinity and feminity "favored gender traditionalism" and pathologized gender deviance if not conforming to the cultural requirement.

Yet highly creative people have often not limited themselves by these rules. Donald MacKinnon captured this aspect in the IPAR (Institute of Personality Assessment and Research) based on extensive studies of highly creative persons across fields at the University of California, Berkeley[28]: The more creative a person is the more apt they are to reveal:

> ... an openness to (their) ... own feelings and emotions, a sensitive intellect and understanding self-awareness, and wide-ranging interests including many which in the American culture are thought of as feminine.... In the language of ... Carl G. Jung ... creative persons are not so completely identified with their masculine persona roles ad to blind themselves to or to deny expression to the more feminine traits of the anima.

Ravenna Helson, who researched creative women mathematicians at IPAR found women didn't show stereotypic masculine interests. However, they were "like creative men in most other personality traits."[29] She concluded that introversion, and self-direction among other traits made them less susceptible to cultural pressures.

In the book I edited called *Everyday Creativity and New Views of Human Nature*, androgyny came out in areas that were both personal and social, as one of the 12 integrating themes.[30] For instance there were benefits for peaceful democratic process, e.g., in Scandinanvia, as noted by Riane Eisler, where roles were less restrictive and "partnership" models of governing were more the rule.

Openness to Experience

Meeting someone with high OE, we find more curiosity than concern, more wonder than fear or anxiety. How brave they are, in one sense, since they don't really know what they will find. Yet they (or we) can enjoy this mysterious quest; it is one part of it. Our openness can help keep us moving, keep us engaged, seeing the world in new and original ways. As Frank Barron (1963) noted, "originality is almost habitual with persons who produce a really singular insight".[31]

Here is a definition of OE[32]

> ... involves the active seeking and appreciation of experiences for their own sake. Open individuals are curious, imaginative, and willing to entertain novel ideas and unconventional values; they experience the whole gamut of emotions more vividly than do closed individuals.

From his research, S. Kaufman's subdivides this into 3 areas of engagement, which don't necessarily arrive together to the same degree: intellectual, affective, and aesthetic[33] This might be expected since we each have different interests. Yet the openness itself is notable. Of further note is relationship of OE to what keeps us going, to our passion and persistence, whether it involves everyday creating, performance, or creative achievement, as shown by Grohman and colleagues.[34] Significantly, in a further study, teacher nominations for passion and persistence predicted for peer-nominations of creativity even beyond the major dimensions of personality.

Our passion can mean everything.

Tolerance of Ambiguity

Tolerance for ambiguity concerns sitting with the unknown and, in our popcorn analogy, more or less letting the popper get hot—to see what will emerge—rather than jumping to conclusions for the satisfaction of an answer. It involves "individual differences in cognitive reaction to stimuli perceived as ambigious...".[35]

It can be tempting at times to reach premature closure. Yet if one cannot sit with the unknown and keep one's mind open, many an insight will be missed—in our analogy, much good popcorn will never have the chance to heat up.

Various cognitive capacities in creativity involve aspects of personality. Tolerance of Ambiguity has this complex mixture; it can draw on a cognitive (or affective, or motivational) combination of qualities, in the process of solving—or waiting to solve—a problem.[36] The next two areas are even more involved with mental processing.

Preference for Intuition

What then is intuition? How often might we ourselves turn toward it? How, as Damasio said, can one "arrive at the solution of a problem *without* reasoning toward it."[37] Examples involve sizing up someone, deciding if a story is true. One gets a feel for the answer. If some call "intuition" an ability or capacity, distinct from and often preceding "insight,"[38] *we are going to promote it here as well to the general category of "cognitive style," including the element of "preference."* It can very much be a preference, and in some spiritual traditions, even a goal in distinction to conceptual thought (which has limitations in our *past*, where categories have been generated)[39] SB Kaufman's findings on "belief in intuition"[40] and correlations with creativity assessments, help support this stylistic preference. Findings of links with features such as low latent inhibition—a looser gating of what we let into our generative creative minds, discussed elsewhere too[41]—further build the importance of intuition.

Is intuition then about "gut feelings and inner knowings—those unconscious nudges..."[42] If so, meaning exactly what? More than one function may fall under this term[43] The process can draw on hemispheric specialization, unconscious knowledge, procedural or body memory, lived experience, holistic knowing, and emotional aspects as well as cognition. These may be accessed without full conscious awareness. Some even turn to transpersonal explanations.[44] If there is not unanimity on "intuition" (nor enough discussion of its nature, one might say, in creativity writings), there are very useful resources, including that of Frances Vaughan or Osho[45] for increasing one's intuition!

Is intuition about mental processing or personality or both? Intuition as a preference or alternative, invoking cognitive style, or ways of processing related to underlying personality trends, would encompass a larger field of mind. Steve Jobs called intuition "more powerful than intellect."[46] His history with Zen Buddhism may have helped find this direction.

A link with the Default Mode of processing as Kaufman and Gregoire indicate makes excellent sense—this being the faster, and more inwardly directed, mode of thought, and indeed where a person may quickly reach a conclusion. Jonas Salk stated however that overall creativity draws on "a merging of intuition and reason."[47] This fits with the balance that has also been recommended for our Systems 1 and 2 thinking modes. The Default Mode needn't stand alone. In courting insight, let us also not forget about the enabling qualities of certain alterations of consciousness, which may well enter here too.

There is still a great deal more to be learned about this intuitive processing. However, most people do know it experientially—have lucky hunches, get a feel for something, sense a bit of a clue. This is part of our universal equipment and is linked to our everyday creativity.

Last is another stylistic creative tendency that has been in the literature for years.

Overinclusion

This stylistic preference with a cognitive aspect also shows association with creativity.[48] *Overinclusion* is not just about a flurry of divergent responses to a Torrance Test item (although it would help), but a general way of thinking. One finds a great many responses within a set or category, with some more unusual or tangential. Interesting the tendency may be found as well in certain families.[49] Included can be both *Behavioral and Conceptual Overinclusion*. The first is quantitative not unlike *fluency*—having a lot of ideas. The second can be more subtle, and includes categorization rules that may be vague, distant, shifting, or developmentally "primitive."

Included are cognitive styles of varied developmental origins. This example is about shifting classification rules, including earlier modes of thinking used as a young child. This is not necessarily a problem. How nice when a creative adult can go back and access alternative ways of viewing things.

Take for instance, a little girl almost two, well known to me, happily said several different things were "cow!"[50]

   (a) a chain saw (the buzzing sounded a lot like a "moo"),
   (b) a black and white patterned fish at the aquarium (it had the right markings); and finally the
   (c) domestic animal...

For a young child, these collections can reflect *complexes*, a child's work in progress, while adult *concept* formation is being learned as per Lev Vygotsky.[51] Then these are often put aside. Yet with higher creativity, they may remain active below consciousness. The creator has access in memory material of "different developmental origins."[52]

For an adult why not access this material? Connecting cow and a chain saw could be powerful and a unique association in a drama or a comedy routine. Plus there is, in itself, healing in knowing ourselves more deeply, in accessing long buried associations, capacities, and "making the unconscious conscious."

Balance Is the Key

This is what Neo-Freudians long have referred to as "*regression in the service of the ego*," keeping a balance between access to deeper material below consciousness, and a loose overriding set of executive functions to adapt the results to our "consensual reality." Like a medicine, the right amount can be lifesaving, too much can even be lethal. The curvilinear issue of *balance* is critical in creativity, has led to misunderstandings about mental health, and is dealt with more in the next chapter.

Russ sees much of this rich capacity born in childhood and pretend play—a safe place where "forbidden and affect-laden thoughts and feelings can be expressed." And also experienced, while manipulated, imagined as real while seen for what they are. The child can work with Freud's *primary process*, "from his theory of the unconscious, where thought is "drive laden and not subject to rules of logic…"[53] Further, for the creator, young or old, they are directing this "play," it has its own logic and it all makes sense.

What Can We Become?

Humanistic View and Ongoing Growth

Here is a promising and positive context for our potential for ongoing growth.

Continual development is central to humanistic psychology. If a person feels, say at age 40, that they have somehow missed a creative boat—well, not at all! The main goal is to keep growing and pursuing our higher human potential, expanding, unfolding, developing what we can be—and this can be continued at any age. Even if we are a little stuff in the knees.

Abraham Maslow foreshadowed positive psychology by studying self-actualizing (SA), or high functioning, highly ethical people, who were developing their fullest human potential. In his private journals,[54] Maslow said he saw these men and women hopefully, as a cutting edge of humanity, "the growing tip." Here were models of individuals, who will, taken together as a group, he said, hopefully "manage to flourish in a hundred or two hundred years, if we manage to endure"[55] Further detail on the humanistic view is found in Chap. 17, including patterns of values and lifestyle. Meanwhile work goes on adapting this positive growth-oriented humanistic model to the circumstances of the twenty-first century.[56]

Although admittedly there can be a "dark side" to creativity,[57] such humanistic process and person-oriented qualities in this population seem particularly consistent with (and suggest that, all else being equal, they will predict for) a good and peaceful and caring life. These persons reportedly lived more[58]:

... in the real world than in the verbalized world of concepts and abstractions. There was less blocking, less self-criticism, more spontaneity. As with "the creativeness of all secure and happy children," it was "spontaneous, effortless, innocent, easy, a kind of freedom from stereotypes and clichés"

Their creativity was about creative process more than product, awareness and authenticity, being alive in the moment, and in general, and as we see more later, doing something useful in the world as well as for self. Of particular interest is equating SA in general with SA creativity—that these are not so terribly different.[59] Might *everyday creativity* be an earlier step in the right direction?

SA (self-actualizing) creativity stresses first the personality rather than its achievements, considering these achievements to be epiphenomena.... It stresses characterological qualities like boldness, courage, freedom, spontaneity, perspicuity, integrity, self-acceptance ... (and) the expressive or Being quality ... rather than its problem-solving or problem making quality

Who Says Personality Is Fixed?

Some time ago, when I was in graduate school, we were told that personality didn't change much. The message: We are what we are. Definitions, such as that of Feist, above, involving a "relatively enduring set of behaviors, feelings, thought, and motives" were taken more literally to suggest a habitual and set personal constellation of qualities.

In Feist's definition, there is still much to be said for the term, "relatively enduring," since many people do not change or want to change much. Furthermore, changing habits and longstanding patterns take major efforts.[60] Yet it can be done. We can instead can put our pointer on the *relatively* enduring. Change can be possible. Especially in the evolutionary unfolding of creativity, and of us.

What if key qualities can—perhaps even by the end of the year, as per our New Year's Resolutions—can change noticeably in us. (We had better cancel that scheduled creativity class if it is not true!) Our *epigenetics* also plays a role in this, in the expression of our personality—what if a time machine transported us to another or even another era. Or if we did this voluntarily. A year in Paris? Just think about it.

Summary and Next Steps

The sustaining power of our creativity may draw from the personal qualities we manifest. Personality can be a complex (and sometimes shifting) biopsychosocial-environmental mixture drawing from powerful epigenetic as well as genetic origins. Aspects of creative personality including cognitive, social, affective, and motivational factors were noted, examples given, and a humanistic view of development introduced to honor the possibility of ongoing unfolding of personal qualities (versus fixed patterns). Since environment can help reveal aspects of our potential that might have remained hidden, we also ask if it is possible deliberately to identify and supply contexts for our personal and social wellbeing. Can we bring out our creativity more? Perhaps more of our humanity too? This is where we go next.

Notes

1. Barron and Harrington, "Creativity, Intelligence, and Personality"; Sternberg and Kaufman, "Afterword: The Big Questions," 376. Degree of domain specificity for creativity remains controversial.
2. Richards, "Relations Between Creativity and Psychopathology."
3. Dacey and Lennon, *Understanding Creativity*, 153. Early in creativity studies, a cognitive model was primary.
4. Amabile, *Creativity in Context*.
5. Richards, "A Creative Alchemy," 119.
6. Richards, "When Illness Yields Creativity," Richards "Everyday Creativity, 199.
7. Ibid., 511.
8. Ibid., 512.
9. Moore, *Developing Genome*; A. Milne, *Two Wings to Fly*, 4, www.tlc.ac.nz; Environment helps shape us while we shape it. Notable are programs for creative arts designed to transfer creative behaviors into daily life, even furthering cultural change.
10. Gleick, *Faster*.
11. Richards, "Relations Between Creativity and Psychopathology"; also Cropley, "Creativity and Mental Health in Everyday Life."

12. Feist, "The Function of Personality in Creativity," 114.
13. Moore, *The Developing Genome*, 14.
14. Ibid., 8.
15. Ibid., 14.
16. Pfaff, *The Altruistic Brain*.
17. Shenk, *The Genius in All of Us*.
18. Rosenthal and Jacobson, *Pygmalion in the Classroom*.
19. Feist, "Function of Personality in Creativity," 114–115, 117.
20. Kaufman and Gregoire, *Wired to Create*, 83.
21. Russ, *Pretend Play*, 71.
22. Keller, *Feeling for the Organism*. Later elected as Nobel Laureate, Dr. McClintock visited Stanford to help a colleague solve a genetic problem, with her approach. Not only did she do that, but seven days later gave a seminar on the findings.
23. Lin-Manuel Miranda, "Stephen Sondheim," 145.
24. Russ, *Pretend Play*.
25. Dacey and Lennon, *Understanding Creativity*, 107–111.
26. Richards, "Twelve Potential Benefits," 290, 307–309.
27. Dacey and Lennon, *Understanding Creativity*, 111.
28. Ibid., 109.
29. Ibid.
30. Eisler, "Our Great Creative Challenge," 270.
31. Barron, *Creativity and Psychological Health*, 139.
32. Costa and Widiger, "Introduction," 3.
33. Kaufman and Gregoire, *Wired to Create*, 83.
34. Grohman, Ivcevic, Silvia, and S Kaufman, "The Role of Passion and Persistence in Creativity," 380–381.
35. McLain, Kefallonitis, and Armani, "Ambiguity Tolerance in Organizations," 344.
36. Cropley, "Creativity and Mental Health in Everyday Life," p. 231.
37. Damasio, *Descartes' Error*, 188.
38. Richards, "Everyday Creativity," 200–201.
39. Myers, *Intuition*; see Osho, *Intuition*, for its development.
40. Richards, "Everyday Creativity," 200.
41. Kaufman and Gregoire, *Wired to Create*.
42. Ibid., 61.
43. Richards, "Everyday Creativity," also Myers, *Intuition*.
44. Richards, Ibid., 200.

45. Osho, *Intuition.*
46. Kaufman and Gregoire, *Wired to Create*, 61.
47. Damasio, *Descartes' Error*, 189.
48. Richards, "When Illness Yields Creativity," 491.
49. Richards, "Relations Between Creativity and Psychopathology." Allusive thinking was found within families.
50. Richards, "When Illness Yields Creativity," 498. My daughter was "thinking in complexes."
51. Vygotsky, *Thought and Language.*
52. Richards, "Beyond Piaget."
53. Russ, *Pretend Play*, 34.
54. Maslow, *The Journals of Abraham Maslow.*
55. Ibid., 168; and Maslow, *Toward a Psychology of Being.*
56. House and Kalisch, *Humanistic Psychology.* We humans are aware and self-aware, can reflect on our actions, affect our cultural evolution, modify our epigenetic parameters, and seed a more prosocial caring direction like this or, frankly, a more destructive one.
57. Cropley et al., *Dark Side of Creativity.*
58. Richards, "A Creative Alchemy," 123.
59. Maslow, *Toward A Psychology of Being*, 145.
60. Feinstein and Krippner, *The Mythic Path.*

10

Creative Space

*The weaving together of intense experience and quiet reflection was particularly
effective.... I think I learned more about teaching than anything else.*
N.Y.U. Law School Professor, Outward Bound, Hurricane Island, ME

*I shall never forget the tranquility and majesty of the canyons and rivers ...
my 'solo' with a green apple and sleeping bag ... the importance of
cooperation and teamwork .... a true learning experience*
Educational Change Professional, Outward Bound Course

Here is the power of environment, first via two shorter examples, in terms
of the resulting harm or help in a situation. Then a longer third example
involving risk and growth for at-risk youth in a wilderness setting. This is
first framed using a humanistic (more positive and growth-oriented) model
of unfolding human potential, also in resonance with interconnected and
feedback dependent models of self-in-world of chaos and complexity theory. There is also empathetic connection and mutual empowerment as per
Relational Cultural Theory. Creativity has been a natural in humanistic psy-

(continued)

© The Author(s) 2018
R. Richards, *Everyday Creativity and the Healthy Mind*,
Palgrave Studies in Creativity and Culture,
https://doi.org/10.1057/978-1-137-55766-7_10

We see here the power of environment, just not to provide a little push in some direction but, at times, even to help determine who we will be in a setting, or might be—what schemas from our vast repository of possibilities—we may withdraw to face a situation. Although "creative people" may be a bit more "field independent,"[1] conscious and able to evaluate and resist certain contextual demands and cues, we all carry this more conformist potential. It is sometimes for good purpose too, where we humans are social creatures who work and relate within groups and benefit greatly from being attuned to each other and a common purpose—including co-creative ones.[2] Charles Darwin himself commented, for social creatures such as ourselves, on the many benefits of our affiliations.[3] Yet at times we may be swayed by a group where it is harmful to all.[4] Two extremes follow below, negative and more positive, the first more automatic and conformist, the second involving some interesting conscious decisions over time.

Influenced in Different Ways?

How much sometimes happens outside conscious control—a lot![5] Our environment definitely can make a difference, particularly in settings where not much is known about the individuals; cues can come from generalizations about a setting and expectations. How are we supposed to behave at this fancy gala benefit (if we have never been to one before). One finds, first, accidental and harmful results, on the negative side, dramatically illustrated in the outcomes of the so-called Stanford Prison Experiment.[6]

Stanford Prison Experiment

Undergraduates who volunteered for two weeks of role-playing in the basement of a psychology basement were randomly assigned. You were a prisoner or you were a guard. And so it began.

After settling in, guards—wearing standard uniforms, sunglasses, and at times carrying heavy sticks—became brutal, even abusive. Prisoners became became rebelious or cowed and frightened. Participants were believing their roles. Remember, these were just regular college under-graduates randomly assigned for a time-limited research study. Yet this experiment was stopped early. Some participants even sought psycho-therapy. (Institutional Review Roards monitoring research now prevent this type of study, and risk to participants). If this example seems an unlikely event, and one we could never see in real life, just think of the humiliation, mocking and abuse of prisoners by our own armed forces at Abu Ghraib.

The Shadow Box

This pendulum can swing the other way too. Important to know how it the experience of participants, especially when helping can emerge, this time in resistance to, rather than conformity with, system rules. Might one learn from epigenetics how to increase the odds of this—including what can encourage us to be kind, to be generous, to take the viewpoint of another, and to resist a structure to be present to another's needs. This includes helping (in this case) a partner in an experiment even over the researcher's given instructions. Interesting indeed.

In a "Shadow Box" experiment, according to Howard Gruber,[7] one sees both how a "unique point of view makes each person special .... (and sometimes) opens the way to the individual's making a unique contribution to the partnership." This is in contrast to being fixed and unyielding in one's own view compared to that of others.

In this study, there literally was a box, with an unknown object within, and lit from behind, such as to cast two different shadows on two different screens. The participants each got one of the two views and screens. They were asked to talk, to find out what was within the box.

Results had complexities since the partners could need time to learn to communicate! This might include developing trust versus a reaction occurring from some along the lines of "you must be crazy!... How can you see a square? I see a triangle." As Gruber said, "If you were to watch some pairs of subjects for only 10 or 15 minutes, struggling to come to terms with each other about a relatively simple problem, some of your worst fears about humanity might seem justified." He added, "Fortunately, we watch them for longer than that."[8]

Among other very interesting results, we turn to one on cooperation. In this case, participants were asked to tell their partner what appeared on their screen, but were then asked to work out the solution, on their own. What happened is "Many disobeyed us, even after repeated urgings to follow our instructions." It was a "spontaneous sharing" "... cooperative work directed toward a goal."[9] Gruber was very gratified to learn that there are some situations in which "a cooperative synthesis of different perspectives is a natural and obvious thing to do—and more, one that is difficult to avoid."[10]

How marvelous. Let us learn more about such situations. Especially since the group goal and success became more important than not only an individual views, but the experiment itself!

Who Is Running This Show?

What is the unconscious and conscious influence on behavior in each case; what is the role of deliberate decision-making, self- and group-awareness and choice? How is the environment drawing us out, and in what way, and how much are we aware of this? With greater mindful awareness of our own habitual tendencies and responses, how effectively can we shift to change our automatic response?[11] For instance in the Stanford Prison Experiment, could we have said "No! Forget it!"? Higher "field independence" has been linked with creativity, as in ability to distinguish an embedded figure from its background field[12] To what extent can creative traits further assist, for instance, in nonconformity and lowered tendency to go along with a crowd?

In our later example, in a wilderness setting, one sees positive creative potential yet reluctant creators, who may have developed their own conscious and negative responses and ways of resisting in earlier environments. They begin in this new setting with silence or by holding back. They may know well their inhibitions and what they want to keep private from others (and perhaps from self).

Yet one sees things change, and in a certain way this is like the Shadow Box situation. They change, and relate more fully, and honestly, to each other. This involves a conscious decision to take the risk. Somehow, within this group, with development of trust, support and encouragement, plus enthusiasm for risking-taking and *process*, a hidden potential comes to the fore for some young people, almost to their own surprise. Something new has begun to bloom.

Creative Press: Dynamic, Open, Caring, Connected

Now a bit of a theoretical interlude, after which we list six key features of humanistic psychology[13] for out purposes and Abraham Maslow's original hierarchy of five needs. The interlude includes aspects of chaos and complexity theory, which has perhaps been underappreciated by some in social sciences until now—although this is beginning to change. How powerful it can be.

Humanistic Psychology, Creativity, Arts

Let us look at humanistic psychology as a dynamic model for what is possible with growth-oriented ever-changing humans, truly as processes-in-motion. This works for the wilderness example below. We are connected to others; we are risking new growth and self-discovery in authentic supportive community, toward higher human possibility.

Creativity has always been a natural for humanistic psychology—in fact a student of cofounder Abraham Maslow who started one of the first humanistic programs, Myron Arons, when doing a Ph.D. in France, even got "creativite" into the French dictionary![14]

Mike and I later coauthored a piece for the *Handbook of Humanistic Psychology* calling these, "Two Noble Insurgencies."[15] The new 2018 edited *Humanistic Psychology: Current Trends and Future Prospects*, a chapter from Louis Hoffman, from me and Steve Pritzker, continues with creativity, arts, and issues of diversity.[16] Then there is Person Centered Creative Arts, from Natalie Rogers (daughter of humanistic psychologist Carl Rogers) based on similar principles including process, person orientation (to process and growth, not the physical project) and drawing on Carl Rogers's guidelines for client-centered therapy. Expressive arts also uses and unique multimodal approach and group effects which are powerful.[17] Many such principles come up in the wilderness example later, although these programs weren't designed using them.

Qualitative research (with sometimes quantitative aspects) has shown emotionally moving and effective expressive arts programs in diverse contexts, and for personal and social growth and healing, including: workplace transformation, bridging different cultures, adolescent anger, elders with dementia, patients with cancer, grief and mourning, veterans issues, and spirituality in young people.[18]

Positive Psychology, Relational-Cultural Psychology, Chaos and Complexity Theories

Viewpoints that resonate with humanistic psychology also include the newer positive psychology it helped inspire, also exploring positive human potential, thoughts, feelings, intentionality, subjectivity, values, attitudes, behaviors and much more, and in a mind-body context as well. Also resonant is relational-cultural theory, from the Stone Center at Wellesley College, further highlighting authenticity, mutual empathy, and empowerment, along with engaging and deepening connections based not just on human universality, but on difference.[19] Connection is also seen as primary, and our selves in relation, our larger contexts essential. I found this approach transformative doing inpatient mental health work, for instance, as well as resonant with Eastern philosophies.[20]

How confirming too that these views relate so exquisitely well to chaos and complexity theories, yet it is not surprisingly so. One considers again, interdependence, deep connection, systems thinking, change and sur-prise, recursion and feedback, ourselves as open systems in a larger context, and self-organization with new emergences (the whole is greater than the sum of its parts—and recall that larger whole is often us, together, as well!). We exist within multiply embedded complex adaptive systems.

Stanley Krippner, humanistic psychologist, and expert on psychology of consciousness, shamanism, and dream studies, wrote a prescient article in 1994, on the natural affinity of humanistic psychology and chaos theory.[21] Chaos and complexity theorist and psychologist Stephen Guastello saw relations to creativity clearly back in 1995[22] leading to major sections of his own textbook. Others of us, from 1989 on in my awareness, were also writing about this area over 20 years ago!

David Schuldberg has also long written about nonlinearities in health and wellness[23]; he is currently Chaos Society (in Psychology and Life Sciences). In fact in 2017. Pincus, Kiefer and Beer, reviewed a long research history up to the present while writing about the marriage of "Nonlinear Dynamical Systems and Humanistic Psychology."[24] Even more interesting that clinician, futurist, and humanistic psychologist (former student of Carl Rogers) Maureen O'Hara offered in the 2018 *Humanistic Psychology: Current Trends and Future Prospects*, a "cultural praxis for an emerging world," drawing on nonlinear dynamical systems and (after her mentor Carl Rogers) "faith in both self-healing and self-organizing capabilities of living systems."[25] It all makes sense.

Humanistic Orientation: A Natural for Everyday Creativity

Humanistic and Creativity-Based Tenets

For convenience, here is a short schematic of certain tenets of humanistic psychology, with a few comments. Creativity, is included as per Rogers, plus his three-client centered principles, now used for expressive arts programs too. Also present is Maslow's original hierarchy of needs, and where self-actualizing *creativity* is also seen as part of *self-actualizing* at its peak.[26]

Several Humanistic Features

These illuminate pathways to development, plus how creativity can fit in:

- **continually evolving humans** (compare relatively value-free behaviorism or deficiency-focused psychoanalysis, two dominant alternatives at the time)
- **Hence a direction**, and energy, toward a positive unfolding, inherent individual change toward healthy balance and a greater good (does not ignore evil—but sees it as a lower manifestation, born in personal misfortune, which can be helped).
- **Holistic approach**—including physical, mental, emotional, and spiritual aspects
- **Self-exploration, free will, authenticity**—intention and agency to drive change. Note that his also resonates with potential for conscious awareness and meta-awareness (not blind conformity, or life as an automaton), along with caring, authentic involvement, presence in the moment, and growing trust with each other.
- **Own individual and group self-exploration**—from innate potential; it needn't bow to experts and hierarchies, although help can certainly be sought where useful.
- **Creativity as purview**—creativity as ongoing interest of humanistic and positive psychology, consistent with healthy growth and change and varied other features above.[27]
- **Creativity catalyzed**—our efforts can be best stimulated, as Carl Rogers put it, amidst process-oriented features we met before (e.g., guidelines in "client-centered therapy") We apply these to arts and creativity, shortly, below.

  - unconditional positive regard;
  - nonjudgmental climate, and
  - empathy and understanding with enhancement of psychological safety.

Maslow's Hierarchy of Needs

Abraham Maslow's hierarchy[28] has become well-known, even in general psychology textbooks. We tend to satisfying our lower needs first, then opening more to higher ones. The order is not fully invariant, as Maslow himself acknowledged; e.g., skipping meals toward helping a loved one, or pursuing higher development.[29] The original five are:

(a) **physiological** needs (eat, sleep, shelter)
(b) **safety**
(c) **love and affection**,
(d) **esteem** or respect,
(e) **self-actualizing** needs, unfolding one's higher potentialities.

With Maslow's hierarchy, one tends to satisfy the lower needs first (physiological, safety, etc.), then higher—although as Maslow himself acknowledged this is not completely invariant. *Self-actualization* was the highest in the original model (See Chap. 17, for one more), and is similar in many ways to the freshness and presence of everyday creativity. It is also aligned with values, being needs and positive intent.[30] One may recall this spontaneity, ease and presence of participants while adhering to higher ideals. They were:

> "Spontaneous, effortless, innocent, easy, (and had) a kind of freedom from stereotypes and cliches." At the same time they appeared more mature, their work like a calling, their movement from "deficiency" needs (personally focused) toward "being" needs, including love, truth, justice, beauty, a more universal caring, and interestingly "aliveness."[31]

Why Important Here?

The humanistic and resonant views here are very helpful in looking at environment *press* (which can potentially also include epigenetics) in creativity. Put simply, for us as creators, in our dynamic and interconnected relationship of self and world, the environment is never separate from us. In our personal unfolding, and our deeper connection with existence and each other, we can find a more expansive awareness and a fuller creativity.

Let us proceed now up a high mountain trail, into the wilderness. Yet where to go?

Creative Space: In the Wilderness

NOTE: A cousin of mine still says how, decades ago, the Outward Bound Hurricane Island experience in the State of Maine "changed my life." (Also, see testimonials that head the chapter). Since then, I have met one of the former instructors, and also encountered varied other types of wilderness experiences. In the right circumstances, and whatever the setting may be for us (it may not be high mountains or rough seas), we may find the chance to flourish, heal, grow and, with this, grow our personal creativity, and our culture we can co-create together.

Yet this section is not about wilderness experiences *per se*—rather about going beyond our usual norms, and habitual environments, so to discover self and others. As an example here, a wilderness frame works well. Plus, in programs here (not all programs) examples draw in part from some of the theoretical and practical tenets above. The sources used are all written and referenced; one may read further about these particular experiences.[32]

Wilderness Treks: Creativity on a High Path

Here are types of environments that, at best, let higher potential of a participant come forward.

In various ways the examples are consistent with a humanistic model. I have spoken with participants and instructors from several types of programs, including Outward Bound, also from a high school based required program for all students, and a therapeutic wilderness experience. These are all different, draw from different groups, and—let us add—are not for everyone.

Furthermore, and very important: Various programs differ in quality as well as philosophy. If interested, look carefully. No recommendations here.

Yet, a therapeutic example is useful to picture here because (a) the context is 24/7, a true wraparound environment, (b) it honors values different from certain mainstream ones, and (c) draws from a population lacking a history of conventional social success. Focus here is more on expressive aspects, than climbing mountains. The example draws from published materials,[33] and also connects with what I've learned. I would pose the question of what connections and resonance may exist (despite physical challenge and hardship) with the "have fun" divergent thinking group, when these youth shared creative expression.

Settings and Situation

There is more than one cohort here. Yet imagine a group of teens, some surly and closed back home. They were now learning to trust someone else to be there for them—to really *be there*—and to hear their deepest revelations. Some of course were more eager than others to do this. But worth hearing from youth who really valued this.

Honestly how well could we do this, ourselves, first the rigors of the mountain trek, but then the self-revelations that became common. How many people do we know whom we would let in to witness our freshest personal insights. People we could trust, no matter what? People where we could take the risk because of a common bond, our respect for each other's *trying*, for our *process of growth, and our willingness to be honest with each other* (or at least, at times, to try).

Where were they? Far from civilization. Western state, Spring or Summer. Cold at night. Miles from the nearest road, in the high desert, with peers one must remain with day and night, teens the kids had only met a week or so before, to be sharing their deepest secrets with (when they rarely told their families anything)? Further, to trust they would still be accepted after doing so. Even, for instance, if they had been stealing or lying. Even perhaps, if they could not fully accept it all themselves?

It surely helped that there was an introductory structure, before a new camper fully joined the group. It surely helped that days involved long hikes and cooperation to make it on the trail. Plus cooperation was needed to haul all the supplies across country, fix a meal, set up for night-time. It helped that nature was there without special favors for anyone, and open to each person in the moment, and whatever their past may have held. It no doubt helped even more that some of the counselors—who were young people always willing to listen—had once been campers themselves.

Campfire Sharing

Here's Chris and he stole. A 240 pound teen, sent to a Wilderness program. Dark knit hat pulled deep over brow, lumpy and inert, withdrawn and quiet. For a long time he said nothing. He was not going to share. But one night, around a flickering campfire, he finally tried it, even dug down a little.

He said it felt good, Chris began, almost inaudibly—to steal. He liked the feeling he got, it made him feel happy. At other times he'd feel lonely and depressed. Chris had been stealing for years, thing large and small. It could be hard to resist.

Some boys in the group fidgeted a little and one finally asked if Chris had done and stealing out there, with them, in this wilderness. Sheepishly and very softly Chris responded: "... I'm trying hard right now, but..." The boys look at each other. Several other kids were nodding.[34]

> No, Chris was not kicked out of the group.
> It became stronger than ever.

These were teens on the margins of the conventional world. They were seeking themselves in a fresh new setting. After early resistance, many found magic in the high desert, scrub trees and scattered flowers, rugged mountains, harsh terrain, an unforgiving nature, but also a beautiful one, accepting no BS, lies or promises. The high country accepted them, falws and all, along with the hedgehog and horse and coyote, in a way that was fair and clear and equal. They became part of a tribe. (Notably, the boys' tribe was independent of a separate girls' tribe. Outward Bound and other programs may also separate the genders.)

Some young people discovered new norms they preferred to the troubled world they had left behind. From one girl,[35]

> ... we placed emphasis on such different things ... introspection, values, teamwork and acceptance, instead of money, greed and power

I am putting the "V" and values first, to give her list a memorable acronym: VITA, Values, Introspection, Teamwork, Acceptance. She had found her place, she tried (so many times, not always successful) and felt accepted even if she stumbled. Values and Introspection, for her, meant seeing not just the world without but the world within, being honest with herself, and open, taking risks, sharing the "real me," while supporting the growth process of others, working as a team, and learning how essential this dynamic is for psychological survival—for growth, joy, creativity, caring, and *self*-caring. *Emphasis was on process and change, on growth and direction*, not some absolute achievement, and not just for one person separately but everyone together. Plus acceptance what central, of who people were or were becoming as they struggled together—with a few exceptions for safety—no matter what.

Poetry Slam

One assist was, interestingly enough, the arts. The baring of souls in a performance context. The norm was for people really to let it out. Not everyone did. But creativity flowered in may ways and, as part of it, creative expression. Even for those who had never tried before. A few lines of song, a drawing, a new game. "There were so many poems, so many stories!" said one girl. *It was part of the culture.*

Mutual respect grew, based on an authenticity, sharing, and one's *path of becoming.* On trying, on sharing, on authenticity. Not on whether one was a young Shakespeare, or any others of a past list of deeds (or misdeeds) or accomplishments. The goal was not to compete with your neighbor—not at all. It was to witness, to help others, and to take the risks of sharing oneself.

The norm was honest expression from within (but expression thought out and composed—not hurled at others in impulsive rage). Here was a safe, or at least safer, container for anger and frustration fears and self-doubts.

Here's a sample and it gets even more raw. All the more devastating these days with so many women coming out forcefully about the huge amount of abuse women have endured from men with power in their lives. Then if they say something not being believed, or where they didn't dare to speak out in the first place.

Imagine, in this culture of silence, the experience of finally being heard[36]:

> F___ around with your boss just to keep your job,
> Being told you can't do shit by plastic surgeon Bob;
> Marry men with lotsa cash just to take a trip
> Getting laser surgery because you got a nick…

Let us go back to the young man, Chris; he finally commented on what it was like to speak out[37]: "I think there's something about this place…. It's ok to look at things you were pretty sure you didn't want to look at."

These examples are not to romanticize a challenging situation, nor was every problem solved. Yet the teens could make remarkable progress. One staff member, prior to a certain camper's departure ceremony, wrote this poem for him, and was perhaps as moved himself by the moment as the camper.[38] The teen had shown tremendous growth after a rough beginning.

> Out here is where the magic happens,
> here in the quiet, gentle hills.
> Here is where you have cried out
> With moans as deep as the earth.
> Here is where you have found your long-lost
> precious self that madness took away.
> You will leave part of yourself here,
> but you will take all the hope in the world with you.

So when you get back to those people
who talk big in large rooms, you will know this:
You have been silent in places too beautiful for words.

*   *   *

I was struck by another situation as well. A young teen back from a wilderness experience, evidently doing ok, still didn't return to his usual routine in the house. His mom told his doctor that every night he would sleep outside in the backyard in his sleeping bag. She was worried. They didn't understand. Why was he doing that? For the boy, it sounded like something was missing.

What? We can only guess. Likely more than a wish for a crisp night under the stars in a sleeping bag. Perhaps he didn't understand it himself, yet one wonders if this teen was desperately trying to hang on to something, to some piece of an experience—some part of a context, of a whole different culture—that was rapidly fading, becoming more distant, and even unreal in all it had once promised, hundreds of miles away, and far from his urban center, high in the mountain desert. A culture, a world, a lifestyle, an acceptance and community that allowed him to open, to risk, and blossom.

Back home amidst the life he had known before—where was it now?

About More than the Wilderness

This section is not really about wilderness programs, and not only about the teens or young people. We all have our troubles. We live in strange settings, compete brutally with each other, endure crazy pressures that get worse and worse, don't dare at times to be ourselves, in a world beset with violence and suffering. How often might we suppress our best selves?

This example is not really about wilderness programs—not only—but about places that honor creative and artistic openness, mutual acceptance (on our path of process) and a different way of living, sharing, and of rediscovering self, and together, in a setting of trust. It is not necessarily about this model. Plus once again, keep in mind that models and programs can differ dramatically. Nor is it about even taking a mountain trek but, rather, somehow to shift our setting and see more consciously its assumptions.

Can we also learn to see more options for humanity and help redesign the way we live now?

Summary and Next Steps

We risk self, we go beyond self, we speak from the heart, we risk all with each other and end up bonding in a greater process and risking we share. We connect as processes-in-motion, seeing self among those who risk and support each other, in the endeavor of change and growth. Can this happen routinely or just in certain special instances? We see principles for creativity coming out in a physically and psychologically demanding high-mountain setting among youth at risk, many of whom may never have shared in this way—or at all—before. Discoveries some youth made involved features of our so called normal society that are not necessarily healthy: Values and bottom lines that favor, above all, profit, and too often a zero-sum game (you win, I lose), along with presentation of less than our true selves. Plus self-interest may dominate without a broader capacity (if perhaps a willingness) for compassion and caring. Outcomes are resonant with humanistic, positive, and relational psychology as well as chaos and complexity theory. Do these tales pluck a heart-string or two, where we too might wish to take part? Perhaps we needn't seek a perilous cliff or refuge miles from civilization. The next chapter shows recent developments that may bring new hope.

Notes

1. Dacey and Lennon, *Understanding Creativity.*
2. Milne, *GO! Art of Change.* Here is a context, www.tlc.ac.nz that even helps us find our creative selves, and bring creative ways of being to society, while personally establishing a "sustainable creativity."
3. Loye, "Telling the New Story."
4. Zimbardo, et al., *Psychology,* 465.

5. Mlodinow, *Subliminal*, 11.
6. Zimbardo, *Psychology*, 465.
7. Gruber in Runco and Richards, *Eminent Creativity, Everyday Creativity, and Health*, 463.
8. Ibid., 473–474.
9. Ibid., 474.
10. Ibid.
11. Shapiro and Carlson, *Art and Science of Mindfulness*.
12. Dacey and Lennon, *Understanding Creativity*, 163.
13. Maslow, *Toward a Psychology of Being*; House et al., *Humanistic Psychology: Current Trends and Future Prospects*, Ch. 1.
14. Richards and Whitehouse, "Subtle Mind, Open Heart: Mike Arons Remembered."
15. Arons and Richards, "Two Noble Insurgencies: Creativity and Humanistic Psychology."
16. House et al., *Humanistic Psychology*.
17. Goslin-Jones and Herron, "Cutting Edge Person-Centered Expressive Arts." Also see Rogers, N., *Creative Connection*, and www.ieata.org.
18. Creswell, *Research Design: Qualitative, Quantitative, and Mixed Methods Approaches*.
19. Jordan, *Relational-Cultural Therapy*.
20. Richards, "Relational Creativity and Healing Potential."
21. Krippner, "Humanistic Psychology and Chaos Theory: The Third Revolution and the Third Force."
22. Guastello, *Chaos, Catastrophe, and Human Affairs: Applications of Nonlinear Dynamics to Work, Organizations, and Social Evolution*.
23. Schuldberg, "Visions of Stability and Change in Physiological and Social Systems." Also Schuldberg, "Living Well Creatively."
24. Pincus, Kiefer, and Beyer, "Nonlinear Dynamical Systems and Humanistic Psychology."
25. O'Hara, *Humanistic Psychology*.
26. Maslow, *Toward a Psychology of Being*.
27. Rogers, *On Becoming a Person*. Also Arons and Richards, "Two Noble Insurgencies," 161.
28. Maslow, 1968; Zimbardo, Johnson, & McCann, 372.
29. Ibid., levels are not completely invariant, as per Maslow himself.
30. Richards, "Everyday Creativity: Our Hidden Potential," 41–43.
31. Ibid., also Maslow, *The Farther Reaches of Human Nature*, 138.

32. Flavin, *Kurt Hanh's Schools and Legacy*; Wilson, *Inside Outward Bound*; also Vorrath and Brendtro, *Positive Peer Culture*, for underlying values of caring and helping.
33. Ferguson, *Shouting at the Sky: Troubled Teens and the Promise of the Wild*.
34. Ferguson, *Shouting at the Sky*, 187.
35. Ibid., 237; compare values, Vorrath and Brendtro, *Positive Peer Culture*.
36. Ferguson, *Shouting at the Sky*, 211.
37. Ibid., 187.
38. Ibid., 116.

Part IV

NORMAL AND ABNORMAL
(Not What Some Think)

11

Deep Sea Diving

Writing is easy. Just put a piece of paper in the typewriter and start bleeding.
Thomas Wolfe

The needle that prods into what really happened may be the same needle that writes a good line, I think …. poetry … has to strike fire somewhere, and truth, maybe unpleasant truth about yourself, may be the thing that does that.
Robert Lowell

Hidden Creative Palette

In writing have you ever found something come to mind that seems totally unacceptable? You think you could never share it with anyone? (Perhaps we have not even shared it fully with ourselves?) Yet somehow—and sometimes—do you go ahead and share it anyway? For me, I find that, quite often, that this turns out to be one of the best parts.

Here is where we can tap into a universal strand, a piece of the human experience, and sometimes one that is not much spoken (or thought) about. I recently saw the 2017 Tony Award Winning top musical, *Dear Evan Hansen*.[1] I even get misty eyes writing about it. Or hearing the

© The Author(s) 2018
R. Richards, *Everyday Creativity and the Healthy Mind*,
Palgrave Studies in Creativity and Culture,
https://doi.org/10.1057/978-1-137-55766-7_11

award winning music. The pain of teenagers in general, the isolation of some, the doubts … the huddling in one's room with social media (perhaps to feel further excluded or diminished there as well), the depression and anxiety, the … teen suicides.

Very moving was the number of parents with kids who attended.

The hero (a teen himself at risk) had lost a classmate to suicide, and attempted to help the classmate's family. Unfortunately this entangled Evan Hansen, our hero, in a lie. And the lie, as many do, unraveled. The plot was much more lively and hopeful than one might think, including the evocative music and a set with changing social media backdrop. There were multiple return visits, in spirit, of the deceased young man, who made humorous quips showing he wasn't the only one who knew this pain. Admist various problems and misunderstandings, there was a final coming together of a entire community, to support and give help to youth who are hurting in their isolation and depression. Finally—or so we are left to hope—is the suggestion of a romance for our hero, one that might still happen.

Why do we tear up (and many did, more than once!) at this drama. Perhaps because we in the audience are brought together in a moving way, around some universal themes, and trials of living, buried in our unconscious minds. Yet now they are shared, publicly and in community. And we thought we were alone.

Deep Sea Diving: Into Our Minds

After that, do we want to go deep sea diving? Into the depths of our minds? Remember, there is positive and wondrous material there too. Plus, even where there is pain, when revealed and well-integrated, ironically, it can help us feel much better than we did before. Some of us may already explore our experiences in blogs, or vlogs (video blogs), poetry, morning pages, or talks with a friend, a coach, counselor, religious leader.[2] Or in a very private journal, only for oneself. Or in programs such as *Personal Mythology*, which can help us find the unconscious stories of our lives. (Yes, the stories do indeed exist!)

It is telling, at minimum, the inner doors such paths can open. And also how this (if not right away—after some initial discomfort) can heal. Of course this does means going into the depths of our minds. It can mean, at times, going very *deep*. And then working with it consciously and deliberately. Some are more comfortable doing this than others. Yet we all can do it, and can do it more, through artistic creative, and other, means.

Arts and Arts Appreciation

Arts, poetry (recall the wilderness youth), visual arts, improvisation—many ways to reflect more deeply, holistically, and emotionally, through our works.[3] Reflection can come from others, too, for our appreciation, as with *Dear Evan Hansen*, or what I and others have found a powerful and multiperspectival look at bipolar disorders in an Oscar Winning movie, *Silver Linings Playbook* (Jennifer Lawrence, at a record young age, won an Oscar for Best Actress).

Silver Linings received 5 out of 5 stars in the 4th Edition of Danny Wedding's guide *Movies and Mental Health*, for which I wrote a Foreword along with Dr. Steven Pritzker. Do note that Dr. Pritzker, a creativity researcher who once wrote prizewinning sitcoms for Hollywood, including the Mary Tyler Moore Show, contributed a chapter on Videotherapy for my edited *Everyday Creativity and New Views of Human Nature*.[4] He shows there are modes of "audience creativity," ways we can actively get more out of appreciating others' work. *Movies and Mental Health* helps us with excellent examples and issues involved where the videos pertain to mental health.

Happier Moments Too

Please note that deep discovery is not just about sadness, tragedy or pathology. The revisited memories may be about an adventure with a friend, a first date that is miraculous, a happy stroll of a young man back into his childhood (what magic he found there). In Ray Bradbury's, "The Sound of Summer Running," *Classic Stories, I*[5] a young boy remembers his first tennis shoes, and back over a great many years all the waves of summer heat and childhood excitement, smells of rubber and of canvas, a full spectrum time-travel revisiting of a time and way of life. I first heard of this one, with huge enthusiasm, from a senior consciousness expert, chaos theorist and psychologist. Bradbury was far from the only one to experience this magic.

A Vast Unconscious Mind

Unconscious Mind

What then is this *unconscious* mind? We are not typically aware of this unconscious content—by its very definition. We may sometimes have a hint of subconscious or preconscious content. The unconscious can be defined as "internal qualities of mind that affect conscious thought and behavior, without being conscious themselves."[6] Awareness of an unconscious goes back at least to ancient Greece where Hippocrates identified four basic temperaments based on bodily humors—sanguine, melancholic, choleric, and phlegmatic—said to shape behavior along with more rational processes.[7]

Many developments have followed and some people come to link the unconscious with Freud, and with deeper problem or hidden issues, as well as the id, ego, and superego, as parts of the personality.[8] These have not been identified biologically but have still yielded clinical value. Still, what is now called the "new" unconscious shows a greatly more extensive set of functions that take place outside of awareness and for which there is also neuroscientific evidence.[9] Examples are sublimation, perception, implicit memory, hypnotic phenomena and more.

Our Hidden Lives

For us and creativity studies, we are more interested in the personal unconscious, of thoughts feelings wishes, memories dreams symbols, metaphors, archetypes, and more, which we don't necessarily experience in waking awareness. Material may be positive, negative, or neutral, on occasion just lost in the mists of time. Negative material includes content (whether framed by Freud of another such as Jung) that is fully shrouded and banned, as in resistance to Jung's *Shadow*,[10] material we reject outright as having to do with us (however central it may be). We all have some of this. "No I'm not like that," they say. "I never get rageful or furious!" Oh, really?

Material can still can be uncovered with integration toward a much healthier state of being, at times with much effort. In the Jungian metaphor, our unconscious is like an iceberg with the vast part of it, let us say 90%, underwater. What we see and believe is "us" is really just a tiny fraction. Do we know ourselves? How can this be expanded?

"We," as represented by our conscious mind, don't know all that much about the rest. We look in the mirror. If in effect we are seeing just "10%" of ourselves. Yet some good news is that highly creative people know a lot more than others about what is below the surface of our conscious minds. This is not necessarily reserved for artists, but anyone comfortable with creative process modes. The practice we are calling deep sea diving, into our minds, or "regression in the service of the ego" (neo-Freudian) or something else[11]—includes drawing on the "core" creative quality of "openness to experience"—and makes our inner world more accessible.[12] We take the plunge.

"Yet I Feel I Know Myself..."

Someone may say that, it may *feel* true; yet let's take one example, and there are many, for instance, in Mlodinow's book *Subliminal: How Your Unconscious Mind Rules Your Behavior*.[13] Even the book's cover, or back cover shine with almost hidden messages, on top of title and the usual information, when seen at a certain angle. "Buy! Buy! Buy!" is what is shown on the back. (I did buy it, but over the Internet.)

One example seemed particularly delightful. Did you have any idea? People tend (without conscious knowledge) to be more likely to marry someone with the same name as their own. Imagine that. A study of the five most common surnames in the U.S., namely: Smith, Johnson, Williams, Jones, and Brown, showed this dramatically. For instance, "Smiths" are *three times* more apt to marry Smiths than any one of the other names.

Subliminal goes on to speculate about possible reasons. However, for this purpose, let's just contemplate that it happened at all. We can then ask the larger question: To what extent is our unconscious mind running our own show? (We saw a bit of this in Chap. 3.) How then can we be more creatively aware, and delve a little deeper?

Going Deeper: A Balancing Act

"Regression in the Service of the Ego"

This is a common and once well-known Neo-Freudian term for this process of going deeper—while holding the magic of a delicate balancing of functions.[14] "Ego," here, in the Freudian sense, is about "adaptation to reality." We find it, and then know how to use it, adaptively, in the manifest world, to make it work for us. We, the creator, can slip back into material that might have been below threshold. Yet it doesn't take over. We know what to do with it. Now it goes in our painting, our curriculum, our newest research. Our evenings with our child, our workings with people at the office. Here is a creative process art, a delicate and sensitive balancing within our minds, that can lead to *emergent* new wisdom.

A foundational creativity researcher, and major influence on me, and a psychologist I was fortunate to meet, was the late Frank X. Barron. Barron, with others including Donald McKinnon, Ravenna Helson, Harrison Gough, at IPAR, the Institute of Personality Assessment and Research, mentioned previously, at the University of California, Berkeley, pioneered a remarkable "living-in assessment" model for a power series of studies of creative persons across fields. The method plumbed many aspects of their lives, and experiences, in field including arts, architecture, science, mathematics, business… Some famous people were included. Today IPAR continues, but is called IPSR (Institute of Personality and Social Research).[15] A famous quote from Frank Barron in this era[16]:

> It appears that creative individuals have a remarkable affinity for what in most of us is unconscious and preconscious … to find hints of emerging form in the developmentally more primitive and less reasonable structured aspects of … mental functioning
> —Frank X. Barron
> *Creative Person and Creative Process*

Bringing New Possibilities into Being

Toward later discussion in Chap. 17, there are further depths of possibility within the unconscious along with expansive potential toward "higher mind."

Now where do creations come from to begin with? This question is at once subtle and vital. Martin and Wilson add a "discovery" aspect in defining creativity, and across diverse fields. This concerns creating as "discovery and bringing into being of possibility." Within mind are worlds of "dispositional propensity"[17] which one can plumb, and bring forth conscious possibilities and future visions of many kinds. The new doesn't pop up *ex nihilo* but results from a process of production to discover what is possible. Hence creators are *finding*, rather than *producing*, in a complex process where the new emerges. This approach fits with our current complex adaptive systems view in this book, and also with the remarkable discovery strategies noted here and more deeply in Chap. 17, around Theory U.[18]

The goal here involves "bringing in the future," as with business planning based in group process and a certain awe and humility, meanwhile opening doors for a greater good which is yet to be discovered. The seeking process also includes a central component of meditation. Here, a group "discovers" together, intuiting where the energies of the future may lie and are flowing, and working with this. It is a very different situation than imposing one's will on the future. Again this mode is closer to the Aikido Master coming to know a larger evolving picture, and finding the best points of intervention. How deep one may sometimes be able to go! For us practitioners, a deep inner growth process may even ultimately reveal "the deepest level of the 'current reality iceberg'."[19]

On a more routine level, consider the huge benefits of Zabelina's[20] powerful strategies of *flexible attention,* as one excellent way we have of seeking more deeply within. Here is shifting between focused and broad attention, as well as a balance of analytic and associative modes. While a valuable and productive mix, the point right now is that overall this feeds an internal process of "discovery."

Now turn to an even larger canvas, within organizations, Scharmer and Kaufer's (proponents of Theory U) citation of Confucius's "seven states of leadership awareness," from Confucius's "Great Learning" essay, along with paths of meditative awareness, are offering creative openness to new approaches within organizations. Discovering self may be a remarkable yet unanticipated benefit. Growing in effective leadership, the individual—looking within, looking without, open and eager to discover beyond ego and personal agendas, may bring into being in our manifest world, something profoundly transformative. This is not just about a creative product within an organization but about one's own creative process and person, and beyond, as evoked in this context. At best it happens along lines of higher consciousness or spiritual realization—a vaster awareness that can also stabilize, meanwhile with diminished personal faults and obscurations. Here, indeed, can emerge a benevolent leader, who works toward a greater good.

Quoting from Confucius, Scharmer and Kaufer share a shining possibility[21]:

> The underlying matrix of mind and matter being investigated,
>   Awareness becomes complete.
> Awareness being complete, thoughts then become sincere....

Presence on Our Figurative "Creative Palette": Now We Can Use It

On a more mundane level, creators, finding healing and new insight, will have expanded access to this emerging material in their deliberate mental functioning. They *can* have as a result, more, and more available content on their figurative creative palettes. Compare another individual with (a) no access, or with (b) problematic access (e.g., they become obsessed by it, so their behavior is distorted in some way and use is not fully within conscious control). The first creator can consciously access and work with this content, more or less as wished.

Here are the brilliant or subtle figurative colors open to the creator, the available forms of fact, fantasy, truth or possibility, open to their imaginations and use. With an artist's palette, one recalls, the creator holds the board and brush; the creator is able to pick, mix, and use colors as they choose, with awareness, selected for our own adaptive creative purposes. In the broader unconscious, or even unconscious somewhat explored, those "colors" might not be as consciously and deliberately available.

From the previous section, one hears the palette may hold hidden wonders of which we are not yet aware. We learn as we go—and we grow as we go. With openness and personal risk-taking, access for our adaptive creative work is possible. One is thus willing to encounter hidden or perhaps even "new" colors, still deeper than we can imagine, still invisible to us—yet in effect somewhere "on the palette"! Let us also not forget their dynamic and ever-changing nature. An example may help.

Example: Dynamic Palette, Parts Hidden Until Called Upon

I mentioned before the remarkable novelist, the late Ursula LeGuin, and the spontaneous evolution she found happening in the depths of her own imagination. It was thus in her available creative palette, if not yet "visible," for future creations. She did not see what might emerge until she went to take a look! This time, LeGuin describes the coming forth of a new character.[22] (LeGuin's example involves *Earthsea: The Other Wind*.)

> Alder, Seppel, Seserakh, each came forward when their moment appeared....
> The one who most surprised me was Seserakh. I was never sure what she was going to say or do next. I didn't even know what she looked like till she burst out of her red tent...

The Creative Person Misunderstood

The successful creator, having traveled to such realms of mind and possibility, having "met" such astonishing personages, having taken risks of discovery not all of which work out, may find aspects of their achievements are misunderstood. The creator's producing less conventional content, more idiosyncratic findings, or sharing how these insights occurred, might lead certain others wrongly to pathologize this creative person or their process.

"That dog looks like a rocket ship!" Huh?" Surely, this is a less obvious association. Can you figure it out? (Will the person suspecting pathology even try?)

Important: It is not *what* the creators say but *why* they say it—that delicate balance of functions again, of creative access and loosely held executive functions—that makes the difference. Issues of pathology and creativity are considered more in Chap. 13.

Evoking the Hidden Past: And Healthy Outcomes

Pennebaker Expressive Writing Studies

Expressive writing studies on the original Pennebaker model have multiplied in replication, and extension.[23] Yet the original remains a particularly powerful example of this healing power of creative expression, in fact originally to the surprise of James Pennebaker himself.[24]

Greater wellbeing can emerge, eventually if not immediately, after difficult expressive writing. The personal benefits, even transformations, in this study appeared in follow up assessment a full 6 weeks later. They might have emerged somewhat sooner than the assessment. Yet this was not directly after the writing experience.

Do try this yourself if you want. We take a milder version of the main writing paradigm. Pennebaker originally designed this a bit like a cardiac rehabilitation program, 20 minute sessions three times a week. Yet the total was only four sessions! The activity involved writing about something that happened to you, in the original case, something so difficult that you had never told anyone about it before. Here is a challenge indeed.

You can get a taste, if you want, by trying this writing yourself for just five minutes. Take a piece of paper, and pen or pencil and write what comes to mind about something *difficult you have never shared.* One example: a small secret you kept from someone close. The issue does not have to be the worst thing you ever experienced or even close to it. Yet it is important to deal with the feelings involved.

The effect is likely to be moving, in any case. It is useful to see if the writing evokes an alteration of consciousness, as you are remembering the past, and whether this process brings and new memories or realizations.

There may be a twinge of something—this is a challenging task—since it involves something never before shared. Further examples might be: That little white lie. The time we forgot that it was someone's birthday. When we were *so envious of* so and so getting a—let's face it—seemingly undeserved honor. Try an example that moves you. Do keep the 5 minutes in mind, and then assess. (Remember, as you do this, that we have all issues like these.)

How Did It Go?

Now ... stop, pens up! *What was your experience?* (Was the example a negative memory, a difficult time—perhaps not, but it often is). Worth contemplating how this is subjective learning, drawing from inner experience, and would be counted as a form of qualitative (as opposed to quantitative) inquiry.[25] In general, subjective awareness of lived experience can be an excellent accompaniment to intellectual and academic learning.

How upsetting was this? Were there deeper understandings? It may be you will not choose to let this go, but will keep working with the issues, perhaps in your mind, or perhaps if you wish, through further writing. What has energized this? Why had this situation not been shared before? Were any of the feelings new? Did you have any intuition of, or somehow "know," that something new and difficult might lie ahead?[26]

Artistic Inquiry (or Research) Can Go Deep

When we relive and express something often we find new insights. The experience is holistic and multidimensional. This activity can also be classified with Arts Based Research (ABR), as a form of qualitative research or inquiry. Artistic inquiry can be emotionally as well as cognitively rich, evoke deeper knowing, and dip below personal defenses that might otherwise block knowing.[27]

Appreciating this process is important for us as researchers too because for many years, qualitative research including artistic inquiry (as in interviews, or one's narrative story, improvisational theater, or other expression) was not seen as rigorous inquiry. Yet here is the human experience one would care about most with creativity. Now qualitative has joined quantitative inquiry, for instance in the research division of the American Psychological Association.[28] We can learn a great deal from inquiries such as we find at the theater, as I, for instance, encountered at *Dear Evan Hansen*. All the more, as students of creativity, when we examine our own inquiry, our own lived experience in the making, at the seat of creativity, witnessing what transpires in our own minds.

A favorite research design actually, is "mixed methods" depending on the research question. One can get a larger quantitative picture, for instance from a survey, and then use interviewing to explore in greater depth from the lived experience of a smaller number of randomly chosen participants. Think of the value of interviews, for instance, retrospectively, on experience over time, in the Pennebaker series of creative writing sessions.

Processing This Experience

Process More Than Product

Thus it is not only the details of the *content* but the *process* of discovery and healing which is of interest. What could account for later wellbeing including even greater immune competence?

Why had the participant (or we) not told anyone? *Was this the first time truly exploring this experience oneself?* We may think we are hiding something from others (and may very much be) while also keeping it out of our own awareness. Varied defenses may be involved[29] such as avoidance, displacement, rationalization, suppression, repression, denial, sublimation (as in humor, in this case, we can "trade up" and make something adaptively creative out of our pain).

After all, who wants to think about *that!* The material is present in our unconscious mind, or perhaps with partial awareness, closer, in our preconscious.[30] With no awareness, whatsoever, this material may still influence us in our waking life. An example: A person enters another bad relationship based on an unhealthy early model—this does seem to be a persistent and sad pattern in some cases. Or there might be a partial awareness about something while the creator is holding the pain and keeping it secret from others (and in part from him/herself). Yet events may destabilize it. Meanwhile the control group of participants is not wrestling with emotional issues, but writing about something much more neutral, such as their shoes.

With new awareness, healthy benefits include, eventually, not only greater wellbeing, potential sense of control over one's life, and sounder choices moving ahead, but as later follow-up work has shown,[31] increases in integration of fragmented mental structure and in working memory.[32]

Related inquiries into the lives of others, often eminent creators, have produced books and vignettes and narratives from which we all can also learn. Tobi Zausner's *When Walls Become Doorways*, shows transformations in the lives of selected artists where visual art helped them cope with personal challenges and illness.[33] Morrison and Morrison show adult writers coping with difficulties originating in childhood[34] and Jana Rivers Norton four well known literary women transforming histories of trauma.[35]

Benefits Are Delayed, Yet Gains Are Major

Having gone *deep* to find hidden material, it may take time to integrate it. With Pennebaker's[36] work, topics came up such as, "loneliness," for students alone for the first time at school. Examples of other topics include loss and death, divorce, problems with partners. One person explained how before she would keep thinking about her situation, but had now gotten it off of her mind.[37] Traumas also was mentioned, but it is important to realize that treatment of trauma is demanding and complex, and may require an experienced clinician; it is unlikely to be resolved by taking part in a brief study.

Of interest here was (a) that right away, right after doing this, people in the Expressive group tended to feel pretty bad. Troubled, or depressed or anxious—they presumably carried parts of the experience with them.

The control group had had an easier time. But now (b) six weeks out, the Expressive group was not only feeling good *but had made fewer visits to the college's student health clinic.* For the real skeptic about such interventions one notes the laboratory evidence, where (c) compared to controls, on blood drawn at the beginning and then the six weeks follow up, expressive participants were *higher than controls on two indices of immune function. These were two measures of T-cell activity*—the white cells that can ward off disease.

Mastery Has Huge Benefits

Here, indeed, is our mind-body connection, in action. How did our body "even know" that we were having creative insights about difficult earlier times. If we become relatively more disease resistant, it does seem there may be evolutionary importance here as well. Does Mother Nature "like" us exploring (with appropriate controls) such problems toward greater health and stability? Worth contemplating.

If you did this writing, consider some follow up writing over the next few days, and see how it goes. If we master important inner issues, this material can become part of our creative palette. As in the case of "sublimation" it can become useful in other ways too. Our experience can be used in our future creating, indeed rather than using us. It can even be taken further by the creator to help others.

Other Modalities: Not Just Writing

Nor is this only about writing—there is more plentiful research for writing than for other modalities.[38] Of particular note, Person-Centered Expressive Arts, is designed primarily for the creative *person* for personal growth.[39] To go bravely into deeper places for the purpose of healing.

PCEA is offered to individuals and also in business settings by my colleague Dr. Terri Goslin-Jones. Exploration using a number of media, including movement, dance, arts, writing … and group sharing. Here is supportive group process as a primary ingredient. The founder of PCEA, the late Natalie Rogers, and daughter of humanistic psychologist Carl

Rogers, very much used his three guidelines presented earlier as resonant with wilderness poetry experiences. These are central for group process in PCEA, to repeat, in brief[40]:

* unconditional acceptance
* nonjudgmental climate
* empathy, and understanding, with enhancement of psychological safety.

As one PCEA participant said, about PCEA and workplace coaching, expressive arts helped her to:

> ... get into flow, lose my sense of time (and she) felt refreshed and energized .... offering more creative options at work .... (and could) communicate differently.[41]

Creative Richness in Context: Lessons of Play

We all did, hopefully, play at one time. Maybe we even play now. Here is a way to dip into our creative source. Melanie Klein saw pretend play as the child's equivalent to the adult's free association.[42] Do we really want to cut back on recess (as some schools have done) to have more time for basic classroom learnings?

Russ writes of "primary process," and how kids can dip into this unconscious reservoir. Play has been a "safe place where primitive, forbidden, affect-laden thoughts, feelings, and actions could be expressed"[43] Freud first conceptualized primary process thought "as an early, primitive system of thought that was drive-laden and not subject to rules of logic or oriented to reality"[44]; an example would be some of the thoughts in dreams.

There are of course other perspectives (not unrelated either to *alpha flash* and *brain blink*, earlier neuroscience views). Yet always, we have, down in those depths, below our conventional thinking, also down below beta waves, amidst alphas and even thetas and deltas,[45] some conventional logic-defying possibilities. Not always having to do with problems either. Very important.

Almost Anything We Want

We are playing with possibilities. Roaming into places we couldn't otherwise go. Pirates on an island. Spies hiding in the cities. Mages in the woods (LeGuin). Happy family, unhappy family. Princess Smartypants. Pokemon Go. Flying a spacecraft. Harry Potter, Star Wars, Spice Girls touring the world. Being a rock star. Being a stage star. Being a shooting star. Some parents rediscover their own childhoods when raising their children. They had forgotten how wonderful (at times) it could be.

Then, how to maneuver different interpersonal challenges. I remember when my preschool daughter wanted to play Power Rangers with the guys (remember Power Rangers?) she got rather a lot of sexism. They wouldn't let her play unless she was the Alien Queen. (She then surely was the Alien Queen—and a very powerful one too!.) Remember that, in play, anything goes, and the Alien Queen could be as strong as she wanted or needed.

Play, resonant with criteria for everyday creativity (originality and meaningfulness), not only includes fun, but coping and mastery, individually and with others. Learnings can involve motional regulation, social skills, listening sharing leading following, co-creating. We can try new things we might never attempt in so-called "real life." In play we can bring Openness to Experience and other qualities to the creative possibility—really open those psychological doors, meanwhile building resilience and resources to meet life more strongly later, as an adult.

Play assessments, not surprisingly, have predicted for measures of creativity as well as creativity as an adult.[46] Features such as resilient coping, and emotional regulation are also very important. Russ lists six important aspects of play[47]:

- **Associations.** practice with the free flow of associations that is part of divergent thinking.
- **Solutions.** Practice with different solutions to problems and different types of object substitutions.
- **Symbols.** Practice with symbol substitution and recombining ideas and images.

- **View of others.** Practice taking the view of others in make-believe play.
- **Alternate scenarios.** Generate different story scenarios with different endings
- **Imaginary worlds.** Even learn to develop and manipulate imaginary world.

Going Deep and the Collective Unconscious

Is there also a "collective unconscious" containing material, as Jung suggested, such as archetypes we come preprogrammed with (mother, father, healer, hero, tree, spirit, birth, death?.... What might exist in an evolutionary library?) In our imaginings we don't necessarily access these. Yet they may come, may fuel some of our Aha's! along our way. Such can appear during dream states as well as waking states. One may have shifted to a "different channel of consciousness" as well, as per Chap. 2.

"Making the Unconscious Conscious"

Freud talked about, in therapy, "making the unconscious conscious." The material need not all be negative (though Freud had a more negative clinical orientation). It also cannot all be present consciously at one time in what Bernard Baars calls "the theater of consciousness."[48] Example: childhood memories. For me, 3 years old, four a.m. Time to take a very early morning drive with family on a trip. My younger brother and I each had little red plastic "doggie" flashlights, a fun way to get up soooo early! Off we went (in a still cold car, with pure blackness outside). An adventure, which can still be remembered today.

What early happy memories might you have down there?

Still, some contents are more or less banished, especially what Jung calls "The Shadow," those parts of self we really and truly don't want to know. Some of the best healing comes from precisely there, when it is consciously recognized, understood, and mastered. Some of the best creative material too.[49]

A startling aspect of learning to meditate is that some of this "stuff" can come up, and early too, once we learn to relax the mind. One has the chance to deal with it, and hopefully move on.[50] We hopefully do this, again, with the right *balance* of "executive controls" so it doesn't overwhelm us.

Back to Balancing

To reiterate, *balance*, is the key word for these situations. The creative secret. Here are skills we can develop to have rich creative access for use in adaptive ways. I think of a Bongo Board (do you remember those?) A board on a roller, you stand on both ends, shift your weight, and move left and right sideways, swooping back and forth on that cylindrical roller. A physical therapist I know remembered the Bongo Board, and showed me a newer, safer, all-in-one plastic model they have today. The point remains, though, to find that balance—*but still be able to move creatively back and forth.* This is what we can become expert in, between those deep sources of inspiration, and forces that help us use it and pull it together.

Summary and Next Steps

Our unconscious and subconscious mind holds legions including challenges and rich wonders for our creativity. This is especially so if we learn the delicate balances of "regression in the service of the ego" bringing emergent material to the attention of "ego" functions which can adapt this for conscious use in the manifest world. One could alternatively speak of other balances, of unconscious and conscious, primitive and adaptive, Systems 1 and 2, and yet more. While plumbing ones unconscious depths, others may think us odd, as we adaptively access this creative reservoir. The next chapter asks us why we may even get pathologized for our healthy creative efforts. It appears we may need a new definition of "normal."

Notes

1. Levenson (author), *Dear Evan Hansen*, Music Box Theater, New York City, November 2017.
2. Borkin, *Healing Power of Writing*; Cameron, *Artist's Way*, and others.
3. Leavy, Method Meets Art, 2nd Ed.
4. Pritzker, "Audience Flow."
5. Ray Bradbury, *Classic Stories, I*. Dr. Allan Combs, consciousness scholar, pointed out the power of such memories!
6. Hassin, Uleman, and Bargh, *New Unconscious*, 3.
7. Ibid.
8. Richards, "Relations Between Creativity and Psychopathology."
9. Hassin, Uleman, and Bargh, *New Unconscious*.
10. Jung, selected by Storr, *Essential Jung*, 65.
11. Richards, "Creative Alchemy"; Russ, *Pretend Play*, 68.
12. Costa and Widiger, "Introduction."
13. Mlodinow. *Subliminal: How Your Unconscious Mind Rules Your Behavior.*
14. Richards, "When Illness Yields Creativity"; Russ, *Pretend Play*, 68.
15. Barron, *Creative Person and Creative Process*.
16. Ibid., 88.
17. Martin and Wilson, "Defining Creativity with Discovery," 423.
18. Scharmer and Kaufer, *Leading from the Emerging Future*.
19. Ibid., 141.
20. Zabelina, "Attention and Creativity," 165.
21. Scharmer and Kaufer, *Leading from the Emerging Future*, 143. Also see Scharmer, "In Front of the Blank Canvas: Sensing Emergent Futures."
22. LeGuin, "Afterword," 265.
23. e.g., Lepore & Smythe, editors, *The Writing Cure*. Pennebaker, editor, *Emotion, Disclosure, and Health*; Sundararajan shows further benefit of fine-grained language analysis, especially across cultures, in *Understanding Emotion in Chinese Culture*.
24. Pennebaker, Kiecolt-Glaser, and Glaser, "Disclosure of Trauma and Immune Function."
25. Creswell, *Research Design*.
26. Briggs and Peat, *Turbulent Mirror*, and see *nuance*, Chap. 16.
27. Leavy. *Method Meets Art, 2nd Edition*.
28. www.apa.org, Division 5.
29. Anna Freud, *Ego and the Mechanisms of Defense*.

30. Be aware these are not actual physical places, although the metaphor of iceberg can be helpful.
31. See Lepore and Smythe, editors, *The Writing Cure.*
32. Klein, "Stress, Expressive Writing, and Working Memory."
33. Zausner, *When Walls Become Doorways.*
34. Morrison and Morrison, *Memories of Loss and Dreams of Perfection.*
35. Norton, *The Demeter-Persephone Myth as Writing Ritual in the Lives of Literary Women.*
36. Pennebaker, Kiecolt-Glaser, and Glaser, "Disclosure of Trauma and Immune Function."
37. Richards, "Everyday Creativity," 38.
38. Freeman, *Mosby Complementary and Alternative Medicine, 3rd Edition.*
39. N. Rogers, *Creative Connection*; also N. Rogers, *Creative Connection for Groups.*
40. C. Rogers, "Toward a Theory of Creativity"; Goslin-Jones and Richards, "Mysteries of Creative Process."
41. Goslin-Jones & Richards, Ibid. (in press).
42. Russ, *Pretend Play*, 34.
43. Ibid.
44. Ibid.
45. Freeman, *Mosby's Complementary and Alternative Medicine*, 199.
46. Russ, "Pretend Play and Creativity" (in press).
47. Russ, *Pretend Play*, 62.
48. Baars, *In the Theatre of Consciousness.*
49. Jung, *Active Imagination*, 166–168; also Jung, selected by Storr, *Essential Jung*, 87.
50. Shapiro and Carlson, *Art and Science of Mindfulness, 2nd Edition.*

12

A New Normal

"The world in general disapproves of creativity."
Isaac Asimov

How hard at times to be different, yet how important to challenge the status quo. To destabilize the known, to bring in something new. Yet negative stereotypes of creators exist, and divergence is not always commended, particularly in more hierarchical environments. Teachers may not even recognize creative voices—these students seem troublesome. Yet who, in our culture, better to keep us from a sometimes dangerous conformity or provide a needed ethical voice in the world? In broadening our limits of "normality" we can also better honor the uniqueness we each have and the sparkling diversity of cultures in a shrinking globe.

The world disapproves of creativity, states prolific science fiction and science writer Isaac Asimov? Does the world disapproves of *creators* too? Of us and our friends? Of creative lifestyles? Where did Asimov get this? We all—including you, creative reader—could be in some trouble.

Creativity: Here is this quality many people idealize and say they want, and that the world increasingly needs.[1] Some countries, or areas of a

© The Author(s) 2018
R. Richards, *Everyday Creativity and the Healthy Mind*,
Palgrave Studies in Creativity and Culture,
https://doi.org/10.1057/978-1-137-55766-7_12

country, are even recruiting established creative minds from elsewhere.[2] Yet what about the creator in embryo. For us personally, resisting the benefits of a more active curious creative life could even be "hazardous to our health." Keep in mind the many personal benefits of being creative, including lifestyle factors: being more open, mindful, richly aware of alternatives, resilient in knowing knowing self and coping resiliently with difficulties. We have seen benefits for both physical and psychological health and wellbeing, and even for immune function. The proliferation of expressive and arts therapies among others testify to the healing powers.[3] Certainly there are the numerous and unending benefits for society.

How often are detractors those who are supporting the *status quo?*[4] The creator is typically changing something to bring the new into being, whether a different teaching mode, or new business product. Might we ourselves even have subtle or unconscious biases at times against creativity, creative process, creators? Are creators enough of a threat or nonconformist source of trouble that more people than we think have some ambivalence here?

True, some highly creative people can also sound a little odd—yet for healthy reasons—involving better contact with less conscious sources, and perhaps speaking some of this aloud! As creativity researcher Frank Barron said, from his studies across several fields[5]:

> It appears that creative individuals have a remarkable affinity for what in most of us is unconscious and preconscious … to find hints of emerging form in the developmentally more primitive and less reasonable structured aspects of his own mental functioning.

Stereotypes: Do They Exist; Why Are They Humorous?

Remember the movie *Back to the Future*, and the mad scientist? He was a superb stereotype, actually, with wild hair, wide eyes, and hyper-dramatic manner, played by Christopher Lloyd. Yet does having hair in disarray go along with having great ideas? Or managing time travel? Some viewers may have accepted this portrayal when first watching the film. I did for one, to be honest, and later, too, taking the Universal Studios tour in Los Angeles, and going past that high town "clock" associated with time travel in the film. I bought the whole story.

One can try Googling "mad creator" on the Internet, choosing the Images option. The results are intended to be funny pictures (well, ok, they are funny), often cartoons, of distracted, outlandish, figures, including wild eyed innovators whose eyes resemble red spirals against a white background, or absent minded professors bumping into walls. These are our scientific creators? Where are my creative university colleagues? Not present. Another interesting question one might ask: Where are the women?

Beyond that, so many "creator" images have hair in disarray that you'd think there was a shortage of barbers. Or of combs and brushes. Or creators have their clothes askew. Is there no time, in creativity, for personal hygiene? Are creators so lost in their minds that they've forgotten that there is a big world out there? If not everyone's stereotype, this surely is one of them.

Why these particular images? Some might even ask: "Will I go crazy from being creative?" Why would that arise? (Remember, creating is said be so healthy.) Hence there is a paradox here, one addressed shortly. Very worrisome is the person who has, for example, a mood disorder and stops their medication to boost their creativity, they believe—yet more likely it will do the opposite.[6] Some believe "the crazier the better." This can be dangerously wrong. Keep in mind the nonlinear balancing of creative inspiration with adaptive function, to shape creations for real world use.

One hopes such persons will instead read about the escalating risks for misery and pain without treatment.[7] The morbidity, even mortality. Suffering and unnecessary risks. Meanwhile the appropriate and measured treatments can help relieve pain and meanwhile, at the same time, help *unlock creativity*.[8]

More about pathology and creativity can be found in the next chapter.

Challenges for Teachers Working with Creative Kids

It is a serious problem at times, what creative kids can face in conventional classrooms.[9] Beghetto reports on how often classrooms are, and have for many years been, structured and hierarchical.[10] In one study, of elementary and secondary school students, 75% of the time was spent in teacher instruction, and over 2/3 of that involved the teacher talking. How difficult for certain young people.

Unchallenged, with their style unrewarded, some will withdraw. Others may misbehave or become class clown. This was true for a creative colleague of mine, who found school a challenge, yet went on to get a coveted sitcom writing job in Hollywood. He was fortunate as well as talented. He also found a profitable use for the humor. Yet that is not the usual case.

Teaching Thirty Kids

Let us give our respect to teachers handling a class of, say, 30 young people, to keep them engaged, and doing their work. This is a large class. Yet for creativity, young people, elementary or secondary level, who are developing creative talents, need more individualized attention, a smaller class size, and a chance to work with ideas and expressions on their own. These youth, after all, are *the embryonic challengers of the status quo*. Learning to get 100% of someone's test is only part of what is needed. Plus it is so important to try things and learn from our mistakes.[11]

Creative young people could benefit more in other settings. Fortunately innovations today include newer forms of teacher training, and shifts to different classroom values.[12] Yet this is often not what one sees, and other young people who *might* have emerged more creative and adventurous never step forward to try. Meanwhile, though, it is unfair to put too much blame on an overworked teacher.[13] Imagine you are a teacher just trying to keep peace, among 30-plus pupils, with four of the kids, kind of "cut ups," talking and laughing in the back for the room. You break them up, and then do so again. You just want, somehow, to finish the day's instructional unit.

Author as Guest Teacher Doing Creative Science: Surprise Teacher Reaction

I was guest teacher for a friend's school, as told in my chapter of Beghetto's 2010 edited *Nurturing Creativity in the Classroom*. I had 4th–6th grade kids (in a small country school, one large classroom). I got them doing an experiment in pairs, each with one battery, wire (one wire, only), and a lightbulb. The objective was, to turn the light bulb on.

The pairs worked together, each pair standing at one young person's desk. What?—they were puzzled—how can it work with only one wire? How can we light up the bulb? All the pairs were engaged, were interested, and trying different things.

Then—an eruption from one pair. They had done it! The bulb had lit up. The other kids ran to see what had happened. What howls of excitement there were, what running around, and literally what joy, to see how it worked. Kids would run (yes run!) back to their desks to try it for themselves. First one pair, then another; they all finally did it. Routinely these kids had sat quietly in rows of chairs. Now they were designing and testing electrical circuits. And jumping with joy at the results!

After the experiment students asked some penetrating questions. How does a light switch in the wall work, and so on. These young people would never look at their living room lamp, and the double-wire that leads to and from it, and plugs into the wall, in the same way again.

Afterward, the teacher, a very nice woman, and a dedicated teacher, came up to me, abashed, and she *apologized!* What? I thought. I was very surprised. She was ashamed, she said, at the kids' misbehavior. How could they act that way and with a guest, yet, running around, laughing, howling (and, let us be clear, very happily sharing and comparing their *science results*—which was the point was it not?) "So sorry" she said again to me, and with emphasis: "They have never acted this way before."

I kept this experience with me for years. The fun and excitement of creative learning. Yet how it could be misunderstood in a conventional classroom.

Systems Issue

Again, this teacher could only do so much[14]; this was also a systems issue, dealing with strapped school budgets, large classes, and let us add, a lack of school or district resources for professional development. There were new ways coming out to teach elementary and secondary level science. Many teachers today want instruction in creative methods. In this case it was "discovery science."[15] In fact, when a teacher *models* their own personal creativity, a student is more apt to follow suit.[16]

I was privileged to be Teaching Assistant one summer for the late John David Miller at U.C. Berkeley School of Education, offering a two-week science workshop for junior high school teachers at the U.C. Berkeley teaching center and action museum, The Lawrence Hall of Science. Dave was the ultimate discovery science teacher (and creativity-oriented historian of science), active, present, engaged.[17] He loved learning by doing, and sharing with students (or teachers at the Lawrence Hall), and was robust with the joy of inquiry. The junior high school teachers got as enthused as the 4–6th grade kids had been. Happy voices, loud exclamations! The main difference was that the teachers didn't run wildly around the room.

One could see they would return to their own classrooms where some of this raucous enthusiasm might again reign.

Can We Recognize Creative Youth?

How well does the average teacher even know who a creative young person is, if not given background on creativity? Let us add, since all kids have intrinsic creative *potential*, we are just talking her about teachers spotting those who have already developed some creative initiative. Others haven't even come that far.

Sadly, it was shown, in some classic and well-known studies[18] that teachers (a) weren't sure who the creative kids even were; meanwhile too often (b) preferring the "other ones." You can attempt this yourself with a research-based list of traits from Westby and Dawson's study, where some (but not all) of these descriptors had been found typical of "more creative" kids. Included in the list were: *sincere, emotional, appreciative, impulsive, responsible, nonconforming, reliable, and makes up rules as they go along.*

Try picking four descriptors you would link more readily with higher than lower creativity in young people. Surprisingly teachers tended to choose features *less* distinctive of creative kids. *Less* apt to characterize them. There is, certainly, nothing wrong with being *sincere, appreciative, responsible, and reliable*—words which were chosen, and some creative kids are this way too. Yet the search was for *distinctive* descriptors and for behavior patterns linked specifically with creativity. In reviewing the list below, and best choices, do also remember the word *balance*—which we have used before. Hence no trait would go unopposed (e.g., impulsive) but be balanced by others and modulated with some executive functioning. Those who get somewhere in life do have the option of calling on self-control, and can reflect on their process.

In any case, words in the list more distinctive of creative students were: *emotional, impulsive, nonconforming, and*—who needs this in a classroom, one might think—*making up rules as they go along!* In another study[19] when teachers were asked what students they *preferred*, and were asked to characterize their "favorite" students, it was again this well-behaved first cohort. Not the creative youth.

Very difficult for the creative young people. Especially if the kids feel put down or, even come to feel they have been "bad." Theirs was classroom misbehavior.

Their hair may not be askew, as in earlier stereotypes, and students may even be dressed nicely. Yet here are the challengers of the *status quo*, people we badly need, creative students including those who may be a "handful" in a large class. Here may be persons who, as they mature, help us challenge unhealthy social practices, who will not be conformists who "go along." Who see events and reframe them ethically.[20] Who remain mindfully aware and able to think for themselves.[21]

Remember that science and science fiction writer Isaac Asimov stated that the world will "disapprove of creativity." One might hope for a different lesson in the schools.

Can All Develop Their Creative Potential?

If we believe in universal creative potential, that even more students could be manifesting in this creative way, then think of the talents going undeveloped. So much is being missed—for self and society. Personal benefits for health, wellbeing, challenge, success, for thinking for oneself, for learning to contribute to the world in new ways, to make it better.

New Normal

What do we mean by a behavioral norm? By definition it is what most people do. Yet because something is the average needn't mean it is what we want. Or the norm our culture needs for a healthy future. Especially in our troubled world today. At the worst, how much do we enshrine (and reward) that is lock-step mindless, do-as-we-are-told behavior? This can be an ongoing conflict, especially in overcrowded schools.

This is not to condone kids "doing whatever they want." One parent challenged me as advocating this in a talk I gave on creative education, at the hospital where I was once working. I had been leaning toward the innovative parts of kids' days. I appreciated that she was bringing up the other part, the balancing executive functions. Which includes planning, discipline, time allotment, and much more.

Creative education does not mean anarchy! Or lack of organization. That is another potential stereotype.

At least we have progressed from when kids were quietly "seen and not heard."

Nature of "New Normal"

Still, it would help to have a "new normal" that is (a) not just an average (mean, median, or mode) but also the other part, the (b) variation around it (range, standard deviation)—a broader range of colorful and acceptable behaviors. This would be more consistent with the diversity of our world, as well as the wide variety of ways we ourselves are each unique; this would address Dobzhansky's "phenotypic plasticity" for our creativity—

that we have, within our genetic and environmental constraints—a great many ways to be. In adopting norms (or an idea for one), what if we seek one that is process-oriented, that embraces *trying* (with success or not), learning from experience. And also one seeing within us *self-as-process*, constantly changing, hopefully growing. *Can we rethink and broaden our acceptable limits of normality?*[22]

When Creating Seems Bizarre But Isn't

The late Robin Williams, mentioned earlier, gave us many examples of a gifted stream of consciousness –pure talent and endless delight. Yet even for Robin Williams, it didn't always happen. No problem for the audience, since it was the greatest times that tended to get published or performed Yet some observers might have wondered if so much free association was intentional or whether there was a problem. Again, it's the issue of underlying control. Swain and Swain helped frame this difference in a nonlinear dynamical way[23]:

> The difference, it seems, between creativity and mental illness is very much one of how much control one has over the non-linear wanderings of the mind to places—wither via a chaotic route drifting farther and farther away, or a catastrophic route, making sudden transitions to new states…

Here is that loose or overarching executive functioning. We can also look at this in terms of Kahneman's System 1 and System 2 thinking.[24] Where our Default Mode, is more linked to creative and intuitive thought and that fleeting spontaneous inner process that some creative artists may tap into more frequently; Type II is that slower logical counterpart. We can fly with I and bring in II to tweak or shape things, as needed. Williams also said,[25]

> You're in control but you're not—the characters are coming through you.

However it seems possible that Williams could have called a halt to the process had he wished to do so. The characters came through when he left the mental door open.

Now imagine we are having these many ideas, are being spontaneous, intuitive, risk-taking, flexible, "throwing things out there," enjoying it; we are not judging, doing "divergent thinking" (where some ideas work and some definitely don't, as in brainstorming—but that's ok). Yet for someone else, witnessing this, at certain times, especially out of context, it might seem a bit bizarre.

The question involves our "New Normal" once again, if we are exercising this open spontaneous, adventurous (and sometimes delightfully "wrong") process, Of course it may seem strange to someone else, at least at times. Remember though, we *don't* have to "get 100% on every test." *Can this become part of our new norm if we plan to be more open, less censorious?*

Consider some colorful examples of cognitive style in creativity. Plus consider when some people might find the responses bizarre. Yet, again, it is less about the response than the underlying process, and the balancing act that keeps the creator, ultimately, in control.

Cognitive Styles

One style creative people may manifest is *overinclusion*[26] which has been studied in creative situations for decades. As discussed earlier under personality, here are cognitive patterns and habits also related to personality trends. As "allusive thinking" some aspects are even found in certain families.[27] The question now is how this might appear to an outside observer who did not manifest such styles.

In the 3rd example below, with ink blot interpretations, higher scores can also be familial. In each, one finds a rich flood of ideas, colorful, with "loose associations" to some (the first two not unlike, *fluency* and *flexibility* in divergent thinking—which would get high scores, let us add). Overinclusion and unique associations have correlated with varied measures of creativity.[28]

(a) behavioral overinclusion—number of elements in a category
(b) conceptual overinclusion—range of classification rules including ones more distant, vague, developmentally primitive.

Example 1 (behavioral—example) Things with wheels: car, truck, watch parts, wagon wheel as table, earth on its axis, wheels within wheels, Wheel of Fortune.

Example 2 (conceptual—example) A creative little girl I knew when she was almost two years old happily thought several things were a "cow": (a) chain saw (where the buzzing sounded like a "moo"); (b) black and white patterned fish at the aquarium (with familiar right milk-cow markings); (c) the domestic animal.

Original? Flexible?

The first responses, if on a divergent thinking test, could seem original, certainly. But in casual conversation? The second set of responses, drawing on conceptual overinclusion, was drawn from primitive forms of concept formation. This child, not yet 2 years old, was learning concept formation, working with more developmentally primitive conceptual forms, what Russian psychologist Lev S. Vygotsky called "thinking in complexes."[29] I can say she hung onto some diverse creative options later too! Yet if this came from an adult, how might it seem to our outside observer who is looking for more "normality"?

In fact, how wonderful to be able to draw on primitive modes of thought—e.g., chain saw as cow for a comedy skit. Many bases exist for associations, metaphors, comic juxtapositions and more.

Flexible Choice Between Styles

For "regression in the service of the ego" or what we've called Deep Sea Diving into our unconscious (another primitive example), for the creative, open person, in learning adult concepts, the earlier modes have not been washed away. It appears one can retain "flexible *choice* between conceptual styles of different developmental origin."[30] Other vivid colors are added to the figurative creative palette that the creator can access. *When and to whom might this seem bizarre?*

Rorschach-Type Inkblots

We turn more specifically into the clinical assessment. Sort of. Do we pathologize these responses or not? Why is anyone pathologizing people who are not being seen for a disorder?

Responses follow for some Rorschach-type inkblot responses from family members of psychiatrically ill persons, including "psychiatrically normal" individuals, related to bipolar individuals.[31] Taking a clinical instead of creative approach, these were rated with The Thought Disorder Index (TDI). Interestingly responses were said to fall on two dimensions distinguishing manic and schizophrenic thought: *combinatory thinking*, and *irrelevant intrusions*.

Example 3 Without having stimulus images, one can still imagine how these responses could on the one hand be creative interpretations of projective inkblot images:

- "It looks like a mastodon wearing shoes." (incongruity)
- "A beetle crying." (incongruity)
- "Because it's black, dark, darkness, lovemaking" (looseness)
- "Two crows with afros, and they're pushing (fabulized) two hearts together." (combination)
- "An evil witch doing a square dance ... She had (playful) her dress like this and she was do-si-do-ing" (confabulation)

Yet the term which follows indicates a mild rating on a scale for "thought disorder."

The point is precisely, again, about executive functions, and balance. Did the people know better? Were they playing with images and meaning. Were they exercising some overriding control? Was there creative intent? (Yes!) Why, someone might ask, does this person think mastodons might wear shoes? Please! *In imagination they can.*

Not to demean these major studies, beautifully done, and for another purpose. They showed lesser measures of so-called "thought disorder" in relatives of both schizophrenics and bipolars (with different flavors for each). Hence further possible evidence, for a *diathesis* in the family that may come out in varied ways—including in adaptive creative thought.

Hence, the issue is contextual, whether a response is creative (not patho-logical). Studies[32] of features in everyday creative persons, such as symptoms of hypomania, in high functioning college students, have a balance built in.[33] Studies of eminent creative writers, with the Minnesota Multiphasic Personality Inventory (MMPI),[34] showed high scores on multiple aspects of psychopathology. Worrisome? They had the very unusual result, at the same time, of a high score on ego-strength. Here was evidence of those adaptive executive functions. Balancing factors. A rich access below consciousness may happen, yet it ultimately remains within the creator's control.

Bizarre?

Not necessarily bizarre at all. The problem involves people who automatically conflate everyday creativity and psychopathology, and in various ways. This includes people who are ill and are suffering, yet they think creativity is about being ill, and therefore resist treatment. Or healthy creators who are unfairly pathologized for doing something or saying something original that looks odd, to their less risk-taking, and less creative neighbors.

Clinical Sharing Threatens Another

Psychopathology is so important that we deal with it and everyday creativity in the next chapter. Yet here we raise ways some people can feel unheard when others (often with their own fears about their own mental health) resist listening to the first person's clinical stories or experiences.

The first person may just want support, want to be heard and understood. Yet a would-be listener shies away from the topic. Why? Does it scare them? Do they carry their own strange stereotype derived from, for instance, the movies. Varied mental health problems are rather common, actually. *Each year*, almost one in five Americans suffers from some form of mental illness[35] Some people may displace their fears for their own mental health on others—it is all about the other person, not me, they would like to think—yet, truth be told, often it *is* about them too, about all of us.

A friend I know was recently very distraught when she felt cut off, trying to share some early clinical memories. She got a strong negative reaction from someone she thought would be more supportive.

Won't Listen?

This friend had clinical issues in her younger years. "Physical illness, fine, even cancer," she told me, "perhaps death." These can be discussed. But mental health? No! "They don't want to hear." She felt hurt, frustrated, and a bit abandoned. Please know she isn't alone in this. I told her about First Lady Rosalynn Carter's mental health initiative on decreasing stigma through education (as well as gaining equity in insurance coverage). I then raised 3 possible fears it seems can limit discussion and keep people bound to a safe, static, non-seeking, even mindless sort of "normalcy."

(a) **Lack of control**. Some deeply fear conditions where one can lose conscious control. This can also be a women's issue, since rates of depression are higher than for men. The condition may be dismissed, as if it is not that bad or simply a matter of will. Deeply depressed? Well "get over it!" Yet things do not always work that way, when there are biological factors.

(b) **Fear of the unconscious.** There it is, the iceberg deep within mind, more massive than the conscious mind, seething with danger, or so it seems, with stuff unprocessed. Creative people have better access, health, integration, need fewer defenses. They might regularly want to have creative access. Yet the resistant non-listener might rather keep that inner door shut.

(c) **Taboo Topics.** Nope (some people say) we don't discuss *that:* mental health! Taboo (*Kapu* in Hawaiian) means both **danger** and **sacred.** Is there something sacred about our unconscious, while also dangerous, on the road to health. We submit the answer may be *yes*, but save it for later.

Creators as Truth Tellers

Why should someone even care if a creative person is sounding little bizarre? Why should it matter? It is their own business, is it not? Still, as above, is not such the listener's reaction sometimes reflecting the resonant fears in themself?

Here is the creator as truth teller, more open to what is "below," in one's mind, through the creative process, and more willing perhaps to say something.

Tobi Zausner, artist and psychologist friend, speaks of the artist (of prosocial art, anyway) as a possible "canary in a coal mine." If you know this saying, the artist (canary) may also, in giving early warning, be risking her life. Such is the deep connection to and awareness of the surrounds, some artists may have, they take the risk to know; they also have a need to express. As Stephanie Dudek notes in "The Morality of 20th Century Transgressive Art,"[36] certain artists specifically may—and let us add here the forthright and open everyday creator in general, not necessarily an artist—show us unwanted truths in the world.

At best, this can also improve us (all else being equal—remember those malevolent creators), and bring us more in touch with ourselves. I have posited this can also help the creator become a better person, can carry some moral import—being honest, aware, and concerned beyond self, taking the risks of expression, and sharing some larger truths. Not everyone agrees that this is a major pattern.[37] Listen to Oscar Wilde:

Oscar Wilde's View

From Wilde's preface to the 1891 edition of *The Picture of Dorian Gray*[38]:

> The artist is the creator of beautiful things…. There is no such thing as a moral or immoral book …. the morality of art consists in the perfect use of an imperfect medium. No artist desires to prove anything…. No artist has ethical sympathies

If sometimes true, for some people, Li and Csikszentmihalyi tell us, this preface was written in response to critics and the reading public finding *Dorian Gray* amoral at the time, for highlighting homosexuality. If on the one hand the above was a stance of "art for art's sake," here anyway was a manifesto of truth and human rights. As Li and Csiksentmihalyi put it, Wilde, "observed professional ethics while ignoring conventional … morality."[39]

Yet one may hope Wilde, using this same truth telling potential of the artist, whether unconsciously or (very possibly) consciously, actually was more subtley helping to advance a universal morality!

Li and Csikszentmihalyi tell too of Nobel Prizewinning scientist Rosalyn Yalow's wish to challenge the conventional morality of her time, while observing universal morality, in general modeling ethical behavior in her work and also consciously empowering women. As she said in her Nobel Banquet speech[40]:

> The world cannot afford the loss of the talents of half its people if we are to solve the many problems which beset us.

More Truth-Telling Creators Speak

In addressing the "moral urgency" of expression, Dudek[41] noted key figures across arts; the last is reminiscent a bit of Oscar Wilde. Included are writer Henry Miller, composer John Cage, and visual artist Davey:

- "Art consists in going the full length so that by the emotional release those who are dead may be restored to life." (Miller)

- "morality if you wish ... to intensify, alter perceptual awareness and, hence, consciousness." (Cage)

- "It is entirely itself. It is not deferring to external value systems. It carries a primary level meaning. Meanwhile ... (NOTE: we witness here the integrity of the artist) ... it subverts cliché, exposes subtle distortions"

There are of course many other artistic examples, one especially gripping to me being Picasso's anti-war black-and-white newsreel of horrors, his painting *Guernica*. There are many other socially active creative examples, of course, outside of arts, in education, science, community development and more. Yet if not all creators are so inclined, there is the fact that many *are*. For some, here even could be steps on *a path toward self-actualization*, as per Abraham Maslow—further ongoing inner integration and development of one's human potentialities.[42] Meanwhile with movement toward higher purpose, increasingly honoring one's *being values* (including as one may recall, Truth and Beauty, Justice and interestingly, Aliveness). Here is a path we can also encourage (vs. arm sales or war making) toward a better future.

Features of a New Normal

Here are some potential advantages of a more open, dynamic, interconnected, and creative "New Normal"

- **Unity.** A new unity within ourselves, as well as view of *self-in-world.*

- **Comfort.** more comfortable sense of self-in-world, including those pop-up Aha's!

- **Process.** Life of flow and process and connection; comfort in dynamic motion, less concern about a seeming static reality (or fixed sense of isolated self)

- **Change as a constant.** Not bound to status quo—or to views advocated by status quo boosters

- **Memory.** higher working memory—more of it has been freed

- **Energy.** higher energy once used for barriers against the seemingly unknowable

- **Immunity.** *Boost in immune function,* seen in physical measureable parameters, including T-cells (which fight disease)—mind-body link with evolutionary import?

- **Presence.** Alive in the moment, direct and honest; immediacy, mindfully aware

- **Intuition.** Better connection with intuition, spontaneity, more immediate knowing.

- **Complex emotions.** Mixed affective states—better able to tolerate difficulties and pain, to transform these, enjoy the mastery over negativity, recreate a better situation.

- **Truth.** Canary in a coal mine? Truth telling, as an aesthetic, and sometimes a duty, plus an early warning system

- **Moral effects.** Creating needn't be a moral prerogative, but creative acts may at times have moral effects. A giving of wider, truer, visions vs. narrow views on life (and even deceptions), could also change the creator.

- **From Deficiency to Being Creativity**. For some, a *self-actualizing path* of higher human development becomes open. This includes a wider look at life, fewer self-focused fears and preoccupations, more immediacy in the moment, a deeper caring for others and wish to contribute something in the world.

The creator will likely be a strong person, and become stronger yet, from challenging the status quo (however small or large the contribution), if people resist their bringing forth something new. All the worse when negative stereotypes are active, or when the creator is misunderstood, especially as a vulnerable young person. Rather than marginalize such a creative person, who can bloom personally, plus help us all—and meanwhile let others be discouraged who may never take the risk—let us have an expanded, more process-based, "new normal," with a greater range of manifestation as well as a different mean. We all need the chance to bloom. We are all human but also gloriously different. This can help every one of us shine in our diverse ways, while bringing further understanding in a diverse world. In this vein, we turn next to other misunderstandings, linked to paradoxes of creativity and a personal/family history of psychopathology. The topic, significantly, is still about pathways to *health*.

Notes

1. Robinson. *Out of Our Minds: Learning to be Creative.*
2. Florida, *Flight of the Creative Class.*

3. N. Rogers, *Creative Connection*; Goslin-Jones and Richards, "Mysteries of Creative Process"; Richards, "Everyday Creativity," 194.

4. Richards, Ibid., 205.

5. Barron, *Creative Person and Creative Process*, 88.

6. Richards, "When Illness Yields Creativity."

7. Goodwin and Jamison, *Manic-Depressive Illness: Bipolar Disorders and Recurrent Depression, 2nd edition.*

8. Kinney and Richards, "Bipolar Disorders." Also Kaufman, ed. *Creativity and Mental Illness.*

9. Richards, "Everyday Creativity in the Classroom."

10. Beghetto, "Creativity in the Classroom," 450.

11. Richards, "Everyday Creativity in the Classroom."

12. Plucker and Dow, "Attitude Change as the Precursor to Creativity Enhancement."

13. Beghetto, "Creativity in the Classroom."

14. Ibid.

15. Shortly after "Sputnik," new science curricula were introduced, including PSSC, Physical Science Study Committee, a discovery approach to physics, and SCIS, the Science Curriculum Improvement Study, for younger kids.

16. Reisman, "Creativity Embedded into K-12 Teacher Preparation and Beyond." It is very important that teachers themselves model being creative.

17. Richards, "Twelve Potential Benefits of Living More Creatively," 313–314. Further tribute to inspiring teacher educator, the late John David Miller.

18. Westby and Dawson; "Creativity: Asset or Burden in the Traditional Classroom"; see also Reisman, "Creativity Embedded into K-12...," 163–164.

19. Getzels and Jackson, *Creativity and Intelligence.*

20. Sternberg, "Creativity in Ethical Reasoning."

21. Goslin-Jones and Richards, "Mysteries of Creative Process."

22. Richards, "Everyday Creativity," 204.

23. Swain and Swain, "Nonlinearity in Creativity and Mental Illness," 139.

24. Kaufman and Gregoire, *Wired to Create*, 65.

25. Russ, *Pretend Play*, 71.

26. Richards, "When Illness Yields Creativity," 491.

27. Richards, "Relations Between Creativity and Psychopathology."

28. Richards, "When Illness Yields Creativity," 492.
29. Vygotsky, *Thought and Language.*
30. Richards, "When Illness Yields Creativity," 500.
31. Ibid., 499.
32. Barron, *Creative Person and Creative Process.*
33. Schuldberg, "Schizotypal and Hypomanic Traits."
34. Barron, *Creative Person and Creative Process,* 72.
35. www.newsweek.com/nearly-1-5-americans-suffer-mental-illness-each-year-230608. (February 28, 2014). Included are depression, bipolar disorder, or schizophrenia, and varied other conditions.
36. Dudek, "The Morality of 20th Century Transgressive Art."
37. Vincent and Goncalo, "License to Steal," 137.
38. Li & Csikszentmihalyi, "Moral Creativity and Creative Morality," 84.
39. Ibid., 85.
40. Ibid., 84.
41. Dudek, "The Morality of 20th Century Transgressive Art," 147.
42. Maslow, *Toward a Psychology of Being,* 1968.

13

Creative (Compensatory) Advantage

*... the creative person is both more primitive and more cultivated, more
destructive and more constructive, occasionally crazier and yet adamantly
saner, than the average person*
Frank X. Barron

We look at research as well as popular thought and misconceptions about
everyday creativity and mental illness—both the bipolar and schizophrenia
spectra of disorders. There *is* evidence for a very real and important creative
advantage. Yet the effect is nonlinear, is not understood by all, and is *more
about health than illness*. It reflects both personal and family history, and
applies not only to patients but to relatives. The formal term is *compensatory advantage*. Other methodological issues also can create misunderstandings, including confounding results on eminent vs. everyday
people—very different populations—or studies of creators vs. people
selected for another personal quality. Of key concern here is awareness of
the nonlinear *inverted*-U effect (curvilinear relationship) for qualities—

(continued)

© The Author(s) 2018
R. Richards, *Everyday Creativity and the Healthy Mind*,
Palgrave Studies in Creativity and Culture,
https://doi.org/10.1057/978-1-137-55766-7_13

(continued)
which may even be healthy—related to psychological risk, which raise the odds of everyday creativity. Creative process requires a sensitive balance of inspiration and adaptive control. These vital issues could affect—and improve—lives of literally millions of people.

There actually *is a basis* to statements about everyday creativity and mental illness. *Yet this is not about being ill* and therefore somehow ending up creative. Because "illness" is mentioned, some get misled. It is actually much more about *health* in a nonlinear model. Here is what we call a creative (compensatory) advantage, one running in *families*. It can affect, and for the better, some relatives too—even some without diagnosed illness. A creative compensatory advantage may even help explain persistence of some genetically mediated familial disorders down through evolutionary history. This is important indeed. Both bipolar *spectrum* disorders and schizophrenia *spectrum* disorders are involved. Considering that full-blown bipolar I (manic-depressive) illness affects near 1% of the population and schizophrenia only somewhat less, *plus the larger spectrum of milder disorders for each condition plus unaffected relatives*, we are talking about a large segment of the population.[1]

There are many roads to creativity, and this chapter is about only one type of phenomenon. However there are lessons for all of us about our own creativity, whether we have a psychiatric disorder or not—and common factors from which we can learn.

Encountering These Clinical Phenomena

I know rather a bit about this area because I have studied it for years, and will add a few of my experiences too. In fact, Daniel Goleman once wrote up our (well-validated) "Lifetime Creativity Scales" and initial bipolar results for the Tuesday *Science Times* section of the *New York Times*.[2]

The focus here is on *everyday creativity*, along with the range of bipolar "spectrum" disorders (including bipolar I, or manic-depressive, bipolar II, with milder "highs" but still major depressions, cyclothymia, with lesser mood swings, and relatives showing none of this (or "subclinically") The bipolar spectrum, for everyday people, is the main example here. Yet happily, it is looking as if a "creative advantage" (with its own unique flavor) may also hold for the schizophrenia spectrum and is included.

Remember: if you don't look at the families you may miss the main effect here

Where we are going:

- **Model: Compensatory Advantage** (Sickle-Cell Anemia analogy and our data)
- **Example: Manic Friend** (can be anything but fun)
- **Brief Overview** (creativity and illness or is it about health?)
- **Special Mix?** (That nonlinear middle-ground or creative balance)
- **Issues Moving Ahead**

Model: Compensatory Advantage

Why this model? Some people think the following sounds rich with promise for creativity: Hear John Ruskin on a state of pure mania.[3] Yet without any brakes to apply, good luck.

> I roll on like a ball, with this exception, that contrary to the usual laws of motion I have no friction to contend with in my mind.... I am almost sick and giddy with the quantity of things in my head—trains of thought beginning and branching to infinity, crossing each other, and all tempting and wanting to be worked out.
> John Ruskin

Creative Advantage

With all thanks to Drs. Dennis Kinney and Steven Matthysse, here is their major insight.[4] I happened to meet them after going to a talk by

Steve during my first year of medical school. I later sought them out, and ended up involved in the research. Life has many sharp turns and bifurcations and, were it not for that talk, I might not even be writing this now. But let us put the model out here.

Consider the nature of compensatory advantage: Dennis and Steve had a key paper on genetic modeling published in 1978 in *Annual Review of Medicine*, on genetic transmission of schizophrenia. They had ingeniously applied **compensatory advantage** to schizophrenia, loosely comparing a sickle-cell anemia model (since schizophrenia surely has more complex genetics and environmental factors). Yet might schizophrenia persist in the population because of a compensatory advantage—rather than fading away? As it turns out, sickle cell anemia—devastating to so many—has such an advantage.

Sickle-Cell Anemia

For sickle cell anemia, the sufferer inherits alleles from each parent, and with inheritance from both parents, this sets the stage for problems and huge suffering, including a devastating anemia, with painful "crises" from rigid sickle shaped blood cells, and chance of early death. Yet for each such person there are numerous "carriers" who have only one inherited allele, from one parent. There can be a mild anemia only. Meanwhile they get the major *compensatory advantage*, namely, resistance to malaria. Significantly, sickle cell anemia grew up in areas where malaria is indigenous.

For schizophrenia, Dennis and Steve, in pursuing a "high density study" in schizophrenic *families*, were exploring various markers for possible advantages for this often heartbreaking full-blown psychiatric syndrome. It, along with lesser "spectrum" disorders, does persist in the population. Note as well that the bipolar spectrum genetic risks are at least at strong. If deleterious, why were rates so stable and not being selected *against*?

I cheerfully brought in creativity interests to do summer work with the "high density" project in schizophrenia. What *positive* features may be found in some very clinically dense families? I came in trailing enthusiasm for creativity—had already worked with it for years, done a relevant Ph.D. dissertation, taught college creativity classes, even speculated about creativity and mental health with graduate students and experienced teachers taking an evening creativity class (see later, below).

Now, faced with actual data, from real patients and families, I saw some unusual word associations—how amazing—among family members of schizophrenics. Long story short, Dennis and I ended up (thanks to Steve and the generosity of Seymour Kety, M.D., head of the Laboratories for Psychiatric Research) able to assess creativity as a variable in a Danish study of schizophrenia and also a study of bipolar spectrum disorders. Out of this too came development and validation of our Lifetime Creativity Scales (LCS), based on real-life creative accomplishment at work and leisure.[5]

We Found It—A Compensatory Advantage!

Rather remarkable. A compensatory (creative) advantage, with an "inverted-U" configuration that fit very well with our carefully mined and "blindly-rated" data. We began studying families with risk for bipolar disorders because potential for success appeared higher. Real-life everyday creativity was rated from interview transcripts by researchers who worked with us where all other information including diagnosis was screened out, most particularly Maria Benet and Ann Merzel. Diagnoses were made in Denmark by totally separate people who were remote from what we were doing, and had no idea who was rated as creative. These were small studies but very carefully done.[6]

If creativity was going to connect with diagnosis it wasn't going to happen by chance in these studies, nor through unconscious bias. It was really going to mean something.

And there it was. We found an inverted-U, curvilinear relationship, first for the bipolar spectrum and then later for schizophrenia. Our measure of overall creativity was *not* highest for those with the most severe diagnoses. Everyday creativity peaked atop our "inverted-U" graph, higher for *better functioning* people, whether on the bipolar or the schizophrenia spectrum. Meanwhile this was not the case for control participants.

Inverted-U

Our curvilinear graph fit nicely with the compensatory advantage hypothesis. If someone was severely affected, creativity tended to be low (on the average—any individual could score anywhere, and for bipolar disorders, there are fluctuant mood states). For control participants with no symptoms—at least persons *not* in a bipolar family in that study—creativity again was lower. But for cyclothymes and persons diagnosed "normal," results were consistent with the *creative (compensatory) advantage*. Overall, when all participants at risk for bipolar disorder were combined, creativity was significantly higher than in controls, yet among those "at risk," it favored "the better functioning individuals."

For schizophrenia too, we also found an inverted-U effect, higher for schizotypy, and peaking remarkably at the subtle stage of "two-plus schizotypal signs." In actuality—and very important—the latter would not even have been diagnosed, or come to clinical attention, outside of our doing a research study that inclued relatives.[7]

Here then was subtle original thinking, and each with its own flavor—related to a bipolar or a schizophrenic family history. Example, for persons at risk for bipolar disorders, one might see in their histories, unusual associations, deeper feeling, strong motivation and self-confidence.

Nonlinearity

Remember, for bipolar and schizophrenia spectra both, there emerged a curvilinear, inverted-U pattern, and thus *nonlinearity*. In psychology many do not think as a rule in nonlinear terms, although we hope this is changing. It is not "the more the better" as we have said elsewhere. Too little medication, and your pain may persist; too much could even kill you. We wonder, for some people, if creative activity at the right time, in the right balance, may even be one of their best medicine, and perhaps even change their life?

Example: Manic Friend

Although everyone is different, let us consider how a bipolar "high" might manifest, taking mania as an example—a full bipolar mood elevation. This example is a composite drawn from several persons (although certain details can be similar across people).

Clinicians and researchers have described qualities of mania, fluency of loose associations, emotional range, energy and confidence that could predict for creativity. We ourselves, plus Kay Jamison, and others,[8] have found that bipolar individuals and relatives can also very much value these. Dr. Kinney and I did a survey at a meeting of the MDDA, The Manic-Depressive and Depressive Association convening at McLean Hospital, involving patients and families.[9] We found on the average that participants felt creativity peaked with a mild high, or mood elevation. It was not full-blown mania! Worth remembering, too, that creative potential and realization are also not the same thing. What other ingredients are needed in this stew, for socially useful creativity to emerge? Consider this example, again a composite of more than one person, from an earlier time in my life.

Manic Episode

I once helped a good friend (and highly creative person, during more down times) who was having a manic episode. She was out of town at a conference and another friend called and was worried. The manic friend was pretty much spending time on the figurative ceiling, so to speak, as "high" as a helium balloon that couldn't come down (nor did it want to). She wasn't sleeping. She seemed hyper, and rather cheery, although there was an edge to it. A lot of the time she wasn't making any sense.

I went to help. This was serious.
This is not clinical advice. I was not a clinician. (Later I became one.)

Yet often our common sense, caring, and persistence can go far. Especially if a person needs someone to trust.

Arrived and there she was—we all met in a dining hall. There weren't many people around. I was glad to see that empty space around us, at that moment.

High? Definitely. Pressure of speech, loose associations, very loud, quite funny at times, even hilarious, and at that point fairly cheerful (though not always the case), yet with ideas coming straight from the stratosphere. She was clearly disconnected from what some might call "consensual reality."

That is to say, she was psychotic.

Let me add that you may have heard that about ½ people with major bipolar disorder can show some form of "thought disorder"[10] ("Thought disorder" is actually higher if we count the creatively adaptive and balanced thought of the last chapter. Yet it is deliberate and creatively monitored so it does not truly qualify.) This friend was surely one of the 1/2, especially at that moment. If she had been in a busy dining hall, crowded with people, staff might well have been trying to hustle her out, and possibly into an ambulance. Or get us to quickly take her somewhere for help. Meanwhile she thought she was fine.

It was certainly worth a try to help her right then and there.

She Could Do Anything

This was mania. She was ultra-high. If euphoric (not dysphoric) people may think they feel so great that the last thing they want is help. Yet they can be dangerously impulsive, spending large sums or taking major risks. They may be experiencing something like Ruskin's "trains of thought beginning and branching to infinity" (earlier quote) and believe it is the best stuff ever. They are so brilliant. Who would ever doubt it? Now they have enough ideas for the rest of their lives.

Please get out of my way, they are saying, so I can write it all down.

Yet they may be the only person who thinks it's all so great.

Potential vs. Realization

The reader will hopefully see here, ingredients for creative thought, at least if more toned down, diluted, under control. This is what we are calling the *creative palette*—material from experience, memory, fantasy which, with self-awareness and reflection, is available for conscious use toward adaptive creative ends. *We use it—it doesn't use us.* Here, for her, were rich associations, positive affect, a largely good mood along with energy, confidence, and motivation to continue; all of these (cognitive, affective, motivational) are advantages which have been reported.[11] Yet here these were not usable.

What then if people are up there on the figurative ceiling making no sense? How does one help if they (sort of) feel fine, believe they are exceptionally creative, and say they need nothing at all (though there can be a franticness in the racing—like outracing an underlying depression). They want nothing to ruin their brilliance, and even worry if an interruption might be a plot? (Yes—that one too. A tinge of paranoia may also arise. Someone wants to stop them from having these great ideas. Fortunately she did not think it was us.)

As a trusted friend, I thought I might be able to get through enough to help her come down a little bit, to relax (to come down from that figurative ceiling—it really felt that way), and slow her down from that fast staccato, high volume, nonstop insistence. She wasn't listening a whole lot either. It also felt as if an undercurrent of not-quite-irritation could break through.

Perhaps if she'd just take a little bit of this medication that she had?
"What!?" she retorted? We tried to reason with her, and she interrupted,
"I don't need it, I don't like it. I have never seen things so clearly!"

Well, some of this continued, without effect. It took a little while even to ease her into listening. Just give it a try, we were saying. It can't hurt. You have had it before. You can always go back to what you were doing before that. You know us, we really care about you. We want you to get a nap. We will be right here (and won't let any malicious forces get to you.) That sort of thing. All that and more.

Took awhile but it worked. It brought the party to an end.

This friend became appropriate enough to realize she'd done some odd things, could easily have been sent to a hospital (she had been in the psych hospital before), and that she was exhausted from no sleep, and might need a little nap. She did keep taking the medication later on. Her local friends got her home the next day where, I am happy to say, she went to see her doctor.

Everyday Creativity and Psychopathology

The creativity for this person, at least on that day, was really not going anywhere.

Remember we are speaking here of individuals in everyday life, not celebrated people with famous creations. We absolutely do not want to *romanticize* any of this.[12] All the more if the persons themselves (as many do) are romanticizing some famous figure, and perhaps identifying with them. Meanwhile we are talking about highly painful disorders. Misleading literature exists on famous, charismatic, and highly talented people who "have had" one disorder or another. Does that mean B causes A? A simple relationship? Become manic and get creative? Not at all. Remember Ruskin's "rolling like a ball." Colorful but uncontrolled. Yet many are the reports about individuals. They have been creative. They carry a serious diagnosis. Some can mistakenly equate those poles.

Now, says the manic friend, there is also a *book* about them, about my heroes, my role models. Isn't that great (and they might add), could there also be a book about me?

This does not mean a disorder "caused" anyone's creativity. But for some, in an imagined linear model of causation, that can be a facile conclusion. They may hope that, by being sick themselves—*the sicker the better, even*—that they can be hugely creative. Tragically, some even stop their medications. This can at times be very dangerous. Creativity will be hurt and meanwhile their health, even their life, may be forfeit.

Some Findings—Keeping Well in Mind the Need for Balance

If you heard folklore about creativity and mental illness, it truly is more complex than that. Yet there is something here. One even finds mentions in ancient history.[13] Sayings exist going back to at least Aristotle on depression, and there is case study research and clinical reporting from the nineteenth century. As Dryden wrote:

> Great wits are sure to madness near allied;
> And thin partitions do their bounds divide.
> —John Dryden

This does not sound very hopeful? Then do put your pointer of the "thin partitions." Demands of creative process may be delicate, but remember that creative people get very good at this. In fact, one may recall, doing this can be a pathway to health.

In any case, the later research is stronger than the first studies, but still has its weaknesses.[14] However, results taken together converge powerfully to support, rather definitively a connection between creativity (variably defined) and aspects of psychopathology–in particular for the bipolar spectrum, and perhaps also for schizophrenia spectrum, as follows:

(a) relationships within both individuals and families,
(b) favoring people (whatever their diagnosis) who are relatively better functioning and even
(c) persons without a diagnosis who are first-degree relatives of someone with one of these major psychiatric disorders. Can also apply to
(d) Individuals with depression who *do* have a bipolar family history.

It is not possible to go into all aspects here. Yet very good books and monographs exist, both older literature[15] and more recent sources.[16] Do not forget to include additional references on creativity and health, and the positive side of the question.[17] These will need to fit together! Kay Jamison[18] notes five types of studies (a) biographical; (b) mental disorders in living artists and writers; (c) large population studies looking at diagnosis, performance and jobs; (d) creativity and mental psychiatric states; and (e) genetic and imaging studies. In particular, our own work on everyday creativity and both bipolar and schizophrenia spectra, looking at individuals and relatives is well summarized in Kinney and Richards.[19]

The best known past research to date has studied eminent people—a different question, and different group of participants—especially in the arts, exploring issues of mental illness.[20] These are eminent figures who have succeeded enough professionally to qualify for such research. Thus one needs to be careful in generalizing beyond such special, and remarkable, groups! Fascinating and important work, yet it doesn't apply automatically, nor to everyone, and not necessarily to everyday creativity. Still some people may tend to think so.

These were selective and specific populations, e.g., award winning writers—important in the study of exceptional literary achievement, certainly, and understanding conditions for "eminent" creativity. In the various studies, e.g., of artists or scientists, these were high-functioning professionals, at least when working. Relatives were sometimes included, sometimes not. Yet we have seen there are *family* associations, and that better-functioning relatives may be of particular interest. Furthermore, that one's creative potential may come out in a great many ways, at work and at leisure.

Different Story: Everyday Creativity in the General Population

It can be another story here.

We at McLean Hospital, and others, as below, weren't exploring a few famous and highly functional (or functional at least at work, or at least at times) people in a specific area of exceptional creativity—e.g., writing—however talented or influential or even transcendently inspiring they might be. We, in particular, began with *all* people, chosen for a particular diagnosis, and their relatives as found through an exhaustive search. The goal was to see whether and in what *form their creativity or their "originality of everyday life," might come out.* It could be anywhere. How easy it could be to miss it. Here is a totally different group, and a different question—this one potentially affecting millions of people.

See Silvia and Kaufman[21] for further perspective on creativity and mental illness and some research design issues.

Now there were other studies of creativity more generally defined (not just about "eminent" creativity in a particular field). One major study with Big Data, using "more" or "less" creative job or occupation is given below. This type of research will miss many forms of creativity, certainly, but the huge numbers give it its own power, and findings can include effects in families.

We by contrast, developed our own assessment, based on real-life activities, and personal interview, so we could address creativity in just about anyone, employed or unemployed and in various leisure or home-making activities, whatever they might be. This was a time-intensive process. Working with Dennis Kinney and associates at Harvard Medical School and McLean Hospital[22] we broadly explored "real-life" creative accomplishment at work and leisure in "major enterprises" over the adult lifetime, to find their "peak" (yet ongoing) creative periods. This was especially important for individuals at risk for major psychopathology, since they could have good and bad periods and even years. We were looking for "peak" accomplishment in a major enterprise—what they could do at their best, and in whatever area, job or hobby. Thus we could begin to "catch" it, the creative potential as actually *realized*, wherever it might come out. This included, homemaking, office management, teaching, landscaping, amateur archaeology. It is fortunate we separated vocational and avocational date (job and hobby) and then combined them for an overall score. For schizophrenia spectrum participants we found creativity more apt to be in a *hobby* than *job*.

To Repeat Our Caution

The eminent and exceptional, however ill, already have some strengths amidst the rest of their experience or they would not have been able to "make it" professionally. They are a unique population, plus homogeneous for their field of endeavor. Their highest creative work is uniquely distinguished. It does occur, even with their success and advantages, and despite their inspiration, and brilliant work, and joy in doing it, that without, and even with help, some come to a heartbreaking end. Theirs is a different path with different pressures; their gifts are also unusual. Importantly, this is a different population than that of the everyday creator.

Meanwhile, in general, it is not true to say: "The sicker the better." Taking a bipolar disorder for instance, a great many are suffering terribly; from deep and despairing lows or from uncontrolled highs which depart from reality, and may have their own undercurrents, too, with mixed states (perhaps with an urgency to outrun something happening under the surface), perhaps anxious, depressed, frightened. There are a great many ways these disorders can manifest. Yet it is not about "the sicker the better."

If a mania sounds fun—and it can surely sound that way to some at times, being quick witted and witty, full of fun and fire—I've also seen someone in mania who thought they could fly off a roof. Fortunately they didn't have the chance to try. This is not some cheerful risk-free situation. It can be very harmful, even lethal. One cannot overemphasize this enough. Nor is it just morbidity, but sometimes mortality. This is not a situation to romanticize.

Changing Lives and Channeling Creative Potential

All the more important to note, and to contextualize and communicate, what a higher creative *potential* might mean among people at risk. To let them know they have a possible advantage—which they may not realize, and could cultivate toward greater health, as well as accomplishment and satisfaction. To let them know there are good ways to help potential become "realization"—whether via medication, therapy, coaching, meditation (yes, it can help), group support, various psychophysiological forms of emotional regulation and more. More personal work and self-regulation is involved here than running with a mania, but one can feel so much better. Some also start finding the beginnings of peace, satisfaction, self-esteem, hope for control, productive change, and having a real life in the world.

Creating can boost resilience, ability to cope with conflict and stress—which some are running from—and can help a great deal in the challenges of trauma recovery. Meanwhile it can also boost the potential for creative post-traumatic growth.[23]

Then there is another big one—what might treatment *prevent?* My colleagues and I wonder especially if people at risk could be identified sooner, might there be

1. With some who are very young, potential for a full primary prevention
2. differentially strong and positive (nonlinear, unusually strong) response to creative interventions.

- **Overall—Inverted U Patterns.** Somewhere in the middle—at the top of the inverted-U—can peak a subtle "creative advantage," a *balance* of factors, delicate and nonlinear, favorable to creativity. From separate studies, e.g., earlier work on thought disorder or overinclusion, or unusual associations, we can speculate perhaps more and richer loose associations, deeper emotions, excess energy and confidence, In schizophrenia spectrum magical thinking, and other unusual modes. Yet this is *balanced by the executive functions to pull it all together.*
- **Evolutionary implications.** *It is even possible that such* creative contributions (and creative appreciation and integration of others' work) could influence our ongoing "cultural evolution" and help keep these risk factors in the population.

A Special Mix?—Reflections from College Teaching

What Could Account for this Creativity?

The scene is a general Psychology of Creativity class offered at the graduate level, Boston University School of Education. I am teaching from books including Frank Barron's *Creative Person and Creative Process.* We are talking about psychopathology and creativity.

What Do You Make of This?

This was a question I would ask the students—many of whom were public school teachers—about Barron and his associates's findings at IPAR (Institute of Personality Assessment and Research, University of California, Berkeley), with their "living in assessment method."[24] There were some unusual findings for participants, creative people across fields including writers, mathematicians, architects and others, compared to their less creative peers. Why did this occur?

Eccentric on Top of It All?

Here is this data, I pointed out, especially on well-known creative writers, who were studied by IPAR. The writers (in this case) got high scores on *multiple* scales of *psychopathology*. Not that they necessarily carried any diagnosis in their day to day lives. Hence the findings were rather unusual. High scores on scales such as Depression, Hysteria, Schizophrenia, Hypomania—actually pretty much all of the pathology scales on the MMPI (Minnesota Multiphasic Personality Inventory). The writers were high in the abnormal direction, scoring in the top 15%. How can we explain this?

Actually, writers were high on all pathology scales but paradoxically not on one other scale. This was *Ego-Strength*, which is almost always *low* with psychopathology, these folks showed scores that were exceptionally *high*. Thus, they were exceptionally high in "adaptation to reality," in ego strength in the capability of "holding it together." Whatever odd thoughts they could muster, these writers also had what we have called executive functions. They were high in the control aspect of what has been called "regression in the service of the ego." On other IPAR assessments as well, in interviews, observations, and varied ratings, these folks showed a good many strengths. What was happening?

In my classroom, the graduate students, including public school teachers, loved it. They often could think of examples. We, as creators, need to be free to imagine, to think, and so on. (Of course it was the more creative teachers who tended to take the psychology of creativity class to begin with!)

We have students like that, some of them said. Yes these students are sometimes misunderstood. (So we have seen.) Perhaps you are aware that the Greeks called creativity "divine madness." Hear Dr. Barron from IPAR again[25]:

> … the 'divine madness' that the Greeks considered a gift of the gods and an essential ingredient in the poet was not, like psychosis, something subtracted from normality; rather it was something *added* (italics here also added). Genuine psychosis is stifling and imprisoning; the divine madness is a liberation from 'the consensus.'

How do we free our students to explore while still providing boundaries and the academic backgrounds they need? Remember, these were the creative teachers in this graduate course. Onward they went, to explore further their own creative methods. Hopefully I continued this too in my own way.[26]

Fast Forward

For many reasons I'd gotten more interested in clinical work and research, while continuing creativity studies, research I'd begun with my own Ph.D. on methods of assessing creativity. I tried out some courses, co-led a parent-adolescent group, and ended up in Harvard Medical School on a trajectory toward psychiatry. I was also happy to bring back my own "hard science" and math background (B.S. in physics, with distinction, and a minor in math—a big gender issue for women back then, where seen less as distinguished and more as "strange"[27]).

I was picking up new findings, all the time, about creativity. Then I got involved with Drs. Kinney and Matthysse at Mc Lean Hospital, as above. My last year in medical school I published a monograph on creativity and psychopathology for a senior project.[28] This includes some of what I learned about *overinclusion*, below. Happily this led to the assessment of everyday creativity in the Danish studies of Seymour Kety and associates, through McLean Hospital.

Special Balance? Or Divine Madness?

As you know, there are now many more clues on psychological and neuropsychological underpinnings pf creativity. Overinclusive tendencies (last chapter) do predict for creativity, in groups notably including writers.[29] Openness to Experience (OE) has been a strong predictor, when balanced with strengths, e.g., as found for instance in high achievers.[30] Similarly, that important neurological gating mechanism, low latent inhibition (LI) allows for more free flow of ideation, yet also needs adaptive control; it is high, yet without creative benefit, when it occurs in chronic schizophrenia.[31] Meanwhile it is high indeed in groups including high achieving college students, with stronger organizational functions.

Again the issue is one of balance. LI does correlate with OE and with measures of creativity—as one might think—but only in such high functioning groups. Research on prediction of LI and creativity by "faith in intuition" suggests not only a loose control but a sense of self-efficacy in using these subtle factors.

Let us also not forget we are dealing with multivariate systems. These are never one or two measures in isolation. If one has a high level of Variable X, will one be creative no matter what? Not at all, and as mentioned relations with clinical symptomatology also tend to be curvilinear and more complex. With an Inverted U: Too much doesn't work. Too little isn't effective either. Not unlike digitalis for heart disease where the right amount can reengage one's failing heart. Yet too much can be lethal.

It is all about balance.

Issues for the Future

Huge Swedish Study

It is helpful to begin with a huge and new Swedish study, one of several, which shows the power in looking at families, and of using Big Data, on thousands of people.

Creative Professions in Arts and Sciences

Kyaga and colleagues[32] in 2012 used "creative professions" in arts and sciences as a measure of creativity. This was for people with bipolar and unipolar depressive mood disorders, in schizophrenia, and control families. They used accounting and auditing for comparison jobs, viewed on the average, as "less creative" professions. Diagnoses were from hospital discharge—hence officially performed and including individuals with some serious conditions. Plus what high numbers of participants! A full 30,000 carried a diagnosis of a bipolar disorder, 218,000 with depression, 54,000 with schizophrenia. IQ was available for men from mandatory armed services records, showing that IQ did not account for the results which follow.[33]

People with Bipolar Diagnoses

* People with bipolar disorders were overrepresented by 35% in "creative professions" in arts (more than sciences) in particular.
* People with depression, were slightly *less likely* than control individuals to report a "creative profession" or job, (see also below)
* First-degree relatives (siblings, parents, offspring) of people diagnosed bipolar were also higher on work indices; compared to control participants, work was concentrated more in the sciences than arts.

People with Schizophrenic Diagnoses

Here too, subjects were also *more likely* to report an artistic profession, *less likely* a scientific one, yet findings are:

* complex to interpret, since only 45% actually had official jobs, and furthermore self-reports were used. It does seem hopeful at least that these individuals *felt more creative* (or artistic), even if creative potential is not realization.
* Beyond this, siblings, aunts, and uncles were also more apt to have a creative profession!

Comparing Everyday Creativity Studies

First, these are incredibly valuable and huge studies using the resources and excellent records of Sweden. Unlike studies of famous people, who are all engaged in writing, or arts, or sciences or leadership, these are everyday people plus not chosen for creativity. Results this have a much broader importance for people in general. This certainly includes seeing some differential job patterns and enhanced creative work patterns within bipolar and schizophrenic families.

Something important is happening here.

Below are selected issues we wish that these and future studies could explore even further:

Compensatory Advantage

Unlike the small but rigorous Danish studies which Dr. Kinney and I headed, which included not just the primary illness, but spectrum disorders in bipolar and schizophrenia spectra, and included unaffected relatives, the Swedish work could not show variation in severity among individuals, and hence curvilinear relations between clinical status and creativity (and with creativity peaking with better functioning status). Nor could it address the issues of *a creative (compensatory) advantage.* A spectrum of manifestations, including different degrees of severity is required.

Without this type of data, and despite the thousands of subjects, some readers could still conclude "the sicker the better." Or that all bipolar disorders (for instance) are comparable. In fact, these can differ a great deal in frequency, severity, and other features between people. Simply linking a history of bipolar disorder with jobs in the arts is an advance, to be sure—and one that is not just about a handful of eminent people. Yet it leaves many questions unanswered. It can be open to misunderstanding. What are the finer details? A five-part typology of relations between creativity and psychopathology, by this author, may be helpful here[34] as well as the "shared vulnerability" model of Shelley Carson.[35]

Hopefully, other research will look specifically for these more subtle effects, nonlinear inverted-U relationships, and conditions facilitating a creative (compensatory) advantage.

Important: Creativity in Depression Depends Upon Family History

Our group from Harvard Medical School and McLean Hospital also found significantly and dramatically more creativity in people with depression who *also had* a bipolar family history than those who lacked this family history.[36] This suggests that potential subclinical (and not necessarily pathological) features could appear related to mood elevation in a bipolar diathesis—for example, deeper mood sensitivity, or richer associations. These could enhance creativity for those with, compared to those lacking, a family history of bipolar disorder.

We thus believe it is hard to draw conclusions about creativity from a diagnosis of individual depression by itself. Furthermore, a large number offspring in a bipolar family with mood disorders are diagnosed unipolar rather than bipolar.[37] We hope more researchers will track family history as well as look for subclinical bipolar features in people carrying a diagnosis of "unipolar" depression. Such features may be productive and friendly to creativity. Sometimes clinicians only look at what is going "wrong," not what is going "right."

Importance of Broadly Surveying Vocational/Avocational Creativity

With the LCS we assessed a wide range of real-life creative activities at work and leisure. Jobs found in art and science, in the Swedish study are vital, but people do many other creative activities too in the course of their lives—at work and at leisure. If no one asks about these creative activities, they will get lost!

People from the families with schizophrenic, in particular, in the Swedish study, may have had activities overlooked. As noted, in our own research with the schizophrenia spectrum, the highest creativity was not in jobs anyway, but within diverse hobbies and leisure activities. Silvia and associates are developing promising approaches, more able to capture individual patterns through sampling. We very much recommend a broader assessment of real-life everyday creative activity![38]

Progress in Linking Clinical Features with Genetic Patterns

Newer work in Iceland, Holland, Sweden with 90,000 people is finding specific genetic patterns linked with bipolar disorder, schizophrenia, and with measures of creativity.[39] Including further clinical and creative detail in assessments may reveal yet more subtle links with individual and family history.

Diverse Paths to Creativity and Many Questions

Multiple Roads

There are many roads to creativity, yet they do often seem to link creativity with health. Health appears as a condition for using certain advantages such as low latent inhibition (LI) and can be a consequence of real-life effective creative achievement. Included is healing through creative expression, or problem solving and adaptive resilient coping, in diverse situations of conflict or illness. Creative person-traits, such as openness and nondefensiveness, well-balanced by strengths, can lead to personal growth.[40] Our *creative palette* offers the material a creator can consciously and intentionally use—rather than being used by it.

Subtle Effects on Creativity Within Families

Varied categories of across-family (vs. within person) patterns of pathology and creativity are compelling and worth further attention[41]: For example where *no pathology* is diagnosed within a creative person showing high creativity, in a family with significant bipolar or schizophrenic pathology—hence a "normal relative"—when is this someone with subclinical (and not-at-all problematic) features, reflecting genetic factors and a "diathesis," one that needn't always come out in a pathological way. That control participants lacking the family psychiatric (bipolar) history can show less of a "creative advantage" is important.

Recall in Ch.12, for example, that mild so-called thought disorder (unusual responses intentionally generated by participants to a Rorschach type stimulus) can appear very creative. These would obtain high scores on a divergent thinking test! To an observer not knowing the circumstances for intentionally generating such material, this creativity could well look symptomatic and end up being pathologized. In studies by Heston, and by Kauffman, with adopted away non-schizophrenic offspring of biological mothers with schizophrenia, some showed unusually great creativity at work and leisure compared to controls)[42]

Disjunction of Bipolar Symptomatology and Creativity

Clinical symptoms and creativity can run in the same family but may or may not end up manifesting in the same person. Rather than assume that "genetic risk factors" are always deleterious, it is worth considering if a GxE diathesis (genetic and environment interaction). What other factors might intervene? Three outcome patterns:

- **Creativity high, pathology present.** Found together (but would the person have done worse without the creative outlet?—how can we know?)
- **Creativity and health present.** Seen in many healthy relatives—yet membership in the diagnosed family is somehow also important here.
- **Creativity low, pathology present.** An ill person is not manifesting much creativity (although the potential may be there but unrealized.)
- **Creativity low, pathology low.** (Combination added for completeness.)

Varied Outcomes from Big Data

Jamison[43] cites research with poignant results for individuals diagnosed as manic-depressive without a strong prognosis. Outcomes emerge as varied, although, for uncertain reasons, some people did much better than expected. This reminds us that many factors interact and that—be it health or illness—very importantly, we do not know them all.

Swain and Swain[44] remind us, again, about the balancing of factors, in a nonlinear dynamical context. Dynamics may be complex, even sudden, in chaotic or complex systems with serious pathology, where an overriding control is not adequate. For example, the mind may drift away, there may be sudden bifurcations to totally new content, there may be self-organizing processes that change mental state. Again it is a delicate balance that can further creativity.

Epigenetic Factors

Also recall Smith[45] on *epigenetics* that "… it has been a hidden mechanistic layer operating at the environment-genome interface." Further study may help illuminate issues such as the above. They may include, we hope, evidence on situations that may prevent pathology or improve outcome. Hopefully there will be even more research that explores:

* Where creative activity might help in **primary prevention.**
* Where creativity might be a particularly effective **treatment** for persons at risk.

Gekoubg People at Risk Learn More About Creativity and Health

With dissemination is a chance not only to (a) open up the creativity of someone at risk toward more productive ends and enhance personal healing, but further to (b) advance creative talents which can benefit, not just the individual, but all of society. Still, many people know little about this phenomenon. When presenting at conferences, I often mention mental health and creativity, even when not the primary topic. In a recent conference in Asia, and another in the U.S.A., with a person from Australia, these international persons came up afterward, shared a bipolar history, and said this was fully new information to them.

Dissemination of knowledge helps decrease stigma of mental illness,[46] as per efforts of Former First Lady Rosalynn Carter with mental health journalism, and can provide new confidence and hope. I was honored to be part of one of the Carter Center's *Conversation* evenings (also broadcast on Georgia Public Radio), providing a brief academic overview that framed presentations by highly creative individuals who were also public with their issues with psychopathology. Here indeed one saw a creative (compensatory) advantage.[47] As well as healthy coping and, in this case, a wish to share publicly with others, who might also come to thrive.

Although some of the persons, above, had achieved eminence, this creative advantage, again is not just a benefit for a select few (however remarkable they may be). When an underlying creative potential is developed, benefits can affect millions. This includes individuals with a personal or family history of major psychiatric disorder, including the schizophrenia and bipolar spectra, plus their unaffected relatives. Such benefits can come to many *millions* of people in this country, and also around the world.

Summary and Next Steps

We have looked at some of the complex issues involving everyday creativity and a personal/familial history of bipolar or schizophrenia spectrum disorders, and the phenomenon of *creative (compensatory) advantage*. The main outcome—one of relative *health* in connection with creativity—fits with other healthy benefits of creativity, as found in other populations. What hope rests here! There are even some considerable advantages, properly guided, for creativity—as well as ways we all can learn from these features. How tragic it can be if an individual does not opt for a healthy path, increasing their suffering, while decreasing creative potential. Misunderstandings about creativity and psychopathology (some of which may stem from overlooked nonlinear relationships and subtle balances) may also help explain a pathologizing of creativity in general. The next chapter moves to other healthy benefits of creativity, ones not as often discussed. In fact, these are readily available and can be seen as the birthright of all of us.

Notes

1. Goodwin and Jamison, *Manic-Depressive Illness, 2nd Edition*; See Richards, "When Illness Yields Creativity," 491. If 5% of the population shows some variant of mood disorder with a bipolar family history (adding, in addition, "spectrum" disorders and "normal relatives" showing subclinical effects) a large segment of the population may be involved.
2. Goleman, "A New Index Illuminates the Creative Life."
3. Jamison, 1993, *Touched With Fire*, 29.
4. Kinney and Matthysse, "Genetic Transmission of Schizophrenia."
5. Richards, Kinney, Benet, and Merzel, "Assessing Everyday Creativity"; Kinney, Richards, Southam, "Everyday Creativity, Its Assessment, and *The Lifetime Creativity Scales.*" (Actual scales are included.)
6. Richards et al., "Creativity in Manic-Depressives, Cyclothymes, Their Normal Relatives, and Control Subjects"; also Richards et al., "Everyday Creativity and Bipolar and Unipolar Affective Disorders."
7. Kinney, Richards, et al., "Creativity in Offspring of Schizophrenics and Controls"; see also special issue commentary, Richards, "Creativity and the Schizophrenia Spectrum: More and More Interesting."
8. Goodwin and Jamison, *Manic Depressive and Depressive Illness*; Runco and Richards, eds. *Eminent Creativity, Everyday Creativity, and Health.*
9. Richards and Kinney, "Mood Swings and Creativity,"
10. Goodwin and Jamison, *Manic-Depressive Illness, 1st Edition.*
11. Richards, "Relations Between Creativity and Psychopathology"; Jamison, in Runco and Richards, editors, "Mood Disorders and Patterns of Creativity in British Artists and Writers," 24.
12. Richards, "When Illness Yields Creativity"; Jamison, *Touched With Fire.*
13. Goodwin and Jamison, *Manic-Depressive Illness*; Becker, "A Socio-Historical Overview of the Creativity-Psychopathology Connection," 5.
14. Richards, "Relations Between Creativity and Psychopathology."
15. Richards, Ibid., Richards, "When Illness Yields Creativity"; Goodwin and Jamison, *Manic-Depressive Illness, 1st and 2nd Editions*; Jamison, *Touched With Fire.*
16. Kaufman, editor, *Creativity and Mental Illness*; Jamison, *Robert Lowell: Setting the River on Fire.*
17. Maslow, *Toward a Psychology of Being*; Rogers, *Creative Connection*; Richards, editor, *Everyday Creativity and New Views of Human Nature*; Kaufman and Gregoire, *Wired to Create*; Robert and Michele Root-Bernstein, *Sparks of Genius.*

18. Jamison, *Robert Lowell*.
19. Kinney and Richards, "Creativity as 'Compensatory Advantage.'"
20. Runco and Richards, editors, *Eminent Creativity, Everyday Creativity, and Health*; Ludwig, *Price of Greatness*; Ludwig, "Creative Achievement and Psychopathology."
21. Silvia and Kaufman, "Creativity and Mental Illness."
22. Richards, Kinney, et al., "Assessing Everyday Creativity"; Kinney, Richards, Southam, "Everyday Creativity, Its Assessment, and *The Lifetime Creativity Scales.*
23. Forgeard et al., "Bringing the Whole Universe to Order: Creativity, Healing, and Posttraumatic Growth."
24. Barron, *Creative Person and Creative Process*, 54.
25. Ibid., 73.
26. Beghetto, "Creativity in the Classroom"; Richards, "Everyday Creativity in the Classroom."
27. Spender, *Women of Ideas*.
28. Richards, "Relations Between Creativity and Psychopathology."
29. Ibid.: see also Richards, "When Illness Yields Creativity," 505, for association with chaos theory.
30. Kaufman and Gregoire, *Wired to Create*; Carson, "The Shared Vulnerability Model"; Richards, "Everyday Creativity," 201.
31. Richards, Ibid.
32. Kinney and Richards, "Creativity as 'Compensatory Advantage,'" 303.
33. Ibid., 304.
34. Richards, "Everyday Creativity," 200, a five-part typology.
35. Carson, "Shared Vulnerability Model," 265.
36. Richards, Kinney, et al., "Everyday Creativity and Bipolar and Unipolar Affective Disorder."
37. Goodwin and Jamison, *Manic-Depressive Illness*, 2nd Edition.
38. See Silvia, "Creativity in Undefinable, Controllable, and Everywhere." Happily Silvia and colleagues are interested in an everyday ecology of creativity and use of ecological sampling and assessment methods in creativity research.
39. Kinney and Richards, "Creativity as 'Compensatory Advantage.'"
40. Richards, "Creative Alchemy"; Richards and Goslin-Jones, "Everyday Creativity."
41. Richards, "Relations Between Creativity and Psychopathology."
42. Kinney and Richards, "Creativity as 'Compensatory Advantage,'" 311.
43. Jamison, *Robert Lowell*.

44. Swain and Swain, "Nonlinearity in Creativity and Mental Illness," 139.
45. Moore, *The Developing Genome*, 15.
46. Stigma is a concern of Former First Lady Rosalynn Carter and her Mental Health Task Force. Journalistic fellowhips have been awarded to professionals helping disseminate important and accurate information, and are helpingange the culture. www.cartercenter.org/health/mental_health/fellowships.
47. Richards, "Everyday Creativity: Our Hidden Potential"; also Richards, "Arts and Self-Expression in Mental Health," Conversations Series, Carter Presidential Center, March, 2004, with broadcast on Georgia Public Radio.

Part V

NEW DIRECTIONS (Going Deeper)

14

Empathy and Relational Creativity

Where empathy and concern flow both ways, there is an intense affirmation of the self and, paradoxically, a transcendence of the self, a sense of the self as part of a larger relational unit. The interaction allows for a relaxation of the sense of separateness; the other's well-being becomes as important as one's own.
Judith Jordan, PhD

Empathy, popularly described as "standing in another's shoes," is central to survival, society, interrelationship and more, and not only for humans. Darwin too spoke of empathy (as sensitivity). At best empathy is also highly creative—as both product and process—being both original and meaningful. Empathy involves a deep dance in the moment, one of life and caring, and honoring uniqueness while bridging to unity.

Favorite quote, and a favorite book, above, from Dr. Judith Jordan, and the "relational" model of development from the Stone Center at Wellesley College[1] This is *empathy*.

© The Author(s) 2018
R. Richards, *Everyday Creativity and the Healthy Mind*,
Palgrave Studies in Creativity and Culture,
https://doi.org/10.1057/978-1-137-55766-7_14

Empathy can be defined in multiple ways, as one will see, but now, for a working definition consider the popular image of, "standing in someone's else's shoes." Empathy is found not only across cultures but also across species. It is fundamental to survival and more. We know it well, and without complex definitions, whether comforting a child, enjoying someone's surprise party, or telling a friend "I know just how you feel."

Even more is when empathy is acted upon. (See Ekman's three-part definition below). In the relational model, of Jordan and colleagues, mutual connection and action may result, termed mutual empathy or *mutuality. Empathy*, at best, evokes caring and hope, even intimacy, whether for friendships, marriage, families, work-life—or conflicts in our crazy world. We, our usual human selves, are in some ways a miracle, yet not always quite "with it," with each other—preoccupied, distracted, tuned out from our neighbor. Yet we mindfully can shift, see each other, and engage. We can *be there*, and also *be with*, the other person.

To live more this way is a hope of this chapter.

Qualities of *everyday creative* process, as a way of life, are important in empathy—for instance including being open, aware, present, non-defensive, while taking big risks in a conflict, and choosing to hear things as they are presented, when we might rather skip them. Conflict and diverse ways of life can help empower learning and growth, if we attend and we care. If we engage the other with spontaneity and fresh-ness, seeking deep connection, we meet criteria for everyday creativity, *originality and meaningfulness.* This means we opt for connection and response, for potential change and honoring the relationship over self-interest, for dynamic movement over predictable stasis. It is a spontane-ous dance of relationship. We consciously show up, mentally, move toward co-creating and, as per the opening quote, possibly co-evolving into something more, not just individually but together. Ultimately, how good it can feel.

Thus, whether with kids, friends, loved ones or even strangers, we are figuratively holding hands. We are creating who knows what it is, yet pos-sibly new chances for happiness even when doing nothing. In a world of pain and misunderstanding, of rush, anonymity, and seeming control by larger forces, we become newly empowered.

Not to mention, we are no longer alone.

Love Is All We Need?

The saying sounds good, as did the popular song by this name. Yet let us explore this further. C.S. Lewis had wise thoughts here, discriminating four types of love, *affection, friendship, eros, charity*. He also added "goodness" in discussing *charity*, in this Western mix our intentions also matter.[2] In Buddhism, *metta* (lovingkindness), or *karuna* (compassion) for instance, bring many other virtues along with them, as will be discussed. For starters, each presupposes the other.[3] Can there be *metta* where we do not also want to help? Yet does *empathy*, as we typically use it, automatically involve caring and helping? Not necessarily—and see Ekman again, below.

Still some of life's greatest joys involve empathy—let us add a touch of caring and compassion—in our direct contacts with others, for instance in our friendships, in our romances.[4] We can also find this in lives we embrace secondarily through great art, theater, music, in coming together and finding something higher, even wondrous, as explored in the next chapter.

Now empathy has a built-in alerting mechanism, which is wonderful, our *mirror neurons*, below. Beyond that, our thoughts and feelings, our intentions are also important. Response is not of one sort, nor automatic. Often people we know have times of huge challenge and need, very demanding of friends or family, sometimes difficult at first for us fully to engage. The totality may take awhile to engage. Yet, are we not glad when we eventually do this?

At certain other times, we are thrust into an urgent and fearsome situation with no choice. New strength and immediacy sometimes can be found, in the moment and almost a heightened reality with our fellows who are with us at those times; have you heard people talk about how alive they felt on the battlefield, or in helping in a natural disaster? How they connected and forged bonds with brethren as deep as any? Let us hope, however, that we do not need a war or dreadful disaster to experience this.

Mirror Neurons

How amazing to have these mirror neurons. At times we tune in to each other in a very immediate way.

A newborn in a nursery cries, and suddenly many other babies are crying too. What is happening?[5]

Our inborn biological equipment is a help in understanding this, notably this phenomenon of *mirror neurons*, first described in the 1990s.[6] Here are neurons combining perceptual and motor sensitivities which can connect us rather remarkably, across living beings. The discovery in Italy of mirror neurons, as it occurred, was somewhat accidental[7] Yet it stimulated fascinating and extensive research reaching even into mental imagery.

Not only do these neurons show a connection between the perceptual and motor areas, but phenomena support presence of shared intentions (the effect does not occur without a planned action), and ability to image or imagine an outcome. When a book drops on someone's foot, and we say "Ouch!," we may in fact also be seeing it hit us, and ourselves are feeling some of that pain.

Here are primary and even built in modes of connecting for strongly social creatures. Plus we can build on the basic responses. This happens for humans certainly, and for other beings as well. There once were a couple of wonderful small dogs in residence at our home, from whom one could learn a great deal. Now one finds "therapy dogs" in many places whose healing powers are prodigious for people who are ill, are shut ins, and have various other problems. We might learn from them with our own *mirror neurons*.

Let us now turn to a natural disaster over a decade ago—where one might or might not have responded so immediately at first, to the reports shown on television, but perhaps later, very deeply.

Hurricane Katrina

The month was August 2005. Do you remember this devastating hurricane, Hurricane Katrina, hitting New Orleans. We have had an excess of other devastating disasters more recently, hurricanes, earthquakes, fires and floods, especially from 2016 on. How dreadful when the help does not arrive. Yet we may watch these events on television, where it sometimes does not always feel quite as real.

Then for me, in August, 2005, this woman's group emails began arriving.

First think back if you can. August 2005. A full 80%, eighty percent!, four-fifths, if you can imagine, of the city was underwater. Lives, homes lost. Recall the newsreels of people waiting on their roofs, water coming way up the sides of their houses, waving their hands, waiting for rescue. Boats arrived at times or they did not. Some people refused to go anyway because, back then, many rescuers would not take their cats or dogs. Almost 50% of children, afterward, in one study of 4th graders, met criteria for psychiatric referral—and not surprising—included depression, frightening memories, trauma, aggression.[8]

Looking Back a Year Later

As it occurred the American Psychological Association was already planning its 2006 Annual Convention in New Orleans just a year later. We went as we would have anyway, but this time also to support the rebuilding of New Orleans. Several of us did a symposium on *empathy*.[9] Just around the town, I found many of the shopkeepers and others we encountered were grateful if initially shy to talk about the hurricane. And where was our APA meeting held? Not only in the still badly bruised City of New Orleans (the Lower 9th Ward devastated and still without power) but in the very same building, and perhaps even in the very same room of the New Orleans Morial Convention Center where some of these refugees had taken shelter.

People had come to the seminar for many reasons, including getting professional continuing education credits or CEUs. But others were there for the topic, for empathy, and we even had some Katrina "first responders." All became subdued, and one woman ended up openly crying.

* * *

I had been collecting those emails, which were like messages in a bottle after a shipwreck—sent from a destitute desert isle.

This woman had been in housing that collapsed. She and others were then bussed to the New Orleans Convention Center (the same place where we were speaking of her at that very moment, in the empathy seminar—just one year later). FEMA and other services were to be provided, but were they? Although first responders did their best, and the Morial Convention Center had certainly opened their doors, remember there were other systems failures, at both the local and federal governmental levels.

This woman saw more and more people brought to the Convention Center for shelter. Again, this was right where we were, and were now talking about her.[10] Yet we were sipping Starbucks coffee out of paper cups. For her and others, still no provisions arrived.

At first, she and others felt hope. Yet the trucks, day after day, passed by the Center without stopping, without bringing food and water. Some soldiers waved to the refugees. Some gave a thumbs up. Yet meanwhile people were dying, and several right next to this woman. From medical ailments, exposure, or lack of provisions—including food and water and lifesaving medications.

Some people joined together to try to escape. I even remember this one from the television news—a bridge near the Morial Convention Center gave an exit to town. I can even picture it in my mind, and saw it in 2006. A lifeline. Yet unbelievably the bridge had been blocked. It was guarded. The people were turned back. There was—what?—fear of looting by the refugees. Fear that windows would be broken and stores robbed of their goods.

The people had to go back.

At this point, the woman said, she and others felt they had been "sent there to die."

Could it get worse? Some young men with guns showed up. Surprisingly, it turned out they became the main ones helping—they began to keep order, amidst the many huddled at the Morial Center. Here was a desperate community but, thanks to some of the perhaps most unlikely people, it had begun to pull together.

Remember we convention-goers were speaking from near if not exactly where she herself had had felt this despair. We so wished this woman could know, wished she could feel, the power of the people on her side, and wanting to help a year later. We were witnessing her pain, her situation, the more than unfairness. Perhaps she and others can still somehow know we were talking about this, and that we care. That they (and others more recently—including the desperate people in Puerto Rico after Hurricane Maria) can feel they are not alone.

In her case, this woman did escape. People from outside came and picked her and others up. Gradually there was relief to the area. But not everywhere and not for everyone.

This was APA 2006, the American Psychological Association Annual Meeting. Yes, we had academic talks about empathy at the Morial Convention Center a year later. But what really drew us was connecting with the real-life lived experience of those who went through it.

How Does One Manage When Events Are Overwhelming: Empathy and Compassion

All the more, let us bow to audience members who helped after Katrina (and a couple of our Saybrook University students among others went to New Orleans to assist). Imagine that your home washed away. Your city washed away. The Lower Ninth Ward, a year later, still had zero power. Many people moved elsewhere, never to return to their beloved city. The large number of traumatized children will carry this with them for years. (Some of their art therapy drawings are hugely moving—giant monstrous clouds descending. Yet feelings were expressed, and art always allows for further additions, and transformation.)[11]

Being Present Can Be Challenging

Still, how do we all cope, including those who help? Sometimes we have our personal work to do, both in tuning in to the extent of a situation (especially a huge one like an overwhelming hurricane, disrupting resources for months), or if involved, staying as immediately connected despite the great pain around us everywhere. Not surprisingly one can experience "secondary traumatization" from helping those who were traumatized. Joanna Macy, Buddhist activist has led workshops on how to continue working when events are overwhelming. How to find the strength, how to nourish oneself while dealing with giant hardships of others. How do we face—just think about it—face the "pain of the world"?[12]

Macy recommends an ongoing opening up, with each other, in groups, an open sharing, repeatedly, and not at all to be alone with it (no one can solve this by themselves). A connecting around the pain and despair, whether from war, oppression, violence, environmental destruction, in New Orleans or elsewhere, and the many other problems for which we humans have yet to devise larger and better solutions.

Along with this, vitally, a turning to spirituality, and a broader sense of our interdependence, our work together as part of a whole, informed by our values, caring, our spiritual beliefs and tradition. "Do unto others as you would have them do unto you" holds power across traditions. To offer universal "compassion" along with wisdom. We personally may be far from Christian saints, Buddhist Bodhisattvas, or benevolent sages across traditions, yet we can touch a bit of this. We can emulate such shining figures while part of a community of meaning and caring and love.

More Than One Kind of Empathy—Finding the Benevolent

Consider three examples, related to Paul Ekman's[13] conceptualizations of empathy, further below. Which among these three examples qualify as potentially empathetic in a caring way? (Which might potentially be creative?)

1. **What about this one?** You are at the breakfast table with some one. They are reading the paper and you are trying to tell them something important. They are distracted and just say to you "uh huh uh huh…" (if it is about "standing in someone's shoes" they are not yours)
2. **Or *this*?** You're at the breakfast table, and in psychological pain, and almost in tears. They are reading the paper. They put it down and ask you to tell them what is going on. You look so miserable. You tell them

and they say "I know just how you feel; I lost a job once too." (Yes! Thank you. Hope, by the way, you have never had the painful experience many have, of losing a job.)

3. **Or *this*?** Same table, same job loss. A well-disguised con artist sits down, you tell the tale; they know just how much you (without that job) could use a door-to-door sales job that, they are telling you, will quickly increase your income, within three months. They pitch it, they give you some figures, while knowing your needs, and you buy in. (Alas. A scam.)

Paul Ekman distinguishes these three aspects of empathy,

(a) **cognitive** empathy (perspective taking);
(b) **emotional** empathy (when you physically share parts of the experience), and
(c) **compassionate** empathy (we not only understand and feel, but are moved and able to help).

Which Examples Show Empathy?

Of these three examples, as far as empathy goes, the first person seems indifferent (or if they could engage, they have not yet done it). The second is potentially caring with a cognitive and emotional connection (and hopefully will be compassionate and giving), showing promise of all three aspects. But it may just stop at the co-experiencing. (We see the story on the news, we feel bad, but go on to something else.) Although the third is manipulative, and it seems counterintuitive, there actually is empathy by *this* definition; in some way this person is tuned in. Yet they could perhaps even be sociopathic, taking advantage of hardship, a con artist who is showing the first part of empathy (taking perspective), and might be able to tune into the feelings as well (share the experience). Yet it is all about turning it to a bad end.

A caring empathy, which morphs into an active compassion and spurs efforts to help is the one of real note here.

Which Examples Show Creativity?

Which, then, of the three are creative? As we defined it, using criteria for *originality* and *meaningfulness* in the moment, being present, connecting and responding in an authentic and spontaneous way, the 2nd and 3rd may both qualify, but for very different reasons. The second person is listening and is potentially engaged and helpful, the 3rd is "reading" the person, both cognitively and emotionally, and using originality to—alas—cheat them. Worth recalling earlier research linking the Default Mode and creativity, which showed *empathy* too as a correlate.[14]

Acting on Compassion

Ekman's third type of empathy is more apt to lead to active help. With compassion there can be a wish to do something. One learns, however, that attitude change does not always automatically create behavior change.[15] Still not absolute guarantee. There can still be a long road of changing habits and reactions, priorities, and much more. One hopes to see caring become linked with a strong practice of acting whenever one can be of help in some way.

Creativity Overlooked?: What Is Lost If the Type of Event Is Common?

The issue is—as with everyday creativity, in general, found throughout our lives—if we also show an empathetic creativity quite commonly, yet it is outside of awareness. We just haven't seen it or named it. Why might such relational creativity in a conversation be overlooked? It is not unusual. For example, in the connection made by person #2. A conversation with deep listening, spontaneous exchange, response including empathetic resonance and perhaps advice in the moment, with a capability of affecting, even changing, both parties, could be precious. It might well also be highly *original* (and also very *meaningful*), hence very creative. Yet unrecognized.

How much richer life could be if such caring, touching, connecting, creative moments were widely acknowledged? Some people are better at this than others. Its presence can surely help build the intimacy into a relationship.

Changing contexts, such interactions might be called conventionally creative if it they were a dialogue a play, and where set lines had been learned and were delivered with this same seeming conviction and evident spontaneity and feeling. How much more so then in this deeply felt "improve" situation in real life?

Yet again, empathy, relationship, creative conversation are not always given credit. How can they all be *creative?* say some people. Among biases may be that there are (or could be) in everyday life, only so *many* perceptive spontaneous and creative interchanges. We are still looking for that rare creative act—even an act of "genius."

If that makes the act of "having a conversation," in itself less unusual—really, how important is that? It is in the deep understanding, intimacy, presence, resonance, verbal and nonverbal signs and signals, creative interactions, and much more, in the individual contact, in which creating, feeling, and deep meaning, lies. These can be the types of things we remember most fondly at life's end.

Yet meanwhile the malicious conversation by the con artist in #3, which we hope happens very rarely, might get credit must faster for creativity (original, meaningful—and what a great and unusual con). Maybe even a TV series. Not fair, is it?

Why cannot creativity be happening all of the time in everyday life, and be acknowledged and treasured as such? In personal relationships, one could only hope for this.

Not Always Positive—Morality of Creativity

On the other hand...

We can sharpen our discernment. Who is doing what and *why are they doing it at all?* Is there a greater good down the road or not? If it is not frankly evil, is there something self-involved or thoughtless, that may yet not serve others well?. Why do we do what we do, and how often does one stop to think about this—or the expanding (systems) effects of what we do? Too many creativity books are saying *how* to be more creative without really looking at *why to be more creative, in the first place.*

Important resources here include two edited books, *The Dark Side of Creativity* and *The Ethics of Creativity.* Clearly not every invention or application is in the interests of human welfare. Sometimes people think so at the time, it should be added, but decide they were wrong. Sometimes they do not look. Some say they actually "didn't mean it," if they only had known, once they see what happened; at the time, they were caught up in the moment.

Particularly poignant and tragic, was the case of scientists working on the Manhattan Project (the atomic bomb which ended up responsible for the massive destruction of Hiroshima and Nagasaki, in World War II). Well known and well-intentioned scientists no less spoke of how people just got so bound up with the work (which was also an "arms race" amidst a brutal war), yet were seeing the project on its own, rather than what lay beyond; they just "didn't think." That family at home at ground zero, grandparents, parents, and children, having a meal.

It never crossed their minds.

The horrors of war. Awareness and mindfulness stay #1.

Meanwhile one knows other people can be diabolically clever in taking advantage of, and harming, others. Even finding pleasure.[16] Yet that is not the current discussion. It is how to build awareness so we don't carelessly make a mistake. How to build ethics into our fundamental discussions about creativity and so-called societal progress, so that benefit is not taken for granted. New doesn't automatically mean good. High tech doesn't automatically mean good. Gene editing doesn't automatically mean good. There are discussions now about AI (artificial intelligence) and ways it might go wrong.[17] One concern is about *The Singularity.*[18] Do we want to leave this to a few top government advisers, or to some powerful wealthy companies. As things speed up more, it will only get worse. How do we make the ethics of creativity part, at all levels, of our basic educational and governmental discussions?

Perhaps, someone says, this is about *survival of the fittest?* Did Darwin say that? No, he didn't within our species. Not between you, me, and the next person. He asked us all to exercise our empathy, creativity, our *love* for each other, and—very much our—morality.

The Lost Darwin: He Spoke of Love, Collaboration

Many do not know that some of Charles Darwin's message was not fully transmitted. Darwin, giant of evolutionary theory, is credited with "survival of the fittest" (phase actually due to Herbert Spencer, applied by Darwin to one species versus another—not people combating each other within the species *H. sapiens*).[19] He had more to say about creative cooperation, and survival together.

Darwin in his private journals and his last book, *Descent of Man,*[20] told a different story. Here we are, a highly social and cooperative species. Darwin spoke extensively of empathy, 61 times using the term "sympathy." More remarkably, in *Descent,* he mentioned the word *love* a full 95, moral sensitivity 92 times, and mutuality or mutual aid (cooperation), 24 times!. *We love, we connect, we live important values, we work collaboratively together.* Darwin, in fact, mentioned "survival of the fittest" only twice, once almost to make fun of the term.[21] It may surprise some to know that Darwin, before finding his final calling, had trained for the ministry.[22]

Indeed this is about creativity, "the originality of everyday life," manifested in our original and meaningful efforts together and for a common good. This occurs in human fellowship, in families, societies, and larger cultural groups, bringing sentiments and values we come equipped with. We are designed, Darwin was saying, to bond, care, and co-create with a larger good in mind.[23] On a community level this could be about family, education, staying fed and healthy, even caring for one's garden (since Darwin's kids helped him with this and certain experiments). Yet how are we doing today?

Broader Social Vision and Co-Creative Action?

Seems harder to follow each day what is happening in our complex and exponentially more sophisticated society and world. Plus we may feel such a small part of the whole. What can we ourselves do?

We also know evolution has done some winnowing over the millennia and often rather brutally, as seen in Chap. 7. Not a happy picture for the future. We humans are threatening the biosphere and our future, leading to extinction of many species via our own lifestyles and wastes across the globe. According to Elizabeth Kolbert, in *The Sixth Extinction*, this era may end up being called the Anthropocene.[24] Not a complimentary term or legacy to leave the future. This is not always because of our greed (it sometimes is) but often reflects our short-sightedness, and fixation on our own lives, when we formally need broader ways of thinking. We live in a global society, a shrinking globe and ever-more diverse conditions.

We can leave it to a few individuals in power or be more informed and creatively active ourselves. Can we:

- **Think more in systems terms**—and our populace needs more instruction in methods from K onward! There can be increased awareness of life and its balances, and what we can expect, on a larger stage. (Meanwhile thinking beyond our block or next week!)
- **Use more creative imagination, for instance, "proflexion"**— Thinking beyond what is happening now to what *could* occur, alternative futuristic scenarios, what life would be like for all of us, and how we can work together to modify scenarios.

Proflexion: Seeing Broadly and Ahead—Creative Alternative Futures

Seana Moran[25] has designed a creative college curriculum to help undergraduates master *proflexion*. Here (instead of reflecting back), they learn to predict ahead for us as human societies and cultural groups, to varied consequences of a situation. How will people live thrive? Or not? Here is divergent thinking writ large—plus a book on the method and examples of what can result. Larger carbon footprint? Serious. Perhaps less depressing: Self-driving cars. Faster social media? How will we live, want to live? Can we develop:

- **Conscious awareness** of problems and alternatives and
- **Systems thinking about effects** on the lives we will lead (looking out, looking in, looking more deeply within each other), and
- **Ways to collaborative for change**—locally or globally, in groups that can be heard or exert influence; key skills for the future.

Seen as Part of Creativity?

Whyever not? Can we include in our personal creativity contemplation on how we experience life and each other, how we can locally and globally respond to different visions of the future(s). Might two biases hinder us?

- **Process.** Contemplation of relationship and lived experience involves a more slippery and emergent creative *process* in real-time, compared to a concrete creative *product*—harder to capture this in the ongoing flow of everyday life? (Yet creativity in drama is honored.)
- **Everyday aspect.** Our experience in everyday creative life is, by some, less valued than eminent or "expert" creative efforts? (see also examples under definitions by Ekman, above)

Empathy Deepened, Including Spiritual Aspects

To conclude, let us return to the further complexity and especially higher and shining aspects of empathy, ending with its higher potential!

Relational-Cultural Theory

In Chap. 10, we discussed Relational Cultural Theory and its resonance with humanistic thinking and also with nonlinear dynamic systems, with our interdependent selves and world. We develop in relationship, we are defined by these.[26] Our brain development is very much the product of intersubjective experience.[27] Rather than working toward some mythical separation and an expanding independence our life embraces an increasing capacity for mutuality. Our progress and growth happens in context, involving further complexification and articulation in relation to and within a larger whole. Through our growth-fostering relationships, we are said to gain (1) more energy, (2) clarity of personal experience and with each other; (3) creativity and productivity; (4) a sense of worth; and (5) desire for more connection.[28]

Relational-Cultural Framework

When I first encountered it, this was the *Self-in-Relation* model. I worked with the founders and some quite wonderful clinicians on an inpatient unit at McLean Hospital and Harvard Medical School. Although designed in a women's setting, the model is appropriate for all, and has also been used in couples work. Furthermore the group has been increasingly and intentionally embracing ethnic diversity and the further learning and growth fostered by difference in conjunction with our underlying humanity. Hence the *Relational-Cultural* designation. The book, *Relational Cultural Therapy* was selected by the American Psychological Assocation for inclusion in its clinical book series about important psychotherapies.[29] The home base for the RCT remains the Stone Center at Wellesley College.

The five fundamental qualities we addressed in the inpatient work I did with this group were (and as I have discussed them):

1. **Engagement**—BE THERE! about attending, moving together
2. **Authenticity**—BE HONEST! sharing the truest sense of self and one's inner experience.

3. **Empathy**—BE WITH ANOTHER. In their shoes yet own perspective
4. **Mutuality**—EMPATHETIC SHARING. Connecting together, a dance of openness and understanding which can change both parties.
5. **Empowerment**—ENERGY, PURPOSE via connection (not competition)

Once might well imagine the progression—within a group committed to these principles—from engaging and doing so with honesty and authenticity to greater awareness of self and other, progressive healing, and the richness of empathy and mutual empathy, along and the greater emergent empowerment which continues to energize the system. Empathy within this model is incredibly valuable in a clinical setting, and I found multiple connections to aspects of Eastern philosophies.[30] Further, there was a bit of the magic of the high country wilderness experience, described earlier, found in this inpatient setting. Although people were there in pain, and sometimes in crisis, there was a deeply felt caring, and sense of acceptance as one was, in process—and as one was becoming.

Invaluable Throughout Life

Significantly, empathy is one of the characteristics featured in the Root-Bernstein's[31] important book, *Sparks of Genius: The 13 Thinking Tools of the World's Most Creative People.* From visual art to choreography, to medical training, to working with animals, and much more. Examples including science are found in the next chapter. Empathy is coming more into its own, in the context of creativity, and is also one of ten qualities chosen for Kaufman and Gregoire's 2015 book, *Wired to Create.*[32] If this does not seem surprising to people today, it was anything but the rule 15–20 years ago!

Although empathy may have near automatic aspects, e.g., with mirror neurons, one has seen there are also complex intellectual-emotional qualities. Psychologist and psychotherapist Judith Jordan explained how empathy in treatment involves a complex mix of both intellect and feelings. We appreciate what another is saying, thinking, feeling, we live their story as well as our own. Yet we also know who is whom, even as we change together.[33] It is very much part of a dance, in the presence of the moment. This could be any contact, as well, and not just a clinical thera-peutic one. Or at least a contact with deep connection and feeling. Features include[34]:

> ... a well-differentiated sense of self in addition to a sensitivity to the differ-entness as well as sameness of the other.... Empathy always involves surren-der ... self-boundaries must be flexible .... involves temporary identification with the other's state, during which ... source of affect is in the other. In the final resolution ... affect subsides and one's self feels more separate...

More separate, yet more fully involved, with a deeper appreciation of the other's inner world, and hopefully also of one's own. Some of this comes naturally, some we can refine and deepen. Think how much we could learn from The Dalai Lama!

His Holiness the Dalai Lama: On Feeling Alone

If empathy is engaged with positivity and caring, we will surely feel all the less alone or disconnected or unaided in an unfriendly world. An inter-viewer asked His Holiness the Dalai Lama about loneliness. Did he ever get lonely?[35]

> Quite simply, the Dalai Lama, said "No."
> "No?" The interviewer was astounded.

The Dalai Lama explained he looks at each person in a positive way and creates an affinity, a connection. Apprehension and fear are replaced by openness.

The interviewer asked how the average person might do this and (do recall the aspect of caring and giving in fullest empathy) the Dalai Lama mentioned *compassion*, He explained[36]:

> ... once that thought becomes active, then your attitude towards others changes automatically ... (it will) reduce fear and allow an openness ... you can approach a relationship in which you, yourself, initially creative the possibility of receiving affection or a positive response.

Acknowledging that sometimes, some others might start off unfriendly or indifferent—not so glad to see you—he recommended flexibility and also taking the initiative, rather than waiting for it.

Ah—imagine if we all lived this way.

Vietnamese Zen Wisdom

A Zen master I know, Thich Minh Duc, put this process of empathizing very succinctly and beautifully,[37]

> "You listen, open the heart, dissolve boundaries." But it's not indiscriminate, it is also, both 'in and out.'

He also showed the profound importance of empathy here—profound indeed, if you hear this literally. He was speaking of a very good king, in ancient Vietnam,[38]

> If you take the pain of others as your own, you will become a good king; *you don't need to look for the Buddha* (Italics added)

Happily we are already on this path, with perhaps a ways more to go.

Yet do we recognize the path? If you think about listening to a friend or your child or a coworker of yours you may find you were doing this all the time, and can even identify these aspects. Bad day at school? Picked on? "I know just how you feel"!

Not surprisingly, mindful awareness practices can increase our capacity for empathy.[39] Plus as we've said, for creativity too.

In Each Others' Shoes: Improvisational Theater

One of our graduate students[40] has done improvisational "playback theater" with young people in several contexts, helping them learn perspectives of others while building greater confidence, connection, social skills and much more. She has also worked with youth on ways of coping with bullying. Now she is considering combining these. Truly it is a whole different 360-degree experience when you are playing it out and someone is actually bullying *you!* Well played dramatically, and it feels very real indeed.

A whole different story, at this point. One is "standing in the shoes" of the other. Feeling the pain. How much more is *this* student apt to act on a caring empathy now?

Remember the weapons developers who just "didn't think." These kids are learning to think—and fully to experience the consequences.

That bully might only be thinking about him/herself and just "didn't think" very much or at all about the others, except as they acted in fearing the bully, enhancing ways of feeling more powerful. Here is bullying at someone's terrible expense, with no compassionate empathy for that other. Now *the bullies* are being bullied instead. Who me? How hard it suddenly becomes. Maybe they never even imagined how it could feel. Insights aplenty, if one is open to learning about them, and about oneself. Will they act the same way again?[41]

Four Immeasureables

Here is a shining goal, high on a hill, with empathy a part of the path represented here by compassion—the Four Immeasureables we have mentioned before, and with equivalents in other world wisdom traditions.[42] Higher creativity trails in their wake, and so very much does health.

Immeasureable they are indeed, these four, but we already know them and they are far from impossible! Though they surely can be deepened for any of us. *Lovingkindness, compassion, sympathetic joy,* and *equanimity.* If we love, we will want to help; we will also rejoice in others' good fortune, nor will we hoard it, we will bring benefit to all. Equanimity is not about equalizing with a lack of caring. It's about brining that lovingkindness and the rest, to the world! OK, big goals. Worth trying?

In fact, many of the songs on the radio are about love. The four immeasureables are also called the *Brahmaviharas,* in Sanskrit, the Divine Abodes.[43] Divine? How marvelous it sounds. Might we live there? We can at least try. Zen Master Thich Nhat Hanh tells us in his *Teachings on Love*[44] that these are named *abodes* because,

… if you practice them, they will grow in you every day until they embrace the whole world. You will become happier, and everyone around you will become happier too.

Summary and Looking Ahead

Hence, we have looked at empathy, caring, our interdependent development, the importance of relationships and our bonds as social creatures, as well as value-bound lives. One sees problems when such involvements are lacking. Charles Darwin too shared these concerns in his later writings. Today we see not only their growing importance in psychology, particularly on a diverse and shrinking globe, but also the hope of an authentic and interpersonal dance of creativity. As our view deepens, we see these concerns are not only important but can even, in a spiritual context, be *immeasureable* and can expand to embrace the whole world. We next turn to beauty, nature, and ways that empathy can help us bridge duality and go even deeper. We can be drawn forward with wonder and awe to new appreciations and ways of knowing.

Notes

1. Jordan, "The Meaning of Mutuality," 83.
2. Lewis, *The Four Loves*, 163.
3. Thich Nhat Hanh, *Teachings on Love*.
4. Lewis, *The Four Loves*, 163.
5. Siegel, *Developing Mind*.
6. Siegel, *The Mindful Brain*, 164–166.
7. This chapter deals with empathy for humans and other species too. Since this author has concerns about animal experimentation and humane treatment of living beings, she has omitted an anecdote about accidental discovery of mirror neurons. Buddhist monk, and translator for HH Dalai Lama, Matthieu Ricard, in *Plea for the Animals*, shares that France passed, in 2014, "an amendment to the French civil code … that recognized animals as sentient beings … extended to the entire French legal system." (p. 272). This includes not causing pain. Unfortunately this is not the case in most parts of the world. Empathy plus awareness of situations (often hidden) can hopefully cause us to act.

8. DeParle, "Orphaned."
9. Richards, "Relational Creativity and Healing Potential: The Power of Eastern Thought in Western Clinical Settings."
10. Ibid., 298, I no longer have the original emails, but recounted her story the next year, and in later talks.
11. Malchiodi, *Art Therapy Sourcebook*, e.g., 138.
12. Rothberg, *The Engaged Spiritual Life: A Buddhist Approach to Transforming Ourselves and the World.*
13. See Ekman, www.YouTube.com/watch?v=3AgvKJK-nrk (June 17, 2010); also Goleman, www.danielgoleman.oinfo/three-kinds-of-empathy-cognitive-emotional-compassionate. Retr. 3-10-2018.
14. Epstein and Norris, "Experiential Thinking Style."
15. Feinstein and Krippner, *The Mythic Path.*
16. Baron-Cohen, *The Science of Evil.*
17. Bostrom, *Superintelligence: Paths, Dangers, Strategies.*
18. Kurzweil, *The Singularity is Near.*
19. deWaal, *Age of Empathy.*
20. Loye, "Telling the New Story: Darwin, Evolution, and Creativity Versus Conformity in Science.
21. Ibid., 157.
22. Richards, editor, *Everyday Creativity and New Views of Human Nature.*
23. Loye, "Telling the New Story."
24. Kolbert, *The Sixth Extinction.*
25. Moran, *Ethical Ripples of Creativity and Innovation.*
26. Jordan, Kaplan, Miller, Stiver, and Surrey, *Women's Growth in Connection*; Note too, Guisinger and Blatt, "Individuality and Relatedness: Evolution of a Fundamental Dialectic." Western psychologies have typically stressed the autonomous, independent side of this dialectic, where interpersonal relatedness has been relatively less emphasized. Pressures of natural selection favor both; there are implications for mature development, social policy. See also Montuori, Combs, and Richards, "Creativity, Consciousness, and the Direction for Human Development."
27. Siegel, *Developing Mind*, 233. Includes discussion of supersystems. See too Guevara, et al., "Attractor Dynamics of Dyadic Interaction," exploring children's problem solving, with oscillation between two attractor states; cooperation and coordination was moderately correlated with better performance.
28. Jordan, *Relational-Cultural Therapy.*

29. Each book may be used with a DVD that demonstrates applications in therapy. See www.apa.org/pubs/books//Theories-series-and-dvds.aspx.
30. Richards, "Relational Creativity and Healing Potential," 286.
31. Root-Bernstein and Root-Bernstein, *Sparks of Genius.*
32. Kaufman and Gregoire, *Wired to Create.*
33. Richards, "Relational Creativity and Healing Potential," 292.
34. Jordan, *Relational-Cultural Therapy,* 69.
35. Dalai Lama and Cutler, *The Art of Happiness.*
36. Ibid., 69.
37. Thich Minh Duc, personal communication, Sept 30, 2005.
38. Richards, "Relational Creativity and Healing Potential," 300.
39. Siegel, *The Mindful Brain.*
40. This can involve both role-playing and role-reveral. With thanks to Kady Pomerleau-Corpstein for her dynamic teaching innovations in working with young people.
41. It is worth finding precursors and vulnerabilities in one's life, whether bullied or the one who bullies, and also alternative ways both can handle the situation.
42. Wallace, *The Four Immeasureables.*
43. Richards, "Relational Creativity and Healing Potential," 300.
44. Thich Nhat Hanh, *Teachings on Love,* 1.

15

Beauty, the Sublime, the Hidden

You do not need to leave your room ....
Remain sitting at your table and listen.
Do not even listen, simply wait. Do not even wait,
be quite still and solitary. The world will freely
offer itself to you to be unmasked. It has no choice.
It will roll in ecstacy at your feet.
Franz Kafka

There is pleasure in the pathless woods
Lord Byron

Can one have profound creative relationships even with inanimate objects, beyond separation of self, and with a deeper knowing? How is it that beauty can bring us immediately to awareness, and a state beyond thoughts of self or a more conceptual appreciation. More powerful yet is the sublime, bringing wonder and awe, vastly large, infinite, exceeding our human understanding. Yet in some way do we still understand? Is there something within us, subtle and nonverbal, that responds?

© The Author(s) 2018
R. Richards, *Everyday Creativity and the Healthy Mind*,
Palgrave Studies in Creativity and Culture,
https://doi.org/10.1057/978-1-137-55766-7_15

Empathy, Creativity, and Arts

Inspired by Zen Master John Daido Loori's *Zen of Creativity*[1] I have had students in a seminar go outside and

- find something, not seek it out, but let it call to them
- a flower, a tree, a fence, whatever may be calling
- nor need it be a "thing," i.e., something we have boxed and named
- Perhaps a puff of air, a fragrant moment, the call of bird

Then sit with it. Let it speak. I give people regular 8–1/2 by 11 inch paper plus crayons so they don't get some complex about making "great art"—this is all about presence and creative expression in the moment. When ready, I ask them to draw something, write something, respond in whatever way feels right to them, in brief, or at length, and return in 25 minutes. Then we discuss what happened.

What is there, as Kafka put it, to be "unmasked"? What is "hidden"?—perhaps more than we imagined? (If intrigued, one could try this exercise before going on.) Unlike bringing our personal will and impressing it upon a subject, a flower, let us say—framed as we already imagine it in our mind—unlike controlling the moment with our own agenda, we are opening to other forces and to something deeper in ourselves. Here is a more profound conversation, one to which we are invited.

One award-winning visual artist[2] told me recently how he notes different faces, whether friends or strangers. One of these will sometimes call and speak deeply. He'll make a quick sketch, in the moment, to capture "the quality." It is not necessarily visible on the surface. The result can be a revealing portrait.

Wu Chen and Bamboo

If you wonder how "empathy" got in here, let us say with a flower, well, why not? Or what if, instead, it was a rock—does this seem more unlikely if the subject was not organic? Yet, as said by some, including indigenous groups, and down through the ages and around the world: Everything

holds some measure of consciousness.[3] Intuitive nonconceptual awareness of an object has in fact been described in Eastern traditions, beyond
dualistic knowing.[4]

When and with what can we feel a more-than-intimate connection?[5]

I had the honor to be guest teaching on creativity in Taiwan, at Tung
Hai University in Taichung, and my hostess and organizational creativity
expert, Professor Pei San Yu, along with a colleague, took me to the National
Museum in Taipei—which has incredible artistic richness. Yet alas, it did
not have paintings of bamboo by Wu Chen, c. 1350, as I had hoped. I was
told I'd need to go to Shanghai. It was not to happen on this trip.

I had admired Wu Chen for years, based on a catalogue my paternal
grandmother had gotten years before at a traveling show she had seen in
San Francisco. An illustrated catalogue. Amazing! Even in reproduction,
even in black and white photos, the bamboo looked alive. The bamboo
seemed to move. The page actually *was* alive.

How was Wu Chen empathizing or "standing in the shoes of the bamboo?" Or was it even better than that? The catalogue notes said "This
album might be called, 'Twenty portraits of the artist as a bamboo'"[6] Is
this at all like Martin Buber's "between space" in *I and Thou*?[7] Where
"between" becomes alive in its own right?

From a book on Chinese brush painting[8]:

Paint with love and kindness for the materials and the subject portrayed,
becoming on with both.

Later, I acquired a bamboo painting by a more modern master—very
large, and I placed it at the end of a room. The wind almost blows within
the frame. I treasure the life force there—not the image, not some details
identical to a photographed model—but something more moving and
dynamic, real, present, and *now!* Yet it is there on the paper, the parch-
ment. Similar to the master of calligraphy, the bamboo artist masters the
skills, then, putting them aside, does the piece.

What then is captured? A deeper authentic truth?[9] A novice asked
Master Ching Hao about the art of portraying beauty[10]:

The important point is to obtain their true likeness, is it not?

Ching Hao was clear:

> *It is not.* Painting is to paint.... Likeness can be obtained by shapes without spirit; but when truth is reached spirit and substance are both fully expressed.

Yet How Do We Get In?

Consider: What if we are *already* in?—if we are in fact of it? If we in some way know it quite intimately. We are after all interconnected. As stated earlier, regarding Open Systems, our boundaries aren't so crisp either. Yet we may maintain we all do our independent and self-sufficient thing, so valued by our culture. One thoughtful gentleman, before coming to our www.AhimsaBerkeley.com annual conference in Berkeley, focused on empathy, relationship, and change, had written the following on a piece of paper, with a wish to share. He read it to the gathering, and gave me a copy. (I later published it as part of a chapter on relational psychology and empathy in *Cultural Beliefs and Healing Systems*)[11] Mr. Gladstone wrote:

> Our present way of life encourages us to be self-centered and self-protective.... "Success" means getting ahead of others and leaving them behind .... we need to understand deeply our interdependence with others and with all of life.... Every religion recognizes interdependence in some way, often expressed in terms of love—'God is love,' "love one another," "love your enemies." This loving attitude is a necessary partner to understanding interdependence. Let us open our hearts and minds to this.

For an "empathetic person," what is called *inside* and *outside* may experientially mix. We know they do so anyway, as well outlined in Eastern philosophy, in terms of processes of perception (object, process, organ of perception, for instance, see clear descriptions by Thich Nhat Hanh[12]) also helping reveal how our own views are constructed, in this system. With deeper knowing, we also bring states of mind, and potential ways of appreciation perhaps beyond our conceptual mind. This even includes, and could it be possible, might sometimes exceed, the fast, intuitive, nonverbal, "default mode," of our intuitions, hunches, guesses, and feelings?[13] Can we give credence, for instance, to more universal symbols and archetypes as per C.G. Jung or a "collective unconscious"?[14]

Here the reader is not at all asked to "believe" a report or claim without acceptable evidence, but rather to keep an open mind, at least when many others, including various cultures, give credence to something.[15] We in the West—to put it mildly—still don't know everything.

Furthermore, in our own Western science, there are numerous states, or alterations of consciousness, as we have said, other than what one may call our "ordinary" consciousness, as we have both seen from scientific study[16] and experiential reports of unusual experiences. Recall the father of American psychology, William James who reported altered experience behind the "thinnest of veils…"[17] So near and yet so far. But he wanted us to know it is there.

It is worth doing our personal experiential studies too—seeking our true creative palette! Humanistic psychologist Kaisa Puhakka spoke of aware, empathic, unmediated, interconnection, in an edited collection on *Spiritual Knowing*.[18]

> "Knowing" is a moment of awareness in which contact occurs between the knower and the known. This contact is nonconceptual, nonimaginal, nondiscursive, and extremely brief. "Having knowledge," on the other hand, consists of descriptive or interpretive claims to the effect that "such-and-such is the case" … (with knowing) what is contacted are, to borrow Husserl's term, "things themselves." The act of contact breaks out of our solipsistic representational world of images and meanings, into genuine, empathic interconnectedness.

It still remains remarkable, to me, that the American Psychological Association (APA), and its foreword looking publishing arm, in 2017, put out an entire text by Imants Baruss (albeit this well-respected consciousness expert had already authored *Alternations of Consciousness* for APA in 2003); this new book (snatched up eagerly by consciousness students) was co-authored with Julia Mossbridge. It is called *Transcendent Mind: Rethinking the Science of Consciousness*.[19] The book's highly-documented premise is still very much at odds with some traditional views of mind and brain. In view of new findings in physics and allied fields, it is not a new thought that mind could exist outside of physical brain.[20] Nor is this a problem with varied spiritual belief systems—where the end of physical life is not considered a full-stop to everything. Yet the possibilities in this book remain controversial to many scientists.

In longstanding Eastern views, however, other belief systems hold sway. Some Western reports fit better with these, for instance, research and experiential evidence on Near Death Experiences (NDEs).[21] Here the individual shows clinical death by many indices yet somehow returns to life in our world and reports events it would be hard to know except from "outside the body." Such information is new for many in mainstream psychology, and especially surprising for those initially meeting such reports.

Here for example, from over 15 years ago, reported by Baruss, is a woman having an aneurysm, excised surgically. Her heart was stopped, blood was drained from the head, EEG was inactive. The surgery succeeded, she was revived, and among other things, she reported hearing the saw that was used on her skull, while flat-lined, and described it rather accurately along with the container that held its blades.[22] Now some reductionist scientists still persist in finding alternative explanations, as in this case.

Yet resonances between interdependence in Buddhist and other traditions, and covert and unsuspected links existing even vastly across space, as with instantaneous electron spin transformation in now separated pairs—consider Bell's phenomenon[23]—are indeed compelling. The late physicist David Bohm[24] held that two events cannot be contemplated one separate from the other—even that same pair of electrons now light years apart can instantaneously affect each other. (One may recall nothing had been said to go faster than the speed of light. Well…)

To those familiar with a "holographic" model of Bohm's "explicate order," the so-called reality we experience where an underlying "implicate order" is a more fundamental source (and indeed is reflected in every piece), this would not be a surprising hypothesis. Here, in a famous quote, is how Einstein put it[25]:

A human being is part of the whole ... a part limited in time and space. He experiences his thoughts and feelings as something separate from the rest— a kind of optical delusion of his consciousness. This delusion is a kind of prison for us.

Well, if so—can we know more about this? Might we even get out of this metaphorical prison?

Beauty: In Search of "The Hidden"

Beauty may further help us plumb this "hidden" quality. Let us start with what appeals, give pleasure, is defined below as "beauty"; chaos theory can also help us later. But beauty—what exactly is that? Surely there is already a bit of mystery?

"It is divinity" say the Upanishads.

Here is a gift of life, and given for free! It is a gift for anyone at all, whomever should find it? Plus it is not just for human beings. Further, beauty can be found pretty much anywhere. Beauty has been variably defined, but in this author's view was characterized well by Santayana as[26]:

> ... value, positive, intrinsic, and objectified.... Beauty is pleasure regarded as a quality of thing.

We lack a good word in English for the many aesthetic qualities that may be invoked for beauty. Handsome, elegant, gorgeous, and so on. One speaks of a fine wine. Or a heavenly sonata (it is not just about visual experience, either).

Humanistic psychologist Rollo May spoke of our own personal experience of beauty, it[27]:

> gives us a sense of joy and a sense of peace simultaneously.... Beauty gives us not only a feeling of wonder; it imparts to us at this one moment a timelessness, a repose—which is why we speak of beauty as being eternal.

Is There an Agenda?

Does beauty ask something of us? Or give us something important and ongoing? Could there be an agenda? A friend once got annoyed at me for suggesting just this. In fact, later, in 2001, I published an article about it.[28]

Yet must everything have a purpose, she asked?

We do have epiphenomena. These just happen, and are present, along with other more causal sequences. Yet we know that often there is some hidden purpose in the elegant efficiencies of nature. With *beauty* could it perhaps be a higher one? Regarding a sunset—glorious across time and culture—remember again the Upanishads: "It is divinity."

Kant, actually, spoke of beauty as being *disinterested.* The "judgment of taste" has no further purpose. We look because we look—and it pleases us intrinsically to do so.[29]

That may well be, from our end, where we don't *know* there is an agenda—we look because we look. *Yet* what if there is, after all, *an agenda.* What if beauty *changes us.*

It will, certainly. We remember that sunset. We are merely doing our thing, and the environment is calling to us. We notice. Most people do. Is this happening epigenetically, and setting some sequence in motion? It seems possible. A 2017 book by Richard Prum, Yale Professor of Ornithology, and Head Curator of Vertebrate Zoology at Yale's Peabody Museum, wrote a now celebrated book called *The Evolution of Beauty: How Darwin's Forgotten Theory of Mate Choice Shapes the Animal World—and Us.*

The "Lost Darwin" Returns Again

Let us be glad that Charles Darwin is finally getting other parts of his message recognized. Prum's new book, *Evolution of Beauty*, contains gorgeous illustrated birds as the main exemplar, while documenting more broadly that beauty, for Darwin, was a whole second strand in the process of evolutionary selection. This addresses selection within a species, rather than between them. Here is ascendance of beauty as an evolutionary force. Notable too, and of further interest in these days of #METOO, with women finally being heard and empowered, is selection as made by the *female*. How nice indeed when the male is ornamented for the female of the species!

Darwin's writings, as revealed in Prum's work, have not been as credited by history as much else has, but they are now getting more serious attention.

In this book, the view on beauty, with at times even a transcendent importance, goes beyond sexual selection, while resonating with the Upanishads and other spiritual and religious traditions. Recall that glorious sunset, for instance. Let us keep our attention broad, so as to include potential exploration of realms of higher meaning.

What More May Be Calling Us?

If there is a further agenda, what might one experience? We move from birds back to the sunset and, earlier, a day at the beach: We walk along the California sand, late summer, finding there still is some warmth in the air, and look at the last bits of sunset, a gorgeous display across an ocean panorama of reds and oranges, yellows and golds and touches of a misty blue. It stretches across the horizon and even over our heads.

The moment is special. This sunset is not only important to those with no electricity or heat at home, who have noticed the sun is setting. Now it will cool off. Much more than survival is going on here. Nor is it just for those who can read in the clouds and wind that tomorrow will be another mild day.

One's noticing is not just for those persons who are artists or art connoisseurs, who bring specialized and appreciative experience to this beauty. We can all appreciate it—and right away. No special study needed. We see it, we wonder, and furthermore we somehow know it. Research on aesthetic pleasure across countries (Australia, Taiwan, Netherlands) also shows such an immediate response, and a pleasure, solely for its own sake, that also crosses cultures.[30] The next chapter, Chap. 16, too speculates more about what underlies this phenomenon.

Awareness!—Evolutionary Triumph

We notice, we view it consciously. Then we mindfully reflect on it. What is the experience?

Look! I say to my neighbors. Not only have I been brought to conscious awareness by this display, but now the others have as well. I have passed it along; they looked immediately. It was catching. It only took a nudge and they also paid attention. We can compare aesthetic appreciation in the fine arts, which may happen fast, at first, yet with aesthetic judgments which after perhaps initial wondrous attention, then involve several stages. Across several models, an information-processing series of steps is said to occur.[31]

This too can depending upon one's experiences as a connoisseur, quantitative and qualitative, even including variations in viewing time (median was a short 21 seconds in a careful museum study across diverse forms of art). Worth also noting Tinio's clever "mirror model" for art appreciation, which involves viewer creativity and use of imagination as well.[32] Note this fascinating process takes further time for processing and appreciation. Here in ways, one's art viewing mirrors the original art-making, yet in reverse. Four proposed stages are initialization—expansion—adaptation—finalizing. Viewing corresponds first of all to automatic processing, linked to *finalizing* (the final product). The other stages in contemplation, unfold in reverse, further opening meaning, emotion, and aesthetic qualities.

Might this hold as well for the artistry of nature? Important question.

In any case, for our purposes, here, the focus is on that initial moment. Plus the universality of the appeal. This particular example from nature is, for most people—and over the ages—not at all new. Yet the appeal remains, it is immediate, and people look.

I have written about this elsewhere in the context of *memes*[33] being shared and replicated, units of information, and much more quickly and vastly, and nonexclusively, by far, than with *genes*. Just consider some information "going viral."[34] A spectacular eclipse. A cure for cancer. The glory of life's larger meaning?

Metaphysically, poet Robert Burns (1790)[35] looking upward, resonates with the Upanishads.

The voice of nature loudly cries,
And many a message from the skies,
That something in us never dies.

Other Possibilities

With such a moment, one may also speculate on arts as experienced within varied *structures* of consciousness, as did Allan Combs and Stanley Krippner, related to context at different stages of human history—magical, mythical, mental, and more recently, integral.[36] Nor need integral be the final possibility. As an ongoing "structure" vs. "stage," one may not consciously acknowledge such frames, fading as they will into cultural beliefs or worldview. This current more multi-perspectival integral frame, also offers "an open and translucent quality through which reality is experienced in a clear and less conditioned way."[37] Access to multiple structures at once can be part of this.[38] We know in addition that "states" of consciousness can temporarily flash forth invoking structures not yet dominant—or in cases of deep spiritual experience, yielding a vastly less structured (or unstructured, even the term beyond the conventional) knowing. What is our experience, then, as per Robert Burns, above, here with the art of nature—or of existence. Looking as well toward the next chapter, when might such immediate and astounding events evoke a rare and important *alteration of consciousness.*

Multiple other reasons can be proferred to notice and record beauty, and rapidly as well, including Prum's prescient revisiting of Darwin's second strand on mate selection. There are more complex aesthetic reasons as well, occurring in stages, and potentially in their unfolding, more time-demanding.[39] Yet, above all, and for whatever reason, we have attended—*we have noticed.* And not just for living creatures in a mating dance, but for creations of humans and of nature, including sunsets and mountains, seascapes and tides and frothy waves, wind blowing through the grass, and the plethora of uncountable and miraculous stars. We marvel at galaxies so far beyond our own (and so long ago—recalling the finite speed of light), and the vast expanses of mystery yet remaining in our cosmos.

Beyond this, many other moments, more modestly, more locally, or so it may seem, on the sandy beach, in the nearby parking lot, driving to the store, across diverse motives and possibilities, may provide openings, similar to Kant's, to attend to life, and perhaps the sunset for its own sake, for the *pleasure* it gives. That it gives deeply and immediately.

We Are Changed—Often Quickly

Whatever the reasons—and they may well be numerous—we have been physically *changed*. Plus quickly. This may even take place generically, with a cohort, for instance, that cohort on the beach. I remember once from a mountain top, seeing a mass of smoky curling gas. It actually seemed aesthetic, even spellbinding. I was drawn to it, with appreciation, yet quickly also thought "Fire!" We certainly don't want to miss that one. Likely, few people did, though I was not with a group at the time. The news when we notice is not always good.

Still we remember this moment, in its immediate appearance. Our brains, our visual cortex, other sensory areas and experiences (sand on bare feet, wind on our faces) our short and now long-term memory storage, has now recorded it. The experience was all that glorious. Physically we have grown new dendrites, connecting diverse neurons, we have wired this experience in for the future.

Plus when our noticing is conscious, not unconscious, information may be shared more broadly across brain subsystems.[40] A breathtaking moment—which for some reason is important—has stopped us. Now it has become part of us, and through group participation and repetition too, it may also be part of our culture. Indeed, of many cultures.

Creative Palette

This material can now participate in further thoughts, wishes, memories, tales we tell our families or roommates on returning home. One might call it an "informational palette" as I did some years ago. However, *creative palette* seems more apt as we go forth to use it in creating our lives.

The moment, the experience, ignites, both then and later, further thought streams, links to other memories, feelings, possibilities, expands our repository of experiences, our creativity, our creative "palette," that is, our basis for new and original thoughts and creations now and in the future. Here we don't need one sole reason for recalling this moment. Perhaps we remember the sunset in meditation. Or if we can't sleep at night. Or if we are planning a trip with our kids. It needn't be about painting a picture.

Mindful Awareness

Let us return again to that sometimes elusive *awareness* from Chap. 2. It is also *mindful awareness*, at least in retrospect, when we notice, are self-reflective, and say "Oh! That was amazing." That state which, for instance, came upon me unannounced—and also in a breathtaking way—during that drive on the Oregon backroad. I passed the moment on immediately to others and without any thought. ("Look!") In that case, too, we were totally in the moment, beyond self-preoccupations (had not been true the instant before). We were aware together of something grand and precious, and with self not particularly separated out, a wondrous holistic experience. Reminiscent to me, also, of Rollo May's earlier experience of "joy and a sense of peace simultaneously."

In a flash, we experienced more direct knowing, transcendence of self, deeper identity with nature, even the cosmos. Our consciousness was expanded.[41]

Only in Nature?

Does this only happen in nature? Surely not (plus, remember, we are *part* of nature!). Yet it does happen in nature frequently. E.O. Wilson, sociobiologist, writes of *biophilia*, including in his edited book by this name.[42] We *want* to see nature, we even feel a *need*, at times, to be in nature.[43] Actually, we do rather desperately need the plants, physically speaking, or we'd suffocate. The trees, plants, greenery are our external lungs, turning carbon dioxide into oxygen. Yet we needn't seek out the trees and plants for this. Still, we do. How common to take a National Park or beachside or lakeside vacation escape. A mountain cabin. A visit to a foreign country with special trip to a rainforest. A hike to a distant waterfall.

The next chapter considers this more fully along with the fractal forms of nature.

Have you ever had the experience, block after block of cement and cars and street. (I recently heard on the radio that 1/4 of Manhattan is said to be streets, or paved). Initiatives have vastly boosted trees and parks, in New York City and other boroughs, including an impressively large number of community gardens,[44] and organizations including The Green Guerillas, which brings together gardeners, communities, and includes volunteer projects for students and more. Here are models for many other cities and areas which may not be as "greened." Yet is there a more intrinsic pull here than one may realize? E.O. Wilson spoke of a "biophilia," a need to be in nature.[45]

Imagine you are in such a "concrete jungle," and suddenly see a tree. A bit like an oasis in the desert? I sit here with some houseplants cheerfully approving this paragraph. I am glad they are here, the geraniums in bright bursts of red. We shall return to nature soon in Chap. 16, with chaos theory and fractals.

The Sublime

The Unbounded

Some differentiate *beauty* from the *sublime*, and Immanuel Kant (1790/1964) carefully defined the differences, well worth noting here and for the next chapter. Where beauty was bounded, knowable, finite, for Kant the *sublime* went far, far beyond.[46] In fact, it was dependent neither on any sense (sight, hearing, etc) or an understanding (finite knowledge we could manage). We meet awe and magnificence, sublimity itself because we cannot encompass our experience and astonishment.

Kant defined both the *mathematical* and *dynamical* sublime. The first renders all else small—immense numbers. (Remember we have as many neurons in our brains as stars in our galaxy, but can we even begin to appreciate this immensity?)[47] There are the towering Himalayas, the immensity of space and galaxies and matter and dark matter and dark energy too—unknown to Kant, and how astonishing. The imagination reaches an upper limit in ability to encompass all this.

Yet here Kant saw a paradoxical triumph of reason, one even having moral overtones. Our noticing, our awe, our ability to encompass this in our own way reminds us we have "a faculty of the mind surpassing every standard of sense.[48]

The *dynamical* sublime involves immense forces that appear to have ultimate power over us—earthquakes, fires, volcanoes, hurricanes. These days with our natural disasters, we might agree more than ever agree. Yet here too, Kant saw our human strength, in our appreciation, that "our person remains unhumiliated".[49]

Gregory Bateson[50] is insightful, too in appreciation of beauty through an honoring of mind:

> The primrose by the rivers' brim' is beautiful because we are aware that the combination of differences which constitutes it appearance could only be achieved by information processing, i.e., by *thought*.

Bateson's next line is extraordinary[51]:

> We recognize another mind within our own external mind.

Infinities

There exists more than one order of infinity—just ask a mathematician. But the single word will suffice here, being in itself extraordinary, awesome, beyond belief, and enough to bring awe, respect, awareness, humility and wonder. Zausner[52] compares transcendent religious states of awe, "an encounter with the infinite, structured by the familiar." She contrasts panic which can bring fears of obliteration. Awe may at best open us to ecstatic states, with "an intimation of eternity, and potential for personal transformation."[53] These can be valued across cultures.

Kant again, on the *sublime*,[54]

> Nature is sublime in those of its phenomena where intuition brings with it the Idea of their infinity.

We go forward with this view in the next chapter, even daring to ask if the small, familiar, and seemingly comprehensible, the jagged piece of pavement, with a small green sprout coming through, may also carry, deep within, such hidden power. Are we, as I recall learning Ken Wilber once said,[55] similar to ants on the pavement. We humans know only our own three dimensions of ordinary reality and have no idea of the greater world and realms we inhabit.

In these *everyday creative* explorations, might we then, the inquirers, find life and mind and creative inspiration going deeper than we ever imagined? Considering evolution, at least as we humans understand it, and our estimated 14 billion years so far, might it be precisely our human job, at this time in history, to seek new awareness and clarity, and to so explore it?

We have seen profound relationships with even inanimate objects, a deep connection that seems to go beyond a duality, a knowing that feels profound. We may see this in our life or someone else's creation. Further, beauty can bring us immediately to awareness, and a state beyond self and more conceptual appreciation. All the more the awe of the sublime, powerful, large, infinite, exceeding our understanding. Yet in some ways it seems we do understand. It calls to something deep within us. We go further with this potential awareness in the next chapter.

Notes

1. Loori, *Zen of Creativity*.
2. Character studies by Russell Mehlman, from www.bwac.org.
3. Rao, *Consciousness Studies: Cross-Cultural Perspectives*. See also Baruss and Mossbridge, *Transcendent Mind*.

4. Rao, *Consciousness Studies: Cross-Cultural Perspectives*, 214.

5. Pope, *Chinese Art Treasures*, 152.

6. Buber, *I and Thou*.

7. Cassettari, Chinese Brush Painting Techniques, 7.

8. Richards, "A New Aesthetic"; Richards, "Twelve Potential Benefits of Living More Creatively," 301.

9. Ross, *World of Zen*, 91.

10. Richards, "Relational Creativity and Healing Potential," 301.

11. Thich Nhat Hanh, *The Heart of the Buddha's Teachings*.

12. Norris and Epstein, "An Experiential Thinking Style."

13. Jung, *Archetypes and the Collective Unconscious*.

14. Richards, "Will the Real Scientists Please Stand Up?: Taboo Topics, Creative Risk, and Paradigm Shift."

15. Baruss, *Alterations of Consciousness*. Also see Wise, *The High Performance Mind*.

16. James, *Varieties of Religious Experience*, 298.

17. Puhakka, "An Invitation to Authentic Knowing," 9.

18. Baruss and Woodbridge, *Transcendent Mind*.

19. Ibid., 27.

20. Ibid., 107.

21. Baruss, *Alterations of Consciousness*, 217.

22. Gilder, *The Age of Entanglement*, 3.

23. Ibid., 252.

24. Dossey, "How Healing Happens," 15.

25. Santayana, The Sense of Beauty, 31.

26. May, *My Quest for Beauty*, 20.

27. Richards, "A New Aesthetic for Environmental Awareness: Chaos Theory, The Beauty of Nature, and Our Broader Humanistic Identity."

28. Ibid., 61.

29. Prum, *Evolution of Beauty*. Not at all the female as ornament for the male (known in species including ours).

30. Blijlevens et al., "The Aesthetic Pleasure in Design Scale." This immediate asthetic pleasure, for its own sake, and across cultures, was demonstrated in a visual design context, although transfer to other senses was suggested.

31. Smith, Smith, and Tinio, "Time Spent Viewing Art and Reading Labels."

32. Tinio, "From Artistic Creation to Aesthetic Reception: The Mirror Model of Art."

33. Richards, "When Illness Yields Creativity," 489; also Richards, "New Aesthetic," 64.
34. Nahon and Hemsley, *"Going Viral."*
35. Burns, "Sketch—New Year's Day: To Mrs. Dunlop."
36. Combs and Krippner, "Structures of Consciousness and Creativity."
37. Combs and Krippner, p. 143.
38. Combs, *"Radiance of Being: Understanding the Grand Integral Vision."*
39. Smith, Smith, and Tinio, "Time Spent Viewing Art."
40. Combs, *Consciousness Explained Better*, 62; Perceptions also join the "informational palette" for future use, Richards, "A New Aesthetic," 64.
41. Combs and Krippner, "Structures of Consciousness."
42. Kellert and Wilson, editors, *Biophilia.*
43. Roszak, Gomes, and Kanner, editors, *Ecopsychology.*
44. Green Guerillas, www.GreenGuerillas.org; from 1973. Today over 600 greater New York City community gardens exist, a nonprofit resource center, and programs to reclaim urban land, stabilize city blocks, and to help people and communities work together.
45. Kellert and Wilson, editors, *Biophilia.*
46. Richards, "New aesthetic," 70.
47. http://www.human-memory.net/brain_neurons.html. The human brain has about 100 billion neurons. Estimates of memory capacity vary widely from one to 1000 terabytes; data from the 19 million volumes in the Library of Congress represents about 10 terabytes!
48. Richards, "New Aesthetic," 71.
49. Ibid.
50. Ibid., 70, and see Bateson, *Form, Substance, and Difference: Steps to an Ecology of Mind.*
51. Ibid.
52. Ibid., 71. See also Zausner, "Trembling and Transcendence."
53. Ibid.
54. Ibid.
55. Ken Wilber compared humans in our usual realms to ants on the pavement, roaming in the dimensions we know, believing this is the totality, while unaware that there is vastly more to the cosmos than we have ever imagined.

16

Fingerprints of Chaos, Nuance, and Creativity

All beings are flowers
Blooming
In a blooming universe.
Soen Nakagawa

It seems we meet the infinite in everyday life, if unknowingly, in the self-similar fractal forms of nature. Here is awe, wonder, and great beauty, in patterns of dynamic potential, the "fingerprints of chaos" showing traces of the life force in action, whether in world or self. Nuance, then can call us to new wonder and creativity, beauty and truth, from beyond words, perhaps linked to "intimation," in creative process, and further fractal or chaos linked phenomena. We are drawn in, finding new potential for creative exploration and discovery. Is our nature even somehow receptive to being "called" in this way?

Fingerprints of Chaos: Path to the Infinite?

Chaos and complexity theory opens new panoramas here—including the phenomena of fractals, which visually, for example, show us "self-similar"

© The Author(s) 2018
R. Richards, *Everyday Creativity and the Healthy Mind*,
Palgrave Studies in Creativity and Culture,
https://doi.org/10.1057/978-1-137-55766-7_16

patterns that move to *infinity*! A tree is a natural fractal, alive in nature—trunk to limbs, to branches, to branchlets to twigs to little shoots that have barely begun. Not unlike the veins found in a leaf, let us add. Compared to nature, a mathematical fractal on such a branching pattern would never need to stop, in theory each new "self-similar" part becoming smaller and smaller and onward and downward indefinitely (or alternatively, becoming larger). Here is a map, in a sense, of the life force in action, "… an infinite series, a process in motion, an ongoing possibility."[1] Not surprising perhaps that such self-similar forms appear in Asian sacred art—be it "swirling clouds or fires of transformation."[2] Most people like fractals, even love them; they can be exquisitely beautiful.

Fractals, have been called "fingerprints of chaos,"[3] related to the microstructure of "chaotic attractors"; our fractals leave a clue and tell us "chaos is here." Or as per John Briggs and David Peat in *Turbulent Mirror*, "Wherever, chaos, turbulence, and disorder are found, fractal geometry is at play."[4] Yet this is not announcing full randomness or sheer anarchy—but rather a beautiful, deeply complex and underlying order. A fractal is "an irregular shape with *self-similarity. It has infinite detail, and cannot be differentiated.*" (Note: For differentiation in calculus one needs a continuous curve with a slope). Fractal forms—or fractal sounds or fractals using other senses—are described more below, and exist not only in life forms, or processes but in inorganic nature as well, indeed throughout our lifespace. By definition they look similar at both larger and smaller scales, and are seen in mountains, clouds, trees, oceans, galaxies in space, and in our own bodies.

Fractals can be seen to encode the microstructure of "chaotic attractors," the end state (in phase space) to which a system can "settle down." Yet perhaps they are not so settled—this end state can be infinitely complex! Chaotic attractors are bounded, yet embrace endless solutions within that finite boundary (think again of the branches on that infinite tree).[5] Here is a marvelous structuring, manifesting the sparkling beauty of uniqueness, yet within specific limits (as in the notion of trees), and in a process of growth and change in our fluid and dynamic world. Below, a little more on chaos and complexity theory,[6] and then if you wish you can make a "self-similar" fractal, and in 60 seconds; call it a snowflake.

Science of Change and Surprise

Chaos and complexity theory, popularly the science of change and surprise, is as one may recall, the science of our deeper interconnection, of feedback and recursiveness, where all is a part, is interconnected, and we all play a role.[7] Where "nonlinear" output may be much different from input; where rules are deterministic, and response to the smallest difference can range from minimal to tremendous—a little push, as one recalls, or that last datum, can start the snowy avalanche on the mountain, end a war, or change the world, including our own avalanche of creative insight. Plus there is that huge weather event. Butterfly Effects are everywhere.

Emergences, where "the whole is greater than the sum of its parts," are aplenty and characteristically, by definition, are surprising. Interestingly, awareness of *emergence* goes are back, before chaos or complexity theory in the scientific literature; in the arts as well[8]; examples here have shown awareness in Shakespeare and others.

Included is that good fortune where we, as per Shakespeare, hope to catch the tide at its peak, or else remain "forever in the shallows." Or where a chance meeting can change one's life. This science of profound connection, holistic order and complex dynamic systems, hums beneath a seeming "predictable" order we perhaps thought we knew—and some even thought they might control.

Rather, *this* slippery slope does not play by the older, simpler, imagined and typically linear, rules, with aim to know and predict and control; our is the vastly more complex multivariate layered and co-evolving dynamic world around us. Yet it is also one that is beautiful, wondrous, open with change, surprise, and new opportunity. It is one we have only begun to know formally, thanks today to the new computers; yet we may also have always had a "feel for it" right now, one that goes way back, not just for the present, but that is built into our human apparatus, our instincts, and intuition. Let us suggest that "feel" is often just what we need for moving ahead, for creativity.

Making a Snowflake: A Fractal in One Minute

Is it self-similar? Very much so. We can do this one quickly with pencil and paper. A very simple principle is applied here and reapplied recursively; it can lead to overwhelming complexity. For some there is a profound even spiritual ring to this, the ring of a deeper truth Do try it yourself.[9] This is the von Koch curve. There are several steps.

1. make a triangle, 3 equal sides, no worries, more or less
2. pick one side and divide it into three equal parts
3. Take the middle line segment, 1/3 of the original, and make it the bottom of another new triangle; draw in the other two sides
4. Likewise with the middle segment of the other two sides of the big triangle
5. Now, repeat: This time, take one of those smaller triangles; divide the base into thirds, and draw a little triangle on middle part.
6. Now finish the other sides of that triangle.
7. Now for all the other medium triangles.
8. You could keep on going—though you surely need not continue to *infinity!* But do you see how, in theory, that could happen, if one were able to keep going and going? In our physical "reality" this might occur down to the atomic level, yet in mathematics/geometry unendingly. How amazing that nature manifests this.

Our own versions of course have unique little twists and turns, a triangle not quite centered, an angle not quite 60 degrees. The artistic line of a pencil. No problem at all. Thus too is the uniqueness in all of us, as children of nature. The real-life fractals are what we live with.

Spotting a Fractal

A fractal as per Benoit Mandelbrot,[10] who had amazing intuition for shapes, complexities, and regularities in nature, is *self-similar.* It looks the same at larger and smaller scales (regularities in fact underline logarithmic scaling principles).[11] Here, with triangles, the output could look exactly the same, as one continues, stage after stage, or at least in theory continuing on with a perfect geometry. Smaller and smaller. Or larger too.

In fact, in our manifest world you will have heard the saying that "every snowflake is different." In numerous small ways, while still having that overall "family resemblance" of a snowflake, we have this near-infinite variety as well. All of the flowers (see opening quote), and so on.

For me, personally, they also seem to move, to shimmer, not unlike the bamboo artist's living creation. They shimmer in a way that heralds the next shoots yet to come, honoring the life force active within. This is not a still picture in time but a living portrayal of a process in motion.

For some beautiful images of fractals see these references,[12] including two further references on the scientific and geometric creation and interpretation of such images.

Can these fractals show a connection with our human creativity? Indeed.

Beauty, Fractals, Attractors

Many people love pictures of those "self-similar" *fractals* (similar at larger/ smaller scales, the microstructure of "chaotic attractors"), or the "fingerprints of chaos" signaling phenomena from Chaos and Complexity Theory, with underlying "attractors" structure.

Those fractals: People really like them! We find them on screensavers, T-shirts, calendars, refrigerator magnets, posters and more. They abound virtual landscapes in *Star Wars*, or *Star Trek*, or video games. They look incredibly real. Sometimes they are made or constructed to be a little wilder than the norm in our manifest world (*Wrath of Khan*), showing a higher dimensionality, a more jagged ruggedness.[13] I did a pilot study with art therapist and then doctoral student Christine Kerr,[14] confirming as Frederick Abraham and others had found that mid-dimensional complexity (a fractal in the intermediate range of complexity) may appeal more than one that is too calm or too wild. We had gotten participant written comments on fractals they preferred, and generated the initial hypothesis that highly creative people like somewhat greater complexity.[15]

Fractals, Beauty, Awe

They draw us in; they are beautiful. Why is this? One possibility is Kant's *awe*. Here indeed is infinity—the proliferation endlessly of recursive possibility. Beyond the scope of our minds to take in, at least in a more numerical way. These fractals can feel, almost, in a way, alive, like the bamboo, like the brush of the artist capturing life energies in motion. Things are happening. As stated, some fractals almost seem to shimmer. Although Kant separated *beauty* from the awe-inspiring and infinitely complex and powerful *sublime*, we are here suggesting—at least for nature—that the sublime and beauty are everywhere *intertwined*. That it is not two separate categories, but all of a piece. Nor is this about immensity and size, sometimes noted in awe—towering mountain, plunging waterfall. That snowflake that tiny descending and shining miracle of complexity can be just as awesome.

Some of life's greater mysteries are thereby suggested. Kant put it well, to paraphrase, our minds know enough to know when there is something vitally important going, and which vastly surpasses our usual capacity. We feel *awe*.

Fractals, named by Benoit Mandelbrot, being fragmented, and jagged, and might sound somehow broken. Yet not at all. *Dimensionality* on the other hand tells us a great deal. A jagged fractal figure, let us say the coastline of Great Britian, considered to have fractal dimension of about 1.3, is somewhere between a line (dimension 1) and such a dense figure is flatly covers the whole plane (dimension 2).[16]

Fractals look remarkably similar whether viewed from close or far away. Picture that coastline from a satellite photo, then an airplane, then viewed from atop a nearby mountain and again, as one walks down a path closer to shore. Still those irregular patterns, smaller within larger but still not only *self-similar* but somehow familiar. In a way, it is as if all mountains look somewhat the same!

Those little irregularities do sprout their own self-similar parts as well. Even if we think we drew a straight line with a ruler on a piece of paper (for our triangle or snowflake) a magnifying glass will show further little bumps and irregularities, in a way a whole fractal coastline beneath the tip of our No. 2 pencil.

How significant that so many people, across cultures, find the traces of these "chaotic attractors" attractive. (These are by far the usual, vs. point or periodic attractors, see below.)

Three Types of Attractor

Where do we find these attractors? Perhaps in a snowstorm, piece of music, a central construct woven into mind or brain as an archetype (such as parent or wounded healer), an odor such as citrus.[17] Chaotic attractors are by far the norm versus simpler ones, "the places in phase space to which a system settles down." These self-similar *fractals*, represent the microstructure of these chaotic attractors, termed in 1999 "the fingerprints of Chaos" because *chaos was here, is here, will be here.* Let us look at some attractors—things are happening.

The chaotic attractors that are most relevant to creativity. We also need differences large enough to reach awareness, so we will creatively and consciously react. For three types of attractors, think of movements of a pendulum which we are swinging.

- **Point Attractor**—the pendulum slows to a stop. Another point attractor, literally, is death. Motion ceases, no more occurs at this point.
- **Periodic Attractor.** "Round and round it goes," our pendulum. Plus it keeps going. In real life, this does not happen; there is friction, a breeze, other forces and small changes. Newton's laws were terrific but still not 100.000%. Even in planets going around the sun.
- **Chaotic Attractor**—infinite possibilities, within a general pattern. Truly infinite. "Awe inspiring." This includes ones which may differ in the tiniest ways from each other. Our snowflake, for example. Also all those branching trees, vessels, rivers, and more. Yet small difference can be deceptive. New creativity may burst forth with just the smallest input stimulating a jump to a new trajectory. To a new solution close at that moment, *very close*, but only for that moment. With "sensitivity to initial conditions," things are now off in an entirely different direction. It is our thunderstorm, hurricane, a stock market boom, a happy tweet gone viral, our long awaited creative insight!

Again we are talking about something dynamic, with an attractor. A process in motion. Realms of possibilities becoming manifest. These can encode where the world can go. Yet if the future seems predicted, encoded (without our intervention, at least) there is still so much complexity that, we, with our human capacities cannot begin to decode it. The weather was hard to predict (at all) until computers took over some of the work. Yet weather still remains a bit of a mystery looking over longer time periods.

We are again dealing with infinities of possibility. Is our awareness (as with the sunset) of these forms and potential, and our response to them, also *built in?* Is it surprising these might leave us in awe?

Might we be even more attuned in advance that we think—and at times have an epigenetic response?

Getting Personal: "Family Resemblance"

We even forget ourselves, initially, go "ahhhh," and become one with the sight. We are beyond personal concerns. We nudge our neighbor. We are part of a greater wonder. From the standpoint of *memes*, we are inscribing, sharing, multiplying, information of importance to all. One talented colleague with Internet background[18] believes a sharing of "something more" is the power behind certain Internet posts going viral. Here is something powerful and universal.

More powerful yet how the fractal forms of nature—including plants, mountains, river streams, also show similarities to those of our own bodies, and minds. Here indeed is a "family resemblance." These self-similar forms, these *fractals* are everywhere in the world around us, and we also hear them in the dripping of a faucet, or the playing of a musical piece; jazz provides one nice example.[19]

Our arteries and veins obey self-similar rules, branching, larger to smaller to smaller, and over time continuing to grow, and expand, arteries, arterioles, and so on down to the tiniest capillaries and branches supplying the individual tissues and cells. Neurons do a similar branching in our brains. Let us leap further from the organic to the inorganic, where patterns of water flow, resemble those same trajectories in the human body.[20] Have shown people slides from a satellite where the guess was: neurons.

Or alternatively, branches on trees. The guesses made sense; a similarity was present. Yet the actual image was the "River Nile from outer space."

Such a broad based "family resemblance" is powerful, there is energy here, a efficient flow, with pathways minimized (and how beautiful this makes them) to optimize the patterns. There is a more eternal wisdom behind these images and their evolution, which for 14 billion years has led to increasing complexity from Big Bang to matter to galaxies to planets to life and to mind! To self-awareness, to meta-awareness to creativity.

Thus creativity is manifesting throughout the cosmos! (We can take a little credit at least for our part) One can expand this into creativity within our minds. The actual objective creations we produce and pass on, can themselves show a general self-similar pattern among themselves, showing variants of a certain style and purpose. These have been described, metaphorically, in stylistic variants of an artist's ongoing work, as a set of instances related to a personal creative attractor. In a larger sense, all is part of the tapestry of life on this planet.

Fractal Memory?

How might brain structure help us generate deeper creative truth and inspiration?

Earlier, Skarda and Freeman's[21] work with odors was mentioned, including the sudden generation of new attractors in brain, to create "wings" or subcategories for smells related to citrus. Now we have lemon. Now we have lime. The brain is poised energetically (negentropically) at the top of a figurative mountain. Like the avalanche, it is ready to "*go!*" with the slightest need, as in the registering of a new smell. The result is a new attractor in our library of smells. Chaotic in nature, with huge numbers of variants possible. Not every lime smells *exactly* the same.

Increasing evidence is supporting a fractal organization within mind and memory.[22] Remember, this is about *memes*, about thoughts and feelings and how they are organized, and retrieved. Plus the further depths of knowledge in the fractal unfoldings, as well as in the interstices between areas[23] This is very relevant to our accessible and useable "creative palette" of mind as we generate the new. A new conversation in happening in a forthcoming special issue of a transpersonal journal, with a key article by Terry Marks-Tarlow[24]and multiple commentaries (not unlike a fractal and its wings).

This brings us to Wallas's stages of creative process and the phenomenon of *nuance*, in creativity, which might be linked to *incubation* or especially *intimation*. That is, below the known and the verbal—clothed in subtle signs, hints and clues—may be potential "seeds of creativity" which can call us. Let us join in speculation here, in the face of such mystery.

Call of Mystery, Creative Possibility?

Nuance

Nuance? What is it? Briggs and Peat, with LaViolette in *Turbulent Mirror* defined it as "a shade of meaning, a complex of feeling, or subtlety of perception for which the mind has not words or mental categories".[25] Overall there is a indication: the *possibility of more*. A clue to hidden depths, to further knowledge, to an unfolding beyond what we know and perhaps even suspect, toward further depth and knowledge. Something is there, but it may not yet be named.

John Briggs and David Peat further posit that "Nuances exist in the fractal spaces between our categories of thought." We are drawn by its promise, and does not this process of unfolding also somehow seem good or positive—important question indeed! One may recall the neurotransmitter "dopamine" and our urge to "explore." Or our Openness to Experience which can very much be engaged by our wish for knowledge, our wish to know. Two examples from the arts:

* **A Germ.** Henry James called it a "germ." A hint, a moment, a phrase that was overheard, a door opening to a new story. James heard a woman at a dinner party commenting about a mother and son fighting over an estate. Not only the basis for a new story, but a whole if vague sense of the totality emerged.

- **Bottomless Bowl.** Virginia Woolf drew unendingly from a childhood mosaic of positive experience and with an inescapable and almost magnetic appeal. For Woolf this involved a sense of: what it was like to be "at St. Ives." It was a "bottomless bowl" she said, from which she could draw, and again. The bowl would never be empty.

Possibilities and Wondrous Moments

Einstein Held One Fascination for a Lifetime

Here was Einstein, age 5. He was home in bed. Sick. His father gave him a compass. To little Albert, this was beyond amazing. Here was a needle that always pointed the same way. Something was happening that was not within the compass. It pointed the same way, each time, in the outside world, no matter how the compass was held. Perhaps Einstein scrambled out of bed to run this place and that with the compass (I am imagining this part); would the needle still hold true? Across the room, down the stairs, the pointer was still showing the same direction! Something mysterious, invisible and powerful was happening—what could it be? Einstein became driven to understand what we know as magnetic attraction.

Have you experienced such a wonder? Were you ever drawn by some *nuance* as described (or a wonder by another name). Age seems no object, either, since one sees 5 year old Einstein, enraptured. Nor is this only about science or art, but might involve anything in life.

Do we have a built in capacity, or urge, to question, to wonder? Is this epigenetically programmed? Will life call to each of us? Briggs[26] gives numerous examples from the world of the arts. What Henry James called "germs" of creativity, are subtle and fleeting but can take root and strongly grow. This relates to an interview study I am doing, called "Seeds of Creativity," asking about the lived experience of having an insight, of working with ongoing creativity, and finally this experience of intimation, of strongly suspecting something is there, without yet knowing exactly what.

Seeking Beauty and Truth? Might *Nuance* Guide Us?

Is our quest, when we are drawn in, when one feels a powerful pull, one almost hard to resist, yet not specific, is it sometimes perhaps the call of a deeper truth, a hidden potential, from our depths of mind below ready verbal or other symbolic expression? Could it be a call of beauty, or perhaps elegance (as used in the aesthetic of science), or of a latent truth, awaiting discovery, and shining with its own beauty?—a buried treasure in one's creative mind, calling to us? Let us further study creators' experiences.

Our artist may be truth-teller, prophet, and sometimes a canary in a coal mine. Toward whatever end, here is an expert at the plumbing of subtleties, a follower of hints, the wisp of an idea, the scent of a discovery. Yet whence this sometimes nonspecific lead, or "clue"?

If the call involves an aesthetic or a new truth near to emerging, such a draw also recalls the *being values* of Abraham Maslow's self-actualizing persons, including beauty, and truth, or justice. Barron[27] found that eminent scientists placed a high value on "esthetic fit" or "elegance" in their scientific solutions. Similar to artists, there was a clear esthetic element. Could such qualities be attracting our higher selves as we unfold our capacities, our higher creativity, toward a fuller understanding? Might the mysterious phenomenon of *nuance* at times help draw us in a direction of such beneficent revelations? Could they resonate with a deeper and more universal knowing, offering new and elegant and more unified mental reorganizations, on the path of discovery? When we get a strong intuitive call, these are questions, at least, to consider.

Philosopher Ken Wilber goes further, while following in the footsteps of Plato or Aristotle, with the Good, the True, and the Beautiful. These were less differentiated in pre-modern times. Largely from the Renaissance forward, the corresponding spheres of Morals, Science, and Arts have become more separate. Yet in a spiritual context, today, Wilber proposes, might they adhere more to each other? He draws on Buddhism, linking beauty and goodness and truth with the Buddhist trinity (Buddha, Dharma, Sangha). First, there is Buddha (and beauty), then Dharma (the teachings or greater truth), then Sangha (or spiritual community, aligned with goodness and justice).[28] Recall again that Maslow's Being Values include beauty, truth, and justice.[29]

Let us ask if such a coming together could (at our human best) support a propensity—be it through arts, sciences, or another route—toward deeper and more meaningful inquiry? An artist can express anything, certainly, although truth is often important, and at times the whole point. A scientist is looking for deeper regularities, explanation, prediction. Some eminent people have spoken to a deeper embedded morality in creative inquiries. Consider, for example:

The subconscious is ceaselessly murmuring, and it is by listening to these murmurs that one hears the truth.
—Gaston Bachelard

Life beats down and crushes the soul and art reminds you that you have one.
—Stella Adler

Art is a collaboration between God and the artist, and the less the artist does the better.
—Andre Gide

The more perfect the approximation to truth, the more perfect is art.
—Maria Montessori

"The most beautiful experience we can have is the mysterious. It is the fundamental emotion that stands at the cradle of true art and true science."
"The ideals that have lighted my way, and time after time have given me new courage to face life cheerfully, have been Kindness, Beauty, and Truth."
—Albert Einstein

Mandelbrot Set

For me—and countless others—scientific wisdom and breathtaking beauty alike are found in images from the mathematically derived, and exquisitely complicated, Mandelbrot Set. There is elegance too, considering that this single small equation, used recursively, unfolds profoundly beautiful virtual universes (and an infinite number of them).

The simple equation is Z*Z (or z-squared) + C (a constant) = new Z. That is all. Plug in your answer, the new Z, for the next round. Then continue. Where this formula converges on finite solutions, and they are displayed graphically, some spectacular visual images are generated. Here feedback and recurrence yield resplendent beauty. At all scales, here are whorls and spirals, not unlike many in nature, generated out of elegant simplicity.[30]

The Mandelbrot Set, is an extraordinarily complex and breathtaking image-in-motion—it moves and changes with each iteration—with its solutions seen endlessly. To be fair there are "complex numbers" in the equation,[31] where C is a constant with a standard part and another part including the square root of minus-one! A so-called "imaginary" number. Complex or "imaginary" numbers aren't really imaginary, let us add, as seen in practical electrical engineering applications, for one. Yet the equation $z*2 + C$. is nonetheless remarkable for its underlying simplicity and intricate solutions. Remember that fractals are self-similar, looking similar at higher or lower magnification—and however far down or up (in mathematics) one goes, it never stops. Here is Kant's *awe*, born and manifested in the infinite.

Wallas's Creative Process: The Two "I's" Before Illumination

One can link nuance, and feature of creative process to Wallas's five stages, and especially to the third, or *intimation*, the stage that is often (and oddly) left out. The series is: preparation—incubation—intimation—illumination—verification. This is a heuristic, a helpful framework is a bit artificial; not every process works precisely this way. Yet it is useful. First, we get ready, secondly we ponder, relax, or take that walk with our muse, thirdly, and remarkably (if not inevitably), we have an intimation that we are getting close, although do not have a clue what it may involve—we just sense it is *there*. We will definitely keep working. Fourthly, we encounter illumination or the Big Aha! Verification, the fifth stage, is pulling it all together.

Let us recall the challenges in "deep sea diving" into the recesses of our unconscious mind. Now we are not only looking for a shining new insight but speculating (or hypothesizing) about how this whole realm is constructed.

Now Incubation

The issue remains about our creative ability to go below the obvious surface of conscious mind and reflection, somehow to plumb the mysterious realms where content can further unfold.[32] What is remarkable is that we, knowing little at all about these hidden depths, may still sense something, feel it, or at least suspect there is huge depth below us, unplumbed infinities of knowledge to be found. Here is our nuance, our hint of "something more." We go deep to seek, to "incubate." If we get close, will we have an "intimation"?

Now swimming in the ocean of mind, we suddenly move out over a whole underwater cliff with many leagues dropping soundlessly beneath our feet. Earlier we also raised the issue of mind outside of brain,[33] with some support—this becomes less problematic if, for instance, one entertains a holographic model of mind or reality.[34] Can one fit this all together? Where are we swimming? We are certainly left with possibilities that can enlarge our contemplation.

The creative step of *incubation* gives our minds a relative leave of absence from the conscious realm to explore in a different way—what a creative capacity for us to develop. Listen to Post-It Notes co-inventor Arthur Fry, who outsourced his explorations to the unconscious[35]: How might we imagine his inquiry unfurled?

> I back away from conscious thought and turn the problem over to my unconscious mind. It will scan a broader array of patterns and find some new close fits from other information stored in my brain.

If we *incubate* creatively around some problem, how much better when we actually"have a clue," a direction, an urge, a hint of hidden treasure, that tells us how to proceed. What we are here calling nuance, or the clue of a "seed" of creativity. Here is where the step of *intimation* might then come in—with the intuition that there is "something there." "Where?" No—that is the wrong question according to Madeleine L'Engle, author of *Wrinkle in Time* and its sequels.[36] Not where.

In moving ahead, from here, let us continue to be unapologetically speculative. This helps illustrate new ideas that are current as well as stimulate our
own open-mindedness about creative possibilities. Consider first the unusual
creative processes of Nobel Prizewinning scientist Dr. Barbara McClintock.
She made genetic discoveries included meiosis and crossing over phenomena. Hence, we entertain her less conventional ways of knowing.

Dr. Barbara McClintock

Imagine this brilliant scientist and geneticist whose work on genetic
transposition went unrecognized for *decades*, even where she, not getting
through to people, and so stopped presenting at conferences. Dr.
McClintock had her own approach, which was not understood.[37] Yet
when the world caught up with her, and could verify her results using
more standard techniques, she not only received a MacArthur Award,
and was elected to the National Academy of Sciences, but became a
Nobel Prizewinning scientist.[38]

With deeper and sometimes artistic ways of knowing in science, Dr.
McClintock and others were harbingers; today we have Arts Based
Research[39] among other forms. Here, where enshrined areas of "science"
and "art," as if totally separate, can thus separate, be barriers to a fuller
understanding. Meanwhile one finds that Nobelists in science often have
capabilities in arts—more so than their less distinguished colleagues.[40]
Meanwhile eminent persons in arts and humanities show greater capacities in sciences than their fellows. How deeply our "silo-ing" of fields and
capabilities can impede our greater knowing.

Here was one experience of Dr. McClintock's which accords quite well
with others who have bridged ways of knowing and even differences with
the subjects of their inquiries or expressions—for example artists Wu
Chen and his portrayals of bamboo. Here is Dr. McClintock and her
process with slides observing chromosomes under the microscope[41]:

> ... the more I worked with them the bigger and bigger and bigger (they)
> got, and when I was really working with them, I wasn't outside, I was down
> there. I was part of the system.... I was even able to see the internal parts of
> the chromosome .... as if I were right down there and these were my friends."

Reflectaphors: Hints of Deeper Knowing

For another colorful deep dive, let us turn to "Reflectaphors" in John Briggs's essay for a volume in honor of the late physicist David Bohm.[42] The essay was subtitled, "The (Implicate) Universe as a Work of Art." Now we ask if ways of knowing, and unusual creative insights, could be born in the myriad part-and-whole and metaphoric relations of an underlying order of "reality," as with Bohm's implicate order.

Theoretical physicist Bohm is known for the *explicate and implicate orders*. What is manifest to us as *explicate order* (as in our world) is said to be a surface manifestation of an enfolded, and intermixed, as in a potentially holographic, underlying order of the universe. Look around at your room or environment. That's part of the explicate order. What we experience—our surrounds and, in fact, let us remember, this includes our own physical selves. A parallel with the movie, *The Matrix*,[43] might not be exact, but could still be useful in visualizing what might happen here.

What then is deeper? Bohm himself said the implicate order wasn't the ultimate source. Not even his *super-implicate order!* His view very much included a fundamental "absolute reality." What we see, as with Shakyamuni Buddha, in our manifest world, is but "a finger pointing to the moon."[44] Whatever one's beliefs, these poems are so marvelously worth reading.

In any case, at the stage, in our manifest reality, of arts and poetry, here is what Briggs said, in characterizing global dynamics of a work, for example, in literature. This could include "irony, pun, motif, symbol and metaphor." In resonance with *implicate order*, reflectaphors provide[45]:

> ... the intersection between its parts and the whole; seedbeds of its 'truth'; the nexes of the mind apprehending and the thing apprehended; and they remain both unchanged and in process. They are the artwork's hidden order.

Let us go beyond words, below conceptual mind: Shall we then find the purity—*and potential infinities*—and intertwined unknowns of deeper experience. Along with enfolded and hidden connections. Here again are possible parallels in ways of appreciating works of art along with parts of the process of creating them, enfolded in an artwork's subtlety is a potential to astonish.

Let us ask, can this also be part of a more poetic and metaphoric tension also *in everyday life*, which can enlarge our experience and communication as well. Particularly if we honor paradox and stretch, and are not tied to conventional logical rules and linear outlines and organization. In whatever way this hypothesis may appeal to you, we are deeper indeed when we got from explicate to implicate order. Such speculation can help further in our voyage—which is now one of creative mind.[46]

Whether we are swimming in "phase space" infinite fractal unfoldings beneath our figurative feet, and/or the implicate order, how marvelous that some aspect of our own subterranean creative mind seems to know what to do next. Knows how? Good question. How important if we can suspect enough figuratively, and intuitively, consciously to dive mentally in that direction. *In any case these phenomena appear very well worth studying!*

Positive Pull to Notice and Care

We follow the energy, open the mysteries. We stand in awe beneath towering redwoods, in the silence of a lushly vegetated wood. We experience E.O. Wilson's profound *biophilia*, this need and love for life. We can sense it everywhere about us, also harking back thousands of years. Through such stunning interconnections, manifested throughout nature, and through paying deep attention, making it conscious, we may further come to cherish our interdependence, view life more in systems terms— and we may, out of the deepest caring, wish more deeply to help preserve and protect the whole.

Not Out of Fear or Guilt

We can thus be drawn to help not out of fear or guilt, despair or hopelessness. But out of joy and awe and wonder, and a wish to preserve the precious, some would say the sacred, in our lives. If this means to relinquish a false hope of control (which out of self-interest, by many, has created spreading circles of damage in our environment and to us humans as well), then let it happen. Our better intentions need not be out of guilt or fear. Rather they can be an act of love. Here, in beauty, in nature, is a way in, to joyously learn about life systems, meanwhile helping preserve them—and ourselves as well.

Potential and Personal Rewards Going Forward

Below are further benefits humans may gain when drawn forward through scientific views and artistic visions of our interconnections with life, beauty, nature.

1. **Expanded awareness** in general and in very fertile areas for inquiry. For some this is a spiritual experience. For all, here is growth, appreciation, learning, awe and wonder, plus new chances to explore and create.
2. **Life Flow:** chance to appreciate life in motion, and for creativity too.
3. **Interconnection:** Working not just for self but for all, but gaining power with others, and seeing at times how small inputs can yield huge returns.
4. **"Family belongingness"**—experiencing in nonlinear dynamical terms, profound similarities between us and other life systems.
5. **Meaning and participation, our common heritage**—however one may define it, finding one is surely part of something greater.
6. **New worldview and view of self-in-world.** Profoundly connecting, co-evolving, dynamically renewing, and embracing our individual role.
7. **Evolution of consciousness**—exploring if potential may exist for a further leap in our collective understanding and potential.

We will become more able to see self as an inextricable part of a broader evolving dynamic, interconnected, even inevitable, ourselves in interaction with the rest. Yet meanwhile we may find a deeper wonder and humility. We know self as unique, yet as only one tiny piece amongst infinities of wonder. We have an identity, an ipseity,[47] or bare awareness of self, plus an autopoetic or self-sustaining keeping of our own flame; we are here and it matters. Perhaps we are standing on the corner of Columbia Street and DeGraw in Brooklyn, New York, or perhaps walking down College Avenue near Ashby Avenue in Berkeley, California. Yet meanwhile, we are of the whole. And so too may be the scope of our human creativity.

* * *

Remarkably we meet the infinite almost regularly; it appears, in nature in the self-similar fractal forms of nature. Here is awe in everyday life; these astound us, and draw us in, possess great beauty and dynamic potential, limning growth and change, the life force of nature, in the world in our own bodies. Phenomena of nuance, as a call to awareness and creativity, from below verbal knowing, perhaps related to "intimation," in creative process, may conceivably draw upon fractal phenomena of mind and memory. They can alert us to wonder, beauty, perhaps truth, and the potential for creative exploration and new discoveries. They also show us how little we know of mind and creativity. Yet, in the next chapter, some examples and exemplars may open a door for inquiry.

Notes

1. Richards, New Aesthetic, 72.
2. Richards, ibid.
3. Richards, "Subtle Attraction," also Richards, "New Aesthetic," 73.
4. Briggs and Peat, Turbulent Mirror____.
5. Mandelbrot, Fractal Geometry of Nature; Schroeder, Fractals, Chaos, Power Laws.
6. Falconer, Fractals; Mandelbrot, Fractal Geometry of Nature.
7. Briggs and Peat, Turbulent Mirror; Mitchell, Complexity.
8. Juarrero and Rubino, Emergence, Complexity, and Self-Organization: Precursors and Prototypes.
9. Falconer, Fractals, 4–6.
10. Mandelbrot, Fractal Geometry of Nature, 42; Schroeder, Fractals, Chaos, Power Laws, 8.
11. Schroeder, Fractals, Chaos, and Power Laws, 33.
12. Peitgen, Jurgens, and Saupe, Chaos and Fractals; centerplates in Gleick, Chaos: Peitgen and Richter, Beauty of Fractals; for visual representations of principles, Frederick Abraham, Visual Introduction to Dynamical Systems Theory for Psychology; Ralph Abraham and Christopher Shaw, Dynamics, Part Two, Chaotic Behavior.
13. Mandelbrot, Fractal Geometry of Nature, see colorplates incl. mountains, valleys, a planet, that never were.
14. Richards and Kerr, "The Fractal Forms of Nature"; also Richards, "New Aesthetic," 83.

15. Richards, "New Aesthetic," 86.

16. Mandelbrot, *The Fractal Geometry of Nature*, 25.

17. Richards, "New Aesthetic"; Guastello and Liebovitch, "Introduction to Nonlinear Dynamics and Complexity."

18. Nahon and Hemsley, *Going Viral*; Mehta, www.servicespace.org, personal communication.

19. Charyton et al., "Historical and Fractal Perspective on the Life and Saxophone Solos of John Coltrane."

20. Bejan, *Design in Nature*.

21. Skarda and Freeman, "How Brains Make Chaos in Order to Make Sense of the World."

22. Kitzbichler et al., "Broadband criticality of human brain network synchronization"; Goertzel, "Belief Systems as Attractors": Goertzel, "A Cognitive Law of Motion"; Pincus, "Fractal Brains: Fractal Thoughts."

23. Richards, "Creativity, Chaos, Complexity, and Healthy Change" (in press).

24. Marks-Tarlow, "A Fractal Epistemology for Transpersonal Psychology."

25. Briggs and Peat, *Turbulent Mirror*, 194.

26. Briggs, *Fire in the Crucible*.

27. Barron, *Creative Person and Creative Process*, 20, 97.

28. Wilber, "The Good, the True, and the Beautiful."

29. Maslow, *Farther Reaches of Human Nature*.

30. Richards, "New Aesthetic"; Schneider, *Awe*. In a humanistic and dynamic context we stand humbled and amazed.

31. Briggs and Peat, *Turbulent Mirror*, 97.

32. Pincus, "Fractal Brain, Fractal Thoughts."

33. Baruss and Mossbridge, *Transcendent Mind*.

34. Rao, *Consciousness Studies*, 144.

35. Kaufman and Singer, "The Creativity of Dual Process 'System 1' Thinking," para 1.

36. L'Engle, author of *Wrinkle in Time, Wind in the Door*. With mind in holomovement, asking "where" might not be a good question, although it is not fully clear why L'Engle kept admonishing, "not *where*"!

37. Also note that women then in science had gender-based disadvantages. See Spender, *Women of Ideas*.

38. Keller, *Feeling for the Organism*.

39. Leavy, *Method Meets Art*.

40. Root-Bernstein and Root-Bernstein, "Artistic Scientists and Scientific Artists."
41. Keller, *Feel for the Organism*, 117.
42. Briggs, "Reflectaphors."
43. Wachowski and Wachowski, directors, "The Matrix," DVD.
44. Thich Nhat Hanh, *Call Me By My True Names*." Astonishing poetry, divided remarkably into two parts, one on The Absolute, and the other on our Relative Reality.
45. Briggs, "Reflectaphors," 414.
46. Briggs, *Fire in the Crucible*.
47. Siegel, *Mindful Brain*, 99. *Ipseity:* experience of life without our constructed self, minimal sense of 'I-ness.'

Part VI

NOW WHAT?

17

Higher Horizons: Three Views

No problem can be solved from the same
level of consciousness that created it.
Albert Einstein

Some speak of "higher consciousness." Or of higher human possibility. Here are three areas to consider, and information from people who have explored or encountered these and attest to something extraordinary. It is for each of us to decide what we think. Interesting that everyday creative qualities might assist on such a path. Could one even find (after Maslow's book by this name) the "farther reaches of human nature"? We would not know what to expect (if anything), yet we do know that evolution has manifested a series of major emergences, from matter to life and then to mind as we know it. Are these over? Interesting that academia is taking more interest in these areas within the discipline of consciousness studies. While pursuing open minded inquiry, and creative new insights, it may be worth our asking if there could be next steps for us humans, and even ones we might meet during our lifetime.

Here are three possible paths to "higher mind." Each involves an exploration of human consciousness. Our creativity, broadly engaged, is relevant, with willingness to entertain the new, and personal qualities

© The Author(s) 2018
R. Richards, *Everyday Creativity and the Healthy Mind*,
Palgrave Studies in Creativity and Culture,
https://doi.org/10.1057/978-1-137-55766-7_17

including awareness, openness, risk-taking, and a non-defensive attention to higher purpose, going beyond self-interest to seek a broader truth.

We do *not* pretend to dismiss the more negative uses of creativity, nor
postures, defenses or other maneuvers that can make this possible.[1] Yet
we do posit that creative qualities can—*all else being equal*—give us
potential for a better life, happier, healthier, more meaningful, both individually and together, and lead to higher ethical awareness and a broader
concern for others.[2]

Furthermore, examples here range into the potential, at some key
point, for a jump to higher consciousness. The three examples here are
based on case studies or group observations by professionals in social sciences or health fields. Far from wishful thinking (and supported by cross-
cultural data across many other countries and many years, in spiritual or
religious disciplines) there seems very much to be "something here."
There could be other examples, as well, but these are presented for your
consideration. As Einstein said, we need to solve our current problems
from a higher state of consciousness than that which created them.

Plus, we can become happier, more at peace, more joyful, more able to
help others in turn. Surely this is an area—as it increasingly is—for serious scientific study in the "academy."

Finally, looking ahead, the Afterword, gives a 12 point summary of
some key issues we have covered. Then an example from the ever-cheerful
innovation called Smile Cards, developed at www.ServiceSpace.com. Use
of these cards brings us a worldview from the *gift economy*, a movement
which has already extended around the globe. Plus this example gives us
something we can all do tomorrow, if we want, and in a few minutes—
plus a simple suggestion.

Projecting Ahead

Who better than a creative person –such as those engaged here—to project ourselves ahead. We can generate possible futures, and also possible
consequences, perhaps to raise the odds of finding some good ones! The
practice of projecting or, rather, as Seana Moran puts it, *proflecting* (rather

than *reflecting*), has been the basis for futuristic explorations she has led with college students. "What might happen if…?" In tracing the spreading ripple effects of innovations, it helps to bring systems thinking into the picture. Take self-driving cars for instance, and now add a decade or two. What are the possibilities?

Further below, three explorations of "higher consciousness," could be part of such an "if" exercise. If we accept the premise, then what if our world, or a lot of the world, were actually like this. How would it affect our own lives, our friends and families, our communities, our happiness, our ways of meeting personal conflicts, local and larger problems, the state of our world. These three exemplars are given out of many others, and you may have powerful ones to add. Each of these involves, in some way, and to some extent, a different way to live—and to experience one's own life.

What the three have in common is (a) they come from educated professionals in social sciences or healing arts (publications from 1905 through present), who base their positions on case study data or (for the group example) observed group practices; (b) they intertwine with everyday creative living or efforts, and predict for jumps or shifts or even radical new emergences for human mind—meaning potentially, if you accept these exemplars, it could mean a jump for you, for me, for everyone.

Further, (c) although creativity can be used malevolently, *that is not the typical case here*. These examples each carry implications for better living, important both for self and others, especially at this crazy time; (d) each suggests new ways of moving toward peace and joy, satisfaction and purpose (even while somehow managing in this crazy world). As noted earlier, humanistic psychologist Abraham Maslow (who returns here again), said, in his private journals[3] that he saw his exemplars as a cutting edge of humanity, *"a growing tip (that will) manage to flourish in a hundred or two hundred years if we manage to endure."*[4]

Finally, the examples (e) may resonate with some great spiritual movements, although this does not necessarily make them spiritual. It depends on a person's own orientation. Yet all of them are very much value-bound, since they look toward a better life for us all. They also acknowledge how much we do not know, as well as nature's profound mystery.

Plumbing Mystery, Finding Meaning

Here, one can speak very generally of spirituality including a connection to something larger than ourselves, and a greater good, while involving a search for meaning in life; this often involves personal practice and experience rather than, or in addition to, adherence to a formal religion.

For some, interestingly enough, the new sciences, including physics and biology and let us add consciousness studies, are providing an entrée to spirituality—when they proceed in a more open, dynamic, non-reductionistic, emergent and interdependent way, taken with a mix of wonder and awe, and a bit of humility that there is still much more to be learned. Theoretical biologist, complex systems researcher, and MacArthur Award winner Stuart Kauffman's has two recent books, *Humanity in a Creative Universe, and Reinventing the Sacred.*[5] In each, emergence is front and center as we contemplate a deep and awe-inspiring order in a cosmos we are only beginning to understand.

Envisioning Possible Futures

Why Project Ahead?

Especially if we cannot know for sure? Better to watch and wait? Yet we are not passive actors; we also can help create conditions, environmentally, epigenetically, and pass on to new generations what learnings we gain. If we wait and see, others will do their own thing. Again we are heir to the actions of certain companies or countries or world leaders of questionable motives—or people we know right on our block. What we do influences cultural and biological evolution (yes, biological evolution too—shall we do gene editing or interface AI "lace" into our brains?). There are the many GxE (genetic times environmental) interactions we are only beginning to understand—why not contemplate them now? Not to give up becoming bionic women or men, if that is the outcome. It is about thinking it through, bringing caution, and honoring other bottom lines than that of profit—moral, ethical; is this good for everyone (or not)? Isn't it time to bring in a second bottom line?

We Humans Are Open Systems, Can See Farther

Since it seems our evolutionary job to keep creating, it makes sense to view the larger picture in doing so. We are open systems, we are auto-poietic (self-maintaining) beings-in-motion, recognizable tomorrow, yet drawing from far beyond ourselves, and affecting much more than ourselves. We are co-evolving, co-creating, alive in a cosmos of emergence. Is it less lonely? More meaningful? Could be. For some this represents a new worldview, as well as view of self-in-world. When we are in connection; when all we do matters. Online, down at the corner store, running for community office. As I write this, kids whose peers were shot in school with assault rifles, as a cohort are marching, and are meeting with state and national legislators. How big or small an effect they will ultimately have, only time will tell. Still, things could change tomorrow. Remember the Aha! The avalanche? The tipping point, which might be near? Whether a small change at home, or efforts on a larger stage, the results at times can be surprising. We may even start a good avalanche.

Looking Within, Looking Without

If we cannot always predict what will happen, we can at least know what we stand for. Our intentions, our values—what we care about, how we influence others. Hopefully we can live creatively and with awareness, presence, courage, openness to options (at least some of the time). Hopefully we have fresh encounters with life—not stereotyping or pathologizing others, or moving through our days like automatons, blindly following someone else's protocol, and missing the best in ourselves.

Meanwhile we can be exploring more deeply, within and without, looking both:

1. **within** our own creative minds, and
2. **without**, into the world we are co-creating and co-evolving.

What If We Just Want a Good Day?

No problem. Don't we all? Let us enjoy a walk, a sunny day, hanging out with friends, playing with kids or grandkids, reading a book, watching a film, making a meal, throwing a party, helping at school. Fun and cheery, yet each action is also still a vote—and a message to our own kids, family, friends and neighbors. Our style—and our intentions, values, authenticity, honesty, caring. And maybe a vote for a "new normal." A proposition in this book is that—all else being equal—an aware and open creative dynamic can help us live (and love) better both individually and together. Amazing if "evolution" is meanwhile keeping us healthier, for so doing, and also more disease resistant?[6]

Evolution of What?: Projections That May Include Technology

H. sapiens exist in a cosmos that generated matter, then life, then mind, then creativity—and then? What is next? The late Harold Morowitz, formerly of Yale, then Clarence Robinson Professor of Biology and Natural History at George Mason University, and author of *Emergence of Everything* (see Chap. 7) turned to Pierre Teilhard de Chardin, who was both paleontologist (including co-discoverer of the Peking Man fossils) and Jesuit priest. After all, Teilhard de Chardin was both an eminent scientist and theologian. Some trajectories and scenarios per Dr. Morowitz[7]:

> Teilhard argues that the emergence of mind along the evolutionary pathway of the hominids was as globally significant as had been the origin of life … just as life gave rise to the biosphere … mind gave rise to the "noosphere," the collective mental activity of *Homo sapiens.* I once regarded noosphere as a rather poetic term … but now I see the World Wide Web as a reification…. Human thought is collective.

Morowitz does see the power of (and potential worries from) our ever accelerating technology and genetic engineering. This view provides[8]:

... a world in which genetic engineering is used for us to become the race of hominids we want to be. Technologically this will be possible, but are we able to be wise enough to avoid unforeseen consequences? And will we know what we want the engineered human beings to be?

Alternatively, Morowitz speculates by opposing tech (in a more negative and less human friendly way) with human spirit, placed on two opposing teams as it were:

> There is every reason to believe that there will be a next emergence, and I think that candidates are on the horizon, possibly in competition. The first concentrates on robotics, genetic engineering, and nanotechnology and looks to a world in which silicon life takes over from carbon life.... To some it is a source of great concern.
> The other view, introduced by Pierre Teilhard de Chardin ... argues that the next emergence following the noosphere will be the emergence of the spirit .... (Morowitz continues) ... The emergent world of the spirit need not relate to past theology, but may introduce novelty. Emergences are difficult to predict before they happen.[9]

A little concerning? Remember we can also have combinations of these scenarios (hence our bionic person may also show "higher consciousness," plus other options). Who can even say? We are this "weedy"[10] species of *H. sapiens*, which, so to speak, can "grow anywhere." How crucial—and hence it is worth repeating—that we humans can also redesign that "anywhere." We can vastly alter our environment. What a powerful role for education—may we contemplate, reflect, and *proflect*. Pfaff's book *The Altruistic Brain*, for one, takes such a considered view.[11]

Finally let us add this, from Morowitz—where, given the state of the world, it seems possible we humans still have some evolutionary work to do[12]:

> Teilhard ... talks about the spirit .... the question for the spiritual ... some aspect of existence that goes beyond the biological (the second great emergence), and beyond the mental (the third great emergence) into the domain of something more psychic, *"a formidable upsurge of unused power."* I think that there is a feeling ranging from the theists to the existentialists that we have not fully evolved or have not worked our way to what we may become.

Yet if "emergences are difficult to predict," as Morowitz said, how can we guess, and what can we do? At least, we can, once more, know what we stand for, and can work to raise the odds of something good emerging. (Here, values of the world's great wisdom traditions, across cultures and over thousands of years, are not bad guides). Visions emerging from the new physics and biology,[13] or movement toward an "evolution of consciousness"[14] might in turn suggest deeper truth, meaning, awareness of our interconnection, wisdom and compassion, and greater overall harmony. Wait—is it *we* who are actually supposed to doing all this? It can sometimes seem impossible.

No One But Us

I do take heart from a passage Annie Dillard wrote in *Holy the Firm*.[15] We humans have stumbled along, but we have also created wonders. Civilizations, cultures, arts, sciences, music, rituals, meaning, sparkling ways of life across centuries and countries and climates from polar regions, to steaming deserts. We have been creative and resilient, thoughtful and joyous. Can we not do so again? She wrote:

> Who shall ascend into the hill of the Lord? Or who shall stand in his holy place? There is no one but us. There is no one to send, nor a clean hand, nor a pure heart on the face of the earth, nor in the earth, but only us, a generation comforting ourselves with the notion that we have come at an awkward time, that our innocent fathers are all dead—as if innocence had ever been—and our children busy and troubled, and we ourselves unfit, not yet ready, having each of us chosen wrongly, made a false start, failed, yielded to impulse and the tangled comforts of pleasures, and grown exhausted, unable to seek the thread, weak, and involved. But there is no one but us. There never has been.

Higher Horizons: Three Views

Here for consideration are three exemplars or possibilities with some support. The reports are brief but you are encouraged to read the original sources. Above all let us keep the door open for further human progress. We have powerful models walking ahead of us. Plus after almost 14 billions years of a remarkable evolution, there will likely still be more creative changes.

1. **Maslow's Next Steps**
2. **Theory U—Emergent Futures**
3. **Higher (Cosmic) Consciousness**

1—Maslow's Next Steps

Abraham Maslow was Professor at Brandeis, founder of humanistic and then transpersonal psychology, initiator of multiple journals, and developer of his well-known "hierarchy of needs." The "self-actualizing person" is very much linked with him. Maslow ended up with much more to say in his later career and in his writings; consider *The Farther Reaches of Human Nature*. Unfortunate indeed that Maslow died before further developing these last directions.

Maslow's original hierarchy of needs, involved (although as noted, not an invariant sequence) of

- immediate physiological needs
- safety
- love (affection, belongingness, attachment, affiliation)
- esteem (respect)
- self-actualization

Later Maslow added a higher self-transcendent stage to the hierarchy, as discussed below.[16]

Self-Actualizing Persons

Worth recalling that Maslow selected and studied persons of highly advanced development on his hierarchy of needs. These persons were opening to and unfolding their fuller creative and human potential, at the then highest stage.[17] He did a series of case studies. Many were eminent although not all, including: Eleanor Roosevelt, Harry Truman, Albert Schweitzer. In this effort and others, Maslow and the humanistic school were foreshadowing many emphases of the later positive psychology.[18]

Can we ascend to a higher level of human development in part because of our creativity? As noted, I and others have argued for the general benefits of qualities such as openness, awareness, non-defensiveness, and bravery—at least with all else being equal—for our more positive and ethical development,[19] qualities which also appear predictive of health.

Interestingly, Maslow, for self-actualizers, found self actualizing creativity and self-actualization to be part of one's orientation to life, and almost the same thing![20] These came out in qualities of daily life such as humor, openness, and approaching things creatively. Unlike the more mindless, and unaware person, these persons tended to live more in the present moment, not boxed in or bound by concepts, or abstractions from the past. They were more spontaneous and free, with less censorship, blocking, self-consciousness or judgment. There was a kind of innocence and ease to them, with an almost childlike naturalness.[21]

Yet meanwhile, these self-actualizers were also more integrated, and whole. While they enjoyed life and had fun, they were also committed to serious work, even seeing their work and play at times as related; further, it was often for the benefit of others. According to Maslow[22]:

> The civil war within the average person between the forces of the inner depths and the forces of defense and control seem to have been resolved in my subjects and they are less split ... more of themselves is available for us, for enjoyment, and for creative purposes

They were also strong people, "very easily egoless, and self-transcending"[23] What could at one time have been "deficiency creativity" (motivated by a wish to solve personal problems) had morphed more into "being creativity," in reflection of their higher and more general humanness.[24] Along with this came their *being values*, such as truth, justice, beauty, and of very real interest here in the context of dynamic living in the present moment, aliveness.[25]

Self-Transcendence

Interestingly, Maslow later saw it useful to differentiate two groups within his self actualizers—although there was not a clear line of demarcation. There were those in whom (a) transcendent experience was not so key, and others where (b) "transcendent experiencing was important and even central."[26] Maslow ended up with the terms Theory Y for the first group and Theory Z for the second. Sudden Peak and unitive experiences ("mystic, sacral, ecstatic"), fast and transformative, were more common in the second group; there was also the "plateau experience." This more extended experience was[27]:

> Serene and calm, rather than a poignantly emotional, climactic, autonomic response to the miraculous, the awesome, the sacralized, the Universal, the B values. So far as I can now tell, the high plateau-experience always has a noetic and cognitive element, which is not always true for peak-experiences.... It then becomes a witnessing, an appreciating, what one might call a serene, cognitive blissfulness.

Living in the *being realm*, or B-realm, as Maslow called it, with presence, expansive awareness, meta-motivation by B-values as above, seemed much more characteristic of the second group, as well as their living more beyond ego-needs. It is not that they were strangers to ordinary reality or the D-realm (deficiency needs). Nor were they any less motivated to be involved in everyday life. Maslow rather delightfully called this involvement, for Theory Z, the "Zen notion of "nothing special.""

Maslow found—again in "the most preliminary of explorations" that he was more likely to find these Theory Z persons not only in self-actualizing groups but "also in highly creative or talented people, in very strong characters, in powerful and responsible leaders and managers, in exceptionally good (virtuous) people and in "heroic" people who have overcome adversity.[28]

Thus the transcenders were often but not necessarily self-actualizers; others could have and deeply value transcendent experiences as well.

Particularly moving is this example, of a plateau experience, with the wonder of new life, as seen[29]:

> in a mother sitting quietly looking, by the hour, at her baby playing, and marveling, wondering, philosophizing, not quite believing...

In introducing his book, Religion, Values, and Peak Experiences[30] Maslow summarized that this Theory Z person:

... has a higher and transcendent nature, and this is part of his essence, i.e., his biological nature as a member of a species was has evolved (emphasis added).... The right label would have to combine the humanistic, the transpersonal, and the trans-human. Besides, it would have to be experiential (phenomenological) at least in its basing. It would have to be holistic rather than dissecting. And it would have to be empirical rather than a priori...

Touching base with a range of great world wisdom traditions, Maslow proposed that others who would meet this characterization included the: sage, mystic, Tsaddik, bodhisattva. Here was higher consciousness indeed.

The focus here was on extraordinary individuals and transcendent experience. Maslow[31] did say later that he wished he had also attended more to groups. We now pursue these in the next example.

2—Theory U and Emergent Futures

With this approach in group or organizational development, we, as individuals, are not imposing our will or own specific plans upon a situation. We, as a group, are opening, to an emergent future to see what its developing needs may be, and how we can meet them. Indeed, here is a fascinating example of organizational theory and change for a new era, within complex and emergent systems, as outlined in *Theory U: Leading From the Future as it Emerges* (subsubtitle: The Social Technology of Presencing), by C. Otto Scharmer, at MIT.[32]

The approach connects deeply with *presencing*, as developed by Peter Senge, Otto Scharmer, Joseph Jaworski, and Betty Sue Flowers, in *Presence: Human Purpose and the Field of the Future*. Peter Senge, Scharmer's collaborator and partner of ten years spoke of creativity in the Foreword to *Theory U*:

> A longtime mentor of mine once said that the greatest of all human inventions is the creative process, how we bring forth new realities .... those moments where 'there is magic in the air,' .... It pervades the mysterious state of surrender whereby, in Michelangelo's words, the sculptor 'releases his hand from the marble that holds it prisoner....' Against this backdrop ... Otto Scharmer suggests that the key to addressing the multiple unfolding crises of our times—and the future course of human development—lies in learning how to access this source of mastery collectively.

I think what first impressed me in this model was that, to access greater knowing, people meditated together. This is during the middle of the "U" process, among other practices, to open to the future and the depth of the field of inquiry. "Retreat and reflect to allow the inner knowing to emerge." Here is an altered state of consciousness. Creative magic can enter!

By contrast, picture certain institutions that appear top down and less sensitive to employees's experience. In the Theory U model, individuals were not impressing their will or own ego-needs on their fellows, nor was the group impressing its will on the future. With humility and curiosity, people were sensing, were learning from this emergent future. They then added their own piece. (Again, this is not unlike an Aikido master, in motion, aware, at one with the flow of energy, while working with it.) Recall Nobel Laureate Dr. Barbara McClintock, with corn, who, looking through her microscope, felt she was down there with it. I have been intrigued to indentify parts of this approach, too, in a personal self help context.[33] Here is some very deep knowing. Again from Theory U:

> The gateway into the field of sensing and co-sensing is total immersion in the particulars of the field—in the living presence of the phenomenon. It is becoming one with the phenomenon you study. It is not studying your customer. It is not creating dialogue with your customer. It is becoming, being your patient or customer. It is living in the full experience of that world…"

A medical and psychological example may be useful, a physician and team dialoguing with a terminally ill patient and family. I have, sadly, seen such moments not go well—where parties are not well connected or empathetic—and you also may have seen this. Lack of an authentic connection, awkwardness, anxiety about the prognosis, who knows what to say? Heartbreaking.

What if instead the clinician enters the larger world of patient and family. Four stages may occur for the group toward such greater connection, awareness, openness, authenticity and trust. One moves toward an emergence out of the whole, with a new and perhaps not fully expected vision for the future.

Do contemplate what it means for who we are and want to be, to be willing and able to do this with someone, to let go, to get there! Scharmer sees the fourth stage, **generative systems**, as "the central phenomenon of our time"[34]

The four stages as they might play out, in this example, are:

1. **Autistic** –doctor and family expound, each in their own space, poor listening, little happens
2. **Adaptive**—it starts, something new registers: fear of death
3. **Self-reflective**—further awareness, the system beginning to see itself, to see "we are the system," finding emergent plans.
4. **Generative**—"connecting with the deepest presence and future possibility"; now there is honesty about fears, life expectancy, caring, worries, what cannot be fixed. Now coevolution can occur into how people can realistically be there, and can help.

The group leader, the doctor, helps orchestrate a new structure. Far from "being driven by past patterns and exterior forces," she or he is able to help "shift the inner place from which we operate" while engaging the other in defining this place. Calling on chaos and complexity theory, one can see a shift for the group to a new group "attractor," a whole new frame, and context, and collective understanding, they have sought to discover, while conveying a sense of understanding and hope. The five movements of the U-Process[35] can be imagined hypothetically here, moving down the "U" with #3 at the bottom, and then up again.

1. **Co-initiating:** Listen to others and what life calls you to do
2. **Co-Sensing:** Go to places of most potential and listen with mind and heart open
3. **Co-presencing:** Retreat and reflect and allow the inner knowing to emerge (meditation can be very powerful here)
4. **Co-Creating:** Prototype a microcosm of the new, to explore the future by doing.
5. **Co-Evolving:** Grow innovation ecosystems by seeing and acting from the emerging whole.

Could it be that Theory U is actually prototyping new forms of emergence in general for a more humble, aware, evolving, and creative human future? Might there be movement here toward a more evolved humanity? In this process, we see empathy, group attunement, and advanced moral development toward co-creative solutions and a greater good. Individual uniqueness has its part, to be sure, yet within this larger container. Sometimes something magical truly will happen. Perhaps you have seen such shifts. They can bring chills.

3—Higher (Cosmic) Consciousness

Dr. Richard Maurice Bucke in 1905, a physician, compiled a book which has now become a classic, *Cosmic Consciousness*,[36] framed as a study "in the evolution of the human mind." Dr. Bucke included characterizations, profiles, and sometimes interviews he had done over a number years. Bucke gave 36 instances including great sages such as Gautama the Buddha, Jesus the Christ, Paul, Mohammed, and on to others in arts and diverse other aspects of life. His purpose in his selected case studies of exceptional individuals living and dead, was to illustrate among persons already "more qualified"[37] (typically in their 30s, moral nature, warm heart, courage, and other positive qualities), that these rare individuals can break quite suddenly with earlier functioning, with a death of the old, and birth of the new.

Bucke gave particular attention to Walt Whitman, our exemplar here, and wrote of him in summer 1880, while personally visiting. Dr. Bucke could identify those writings which followed shortly after a sudden transformation Whitman had reported. Of his own impressions, Bucke described Walt Whitman in saintly terms, distinguished, 6 feet tall, never in anger, charmismatic, creating a glow in some who visited him.

What follows is from early in Whitman's folio, *Leaves of Grass*,[38] followed by a different verse and quotation from a prose work. First:

    …. Swiftly arose and spread around me the peace
and joy and knowledge that pass all the art and
argument of the earth;
And I know that the hand of God is the older hand
of my own.
And I know that the spirit of God is the oldest brother

of my own,
And that all the men ever born are also my brothers,
… and the women my sisters and lovers,
And that a kelson of creation is love.

Whitman also wrote:

As in a swoon, one instant,
Another sun, ineffable full-dazzles me,
And all the orbs I knew, and brighter, unknown orbs;
One instant of the future land, Heaven's land.

(Bucke compares a description from Dante:
"Day seemed to be added to day as if he who is able
had adorned the heavens with another sun.")

From the prose of Whitman[39]:

"The thought of identity…. Miracle of miracles, beyond statement, most
spiritual and vaguest of earth's dreams, yet hardest basic fact, and only
entrance to all facts. In such devout hours, in the midst of the significant
wonders of heaven and earth (significant only because of the *Me* in the centre), creeds, conventions, fall away and become of no account before this
simple idea. Under the luminousness of real vision, it alone takes possession,
takes value. Like the shadowy dwarf in the fable, once liberated and looked
upon, it expands over the whole earth and spreads to the roof of heaven."

*   *   *

Evidence abounds in such examples that there can be the profound experience of "something more." For Whitman, let us posit that higher consciousness, going beyond "self" and multiple other limits, to the
extraordinary, ineffable, and ultimately all-knowing, is not on the ordinary continuum at all. There is a jump here.

Yet however rare and extraordinary, this is not for a few—but ultimately, if it is sought, for everyone.

Experiences do of course vary, yet it is useful to compare Pahnke's nine
core characteristics of mysticism; these also encompass William James's
qualities for mystical spiritual experience.[40]

Mystical Experience

One may consider this a study of consciousness, not necessarily linked to a particular spiritual or religious tradition, although it may be. Either way, a greater good may well be an outcome.

Pahnke[41] from extensively reviewing the literature, identified nine core characteristics:

- **unity** (subject-object dichotomy is transcended)
- **noetic quality** (insight into the nature of being)
- **transcendence** of space and/or time
- **sense of sacredness**
- **deeply felt positive mood**
- **paradoxicality** (may violate normal logical principles, e.g., empty unity containing all)
- **ineffability** (cannot be adequately expressed)
- **transiency** (compared to everyday consciousness)
- **positive change in attitude/behavior**

Do note that this, and the two other examples of "higher consciousness" given here represent only a tiny taste of each area, and do not claim full or accurate accounts of anything at all!

Except that: Something important is here! Plus it has consensual validation across multiple persons, and has documentation as well. How remarkable, perhaps, that these are experiences and realizations we too might have. If any of this calls to you, do find and investigate what resonates for you and, of great importance, if possible, seek out a qualified guide or teacher. These are experiential learnings, and promising ones. Four issues/findings that appear very important across reports include:

1. A fit with Pahnke's/William James's descriptors for spiritual experience[42]
2. Those reporting this expanded awareness (while beyond words!) become much less concerned with earlier life issues, with self, less afraid of death, more ethical and purified in outlook, more wanting to help others.[43]
3. A fit with a further level of growth and concern, well beyond the individual and personality, however varied other details, and across time

and culture. Morowitz saw it as further emergence, beyond mind to spirit.[44] He hoped it to be the next emergence.

4. In our troubled world today, this vastly higher potential fits with Einstein's dictum that certain problems can only be solved at a level beyond that which created them.

Chogyam Trungpa Rinpoche, beloved teacher from Tibet, and one of the first to come to the United States, wrote and spoke extensively on being a "spiritual warrior."[45] This is certainly not about proselytizing others, and absolutely not about armed conflict. Rather it concerns offering generously of wisdom and compassion to help those who suffer, to lower the pain, to increase the capacity for joy and healing and growth. (Again this is not unlike many other world wisdom traditions; do know the present author writes from an interfaith perspective). What we do see, beyond academia, is a great many recognized teachers and holy figures reporting other such experiences, framed in different traditions.

His Holiness the Dalai Lama, in his book, *Beyond Religion: Ethics for A Whole World*, proposed "two pillars for secular ethics," seen as uniting diverse world traditions, and potentially all of us. How marvelous this commonality! Focus is on *shared humanity*, and on our *interdependence*.

* recognition of our shared humanity and our shared aspiration to happiness and the avoidance of suffering
* Understanding of interdependence as a key feature of human reality, including our biological reality as social animals.

New Bridges Between Western Science and Spirituality

Entrées into Academia

An important sign to this author is increasing recognition and study of such phenomena in academia, and integration of scientific inquiry into some spiritual traditions. The literature is growing, with fascinating and sometimes surprising results.

Among earlier examples is a 1983 book edited by Ken Wilber, along with Jack Engler and Daniel Brown, *Transformations of Consciousness*.[46] It scientifically explores levels of development as well as stages of meditation across traditions for highly realized practitioners. A chapter by Brown and Engler, for instance, gives stunning detail on such exceptional beings from assessments including the Rorschach (inkblot) Tests!

Among a growing number of newer scientific publications is the celebrated 2017 book *Altered Traits*, by Daniel Goleman and Richard Davidson (mentioned earlier), which integrates many years of careful research. Three levels of meditative accomplishment are compared, throughout, with outcomes including major changes in the actual *physical* brain.[47] For some readers (including skeptics and unbelievers), such physical evidence is particularly compelling.

Meanwhile, the spiritual results, including deep changes in one's life, happiness, and purpose can be phenomenal. Such research is now being disseminated beyond scientists and academia to a more general readership. In fact I gifted several people this last year—including someone who had suffered a severe stroke—with a related CD by Rick Hanson, Ph.D., and Richard Mendius, M.D., *Meditations to Change Your Brain*. Remember, the brain (and we) are open interconnected systems and always changing.

Among other resources for the scholar, one may note a massive compilation by the Institute of Noetic Sciences, of decades of research on meditation,[48] work which continues and expands today. For a quick view, just try Google or Google Scholar.

With regard to exceptional and realized women, specifically, the venerable Tibetan Buddhist nun and academic, Karma Lekshe Tsomo, Professor of Theology and Religious Studies at the University of San Diego, has edited a powerful series of volumes from 1988 to document the experiences of accomplished Buddhist female figures, including *Buddhist Women Across Cultures*, *Buddhist Women and Social Justice*, and *Eminent Buddhist Women*.[49] These collections illuminate the struggles and breakthroughs of accomplished and remarkable Buddhist women, monastic and lay, from diverse countries around the world.

Vietnamese monk, Zen Master, and powerful teacher I am privileged to know, Thich Minh Duc, contributed a chapter to yet another edited volume in this series, *Innovative Buddhist Women: Swimming Against the Stream*.[50] He documented the life and accomplishments of the venerable Vietnamese

Buddhist Abbess and nun, the late Dam Luu. Each of them had worked in Vietnam and in the United States. The many achievements of this remarkable nun and abbess included—after immigrating to the US with less than $20 and no English—founding a nunnery and a major community temple, widely known in San Jose, CA, and surrounds. The founding monastics offered a spiritual and cultural center to many, including those who had come from a war-torn country. I had the privilege of a number of encounters with the remarkable Dam Luu as did my then young daughter, who seemed magnetically drawn to her (and drew pictures in her temple office). After Dam Luu died, her cremation revealed multicolored precious relics called sarira. Visitors came from around the world to honor her, and I too was privileged to be present.

I recall her saying how each new nun was like "the lighting of a candle." May we all help spread the light.

Let us also recall the organizational accomplishments of Tibetan nun and academic figure Karma Lekshe Tsomo and a global network of associates, who founded *Sakyadhita* in 1987. This international organization for Buddhist women, monastic and lay, has initiated activities featuring a series of biennial international conferences throughout Asia and the world. As per *Sakyadhita's* orientation of openness and equity, presenters and attendees include both women and men, with academic professionals also included. Gatherings are, furthermore, broadly open to men, women, and children of all religions or none.[51] Translators are present for multilingual access, and a large book of proceedings is available in several languages. When the first conference convened, in 1987, in Bodhgaya, India, the site of Shakyamuni Buddha's enlightenment, the keynote address was presented by His Holiness the Dalai Lama.

In general, Sakyadhita's guiding objectives involve spiritual and secular welfare for all the world's women, specifically including gender equity in Buddhist education and opportunities, including ordination, and assisted by research, publication, social action, interfaith dialogue, and efforts toward world peace. Let us recall that one is speaking, here, of *more than 50% of the world's population.*

The 2017 *Sakyadhita* conference was convened at the University of Hong Kong, with almost 1,000 attendees from 32 countries. Formal presentations featured varied issues in contemplation, cultural exchange, and social action. Examples of workshops included practices and benefits of meditation, arts and spirituality, and compassionate listening. My former doctoral student Ting Chuk Lai, Ph.D., and I co-presented two workshops involving arts experience based on chaos theory, creativity, interconnection, and collaboration in the present moment (while noting the typical dissolving of limiting gender stereotypes seen with higher creativity (see Chap. 9)—and, also interestingly, with spiritual accomplishment). We opened each workshop reading from Murcott's edited book of ancient "enlightenment poems" of Buddhist women (such poems being a longstanding tradition of monks).[52] Across more than 2500 years, which is to say, remarkably spanning over two and a half *millennia*, "Mitta" spoke to us—just as if she were next door. Mitta's words can readily bring tears (of joy). May all who wish it follow her path.

The 2019 *Sakyadhita* conference will be convened in Australia. Perhaps a reader here will attend one of these international gatherings.

Let us further highlight His Holiness the Dalai Lama as a key influence and exemplar of a spiritual leader who has long bridged, and publicly continues to bridge, science and spirituality, through presentations, publications, and more. Past events include over two dozen meetings with Western scientists along with related publications from his Mind and Life Institute. One notable early book of published lectures is called *The Dalai Lama at Harvard*.[53] As described in the record of the 26th such meeting held since 1987, the objective of the Mind and Life Institute has been[54]:

> ... arranging for the Dalai Lama and leading scientists and philosophers to meet for in-depth conversations, extending up to a week, on topics as diverse as physics, neuroscience, emotions, consciousness, ecology, economics, and wellness .... the Dalai Lama and other monastic scholars engage with experts ... to creatively but critically investigate important themes from the perspective of ... Western science and Tibetan Buddhism. The hope is that such cross cultural, interdisciplinary dialogue will lead to mutual enrichment and new insights about the nature of reality, the human mind, and human behavior.

An earlier event included my long-time colleague from McLean Hospital and Harvard Medical School, Psychobiologist Steven Matthysse, Ph.D., who was moved by this coming together and its insights. Other participants at this event included Herbert Benson, Daniel Goleman,

Howard Gardner, Robert Thurman, and Joseph Schildkraut, where Dr. Benson (author of *Relaxation Response*) helped co-edit the corresponding book, *Mind Science: An East-West Dialogue*. In the Foreword, His Holiness the Dalai Lama said he has

> ... always stressed the importance of combining both the mental and mate-rial approach to achieving happiness for humankind."[55]

The 2017 book noted earlier, which reported on the now *twenty-sixth* (26th) such dialogue, is entitled *The Monastery and the Microscope: Conversations with The Dalai Lama on Mind, Mindfulness, and the Nature of Reality*. This collection opens to us all a new type of meeting, quite dif-ferent in "mission and scope." Edited by Wendy Hasenkamp, Ph.D., Science Director at the Mind and Life Institute, along with Janna R. White,[56] the event drew from dialogues with scientists who met, not in a public forum, or retreat setting but in a monastic environment with literally thousands of monks and nuns in attendance. The event was also live-streamed and ultimately viewed worldwide by more than 10,000 people!

Topics were compelling indeed, and of vast range; the four book sub-sections involved "Quantum Physics and the Nature of Reality," "Consciousness Studies and the Nature of Mind," "Neuroscience and Neuroplasticity," and "Contemplative Practice in the World." One can appreciate H.H. the Dalai Lama's desire to share more broadly, along with an eager public's desire to learn. According to the editors, The Dalai Lama, from his own studies, discovered:

> ... that Buddhism and Western science had much in common, particularly their focus on rigorous empirical investigation ... to discern the truth. In order .... to achieve their shared purpose, these emerging dialogues should not be sequestered in the halls of academia or available only to a privileged few. They (need) to reach out to everyone who might benefit from this shared learning...

There are even pilot programs to teach scientific methods and discov-eries to monastics. The editor of seeing *Monastery and the Microscope*, Dr. Wendy Hasenkamp, while at Emory University conducting cognitive neuroscience research on meditation, helped design a neuroscience curriculum for the Emory-Tibet Science Initiative (ETSI). She spent two summers in India with a small group of monks and nuns to help pilot the program. Several such programs continue.

What enormous scope is now being offered to us across cultures in this modern age—and not just for a limited audience—these extraordinary and boundary-breaking opportunities to learn and explore while bridging Western science and Buddhism—or other world wisdom traditions. Such initiatives are opening scientific inquiry into what might once have been seen as very distinct areas of religious/spiritual studies—meanwhile integrating spiritual inquiry with valuable disciplines from Western sciences.

How provocative the emergent questions can be. The reader may recall that Judith Jordan, Ph.D., who wrote the Foreword to the present book, also participated in one of the Mind and Life Institute dialogues. As per her Foreword, the conversation with her group was important; yet most moving to her above all was the *presence* of His Holiness the Dalai Lama.

What this underlies this powerful presence as well as the benevolence, one might ask, which has been reported in special encounters, and with teachers and sages across other traditions as well? This is surely hard to describe, but I have encountered it a bit myself with certain beings I have met, including some mentioned here. Perhaps the reader has encountered this as well. The personage need not necessarily be a spiritual figure.

What is more, some aspects of this too are being researched. I have been privileged to know Tibetan Buddhist international teacher and administrator/teacher at Namdroling Monastery in India, Khenchen Tsewang Gyatso Rinpoche, one of many Tibetan lamas interviewed over 27 years by Henry M. Vyner, M.D. to explore experiences of the mind. Dr. Vyner's portrayals go far beyond Western mainstream models, as found in his 2018 book, *The Healthy Mind: Mindfulness, True Self, and the Stream of Consciousness.*[57]

How fortunate we are, truly, to be able to learn—by their presence and example as well as their words from—such teachers and figures, across cultures and varied world wisdom traditions. It may seem ever more likely, the more we learn, that some "higher horizons"—whatever these may comprise—could be possible for our human future. Possible for everyone!

Increasing Interest from Professional Organizations and Publishers

Can one readily encounter such learnings and cross-cultural findings? In fact, mainstream presses are increasingly involved here, including Yale University Press, for *The Monastery and the Microscope*. For psychologists and social scientists, it is important that the American Psychological Association (APA) has, in recent years embraced spirituality, (which may be broadly characterized as involving personal and experiential aspects of a path which may, for instance, honor deity, absolute reality, a higher power, or a greater good—that is, many paths). Conference symposia incorporating spirituality have become popular at APA meetings. Furthermore, the 2017 APA publication written by Imants Baruss and Julia Mossbridge, *Transcendent Mind*, already mentioned, is one remarkable exemplar for marshalling evidence to go beyond a mainstream mind-brain paradigm. Things are changing.

Of note for clinicians is the 2017 2nd edition of a major text by Shauna Shapiro and Linda Carlson, *The Art and Science of Mindfulness: Integrating Mindfulness into Psychology and the Helping Professions*. Among others, APA also published a book I edited, in 2007, *Everyday Creativity and New Views of Human Nature: Psychological, Social, and Spiritual Implications*, a precursor in certain ways to the present book. Content in such APA volumes is not limited to well-known mainstream science. Yet these and other books do encompass significant scholarship, and can responsibly work to open new doors.

While taking APA Books as one exemplar (again far from the only forward looking publisher), let us add here books from the State University of New York (SUNY) Press, which published the series by Venerable Karma Lekshe Tsomo, mentioned above, on eminent and accomplished Buddhist women, around the world. These and other major publishers have shown insight and leadership, presenting non-conventional issues and experiences (for the mainstream West) in a careful and well-documented way. Areas of study are thus expanding; things are changing.

Creativity on the Path

To what extent is creativity on this path? Using a process definition of creativity and a focus on the creator, perhaps a lot. Here, for example, is D.T. Suzuki, writing about the arts of Zen:

> The arts of Zen are not intended for utilitarian purposes,
> Or for purely aesthetic enjoyment,
> But are meant to train the mind, indeed,
> To bring it into contact with ultimate reality.

Or Roshi John Daido Loori in The Zen of Creativity.[58] Again, these are arts at a higher level. It is not about any artistic expression. Further, this statement need not be about art at all, but about creative process, including everyday creative living, manifested throughout all of life.

> The creative process, like a spiritual journey, is intuitive, nonlinear, and experiential. It points us toward our essential nature, which is a reflection of the boundless creativity of the universe.

To Ponder: Three examples were provided—and there could be others—examples which are powerful, different than the usual in psychology books, and which bring us something to ponder. Each is based on individual or group experience. Each draws on creativity, and unique paths of consciousness development. Each offers something for us individually, and also together. We live in a dynamic world that keeps changing, and changing faster and faster—will we get drawn in, will we play along? Meanwhile we do have consciousness, meta-awareness, and creative choice. We can entertain new creative outcomes (product), ways to live (process), views of self in-world (person), and meanwhile stack the deck positively (environmental press) rather than leaving it to chance or not so well-intentioned others. This author's hope is, for all of us, in our own ways, to engage what makes life beautiful.

* * *

Summary

We moved from creativity in general to a sharp discontinuity reported across cultures involving "higher consciousness," where creativity can be a key feature on the path. Three examples given here also have some scientific backing. Academia is looking more in this direction, in general. Meanwhile Buddhism, for one, is collaborating more with Western sciences. Will we humans also find new potential in our studies of creativity, specifically, so as to explore (after Maslow's book by this name), "the farther reaches of human nature"? Toward this end, let us nurture our "openness to experience," and explore courageously what may be most important for us and our future.

Notes

1. Cropley et al., editors, *Dark Side of Creativity.*
2. Richards, "A Creative Alchemy."
3. Maslow, *Journals of Abraham Maslow.*
4. Ibid., 168.
5. Kauffman, *Reinventing the Sacred;* Kaufman, *Humanity in a Creative Universe.*
6. Johnson, "Is this the Worst Hurricane Season Ever?"
7. Morowitz, *Emergence of Everything,* 175.
8. Ibid., 177.
9. Ibid., 184.
10. Https://www.merriam-webser.com/dictionary/weed%20species "weed species": having the potentiality for overpopulating an area an upsetting its normal biological balance.
11. Pfaff, *Altruistic Brain.*
12. Morowitz, *Emergence of Everything,* 177.
13. Kauffman, *Reinventing the Sacred;* Rao, *Consciousness Studies;* Ornstein, *Evolution of Consciousness.*
14. Bucke, *Cosmic Consciousness;* Ornstein, *Evolution of Consciousness,* Combs, *Radiance of Being.* Richards, *Everyday Creativity.*
15. Dillard, *Holy the Firm,* 56.
16. Zimbardo, Johnson, and McCann, 372.

17. Maslow, *Toward a Psychology of Being.*
18. Schneider et al., *Handbook of Humanistic Psychology.*
19. Richards, "A Creative Alchemy," 119; also see Richards, editor, *Everyday Creativity and New Views of Human Nature.*
20. Maslow, *Toward a Psychology of Being;* Maslow, *The Farther Reaches of Human Nature.*
21. Maslow, *Toward a Psychology of Being,* 88.
22. Ibid., 90.
23. Ibid., 89.
24. Rhodes, "Growth from Deficiency Creativity to Being Creativity.
25. Maslow, *The Farther Reaches of Human Nature.*
26. Ibid., 270.
27. Maslow, *Religion, Values, and Peak Experiences,* xvi–xvii.
28. Maslow, *Farther Reaches of Human Nature,* 270–271.
29. Maslow, *Religion, Values, and Peak Experiences,* xv.
30. Ibid., xvi–xvii
31. Ibid.
32. Scharmer, *Theory U.*
33. Beck, *Finding Your Way in a Wild New World.*
34. Scharmer, *Theory U,* 361.
35. Ibid., 378.
36. Bucke, *Cosmic Consciousness.*
37. Bucke's contemporary participants were around 30 years old, and male. However, realizations are well-known across gender and age, e.g., Tsomo, *Eminent Buddhist Women;* Kapleau, *Three Pillars of Zen.*
38. Bucke, *Cosmic Consciousness,* 188.
39. Ibid., 189.
40. Baruss, *Alterations of Consciousness,* 183; See also, Pahnke, "Implications of LSD and Experimental Mysticism."
41. Baruss, *Alterations of Consciousnes,* 183.
42. Ibid.
43. Bucke, *Cosmic Consciousness.*
44. Morowitz, *Emergence of Everything.*
45. Trungpa, *Shambhala: The Sacred Path of the Warrior.*
46. Wilber, Engler, and Brown, *Transformations of Consciousness.*
47. Goleman and Davidson, *Altered Traits.*
48. Murphy and Donovan, "*The Physical and Psychological Effects of Meditation: Review of Contemporary Research with a Comprehensive Bibliography, 1931–1996.*"

49. Karma Lekshe Tsomo, editor, volumes including *Buddhist Women Across Cultures, Buddhist Women and Social Justic, Eminent Buddhist Women.*

50. Thich Minh Duc, Karma Lekshe Tsomo, editor, "Dam Luu: An Eminent Buddhist Nun," *Innovative Buddhist Women, 104.* Sarira, as used here, are multicolored pearl-like relics which can be found after cremation of a highly accomplished Buddhist, and which hold great spiritual significance.

51. Wurst, Jampa, Rotraut "Celebrating the Daughters of the Buddha," *Sakyadhita, 26,* 1. Also Karma Lekshe Tsomo, Personal Communication, May 3, 2018.

52. Murcott, editor and transl. *The First Buddhist Women: Translations and Commentary on the Therigata,* 21.

53. H.H. Dalai Lama and Hopkins, *The Dalai Lama at Harvard.*

54. Hasenkamp and White, *The Monastery and the Microscope: Conversations with the Dalai Lama on Mind, Mindfulness, and the Nature of Reality,* 3.

55. H.H. Dalai Lama, Foreword, *MindScience: An East-West Dialogue,* vi.

56. Hasenkamp and White, *The Monastery and the Microscope.*

57. Vyner, *Healthy Mind Interviews: Khenpo Tsewang Gyatso;* plus a 2018 integrated volume by Dr. Vyner of 27 years of interviews with Tibetan lamas, *The Healthy Mind: Mindfulness, True Self, and the Stream of Consciousness.*

58. Loori, *Zen of Creativity,* 1.

18

Afterword: 12 Points to Ponder—Then Smile!

Here are 12 points to ponder. These are followed, on a lighter note (perhaps) by the engaging and now global phenomena of "Smile Cards" and the "gift economy." Here is something we can try even in the next few minutes. What would happen if we all did it? What *is* our human nature?

Twelve Points to Ponder

Here are 12 points or steps along the path taken. These are points I find especially moving in contemplating everyday creativity. I am grateful to be studying it.

- **Missing worlds.** We are missing so much of our world, our lives, our outer lives and our inner lives and possibilities as well. My shift of scenes driving the Oregon roads was a startling example. Alterations of

© The Author(s) 2018
R. Richards, *Everyday Creativity and the Healthy Mind*,
Palgrave Studies in Creativity and Culture,
https://doi.org/10.1057/978-1-137-55766-7_18

consciousness. Good news: we can be mindfully aware, choose what is of benefit, and develop it. At any age, we can be primed by nature (if we embrace it) to advance our everyday creative genius.

- **Change and surprise—new worldview.** We are also missing—or some of us are missing—a lot of what this world involves, changing, shifting, holistically emerging—plus in mysterious ways we cannot always predict. Can we see it? Flow with it? Ride a bifurcation over a bump? Not too late for us to adapt—for change, after all, is the constant. From avalanches to thunderstorms to economic booms to emergent relationships. The wind shifts; things happen. For many this is a different *worldview.*

- **Open systems—view of self-in-world.** We too are part of this picture, are processes-in-motion, are open systems, breathing, eating, listening, speaking, interconnected to life; we are not static and independent objects. Our creating is yet another aspect of a dynamic flow of life. From mountain avalanches to avalanches of mind, witness our Aha! Moments. We all have these, small and medium, at times very large. These can sometimes change our lives. For many, here a different *view of self-in-world.*

- **Ongoing creativity—as way of life.** There is one-shot creating, then an ongoing way of life. "Originality is almost habitual…" said Frank Barron. Taking the "4Ps of Creativity," Product (creative outcome) plus Process, Person, and Press of the environment, patterns emerge with altered consciousness, features of personality, cognitive style, values and more. Our actions may change them; they can also change us. Environmental Press even can be decisive, as influence, and some environments almost magical. Others deadly. Meanwhile epigenetic inquiries are showing us we can be more proactive in creating conditions for what can draw the best from us, and be of benefit. We are products of our biological and cultural evolution, in complex interaction. Best of all, we can share our learning, and down through the generations.

- **Healthier for us—truly it is.** Creating can be healthy and very good for us, physically and psychologically. At best, it can create greater inner integration, awareness, openness, peace and comfort in the world, non-defensiveness, aptitude for spontaneity and play, and can even increase immune function. Is there a mind-body message here to "be well" and keep on creating? Might we also live longer?

- **It can happen—with a "greater good."** Longevity also favors those living with meaning, connection, purpose, and orientation toward a greater good; religiosity predicts less in itself than if allied with such intentions. Maslow's self-actualizing persons show not only higher, "being" or "being values" (B-values including truth, justice, beauty, and interestingly, aliveness) but relatively less concern with deficiency needs (D-values), defensiveness, and lower levels on his hierarchy of needs. Everyday creating may be on a path to higher possibilities with personal qualities of spontaneity, presence, humor, openness, and (as noted a "being value") aliveness. It needn't be. Yet how qualified need we be? As Annie Dillard said, whether in good times or bad, "There is only us." (That is, we are flawed and human yet at times we are amazing. We all have the potential.)

- **Colorful inner life—let us cherish it.** Jung, Freud, Anna Freud, and others identified psychological defenses and barriers to our inner knowing, and learned ways to bridge or soften these (e.g. Freud and dreams, "the Royal Road to the Unconscious," Jung's arts-based inquiries, "regression in the service of the ego") as paths to meeting our deeper selves. Yet we also need balancing strengths (egostrength, executive functions, etc.) for adaptive use of our potential.
Instead of seeking, some can shut down from within, are closed, miss much of inner life, meanwhile defended, resistant, even frightened. Some may start stereotyping and perhaps denigrating the creator (and, alas!, our creative selves) as strange and to be censured. Recall that Frank Barron saw the creator as "both crazier and yet adamantly saner than the average person." Yet by "crazier" he really meant "open," and to many developmental levels. It is more to a figurative automaton

cookie-cutter conformist that one looks odd or sick. Our well-being, which is also well-balanced, lies precisely in a more open, accepting, direction. If our view of self can incorporates a changing *process*, an open engagement with the new, ourselves as processes-in-motion, then we can live in the freshness of this moment. Spontaneous, more richly aware, creatively present, and self-accepting, we can also move beyond worrying about any of this.

- **Pathology.** Paradoxes about psychopathology are related, and can be helped by realizing creativity involves that *balance* of diverse and sometimes primitive processing along with healthy adaptive strengths. This is a *nonlinear* and delicate balance—and learning it is an art of living. It is useful in much of life, not just in creating. A creative (compensatory) advantage in a family/person can indeed predict for creativity, *along* with relative health and balancing strengths. Meanwhile if one is idealizing illness, and worse yet failing to treat it, this can yield tragedy.

- **Evolutionary path.** Being creative very much appears part of our human role, and our joy in life, both in an evolutionary sense, and in what brings challenge and satisfaction to each day. Over billions of years, from emergence of matter to life to mind—well, now what? Creativity is a crowning achievement, and intertwines biological with cultural evolution. Our meta-awareness is a key aspect. We don't like something, we see it, and change it. What is next?

- **New Directions.** A pleasure at times to ponder these universal and timeless concerns, including beauty, empathy, nuance, truth and the mystery of deep creative urges. Darwin himself, who was misunderstood on "survival of the fittest," was very much concerned with our social nature, and love, cooperation, empathy (as sympathy) and values that honor our lives together. Subtle sources of creativity, perhaps carrying not only beauty but truth, are not surprising within one of the most complex human activities. We creators often depart the known, to move toward worlds unknown, endless worlds we have not yet even imagined. What may still await? Pierre Teilhard de Chardin proposed an emergence beyond mind to "spirit." Others such as Stuart Kauffman, have put forth positive views of a more secular nature (or spirituality redefined including understanding from the new sciences) in books such as *Reinventing the Sacred.* Let us use wide lenses in looking ahead to next steps.

- **Look more within, more without.** Higher creativity asks us to *look more within,* into our amazing creative selves, *look more without,* into the vastness of multiple complex embedded systems of which we are at the very same time, intrinsically a part. We can focus beyond our personal day and immediate needs (while not forgetting them) to ponder in dynamic, interconnected, systems terms the larger picture. It is also our picture—one where we too are (always) playing a part.

  Here is purpose and at all levels, potentially, health.

- **Emergence and higher mind.** As Einstein said, "No problem can be solved from the same level of consciousness that created it." What does this mean for us today? Emergence continues in life and mind (including ongoing AI, or artificial intelligence, developments). The details by definition can be unclear, since "the whole is greater than the sum of its parts." Whether larger or smaller changes, too, we also cannot say. Yet we humans do have our creative input. Further work with systems thinking as a way of knowing, and explorations of environment (and us) from Kindergarten onward could be helpful indeed. Deeper exploration of epigenetics can only help. Can we create more conditions for altruism, perhaps, or situations that otherwise raise the odds toward happier paths for all? How much influence can we have? *What is our human nature?*

  Finally, along this path, the author's hope is, for each of us in our own way, to engage what makes life beautiful.

* * *

Time to Smile!

Finally, let us end on something small, or so it seems, as an example. Yet it also helps us ask: *What is our human nature.* Or perhaps better: *What is our higher human nature.* We do have many possible natures, ways of being, sometimes all at once. If at times we shift unpredictably like Dr. Jekyl and Mr. Hyde, at times we may morph very predictably in separate settings based on different external expectations. Our "lower" potential was on display in research such as the Stanford Prison Experiment—and this is about potential within all of us, within humanity! Yes, we too might do those bad things. Yet there is also a reason the world's great wisdom traditions all have some variant of the dictum, "Do unto others as you would have them do unto you." (Darwin also cited this!)[1] In time, this too, and this even more, may come out as part of our higher human nature.

Smile Cards

Smile Cards—have you heard of these? This trend is quite real and growing and has spread around the world. Maybe you even saw these or took part once yourself. A good deed—that is the main point, as explained below. Then you leave your card. Yet at root, this is also about shifts in attitudes and values. Plus, let us add, about finding awareness, creativity, and taking risks toward new and nonconformist ways of living.

Yet is this realistic? Why not? A good deed? Anonymous one, too. Certainly the Girl Scouts and Boy Scouts have long believed in this. One company using this same *gift economy* model, involving associates of the Smile Cards initiators, here toward a larger objective in health care, was made a required case study for Harvard Business School.[2]

What Is This Card? Will You Smile?

It is cute, this small business size card, with a bright yellow smiley face.[3] On it, in large blue letters, is SMILE! And also the message "You have been tagged." Surprise.

Something nice has just been done for you, and without your wishing it or even knowing. Or knowing the person who did it. Now comes the suggestion: to "pay it forward."[4] Money, maybe, but could also be a smile a handshake, assistance at the market, crossing the street, whatever. The next creative step is up to you.

For instance, as a very real example, your car pulls up to the toll both at a major bridge (one of the favorite uses). You are scrambling to pay the toll. The toll-taker (before automation reached this site) is smiling, and says, "go right on through. The toll has already been paid!"[5] He gives you this colorful card, saying SMILE! Perhaps you see a happy car ahead of you, now speeding off, parent at wheel, a couple of grinning children, in back, looking out the window—for you. They gave this gift (perhaps on the parent's suggestion), and everyone is happy.

Or perhaps you never see the car, or the people. This is "an anonymous act of kindness." Significant how this can make us smile.

Smile Cards are a project of the umbrella group (though you will not find them on the card[6]) www.ServiceSpace.org. Do look for other offerings too; these include Karma Kitchen, and Karma Clinic. You can also watch videos on www.YouTube or TEDx, including features by co-founder Nipun Mehta or others. There are blogs, stories, e-newsletters to sign up for and more—it is well worth seeing the larger picture.

For Smile Cards, more directly, you can check an affiliated site (with the lovely motto: "Small Acts That Change the World") www.KindSpring. org/smilecards/. There you can look, read stories, or place an order for, or download, Smile Cards yourself You will not be alone. The site announces: "Over one million Smile Cards shipped to 90+ countries." So impressive. I will also run into people who say "I've heard of those!"

Half a Million People?: Probably More

A number of years ago, I was told that ServiceSpace had over a half-million volunteers—the number must be larger by now. I may be officially registered, because I have ordered and given out Smile Cards; I have also posted a note or two with a www.servicespace.org site. You can sign up yourself, by the way, at Smile Card sponsor www.KindSpring.org

(now has 104,000 members). You can also sign up with the umbrella organization www.ServiceSpace.org, and I recommend one of their inspiring e-newsletters. I have suggested that our students explore various offerings, actually, as an option for part of their coursework, for one of our Creativity Studies course offerings.

I know one of the founders, and have sometimes sent back, from travels, group photos, with each smiling person, from whatever distant place, holding a Smile Card.

New Zealand, Taiwan, the Annual Meeting of the American Psychological Association (APA), in Toronto. APA was particularly promising—where a smiling group of students gave out Smile Cards to attendees from across the USA and Canada. Now conference goers could return home to their own states or countries, and share in turn. Nice, huh?

ServiceSpace.org has also done some research. Certain Smile Cards were created for scanning and were followed on their journeys, with a group of student volunteers monitoring their travels. If you ever saw the movie *Pay it Forward*, one witnesses unexpected, dramatic, and spreading circles of benefit.[7] Not unlike the ripples of a stone thrown into water. In our dynamic and interconnected world, we throw in a bifurcation (the Smile Card appears!). Will there be emergences of potential new structures or influences; can our open systems reach to distant shores? So we might hope.

Origins of www.ServiceSpace.org and a Restaurant Visit

Here is what I first was told about ServiceSpace, from a colleague who saw it get started.

The founders originally did well in the computer business in Silicon Valley. They wanted to share the benefits. They started making websites for needy groups, including homeless shelters. They also helped some well-meaning volunteer non-profit organizations such as ours, www. AhimsaBerkeley.org. ServiceSpace grew.

Two of my favorites are Karma Clinic (healthcare in this model for those at need) and, clever and catching on elsewhere, the unique Karma Kitchen, a Sunday option at Taste of Himalayas, a restaurant in Berkeley,

CA. The latter has since spread afar to other cities. At Karma Kitchen, during a special meal each week, your food is free. In turn, you can pay ahead for the next person.

I once took my brother there for his birthday, but oops!, we got the wrong time for Karma Kitchen. We just had a regular meal and paid in the usual way. Disappointing. Yet we met a guy who had driven down from Oregon, all the way from the northern part of the state, Portland, I think, bringing along his guitar—so eager was he to see this place in person. He made some "free" music, too, in the spirit of giving. (Fortunately he also came at the right time of day.)

Three Questions

I again ask you and also ask myself: Is this the

(a) "way people really are" and/or
(b) the "way people could be" under the right environmental and epigenetic circumstances? Or is this
(c) just one select group of "do-gooders," impressive people to be sure, but only one pattern, and perhaps drawn from well-to-do and privileged people as well, against the unchanging panorama of a more brutal and less giving world. After all, who has the money or time to be giving, anyway. Who can even pay their rent or mortgage?

Then again, it is the giving, isn't it?, and not the value of the gift. The caring, the effort? Plus we have world wisdom across many traditions along the lines of the Christian "Do unto others…" We have His Holiness the Dalai Lama and universal compassion and healing. We have Tikkun. We have Catholic Charities. We have Unitarian Universalist projects. We have numerous others. There is a broader vision. One which crosses traditions, and crosses the ages. A "gift economy" is based on love and compassion, and on shifts toward contribution, trust, community, and abundance, rather than grasping, distrust, isolation, and scarcity.[8]

One powerful hope is exemplified in Pfaff's *Altruistic Brain Theory*.[9] We are intrinsically designed to help. Biologically. How then can conditions be created to further this possible course? At the other extreme we see how some horrific experiences, as in severe trauma, can actually methylate our DNA, attach a molecular unit which dims certain responsiveness (that is, we have actually shut down some of our inherited biological potential). Yet why wouldn't that happen? Our bodies mean well after all—this is done, in theory, for our protection. We won't let it happen again. Yet, as one knows, trauma can do much ongoing harm. In our traumatic world today, I often picture how methylated some of our DNA strands may be. (I mean for any of us.)

We have a lot to learn here, some parts carrying hope; our DNA is not the whole story. Long ago our cells got their marching orders. All initially alike, how did this cell know, for instance, that it would becomes part of an arm, that one part of the brain. Further, our environment and other innate processes interact, create a superstructure, and can call on certain potentials amidst what is there. Even today, we can change our basic programming.[10] Personally I see no harm in opting for the chance of (a) or (b), above, that is, for endorsing or at least exploring, the option of our higher potential, for putting such possibilities to the test. What more might we accomplish in real life, *in vivo*? For our own personal research, this might even include handing out a Smile Card or two, or doing a good deed, or the equivalent.

Longevity and Such

Oh yes, and we may also live longer!—although if that is one's sole objective for doing it, rather than the joy of giving, it may not exactly work. Would not count on it, anyway. (Or, on the other hand, it may end up opening people to broader motives along the way, and their motivations will expand.)

Do see books including the *eighty year* study called *The Longevity Project* by Friedman and Martin, using the Lewis Terman sample of participants.[11] Why do some live long and thrive, others die early? Many and varied factors were explored for healthier aging, even longevity—including meaning making, caring, community, spirituality or higher belief system, religious attendance, and more. You can also learn whether it is better to stay married! There is a separate literature beyond this on creativity and healthy aging. Remember our giving to others is not about self-interest. It is about empathizing and caring, connecting, and finding new meaning in giving, while co-creating in a dynamic world. But ok, we can feel good too. Nothing wrong with that.[12] We are smiling into an evolving and happier picture.

Aravind Eye Hospitals

Aravind, this inspiring vision restoration project, began in India, and from the extended family, actually, of numerous opthalmologists, related to a Servicespace.org founder. The initiator of Aravind, Dr. G. Venkataswamy (known as "Dr. V"), decided after his professional medical retirement to spend further medical time offering service to the community. Multiple medically trained relatives and associates ended up joining.

Did this model ever grow! It is now the largest vision restoration project in the world.[13] The way it works, one paying client allows two poor patients to be treated for free. And now three people can see! Aravind is what grew into the international vision restoration project that was made a required case study at Harvard Business School.

There is also a moving 2011 book, by Mehta and Shinoy, *Infinite Vision: How.*
Aravind Became the World's Greatest Business Case for Compassion.

I wrote an Amazon review in honor of my own ophthalmologist, Dr. Gary Aguilar, in San Francisco, who has regularly volunteered time for cataract surgery in places including Guatemala and China. How well he knows how vision restoration can change a life When the blind can suddenly see. I have met other opthalmologists doing related work in places including Haiti and the Caribbean.

Values, Guidelines, Principles

Do deeper values motivate all this? With Aravind and related projects, certainly, and in this case from a very deep commitment, inspired by revered spiritual leader, Sri Aurobindo. Such inspiration could surely come from other world wisdom traditions, too, and from elsewhere, including secular humanism, with "no spirituality required."

How does this sound to you? Truth told, the four features below seem unrealistic to a great many people. Or is it that they sound this way right now, based on the way one was raised? It is part of the question. What if we had a different worldview—more interconnected, empathetic, caring, open, aware, creatively giving. Might programs such as these be a signpost, on a broader way in?

In any case, with all apologies, I reordered the four watchwords a bit from the original[14] (the original order is also given above) to make a more memorable acronym: ACCT. Perhaps as in "**ACT!**" Or maybe it is a new "**ACCT**," a new "account with reality," with the world, with each other, our kids, our future? An acronym at least helps me to remember the list.

A *gift economy* doesn't mean we do not "watch out for trouble." It still makes sense to stay alert for those who might take advantage of one's generosity. The risk is definitely out there! It is just that we might choose to meet it differently. The four watchwords, in any case, are as follows (mnemonic = ACCT), with some comments:

A   **Abundance**—awash in good fortune, we also give to others
C   **Community**—working together as well. No zero-sum game ("You win, I lose") but rather, a "win-win."
C   **Contribution**—vs. grasping even harder to keep what is ours.
T   **Trust**—we work with each other, also with caring and respect.

Instead of what? Here again is that dreary and depressing list, which also sounds rather familiar in our sometimes crazy impersonal, changing and uncaring world today: scarcity (vs. abundance), isolation (vs. community), grasping (vs. contribution), and distrust (vs. trust). Must it always be this way?

One may connect this one model with our larger framework, of evolving connected humanity and global culture. Here is the *gift economy* from a personal consciousness now raised to global participation. Involvement touches on creative *product, process,* and even to *changing a person* and in culture as *creative press* of the environment—and broadly toward a serious bifurcation in practices, maybe an entire paradigm shift. Thomas Kuhn[15] said that paradigm change can finally occur when the data becomes overwhelming. Well, it does seem a lot is *not* working, right now, in the world today.

Cannot Do Everything: Can Do Something

None of us can do everything by ourselves—to put it mildly. Yet we are also working together. Those cheery white and yellow and blue Smile Cards are one example of a way we can each do something, even in a few minutes. We are one of many; what if we all did "an anonymous act of kindness." Remember, too, with the Butterfly Effect, we never know how close the tipping point is, or which, using the snowy mountain analogy, will be the "last snowflake before the avalanche."

We can at least try the spirit of a Smile Card (with or without a card or something comparable that connects). What if we did this as per a www.Kindspring.org/SmileCards 21 day challenge? Beyond the surprised recipients, how might this *affect us*? If results are really striking, we might even let www.KindSpring.org/SmileCards know.

What Is Calling Us?

This is a suggestion above, to consider, in any case. Whatever else you the reader do, something brought you to this book. I suspect you may intuit deeper potential within yourself—something important, and uniquely yours, yet to be revealed, in the larger picture. Please hang on to that precious everyday creativity, already present, a process which can open us to life, in the moment, and perhaps to higher paths. It is our birthright, your birthright. Plus it can be unusually healthy, and feel very good. Thanks so very much for being here.

Notes

1. Loye, "Telling the New Story: Darwin, Evolution, and Creativity Versus Conformity in Science."
2. Mehta and Shenoy, *Infinite Vision: How Aravind Became the World's Greatest Business Case for Compassion.*
3. www.kindspring.org/smilecards/. One can read about Smile Cards and order or download them.

4. Ibid. Also note the feature video "Pay if Forward" (2009, M. Leder, Director, with Kevin Spacey), entertaining while also illustrating the spreading and sometimes surprising circles of positive effects.

5. Richards, "A Creative Alchemy," 120.

6. On the back of some cards is www.helpothers.org which goes to KindSpring.org. Also on the back, a quote from Mahatma Gandhi: "The fragrance always remains on the hand that gives the rose."

7. Compare "Proflexion," researched by Seana Moran in *Ethical Ripples of Creativity and Innovation*—prediction of effects of innovations; we can seek benevolent outcomes in following the ripples.

8. Richards, "A Creative Alchemy."

9. Pfaff, *Altruistic Brain Theory*, 253.

10. Also see Moore, *The Developing Genome.*

11. Friedman and Martin, *Longevity Project*; Richards, "Everyday Creativity."

12. Some believe that, if we are not made uncomfortable by a good deed, then it "doesn't count." Buddhism by contrast, sees this as a huge source of happiness and joy (more than in receiving a gift). This is not to be confused with giving simply to get benefits for oneself—but in helping others, we can surely feel good too.

13. Mehta and Shinoy, *Infinite Vision*; Richards, "Creative Alchemy," 120, 132.

14. See www.servicespace.org; www.kindspring.org/SmileCards, also Richards, "Creative Alchemy," 120.

15. Kuhn, *The Structure of Scientific Revolutions.*

Bibliography

ABC News. 2017. More Than 1 Million Rally at Women's Marches in US and Around World, January 22. http://abcnews.go.com/Politics/womens-march-heads-washington-day-trumps-inauguration/story?id=44936042.

Abraham, Frederick David. 1996. The Dynamics of Creativity and the Courage to Be. In *Nonlinear Dynamics in Human Behavior*, ed. W. Sulis and A. Combs, 364–400. Singapore: World Scientific.

Abraham, Ralph H., and Christopher D. Shaw. 1990. *Dynamics—The Geometry of Behavior, Part II, Chaotic Behavior*. Santa Cruz, CA: Aerial Press.

Abraham, Frederick David, Ralph Abraham, and Christopher Shaw. 1989. *Visual Introduction to Dynamical Systems Theory for Psychology*. Santa Cruz, CA: Aerial Press.

Achterberg, Jeanne. 2002. *Imagery in Healing: Shamanism and Modern Medicine*. Boston: Shambhala.

Akiskal, H., and K. Akiskal. 1992. *Cyclothymic, Hyperthymic, and Depressive Temperaments as Subaffective Variants of Mood Disorders, Review of Psychiatry*. Edited by A. Tasman and M.B. Riba, vol. 11, 43–62. Washington, DC: American Psychiatric Press.

Algaze, D., Dennis Kinney, and Ruth Richards. 2011. Creativity, Mental Health, and the Potential for "Compensatory Advantage" in Selected Psychiatric Disorders. In *Encyclopedia of Mental Health Issues in America*. Santa Barbara: ABC-CLIO.

© The Author(s) 2018
R. Richards, *Everyday Creativity and the Healthy Mind*,
Palgrave Studies in Creativity and Culture,
https://doi.org/10.1057/978-1-137-55766-7

Allaby, Michael. 1996. *How It Works: The Environment*. London: Horus Editions Limited.

Amabile, Teresa. 1996. *Creativity in Context*. New York: Routledge.

Arns, Martijn, Hartmut Heinrich, and Ute Strehl. 2014. Evaluation of Neurofeedback in ADHD: The Long and Winding Road. *Biological Psychology* 95: 108–115.

Arons, Myron. 2007. Standing Up for Humanity: Upright Body, Creative Instability, and Spiritual Balance. In *Everyday Creativity and New Views of Human Nature*, ed. Ruth Richards, 175–193. Washington, DC: American Psychological Association.

Arons, Myron, and Ruth Richards. 2014. Two Noble Insurgencies: Creativity and Humanistic Psychology. In *Handbook of Humanistic Psychology*, ed. Schneider Kirk, J. Pierson, and James Bugental, 2nd ed., 161–176. Thousand Oaks, CA: Sage Publishers.

Austin, J.H. 1998. *Zen and the Brain*. Cambridge, MA: MIT Press.

Baars, Bernard. 2001. *In the Theater of Consciousness: The Workspace of the Mind*. New York: Oxford University Press.

Baron-Cohen, Simon. 2011. *The Science of Evil: On Empathy and the Origins of Cruelty*. New York: Basic.

Barron, Frank. 1963. *Creativity and Psychological Health*. Princeton, NJ: Van Nostrand.

———. 1968. *Creativity and Personal Freedom*. New York: Van Nostrand Reinhold.

———. 1969. *Creative Person and Creative Process*. New York: Holt, Rinehart, and Winston.

Barron, Frank, Alfonso Montuori, and Anthea Barron, eds. 1997. *Creators on Creating*. New York: G.B. Putnam's Sons.

Baruss, Imants. 2003. *Alterations of Consciousness: An Empirical Analysis for Social Scientists*. Washington, DC: American Psychological Association.

Baruss, Imants, and Julia Mossbridge. 2017. *Transcendent Mind: Rethinking the Science of Consciousness*. Washington, DC: American Psychological Association.

Bateson, Gregory. 2000. *Form, Substance, and Difference: Steps to an Ecology of Mind*. Chicago: University of Chicago Press.

Beck, Martha. 2012. *Finding Your Way in a Wild New World*. New York: Atria.

Becker, George. 2014. A Socio-Historical Overview of the Creativity-Psychopathology Connection. In *Creativity and Mental Illness*, ed. James C. Kaufman, 3–24. Cambridge: Cambridge University Press.

Beghetto, Ronald A. 2010. Creativity in the Classroom. In *Cambridge Handbook of Creativity*, ed. James C. Kaufman and Robert J. Sternberg, 447–463. New York: Cambridge University Press.

Bejan, Adrian. 2013. *Design in Nature: How the Constructal Law Governs Evolution in Biology, Physics, Technology, and Social Organizations*. New York: Anchor.

Blijlevens, Janneke, Clementine Thurgood, Paul Hekkert, Lin-Lin Chen, Helmut Leder, and T.W. Allan Whitfield. 2017. The Aesthetic Pleasure in Design Scale. *Psychology of Aesthetics, Creativity, and the Arts* 11: 86–98.

Bogzaran, Fariba. 1991. Experiencing the Divine in the Lucid Dream State. *Lucidity Letter* 10 (1 & 2): 1–10.

Bohm, David. 1980. *Wholeness and the Implicate Order*. New York: Routledge.

Boon, J.-P., J. Casti, and R.P. Taylor. 2011. Artistic Forms and Complexity. *Nonlinear Dynamics, Psychology, and Life Sciences* 15 (2): 265–283.

Borkin, Susan. 2014. *The Healing Power of Writing: A Therapist's Guide to Using Journaling with Clients*. New York: W.W. Norton.

Bostrom, Nick. 2014. *Superintelligence: Paths, Dangers, Strategies*. Oxford, UK: Oxford University Press.

Bowden, Edward, Mark Jung-Beeman, Jessica Fleck, and John Kounios. 2005. New Approaches to Demystifying Insight. *Trends in Cognitive Science* 9 (7): 322–328. https://doi.org/10.1016/j.tics2005.05.012.

Bradbury, Ray. 1990. The Sound of Summer Running. In *Classic Stories, I*, ed. Ray Bradbury, 342–348. New York: Bantam.

Briggs, John. 1987. Reflectaphors: The (Implicate) Universe as a Work of Art. In *Quantum Implications*, ed. B. Hiley and F. David Peat, 414–435. London: Routledge.

———. 1990. *Fire in the Crucible: Understanding the Process of Creative Genius*. Los Angeles: Tarcher.

Briggs, John, and F. David Peat. 1989. *Turbulent Mirror*. New York: Harper and Row.

Buber, Martin. 1970. *I and Thou*. New York: Touchstone.

Bucke, Richard Maurice. 1905/2010. *Cosmic Consciousness: A Study in the Evolution of the Human Mind*. Mansfield Center, CT: Martino Publishing.

Buckner, Randy, Jessica Andrews-Hanna, and Daniel Schachter. 2008. The Brain's Default Network: Anatomy, Function, and Relevance to Disease. *Annals of the New York Academy of Sciences* 1124: 1–34.

Buddhist Text Translation Society. 2009. *Surangama Sutra (with Commentary by Ven. Master Hsuan Hua)*. Edited by David Rounds and Ronald Epstein. Ukiah, CA: Buddhist Text Translation Society.

Burns, Robert. 1790. *Sketch—New Year's Day: To Mrs. Dunlop*.

Cameron, Julia. 2016. *The Artist's Way*. New York: TarcherPerigee.

Carson, Shelley. 2014. The Shared Vulnerability Model of Creativity and Psychopathology. In *Creativity and Mental Illness*, ed. James C. Kaufman, 253–280. Cambridge: Cambridge University Press.

Carson, S., J.B. Peterson, and D.M. Higgins. 2003. Decreased Latent Inhibition Is Associated with Increased Creative Achievement in High Functioning Individuals. *Journal of Personality and Social Psychology* 85 (3): 499–506.

Carter Presidential Center. 2018. Rosalynn Carter Fellowships for Mental Health Journalism. https://www.cartercenter.org/health/mental_health/fellowships/.

Cassertari, S. 1987. *Chinese Brush Painting Techniques*. London: Angus and Robertson.

Charyton, Christine, John G. Holden, Richard Jagacinski, and John Elliott. 2012. A Historical and Fractal Perspective on the Life and Saxophone Solos of John Coltrane. *Jazz Perspectives* 6 (3): 311–335.

Cheney, Margaret. 1981. *Tesla: Man Out of Time*. New York: Touchstone.

Combs, Allan. 1996. Consciousness: Chaotic and Strangely Attractive. In *Nonlinear Dynamics in Human Behavior*, ed. W. Sulis and Allan Combs, 401–411. Singapore: World Scientific.

———. 2002. *The Radiance of Being: Understanding the Grand Integral Vision, Living the Integral Life*. 2nd ed. St. Paul, MN: Paragon House.

———. 2009. *Consciousness Explained Better*. St. Paul, MN: Paragon House.

Combs, Allan, and Stanley Krippner. 2007. Structures of Consciousness and Creativity. In *Everyday Creativity and New Views of Human Nature*, ed. Ruth Richards, 131–149. Washington, DC: American Psychological Association.

———. 2010. Daylife, Dreamlife, and Chaos Theory. In *Perchance to Dream*, ed. S. Krippner and D.J. Ellis. New York: Nova.

———. 2017. Walter Freeman III and the Chaotic Nature of Dreams. *Nonlinear Dynamics, Psychology, and Life Sciences* 21 (4): 475–484.

Costa, P., and T.A. Widiger. 1994. Introduction. In *Personality Disorders and the Five Factor Model of Personality*, ed. P. Costa and T. Widiger, 1–10. Washington, DC: American Psychological Association.

Creswell, John W. 2014. *Research Design: Qualitative, Quantitative, and Mixed Methods Approaches*. 4th ed. Thousand Oaks, CA: Sage.

Cropley, Arthur. 1990. Creativity and Mental Health in Everyday Life. *Creativity Research Journal* 3: 167–178.

Cropley, David H., A.J. Cropley, James Kaufman, and Mark Runco. 2010. *The Dark Side of Creativity*. New York: Cambridge University Press.

Csikszentmihalyi, Mihaly. 1990. *Flow: The Psychology of Optimal Experience*. New York: HarperCollins.

———. 2013. *Creativity: The Psychology of Discovery and Invention*. New York: HarperPerennial.

Dacey, John, and Kathleen Lennon. 1998. *Understanding Creativity*. San Francisco, CA: Jossey-Bass.

Dalai Lama, His Holiness. 1988. *The Dalai Lama at Harvard: Lectures on the Buddhist Path to Peace*. Edited by Jeffrey Hopkins. Translated by Jeffrey Hopkins. Ithaca, NY: Snow Lion.

———. 1999. Foreword. In *MindScience: An East-West Dialogue*, ed. Dalai Lama, His Holiness, Herbert Benson, Robert Thurman, et al. Boston: Wisdom.

———. 2011. *Beyond Religion: Ethics for a Whole World*. New York: Mariner Books.

Dalai Lama, His Holiness, and H.D. Cutler. 1998. *The Art of Happiness: A Handbook for Living*. New York: Riverhead.

Damasio, Antonio. 2005. *Descartes' Error: Emotion, Reason, and the Human Brain*. New York: Penguin.

de Waal, Frans. 2009. *The Age of Empathy: Nature's Lessons for a Kinder Society*. New York: Harmony.

Dentler, Robert, and Bernard Mackler. 1964. Originality: Some Social and Personal Determinants. *Behavioral Science* 9 (1): 1–7.

DeParle, J. 2006. Orphaned. *New York Times Magazine*, August 27: 26–27.

deVos, Corey. 2017. What Is the Good, the Beautiful, and the True (Introduction to video by Ken Wilber). *Integrallife.com*. https://integrallife.com/good-true-beautiful/?utm_source=integral+Life+Newsletter.

Dillard, Annie. 1977. *Holy the Firm*. New York: Harper and Row.

Dobzhansky, Theodosius. 1962. *Mankind Evolving: The Evolution of the Human Species*. New Haven: Yale University Press.

Dossey, Larry. 2001. How Healing Happens: Exploring the Nonlocal Gap. *Alternative Therapies* 8 (2): 12–15, 103–110.

Dudek, Stephanie. 1993. The Morality of 20th Century Transgressive Art. *Creativity Research Journal* 6 (1–2): 145–152.

Eisler, Riane. 2007. Our Great Creative Challenge: Rethinking Human Nature and Recreating Society. In *Everyday Creativity and New Views of Human Nature*, ed. Ruth Richards, 261–285. Washington, DC: American Psychological Association.

Enomiya-Lassalle, Hugo. 1986. *Living in the New Consciousness*. Boston: Shambhala Books.

Falconer, Kenneth. 2013. *Fractals: A Very Short Introduction*. Oxford: Oxford University Press.

Feinstein, David, and Stanley Krippner. 2006. *The Mythic Path*. 3rd ed. Santa Rosa, CA: Elite Books.

Feist, Gregory J. 2010. The Function of Personality in Creativity: The Nature and Nurture of the Creative Personality. In *Cambridge Handbook of Creativity*, ed. James C. Kaufman and Robert J. Sternberg, 113–130. New York: Cambridge University Press.

Ferguson, Gary. 1999. *Shouting at the Sky: Troubled Teens and the Promise of the Wild*. New York: Thomas Dunne Books/Macmillan.

Field, R.J., and David Schuldberg. 2011. Social-Support Moderated Stress: A Nonlinear Dynamical Model and the Stress-Buffering Hypothesis. *Nonlinear Dynamics, Psychology, and the Life Sciences* 15 (1): 53–85.

Fink, A., and M. Benedek. 2013. The Creative Brain. In *Neuroscience of Creativity*, ed. Oshin Vartanian, A.S. Bristol, and James C. Kaufman, 207–232. Cambridge, MA: MIT Press.

Flavin, Martin. 1996. *Kurt Hahn's Schools and Legacy: To Discover You Can Be More and Do More Than You Believed*. Wilmington, DE: Middle Atlantic Press.

Fleck, Jessica, Green Deborah, Jennifer Stevenson, et al. 2008. The Transliminal Brain at Rest: Baseline, EEG, Unusual Experiences, and Access to Unconscious Mental Activity. *Cortex* 44: 1353–1363.

Florida, Richard. 2002. *Rise of the Creative Class*. New York: Basic Books.

———. 2005. *Flight of the Creative Class*. New York: HarperBusiness.

Forgeard, Marie, Anne Mecklenburg, Justin Lacasse, and Eranda Jayawickreme. 2014. Bringing the Whole Universe to Order: Creativity, Healing, and Posttraumatic Growth. In *Creativity and Mental Illness*, 321–342. Cambridge: Cambridge University Press.

Franck, Frederick. 1993. *Zen Seeing, Zen Drawing: Meditation in Action*. New York: Bantam.

Freeman, Lyn. 2009. *Mosby's Complementary and Alternative Medicine: A Research-Based Approach*. 3rd ed. St. Louis, MO: Mosby/Elsevier.

Freud, Anna. 1992. *The Ego and the Mechanisms of Defense*. New York: Routledge.

Friedman, Howard, and Leslie Martin. 2012. *The Longevity Project*. New York: Plume.

Gabora, Liane, and Scott Barry Kaufman. 2010. Evolutionary Approaches to Creativity. In *Cambridge Handbook of Creativity*, ed. James Kaufman and Robert Sternberg, 279–300. New York: Cambridge University Press.

Getzels, Jacob W., and Philip W. Jackson. 1962. *Creativity and Intelligence: Explorations with Gifted Students*. Hoboken, NJ: Wiley and Sons. See also AAUP Bulletin 48 (2):186.

Gilder, Louisa. 2008. *The Age of Entanglement: When Quantum Physics Was Reborn*. New York: Vintage.

Glaveanu, Vlad Petre. 2016. Introducing Creativity and Culture, the Emerging Field. In *The Palgrave Handbook of Creativity and Culture Research*, ed. V.P. Glaveanu, 1–12. London: Palgrave Macmillan.

Gleick, James. 1987. *Chaos: Making a New Science*. New York: Penguin.

———. 1999. *Faster: The Acceleration of Just About Everything*. New York: Pantheon.

Goerner, Sally. 1995. Chaos and Deep Ecology. In *Chaos Theory in Psychology*, ed. Albert R. Gilgen and Frederick David Abraham, 3–18. Westport, CT: Praeger.

Goertzel, Ben. 1995a. A Cognitive Law of Motion. In *Chaos Theory in Psychology and the Life Sciences*, ed. Robin Robertson and Allan Combs, 135–154. Mahwah, NJ: Erlbaum.

———. 1995b. Belief Systems as Attractors. In *Chaos Theory in Psychology and the Life Sciences*, ed. Robin Robertson and Allan Combs, 123–134. Mahwah, NJ: Erlbaum.

Goleman, Daniel. 1988. New Index Illuminates the Creative Life. *New York Times, Tuesday Science News feature*, September 13: C1, C9.

———. 2007. *Three Kinds of Empathy: Cognitive, Emotional, Compassionate*, June 12. Accessed March 10, 2018. http://www.danielgoleman.info/three-kinds-of-empathy-cognitive-emotional-compassionate.

Goleman, Daniel, and Richard J. Davidson. 2017. *Altered Traits: Science Reveals How Meditation Changes Your Mind, Brain, and Body*. New York: Avery.

Goodwin, Frederick, and Kay Redfield Jamison. 2000. *Manic-Depressive Illness*. New York: Oxford University Press.

———. 2007. *Manic-Depressive Illness: Bipolar Disorders and Recurrent Depression*. 2nd ed. New York: Oxford University Press.

Goslin-Jones, Terri, and Sue Ann Herron. 2016. Cutting-Edge Person-Centered Expressive Arts. In *The Person-Centered Counseling and Psychotherapy Handbook*, 199–211. New York: Open University Press/McGraw-Hill Education.

Goslin-Jones, Terri, and Ruth Richards. In press. Mysteries of Creative Process: Explorations at Work and in Daily Life. In *International Handbook of Creativity at Work*, ed. Lee Martin and Nick Wilson. London: Palgrave Macmillan.

Green Guerillas. n.d. Green Guerillas. *Our History.* http://www.greenguerillas.org/history.

Grohman, Magdalena, Zorana Ivcevic, Paul Silvia, and Scott Barry Kaufman. 2017. The Role of Passion and Persistence in Creativity. *Psychology of Aesthetics, Creativity, and the Arts* 11 (4): 376–385.

Gruber, Howard. 1981. *Darwin on Man: A Psychological Study of Scientific Creativity.* 2nd ed. Chicago: University of Chicago Press.

Guastello, Stephen J. 1995. *Chaos, Catastrophe, and Human Affairs.* Mahwah, NJ: Erlbaum.

Guastello, Stephen, and Larry Liebovitch. 2009. Introduction to Nonlinear Dynamics and Complexity. In *Chaos and Complexity in Psychology,* ed. Matthijs Koopmans and David Pincus Stephen Guastello, 1–40. New York: Cambridge University Press.

Guastello, Stephen J., Matthijs Koopmans, and David Pincus, eds. 2009. *Chaos and Complexity in Psychology: The Theory of Nonlinear Dynamical Systems.* New York: Cambridge University Press.

Guevara, Marlenny, Ralf F.A. Cox, Marijn van Dijk, and Paul van Geert. 2017. Attractor Dynamics of Dyadic Interaction: A Recurrence Based Analysis. *Nonlinear Dynamics, Psychology, and Life Sciences* 21 (3): 289–317.

Guilford, J.P. 1950. Creativity. *American Psychologist* 5: 444–454.

———. 1967. *The Nature of Human Intelligence.* New York: McGraw Hill.

Guisinger, Shan. 2003. Adapted to Flee Famine: Adding an Evolutionary Perspective on Anorexia Nervosa. *Psychological Review* 110 (4): 745–761.

Guisinger, Shan, and Sidney J. Blatt. 1994. Individuality and Relatedness: Evolution of a Fundamental Dialectic. *American Psychologist* 49 (2): 104–111.

Hallowell, Edward, and John Ratey. 2011. *Driven to Distraction: Recognizing and Coping with Attention Deficit Disorder.* New York: Anchor.

Hasenkamp, Wendy, and Janna R. White, eds. 2017. *The Monastery and the Microscope: Conversations with the Dalai Lama on Mind, Mindfulness, and the Nature of Reality.* New Haven: Yale University Press.

Harner, Michael. 2013. *Cave and Cosmos: Shamanic Encounters with Another Reality.* Berkeley, CA: North Atlantic Books.

Hassin, Ran R., James Uleman, and John Bargh, eds. 2005. *The New Unconscious.* Oxford: New York.

Hoffman, Louis, Ruth Richards, and Steven Pritzker. 2012. Creativity and the Evolution of Humanistic Psychology. *Self and Society* 40: 10–15.

———. 2018. Creativity in the Evolution of Humanistic Psychology. In *Humanistic Psychology: Current Trends and Future Prospects,* ed. Richard House, David Kalisch, and Jennifer Maidman, 34–44. New York: Routledge.

Holland, John H. 2014. *Complexity: A Very Short Introduction.* Oxford: Oxford.

House, Richard, David Kalisch, and Jennifer Maidman, eds. 2017. *Humanistic Psychology: Current Trends and Future Prospects.* New York: Routledge.

James, William. 1958. *The Varieties of Religious Experience.* New York, NY: Mentor.

Jamison, Kay Redfield. 1989. Mood Disorders and Patterns of Creativity in British Artists and Writers. *Psychiatry* 52: 125–134.
———. 1993. *Touched with Fire*. New York: Free Press.
———. 2017. *Robert Lowell: Setting the River on Fire*. New York: Knopf.
Johnson, David. 2017. Is This the Worst Hurricane Season Ever? Here's How It Compares. *Time Magazine*. http://time.com/4952628/hurricane-season-harvey-irma-jose-maria/.
Jordan, Judith. 1991. The Meaning of Mutuality. In *Women's Growth in Connection*, ed. Judith Jordan, Alexandra Kaplan, Jean Baker Miller, Irene P. Stiver, and Janet L. Surrey, 81–96. New York: Guilford.
Jordan, Judith V., ed. 1997. *Women's Growth in Diversity: More Writings from the Stone Center*. New York: Guilford.
———. 2010. *Relational-Cultural Therapy*. Washington, DC: American Psychological Association.
Jordan, Judith, Alexandra Kaplan, Jean Baker Miller, Irene P. Stiver, and Janet L. Surrey. 1991. *Women's Growth in Connection: Writings from the Stone Center*. New York: Guilford.
Juarrero, Alicia, and Carl Rubino, eds. 2010. *Emergence, Complexity, and Self-Organization: Precursors and Prototypes*. Litchfield Park, AZ: Emergent Publications.
Jung, C.G., ed. 1964. *Man and His Symbols*. New York, NY: Dell.
———., ed. 1969. *The Archetypes and the Collective Unconscious*. Princeton: Princeton University Press.
———., ed. 1983. *The Essential Jung*. Edited by and Introduced by Anthony Storr. Princeton, NJ: Princeton University Press.
———. 1997. *Jung on Active Imagination*. Edited by and with Introduction by Joan Chodorow. Princeton, NJ: Princeton University Press.
Kahneman, Daniel. 2013. *Thinking Fast and Slow*. New York: Farrar Straus and Girous.
Kapleau, Roshi Philip. 1989. *The Three Pillars of Zen*. New York: Anchor.
Kauffman, Stuart. 1995. *At Home in the Universe: The Search for the Laws of Self-Organization and Complexity*. New York: Oxford University Press.
———. 2008. *Reinventing the Sacred: A New View of Science, Reason, and Religion*. New York: Perseus.
———. 2016. *Humanity in a Creative Universe*. New York: Oxford University Press.
Kaufman, Scott Barry. 2009. Faith in Intuition Is Associated with Decreased Latent Inhibition in a Sample of High Achieving Adolescents. *Psychology of Aesthetics, Creativity, and the Arts* 3 (1): 28–34.

Kaufman, James C., ed. 2014. *Creativity and Mental Illness*. Cambridge: Cambridge University Press.

Kaufman, Scott Barry, and Carolyn Gregoire. 2015. *Wired to Create*. New York: Perigee.

Kaufman, Scott Barry, and Jerome L. Singer. 2012. The Creativity of Dual Process "System 1" Thinking, January 17. Accessed February 10, 2013. http://blogs.scientificamerican.com/guest-blog/2012/01/17.

Kaufman, James, and Robert J. Sternberg, eds. 2010. *The Cambridge Handbook of Creativity*. New York: Cambridge University Press.

Kaufman, James, Jonathan Plucker, and John Baer. 2008. *Essentials of Creativity Assessment*. Hoboken, NJ: Wiley and Sons.

Keller, Evelyn Fox. 1983. *A Feeling for the Organism: The Life and Work of Barbara McClintock*. New York: Henry Holt.

Kellert, Stephen, and Edward O. Wilson, eds. 1993. *The Biophilia Hypothesis*. Washington, DC: Island Press.

Keltner, Dacher. 2009. *Born to Be Good: Science of a Meaningful Life*. New York: W.W. Norton.

Kerouac, Jack. 1976. *Dharma Bums*. New York: Penguin Classics.

KindSpring. n.d. *Small Acts That Can Change the World: How to Use A Smile Card*. ServiceSpace.org. Accessed March 13, 2018. http://www.KindSpring.org/SmileCards.

Kinney, Dennis K., and Ruth Richards. 2011. Bipolar Mood Disorders. In *Encyclopedia of Creativity*, 2nd ed. Santa Barbara: Academic Press.

———. 2014. Creativity as 'Compensatory Advantage': Bipolar and Schizophrenic Liability and the Inverted-U Hypothesis. In *Creativity and Mental Illness*, ed. James Kaufman, 295–317. New York: Cambridge University Press.

Kinney, Dennis, and Steven Matthysse. 1978. Genetic Transmission of Schizophrenia. *Annual Review of Medicine* 29: 459–473.

Kinney, Dennis, Ruth Richards, P. Lowing, D. LeBlanc, M. Zimbalist, and P. Harlan. 2000–2001. Creativity in Offspring of Schizophrenics and Controls. *Creativity Research Journal* 11: 17–25.

Kinney, Dennis, Ruth Richards, and Marti Southam. 2012. Everyday Creativity, Its Assessment, and the Lifetime Creativity Scales. In *The Creativity Research Handbook*, ed. Mark Runco, 285–319. Creskill, NJ: Hampton Press.

Kitzbichler, M., M. Smith, S. Christensen, and E. Bullmore. 2009. Broadband Criticality of Human Brain Network Synchronization. *PLoS Computational Biology* 5 (3): e1000314. https://doi.org/10.1371/journal.pcbi.1000314.Epub.

Klein, K. 2002. Stress, Expressive Writing, and Working Memory. In *The Writing Cure*, ed. S.J. Lepore and J.M. Smyth, 135–155. Washington, DC: American Psychological Association.

Kolbert, Elizabeth. 2014. *The Sixth Extinction: An Unnatural History*. New York: Holt and Company.

Kounios, John, and Mark Beeman. 2015. *The Eureka Factor: Aha Moments, Creative Insight, and the Brain*. New York: Random House.

Kounios, John, Jennifer Frymiare, Edward Bowden, et al. 2006. The Prepared Mind: Neural Activity Prior to Problem Presentation Predicts Subsequent Solution by Sudden Insight. *Psychological Science* 17 (10): 882–890.

Kozbelt, Aaron, Ronald Beghetto, and Mark Runco. 2010. Theories of Creativity. In *Cambridge Handbook of Creativity*, 48–73. New York: Cambridge University Press.

Krippner, Stanley. 1999a. Altered and Transitional States. In *Encyclopedia of Creativity*, ed. Mark Runco and Steven R. Pritzker, vol. I, 59–70. San Diego, CA: Academic Press.

———. 1999b. Dreams and Creativity. In *Encyclopedia of Creativity*, ed. Mark Runco and Steven R. Pritzker. San Diego: Academic Press.

———. 2016. Humanistic Psychology and Chaos Theory. *Journal of Humanistic Psychology* 34 (3): 48–61.

Krippner, Stanley, Ruth Richards, and Frederick D. Abraham. 2014. Chaos and Creativity While Waking and Dreaming. *International Journal of Existential Psychology and Psychotherapy* 5 (1): 18–26.

Kris, E. 1952. *Psychoanalytic Explorations in Art*. New York: Columbia University Press.

Krishnamurti, Jiddu, and David Bohm. 1985. *The Ending of Time*. New York: Harper and Row.

Kuhn, Thomas. 1962. *The Structure of Scientific Revolutions*. Chicago, IL: University of Chicago Press.

Kurzweil, Ray. 2006. *The Singularity Is Near: When Humans Transcend Biology*. New York: Penguin.

L'Engle, Madeleine. 1989. *A Wind in the Door*. New York: Farrar, Straus, and Giroux.

Langton, Chris G. 1990. Computation at the Edge of Chaos: Phase Transitions and Emergent Computation. *Physica D* 42: 12–37.

Leakey, R., and R. Lewin. 1995. *The Sixth Extinction: Patterns of Life and the Future of Humankind*. New York: Random House.

Leavy, Patricia. 2015. *Method Meets Art: Arts-Based Research Practice*. 2nd ed. New York: Guilford.

LeGuin, Ursula. 2012. Afterword. In *Earthsea: The Other Wind*, ed. Ursula LeGuin, 263–266. Boston: Houghton Mifflin.

Lepore, S.J., and J.M. Smythe. 2002. *The Writing Cure: How Expressive Writing Promotes Health and Emotional Well-Being*. Washington, DC: American Psychological Association.

Lewis, C.S. 1960. *The Four Loves*. New York: Harcourt Brace Jovanovich.

———. 2015. *Mere Christianity*. New York: HarperOne.

Li, Qin, and Mihaly Csikszentmihalyi. 2014. Moral Creativity and Creative Morality. In *Ethics of Creativity*, ed. Seana Moran, David Cropley, and James C. Kaufman, 75–91. London: Palgrave Macmillan.

Li, Shanshan, Meir Stampfer, David Williams, and Tyler VanderWeele. 2016. Association of Religious Service Attendance with Mortality Among Women. *Journal of the American Medical Association Internal Medicine* 176: 777–785.

Loori, John Daido. 2005. *The Zen of Creativity: Cultivate Your Artistic Life*. New York: Ballantine Books.

Loye, David. 2007. Telling the New Story: Darwin, Evolution, and Creativity Versus Conformity in Science. In *Everyday Creativity and New Views of Human Nature*, ed. Ruth Richards, 153–174. Washington, DC: American Psychological Association.

Ludwig, Arnold. 1992. Creative Achievement and Psychopathology: Comparison Among Professions. *American Journal of Psychotherapy* XLVI (3): 330–354.

———. 1995. *The Price of Greatness*. New York: Guilford.

Lutz, Antoine, and E. Thompson. 2003. Neurophenomenology Integrating Subjective Experience and Brain Dynamics in the Neuroscience of Consciousness. *Journal of Consciousness Studies* 22: 31–52.

MacFarquhar, Larissa. 2015. *Strangers Drowning: Grappling with Impossible Idealism, Drastic Choices, and the Overpowering Urge to Help*. New York: Penguin Press.

Magee, Glenn Alexander, ed. 2016. *The Cambridge Handbook of Western Mysticism and Esotericism*. New York: Cambridge University Press.

Maslow, Abraham. 1968. *Toward a Psychology of Being*. New York: Van Nostrand Reinhold.

Malchiodi, Cathy A. 2007. *The Art Therapy Sourcebook*. New York: McGraw-Hill.

Mandelbrot, Benoit B. 1983. *The Fractal Geometry of Nature*. New York: W.H. Freeman.

Marks-Tarlow, Terry. 2008. *Psyche's Veil: Psychotherapy, Fractals and Complexity*. London: Routledge.

———. In press. A Fractal Epistemology for Transpersonal Psychology. *International Journal of Transpersonal Studies*.

Martin, Lee, and Nick Wilson. 2017. Defining Creativity with Discovery. *Creativity Research Journal* 29 (4): 417–425.

Martindale, Colin. 1999. Biological Bases of Creativity. In *Handbook of Creativity*, ed. Robert Sternberg, 137–152. New York: Cambridge University Press.

———. 2007. A Neural Network Theory of Beauty. In *Evolutionary and Neurocognitive Approaches to Aesthetics, Creativity, and the Arts*, ed. Paul Locher and V.M. Petrov Colin Martindale, 181–194. Baywood: Amityville, NY.

Martins, M.J., F. Fischmeister, E. Puig-Waldmuller, et al. 2014. Fractal Image Perception Provides Novel Insights into Hierarchical Cognition. *NeuroImage* 96: 300–308.

Maslow, Abraham. 1968. Creativity in Self-Actualizing People. In *The Creativity Question*, ed. A. Rothenberg and C.A. Hausman, 86–92. Durham, NC: Duke University Press.

———. 1970. *Religions, Values, and Peak Experiences*. New York: Viking Penguin.

———. 1971. *The Farther Reaches of Human Nature*. New York: Viking Press.

———. 1982. *The Journals of Abraham Maslow*. Edited by R. Lowry. Brattleboro, VT: Lewis Publishing Company.

May, Rollo. 1985. *My Quest for Beauty*. New York: W.W. Norton.

McAdams, Dan P. 1993. *Stories We Live By: Personal Myths and the Making of the Self*. New York: William Morrow and Co.

McLain, David L., Efstathios Kefallonitis, and Kimberly Armani. 2015. Ambiguity Tolerance in Organizations: Definitional Clarification and Perspectives on Future Research. *Frontiers in Psychology* 6: 344. https://doi.org/10.3389/fpsyg.2015.00344.

Mednick, Sarnoff, and Martha T. Mednick. 1965. *Associative Basis of the Creative Process*. Vols. Issue 1073 of Cooperative Research Project, U.S. Office of Education. University of Michigan.

Milne, Jonathan. 2006. *GO! The Art of Change*. Wellington, New Zealand: Steele Roberts Aetearoa.

Milne, Alice Wilson. 2017. *Two Wings to Fly: An Insider's Guide to Creativity and Innovation*. Wellington: Steele Roberts Aotearoa.

Minh Duc, Thich. 2000. Dam Luu: An Eminent Vietnamese Buddhist Nun. In *Innovative Buddhist Women: Swimming Against the Stream*, ed. Karma Lekshe Tsomo, 104–118. Richmond, Surrey: Curzon Press.

Miranda, Lin-Manuel. 2017. Stephen Sondheim. *New York Times Style Magazine*, October 22: 142–145.

Mitchell, Melanie. 2009. *Complexity: A Guided Tour.* New York: Oxford University Press.

Mithen, Steven. 2006. *The Singing Neanderthals: The Origins of Music, Language, Mind, and Body.* Cambridge, MA: Harvard University Press.

Mlodinow, Leonard. 2012. *Subliminal: How Your Unconscious Mind Rules Your Behavior.* New York: Vintage.

Montuori, Alfonso, Allan Combs, and Ruth Richards. 2004. Creativity, Consciousness, and the Direction for Human Development. In *The Great Adventure: Toward a Fully Human Theory of Evolution,* ed. David Loye, 197–236. Albany, NY: State University of New York Press.

Moore, David S. 2015. *The Developing Genome: An Introduction to Behavioral Genetics.* New York: Oxford University Press.

Moore, James, and Adrian Desmond. 2004. *Introduction: Charles Darwin, Descent of Man.* New York: Penguin Classics.

Moran, Seana. 2016. *Ethical Ripples of Creativity and Innovation.* London: Palgrave Macmillan.

Moran, Seana, David Cropley, and James Kaufman, eds. 2014. *The Ethics of Creativity.* London: Palgrave Macmillan.

Morowitz, Harold J. 2002. *The Emergence of Everything.* New York: Oxford University Press.

Morowitz, Harold, and Jerome L. Singer, eds. 1995. *The Mind, the Brain, and Complex Adaptive Systems (Proceedings Volume XXII, Santa Fe Institute).* Reading, MA: Addison-Wesley.

Morrison, Delmont, and S.L. Morrison. 2006. *Memories of Loss and Dreams of Perfection: Unsuccessful Childhood Grieving and Adult Creativity.* Amityville, NY: Baywood.

Muktananda, Swami. 1972. *Light on the Path.* South Fallsburg, NY: SYDA Foundation.

Murcott, Susan, ed. 1991. *The First Buddhist Women: Tranlations and Commentary on the Therigatha.* Translated by Susan Murcott. Berkeley, CA: Parallax Press.

Murphy, Michael, and S. Donovan. 1999. *The Physical and Psychological Effects of Meditation: A Review of Contemporary Research with a Comprehensive Bibliography.* 2nd ed. Sausalito, CA: Institute of Noetic Sciences.

Myers, David G. 2002. *Intuition: Its Powers and Perils.* New Haven, CT: Yale University Press.

Nahon, Karine, and Jeff Hemsley. 2013. *Going Viral.* Cambridge: Polity Press.

Newsweek. 2014. Nearly 1 in 5 Americans Suffers from Mental Illness Each Year. *Newsweek Magazine,* February 28. www.newsweek.com/nearly-1-5-americans-suffer-mental-illness-each-year-230608.

Nhat Hanh, Thich. 1988. *The Sun My Heart.* Translated by Anh Huong Nguyen, Elin Sand, and Annabel Laity. Berkeley: Parallax Press.

———. 1993. *Call Me By My True Names: The Collected Poems of Thich Nhat Hanh.* Berkeley, CA: Parallax Press.

———. 1998. *The Heart of the Buddha's Teachings.* Berkeley, CA: Parallax Press.

———. 2002. *Teachings on Love.* Berkeley: Parallax Press.

Nooris, Paul, and Seymour Epstein. 2011. An Experiential Thinking Style: Its Facets and Relations With Objective and Subjective Criterion Measures. *Journal of Personality* 79 (5): 1043–1080.

Norton, Jana Rivers. 2016. *The Demeter-Persephone Myth as Writing Ritual in the Lives of Literary Women.* Newcastle Upon Tyne: Cambridge Scholars.

O'Hara, Maureen. 2018. Humanistic Cultural Praxis for an Emerging World. In *Humanistic Psychology: Current Trends and Future Prospects,* 75–86. London: Routledge.

Ockuly, Marta, and Ruth Richards. 2013. Loving or Fearing Creativity? It's All in the Definition. *NeuroQuantology.*

Ornstein, Robert. 1991. *Evolution of Consciousness.* New York: Prentice Hall.

Osborn, A.F. 1967. *Applied Imagination: Principles and Procedures of Creative Problem Solving.* 3rd Revised Edition. New York: Charles Scribner's Sons.

Osho. 2001. *Intuition: Knowing Beyond Logic.* New York: St. Martin's Griffin.

Owen, Keith, A. Steven Dietz, and Ralph Gohring. in press. Strategies for Creating the Learning Organization. In *Nonlinear Psychology,* ed. David Schuldberg, Ruth Richards, and Shan Guisinger. New York: Oxford University Press.

Pahnke, W.N., and W.A. Richards. 1972. Implications of LSD and Experimental Mysticism. In *Altered States of Consciousness,* ed. Charles Tart, 409–439. Garden City, NY: Anchor.

Panek, Richard. 2011. *The 4% Universe: Dark Matter, Dark Energy, and the Race to Discover the Rest of Reality.* New York: Mariner.

Payne, Katherine. 2001. The Progressively Changing Songs on Humpback Whales: A Window on the Creative Process in a Wild Animal. In *The Origins of Music,* ed. Bjorn Merker Nils and Steven Brown Wallin, 135–150. Cambridge, MA: MIT Press.

Peat, F. David. 2000. *The Blackwinged Night: Creativity in Nature and Mind.* Cambridge, MA: Perseus.

Peitgen, Heinz-Otto, and Peter H. Richter. 1986. *The Beauty of Fractals.* Berlin: Springer Verlag.

Peitgen, Hans-Otto, Hartmut Jurgens, and Dietmar Saupe. 2004. *Chaos and Fractals: New Frontiers of Science.* 2nd ed. New York: Springer.

Pelosi, Nancy, and Amy Hill Hearth. 2008. *Know Your Power: A Message to America's Daughters*. New York: Doubleday.

Pelzang, Khenpo Ngawang. 2004. *A Guide to the Words of My Perfect Teacher*. Translated by Dipamkara with the Padmakara Translation Group. Boston: Shambhala.

Pennebaker, James, ed. 1995. *Emotion, Disclosure, and Health*. Washington, DC: American Psychological Association.

Pennebaker, James, J.K. Kiecolt-Glaser, and R. Glaser. 1997. Disclosure of Traumas and Immune Function. In *Eminent Creativity, Everyday Creativity, and Health*, ed. Mark Runco and Ruth Richards, 287–302. Greenwich, CT: Ablex Publishing Corp.

Pfaff, Donald W. 2015. *The Altruistic Brain: How We Are Naturally Good*. New York: Oxford University Press.

Pilisuk, Marc, and S. Parks. 1986. *The Healing Web: Social Networks and Human Survival*. Hanover, NH: University Press of New England.

Pilisuk, Marc, and Jennifer Achord Rountree. 2015. *The Hidden Structure of Violence*. New York: Monthly Review Press.

Pincus, David. 2009. *Fractal Brains, Fractal Thoughts*. http://www.psychology-today.com/node/32616.

Pincus, David, Adam Kiefer, and Jessica Beyer. 2017. Nonlinear Dynamical Systems and Humanistic Psychology. *Journal of Humanistic Psychology* 58: 1–24. https://doi.org/10.1177/0022167817741784.

Plucker, Jonathan, and Ronald Beghetto. 2004. *Why Creativity Is Domain General, Why It Looks Domain Specific, and Why the Distinction Does Not Matter*. Edited by Robert Sternberg, Elena Grigorenko, and Jerome Singer, 153–167. Washington, DC: American Psychological Association.

Plucker, Jonathan, and Gayle T. Dow. 2017. Attitude Change as the Precursor of Creativity Enhancement. In *Nurturing Creativity in the Classroom*, ed. Ronald Beghetto and James C. Kaufman, 2nd ed., 190–211. New York: Cambridge University Press.

Pope, J. 1961. *Chinese Art Treasures: Catalog for Selected Groups of Objects Exhibited in the U.S. by the Government of the Republic of China*. Lausanne: Skira.

Pritzker, Steven. 2007. Audience Flow: Creativity in Television Watching with Applications to Teletherapy. In *Everyday Creativity and New Views of Human Nature*, ed. Ruth Richards, 109–130. Washington, DC: American Psychological Association.

Prum, Richard O. 2017. *The Evolution of Beauty: How Darwin's Forgotten Theory of Mate Choice Shapes the Animal World—And Us*. New York: Doubleday.

Puhakka, Kaisa. 2000. Invitation to Authentic Knowing. In *Transpersonal Knowing*, ed. Tobin Hart, P.L. Nelson, and K. Puhakka, 11–30. Albany, NY: SUNY Press.

Rahula, Walpola. 1959. *What the Buddha Taught*. New York: Grove Press.

Rand, Gunvor, and Per Rand. 1978. The Effects of Working Atmospheres on Creativity. *Scandinavian Journal of Educational Research* 22 (3): 91–106.

Rao, K. Ramakrishna. 2002. *Consciousness Studies: Cross-Cultural Perspectives*. Jefferson, NC: McFarland and Company.

Red Pine, Commentary, Trans. 2013. *Lankavatara Sutra*. Berkeley, CA: Counterpoint.

Reisman, Frederika K. 2017. Creativity Embedded into K-12 Teacher Preparation. In *Nurturing Creativity in the Classroom*, ed. Ronald Beghetto and James Kaufman, 2nd ed., 162–189. New York: Cambridge University Press.

Reuter, Monika E. 2015. Ten Domains That Have Explained Creativity ... Or Maybe Not. In *Creativity—A Sociological Approach*, ed. M.E. Reuter, 16–39. Basingstoke: Palgrave Macmillan.

Rhodes, C. 1990. Growth from Deficiency Creativity to Being Creativity. *Creativity Research Journal* 3: 287–299.

Ricard, Matthieu. 2017. *A Plea for the Animals: The Moral, Philosophical, and Evolutionary Imperative to Treat All Beings with Compassion*. Boulder: Shambhala Books.

Ricard, Matthieu, and T.X. Thuan. 2001. *The Quantum and the Lotus: A Journey to the Frontiers Where Science and Buddhism Meet*. New York: Crown.

Richards, Ruth. 1976. Comparison of Selected Guilford and Wallach-Kogan Tests of Creative Thinking in Conjunction with Measures of Intelligence. *Journal of Creative Behavior* 10: 151–164.

———. 1981. Relationships between Creativity and Psychopathology: An Evaluation and Interpretation of the Evidence. *Genetic Psychology Monographs* 103: 261–324.

———. 1994/2017. *Everyday Creativity: Coping and Thriving in the 21st Century*. Raleigh, NC: Lulu Publishers.

———. 1996. Beyond Piaget: Accepting Divergent, Chaotic, and Creative Thought. *New Directions in Child Development* 72: 67–86.

———. 1997. Conclusions: When Illness Yields Creativity. In *Eminent Creativity, Everyday Creativity, and Health*, ed. Mark Runco and Ruth Richards, 485–540. Greenwich, CT: Ablex.

———. 1998. The Subtle Attraction: Beauty as a Force in Awareness, Creativity, and Survival. In *Affect, Creative Experience, and Psychological Adjustment*, ed. S.W. Russ, 191–213. Philadelphia: Brunner/Mazel.

————. 1999. Four P's of Creativity. In *Encyclopedia of Creativity*, ed. M. Runco and S. Pritzker, vol. I, 733–741. San Diego, CA: Academic Press.

————. 2000–2001. Creativity and the Schizophrenia Spectrum: More and More Interesting. *Creativity Research Journal* 13 (1): 111–131.

————. 2000–2001. Millennium as Opportunity: Chaos, Creativity, and J.P. Guilford's Structure-of-Intellect Model. *Creativity Research Journal* 13 (3 & 4): 249–265.

————. 2001. A New Aesthetic for Environmental Awareness: Chaos Theory, the Beauty of Nature, and Our Broader Humanistic Identity. *Journal of Humanistic Psychology* 41 (2): 59–95.

————. 2004. Arts and Self-Expression in Mental Health. *Presentation to Frame Demonstrations/Performances for a "Conversations" Event, Carter Presidential Center; Adaptation publ in Elites (Italian)* (Georgia Public Radio broadcast the event).

————, ed. 2007a. *Everyday Creativity and New Views of Human Nature: Psychological, Social, and Spiritual Perspectives*. Washington, DC: American Psychological Association.

————. 2007b. Everyday Creativity: Our Hidden Potential. In *Everyday Creativity and New Views of Human Nature*, ed. Ruth Richards, 25–53. Washington, DC: American Psychological Association.

————. 2007c. Relational Creativity and Healing Potential: The Power of Eastern Thought in Western Clinical Settings. In *Cultural Healing and Belief Systems*, ed. James Pappas, W. Smythe, and A. Baydala, 286–308. Calgary: Detselig.

————. 2007d. Twelve Potential Benefits of Living More Creatively. In *Everyday Creativity and New Views of Human Nature*, ed. Ruth Richards, 289–319. Washington, DC: American Psychological Association.

————. 2009. Who Is Gifted and Talented and What Should We Do About It? *Creativity Network Update*, May: 6–11.

————. 2010. Everyday Creativity in the Classroom. In *Nurturing Creativity in the Classroom*, ed. Ronald Beghetto and James C. Kaufman, 206–234. New York: Cambridge University Press.

————. 2010a. Everyday Creativity in the Classroom: A Trip Through Time with Seven Suggestions. In *Nurturing Creativity in the Classroom*, ed. Ron A. Beghetto and James C. Kaufman, 206–234. New York: Cambridge University Press.

————. 2010b. Everyday Creativity: Process and Way of Life—Four Key Issues. In *Cambridge Handbook of Creativity*, ed. James Kaufman and Robert Sternberg, 189–215. New York: Cambridge University Press.

————. 2011a. Age of Empathy: New Views of Health, Human Nature, and Creativity. www.CultureofEmpathy.com (E. Rutsch for www.AhimsaBerkeley. org). www.YouTube.com/watch?v=nA8;khOktcc.

————. 2011b. Everyday Creativity. *www.awakin.org*, December 13. www. awakin.org/?tid=778.

————. 2014a. A Creative Alchemy. In *Ethics of Creativity*, 119–136. London: Palgrave Macmillan.

————. 2014b. Will the Real Scientists Please Stand Up? Taboo Topics, Creative Risk, and Paradigm Shift. *Journal of Humanistic Psychology* 55 (3): 292–322.

————. In press. Chaos, Creativity, Complexity, and Healthy Change. In *Nonlinear Psychology: Keys to Chaos and Creativity in Mind and Life*, ed. David Schuldberg, Ruth Richards, and Shan Guisinger. New York: Oxford University Press.

Richards, Ruth, and Howard Whitehouse. 2008. Subtle Mind, Open Heart: Mike Arons Remembered (1929–2008). *Psychology of Aesthetics, Creativity, and the Arts* 2 (4): 264–270.

Richards, Ruth, and Terri Goslin-Jones. 2018. Everyday Creativity: Challenges for Self and World—Six Questions. In *Nature of Human Creativity*, ed. Robert Sternberg and James C. Kaufman, 224–245. New York: Cambridge University Press.

Richards, Ruth, and Christine Kerr. 1999a. *The Fractal Forms of Nature: A Resonant Aesthetic*. Annual Meeting of The Society for Chaos Theory in Psychology and the Life Sciences, Berkeley, CA, July.

————. 1999b. *The Fractal Forms of Nature: A Resonant Aesthetic*. 107th Annual Meeting of The American Psychological Association, Boston, August.

Richards, Ruth, and Dennis K. Kinney. 1990. Mood Swings and Creativity. *Creativity Research Journal* 3 (3): 202–217.

Richards, Ruth, Dennis K. Kinney, Inge Lunde, and Maria Benet. 1988a. Creativity in Manic-Depressives, Cyclothymes, Their Normal Relatives, and Control Subjects. *Journal of Abnormal Psychology* 97: 281–288.

Richards, Ruth, Dennis Kinney, Maria Benet, and Ann P.C. Merzel. 1988b. Assessing Everyday Creativity: Characteristics of the Lifetime Creativity Scales and Validation with Three Large Samples. *Journal of Personality and Social Psychology* 54: 476–485.

Richards, Ruth, Kinney Dennis, H. Daniels, and Karen Linkins. 1992. Everyday Creativity and Bipolar and Unipolar Affective Disorder: Preliminary Study of Personal and Family History. *European Psychiatry* 7: 49–52.

Rifkin, Jeremy. 2009. *The Empathic Civilization: The Race to Global Consciousness in a World in Crisis*. New York: Jeremy P. Tarcher.

————. 2014. *The Zero Marginal Cost Society*. New York: Palgrave Macmillan.

Rinpoche, Tarthang Tulku. 1994. *Dynamics of Time and Space*. Berkeley: Dharma Publishing.

Robinson, Sir Ken. 2011. *Out of Our Minds: Learning to Be Creative*. West Sussex, UK: Capstone Publishing.

Rogers, Carl. 1959. Toward a Theory of Creativity. In *Creativity and Its Cultivation*, ed. H. Anderson, 69–82. New York: Harper and Row.

Rogers, Natalie. 1993. *Creative Connection: Expressive Arts as Healing*. Palo Alto, CA: Science and Behavior Books.

————. 2011. *Creative Connection for Groups: Person-Centered Expressive Arts for Healing and Social Change*. Palo Alto, CA: Science and Behavior Books.

Root-Bernstein, Robert, and andd Michele Root-Bernstein. 1999. *Sparks of Genius: The 13 Thinking Tools of the World's Most Creative People 1999*. Boston: Houghton Mifflin.

Root-Bernstein, Robert, and Michele Root-Bernstein. 2004. Artistic Scientists and Scientific Artists: The Link Between Polymathy and Creativity. In *Creativity: From Potential to Realization*, ed. Elena Grigorenko, Jerome L. Singer, and Robert J. Sternberg, 127–151. Washington, DC: American Psychological Association.

Rosen, Diane. 2016. Accessing Creativity: Jungian Night Sea Journeys, Wandering Minds and Chaos. *Nonlinear Dynamics, Psychology, and Life Sciences* 20 (1): 117–139.

Rosenthal, Robert, and Lenore Jacobson. 2003. *Pygmalion in the Classroom: Teacher Expectation and Pupils' Intellectual Development, Expanded Edition*. New York: Crown House Publ.

Ross, N.W., ed. 1960. *The World of Zen*. New York: Vintage.

Roszak, Theodore, Mary Gomes, and Allen Kanner, eds. 1995. *Ecopsychology: Restoring the Earth, Healing the Mind*. San Francisco, CA: Sierra Club Books.

Rothberg, Donald. 2006. *The Engaged Spiritual Life: A Buddhist Approach to Transforming Ourselves and the World*. Boston: Beacon Press.

Runco, Mark. 2006. *Creativity: Theories and Themes—Research, Development, and Practice*. San Diego: Academic Press.

Runco, Mark A. 2010a. Divergent Thinking, Creativity, and Ideation. In *Cambridge Handbook of Creativity*, ed. James C. Kaufman and Robert J. Sternberg, 413–446. New York: Cambridge University Press.

Runco, Mark. 2010b. Torrance Tests of Creative Thinking as Predictors of Personal and Public Achievement: A Fifty-Year Follow-Up. *Creativity Research Journal* 22 (4): 361–368.

Runco, Mark, and Ruth Richards, eds. 1997. *Eminent Creativity, Everyday Creativity, and Health*. Greenwich, CT: Ablex Publishing Corp.

Russ, Sandra. 2014. *Pretend Play in Childhood: Foundation of Adult Creativity*. Washington, DC: American Psychological Association.

———. 2018. Pretend Play and Creativity: Two Templates for the Future. In *Nature of Human Creativity*, ed. Robert J. Sternberg and James C. Kaufman, 264–279. New York: Cambridge University Press.

Santayana, George. 1955. *The Sense of Beauty: Being the Outline of Aesthetic Theory*. New York: Dover.

Sawyer, R.K. 2005. *Social Emergence: Societies as Complex Systems*. Cambridge, UK: Cambridge University Press.

Scharmer, C. Otto. 2009. *Theory U: Leading from the Future as It Emerges—The Social Technology of Presencing*. San Francisco: Berrett-Koehler.

Scharmer, C. Otto, and Katrin Kaeufer. 2010. In Front of the Blank Canvas: Sensing Emerging Futures. *Journal of Business Strategy* 31 (4): 21–29.

Scharmer, Otto, and Katrin Kaufer. 2013. *Leading from the Emerging Future*. Oakland, CA: Berrett Koehler.

Schneider, Kirk. 2004. *Rediscovery of Awe: Splendor, Mystery, and the Fluid Center of Life*. St. Paul, MN: Paragon House.

———. 2011. Awakening to an Awe-Based Psychology. *The Humanistic Psychologist* 39: 237–252.

Schneider, Kirk J., J. Fraser Pierson, and James F.T. Bugental, eds. 2014. *Handbook of Humanistic Psychology: Theory, Research, and Practice*. 2nd ed. Thousand Oaks, CA: Sage Publications.

Schroeder, Manfred. 1991. *Fractals, Chaos, Power Laws: Minutes from an Infinite Paradise*. New York: W.H. Freeman.

Schuldberg, David. 1990. Schizotypal and Hypomanic Traits, Creativity, and Psychological Health. *Creativity Research Journal* 3 (3): 218–230.

———. 2007. Living Well Creatively: What's Chaos Got to Do with It? In *Everyday Creativity and New Views of Human Nature*, ed. Ruth Richards, 55–73. Washington, DC: American Psychological Association.

———. 2017. Visions of Stability and Change in Physiological and Social Systems. *Society for Chaos Theory in Psychology and Life Sciences Newsletter*, November: 4–8.

Schwantes, Marcel. 2018. Steve Jobs's Advice on the Only 4 Times You Should Say 'No' Is Brilliant. *www.Inc.com*, January 31. Accessed February 5, 2018. https://www.inc.com/marcel-schwantes/first-90-days-Steve-Jobs-advice-on-the-only-4-times-you-should-say-no.html.

Schwartz, Stephan, and Larry Dossey. n.d. Nonlocality, Intention, and Observer Effects in Healing Studies: Laying a Foundation for the Future. *Explore* 6 (5): 295–307.

Senge, Peter, C. Otto Scharmer, Joseph Jaworski, and Betty Sue Flowers. 2004. *Presence: Human Purpose and the Field of the Future*. Cambridge, MA: Society for Organizational Learning.

Serlin, Ilene. 2014. Kinaesthetic Imagining. In *Grief and the Expressive Arts: Practices for Creating Meaning*, ed. Barbara E. Thompson and Robert A. Niemeyer, 116–119. New York: Routledge.

Shakespeare, William. 2010. *Julius Caesar*. New York: Oxford University Press.

Shansis, F., M. Fleck, R. Richards, D. Kinney, et al. 2003. Desenvolvimento da Versao Para o Portugues das Escalasda Criatividade ao Longo da Vida (ECLV) [Development of the Portuguese Version of the Lifetime Creativity Scales]. *Rev. Psiquiatr. Rio Grande Do Sul* 25 (2): 284–296.

Shapiro, Shauna, and Linda Carlson. 2017. *The Art and Science of Mindfulness*. 2nd ed. Washington, DC: American Psychological Association.

Shenk, David. 2011. *The Genius in All of Us: New Insights into Genetics, Talent, and IQ*. New York: Anchor.

Siegel, Daniel J. 2007. *The Mindful Brain: Reflection and Attunement in the Cultivation of Well-Being*. New York: W.W. Norton.

———. 2012. *The Developing Mind: How Relationships and the Brain Interact to Shape Who We Are*. New York: Guilford.

Silvia, Paul. 2018. Creativity Is Undefinable, Controllable, and Everywhere. In *Nature of Human Creativity*, ed. Robert J. Sternberg and James C. Kaufman, 291–301. New York: Cambridge University Press.

Silvia, Paul, and James C. Kaufman. 2010. Creativity and Mental Illness. In *Cambridge Handbook of Creativity*, ed. James C. Kaufman and Robert J. Sternberg, 381–394. New York: Cambridge University Press.

Silvia, Paul, R. Beaty, E. Nusbaum, et al. 2014. Everyday Creativity in Daily Life: An Experience Sampling Study of "Little c" Creativity. *Psychology of Aesthetics, Creativity, and the Arts* 8: 183–188.

Simonton, Dean Keith. 1988. *Scientific Genius: A Psychology of Science*. New York: Cambridge University Press.

Singer, Jerome L. 2006. *Imagery in Psychotherapy*. Washington, DC: American Psychological Association.

Singer, Jerome, and Scott Barry Kaufman. January 17, 2012. *The Creativity of Dual Process 'System 1' Thinking*. Scientifican American Blog Network. https://blogs.scientificamerican.com/guest-blog/the-creativity-of-dual-process-system-1-thinking/.

Skarda, C., and Walter Freeman. 1987. How Brains Make Chaos in Order to Make Sense of the World. *Behavioral and Brain Science* 10: 161–173.

Smith, Leonard. 2007. *Chaos: A Very Short Introduction.* Oxford: Oxford University Press.

Smith, Huston. 2009. *The World's Religions.* New York: HarperOne.

Smith, Jeffrey, and Lisa F. Smith. 2010. Educational Creativity. In *Cambridge Handbook of Creativity*, ed. James C. Kaufman and Robert J. Sternberg, 250–264. New York: Cambridge University Press.

Smith, Lisa, Jeffrey Smith, and Pablo Tinio. 2017. Time Spent Viewing Art and Reading Labels. *Psychology of Aesthetics, Creativity, and the Arts* 11: 77–85.

Smith, Patrick, Leilani Goodmon, and Sarah Hester. 2018. The Burtynsky Effect: Aesthetic Reactions to Landscape Photographs that Vary in Natural Features. *Psychology of Aesthetics, Creativity, and the Arts* 12 (1): 34–49.

Spender, Dale. 1991. *Women of Ideas.* New York: Harper Collins.

Sternberg, Robert J. 2014. Creativity in Ethical Reasoning. In *Ethics of Creativity*, ed. Seana Moran, David Cropley, and James C. Kaufman, 62–74. London: Palgrave Macmillan.

Sternberg, Robert J., and James C. Kaufman. In press. Afterword: The Big Questions in the Field of Creativity—Now and Tomorrow. In *Nature of Human Creativity*, ed. Robert Sternberg and James Kaufman. New York: Cambridge University Press.

Strogatz, Steven. 2003. *Sync: How Order Emerges from Chaos in the Universe, Nature, and Daily Life.* New York: Hyperion.

Subramaniam, Karuna, John Kounios, Todd Parrish, and Mark Jung-Beeman. 2008. A Brain Mechanism for Facilitation of Insight by Positive Affect. *Journal of Cognitive Neuroscience* 21 (3): 415–432.

Sundararajan, Louise Lu. 2015. *Understanding Emotion in Chinese Culture.* New York: Springer.

Swain, J.E., and J.D. Swain. 2014. Nonlinearity in Creativity and Mental Illness: The Mixed Blessings of Chaos, Catastrophe, and Noise in Brain and Behavior. In *Creativity and Mental Illness*, ed. James C. Kaufman, 133–134. Cambridge: Cambridge University Press.

Tart, Charles T. 1975. *States of Consciousness.* New York: E.P Dutton.

Taye, Jamgon Kongtrul Lodro. 1995. *Myriad Worlds: Buddhist Cosmology in Abhidharma, Kalachakra, and Dzog-chen.* Ithaca: Snow Lion.

Teilhard de Chardin, Pierre. 1975. *The Phenomenon of Man.* New York: Harper Colophon.

The Human Memory. n.d. *Neurons and Synapses.* http://www.human-memory. net/brain_neurons.html.

Tinio, Pablo. 2013. From Artistic Creation to Aesthetic Reception: The Mirror-Model of Art. *Psychology of Aesthetics, Creativity, and the Arts* 7: 265–275.

Trungpa, Chogyam. 2007. *Shambhala: The Sacred Path of the Warrior*. Boulder, CO: Shambhala Books.

Tsomo, Karma Lekshe, ed. 1999. *Buddhist Women Across Cultures*. Albany: SUNY Press.

———, ed. 2000. *Innovative Buddhist Women: Swimming Against the Stream*. Albany: SUNY Press.

———, ed. 2004. *Buddhist Women and Social Justice*. Albany: SUNY Press.

———, ed. 2014. *Eminent Buddhist Women*. Albany, NY: State University of New York Press.

Tulku, Tarthang. 1994. *Mastering Successful Work*. Berkeley, CA: Dharma Publishing Co..

Varela, Francisco, ed. 1997. *Sleeping, Dreaming, and Dying: An Exploration of Consciousness with the Dalai Lama*. Boston: Wisdom Publications.

Varela, Francisco, E. Thomspson, and Eleanor Rosch. 1992. *The Embodied Mind: Cognitive Science and Human Experience*. Boston: MIT Press.

Vartanian, Oshin. 2013. Fostering Creativity: Insights from Neuroscience. In *Neuroscience of Creativity*, ed. Oshin Vartanian, Adam S. Bristol, and James C. Kaufman. Cambridge, MA: MIT Press.

Vartanian, Oshin, Adam Bristol, and James C. Kaufman, eds. 2013. *Neuroscience of Creativity*. Cambridge, MA: MIT Press.

Vartanian, Oshin, A. Vartanian, R. Beaty, E. Nusbaum, K. Blacvkler, Q. Lam, E. Peele, and Paul Silvia. 2017. Revered Today, Loved Tomorrow: Expert Creativity Ratings Predict Popularity of Architects' Works 50 Years Later. *Psychology of Aesthetics, Creativity, and the Arts* 11 (4): 386–391.

Vaughan, Frances. 1979. *Awakening Intuition*. New York: Anchor.

Vernon, P.E. 1971. Effects of Administration and Scoring on Divergent Thinking Tests. *British Journal of Educational Psychology* 41 (3): 245–257.

Vincent, Lynne C., and Jack A. Goncolo. 2014. License to Steal: How the Creative Identity Entitles Dishonesty. In *Ethics of Creativity*, ed. Seana Moran, David Cropley, and James C. Kaufman, 137–151. Basingstoke: Palgrave Macmillan.

Vorrath, Harry H., and Larry K. Brendtro. 2007. *Positive Peer Culture*. 2nd ed. New Brunswick: AldineTransaction.

Vygotsky, Lev S. 1986. *Thought and Language*, Revised ed. Edited by Alex Kozulin. Cambridge: MIT Press.

Vyner, Henry. 2016. *The Healthy Mind Interviews: Khenpo Tsewang Gyatso*. Kathmandu: Vajra Books.

———. 2018. *The Healthy Mind: Mindfulness, True Self, and the Stream of Consciousness*. New York: Routledge.

Wallace, B. Alan. 1999. *The Four Immeasureables: Cultivating a Boundless Heart*. Ithaca: Snow Lion.

———. 2012. *Dreaming Yourself Awake: Lucid Dreaming and Tibetan Dream Yoga for Insight and Transformation*. Boston: Shambhala.

Wallach, M.A., and Nathan Kogan. 1965. *Modes of Thinking in Young Children*. New York: Holt, Rinehart, and Winston.

Wallas, Graham. 1931. *The Art of Thought (Life and Letters Series No. 24)*. London: Jonathan Cape.

Wallin, Nils L., Bjorn Merker, and Steven Brown, eds. 2001. *The Origins of Music*. Cambridge, MA: MIT Press.

Walnut, W. n.d. Power Napping for Creative Gems, Inspiration and Invention. *Wilywalnut.com*. Accessed February 27, 2018. http://www.wilywalnut.com/Thomas-Edison-Power-Napping.html.

Westby, V.L., and E. Dawson. 1995. Creativity: Assets or Burden in the Traditional Classroom? *Creativity Research Journal* 8: 1–10.

Wilber, Ken, Jack Engler, and Daniel Brown. 1986. *Transformations of Consciousness: Conventional and Contemplative Perspectives on Development*. Boston: Shambhala.

Wilson, Renate. 1982. *Inside Outward Bound: Success Story of the International Wilderness School*. Madeira Park: Douglas and McIntyre.

Wise, Anna. 2004. *The High Performance Mind: Mastering Brainwaves for Insight, Healing, and Creativity*. New York: Tarcher.

Wurst, Jampa Rotraut. 2017. Celebrating the Daughters of the Buddha. *Sakyadhita* 26: 1–2.

Yeats, W.B. 1994. Collected Poems of W.B. Yeats, edited by Richard J. Finneran. Ware, Hertfordshire, U.K.: Wordsworth Poetry Library.

Yu, Qi, Shun Zhang, and Jinghuan H. Zhang. 2017. Association of Dopamine D2 Receptor Gene with Creative Ideation. *Creativity Research Journal* 29 (2): 108–113.

Zabelina, Darya L. 2018. Attention and Creativity. In *Cambridge Handbook of Neuroscience and Creativity*, ed. Rex Jung and Oshin Vartanian, 161–179. New York: Cambridge University Press.

Zacharek, Stephanie, Eliana Dockterman, and Haley Sweetland Edwards. 2017. 2017 Person of the Year: The Silence Breakers—The Voices That Launched a Movement. *Time Magaine*, December 18: 34–71.

Zausner, Tobi. 1999. Trembling and Transcendence: Chaos Theory, Panic Attacks, and Awe. *The Psychotherapy Patient* 11 (1–2): 83–107.

———. 2006. *When Walls Become Doorways: Creativity and the Transforming Illness*. New York: Harmony.

———. 2011a. Chaos, Creativity, and Substance Abuse: The Nonlinear Dynamics of Choice. *Nonlinear Dynamics, Psychology, and Life Sciences* 15 (2): 207–227.

———. 2011b. Transcending the Self Through Art: Altered States of Consciousness and Anomalous Events During the Creative Process. *Journal of Consciousness Exploration and Research* 2 (7): 993–1005.

Zimbardo, Philip G., Robert L. Johnson, and Vivian McCann. 2014. *Psychology: Core Concepts*. 7th ed. Boston: Pearson.

Index[1]

---

[1] Note: Page numbers followed by 'n' refer to notes.

CPSIA information can be obtained
at www.ICGtesting.com
Printed in the USA
LVHW101447041219
639272LV00004B/36/P